Children's Peer Talk

Inside and outside the classroom, children of all ages spend time interacting with their peers. Through these early interactions, children make sense of the world and co-construct their childhood culture, while simultaneously engaging in interactional activities which provide the stepping stones for discursive, social and cognitive development.

This collection brings together an international team of researchers to document how children's peer talk can contribute to their socialization and demonstrates that if we are to understand how children learn in everyday interactions we must take into account peer group cultures, talk, and activities.

This book will be of interest to students and researchers in the fields of language acquisition, sociolinguistics, pragmatics and discourse analysis, and related disciplines. It examines naturally occurring talk of children aged from three to twelve years from a range of language communities, and includes ten studies documenting children's interactions and a comprehensive overview of relevant research.

ASTA CEKAITE is Professor of Child Studies in the Department of Thematic Research at Linköping University, Sweden.

SHOSHANA BLUM-KULKA (1936–2013) was Professor Emerita in the Department of Communication and the School of Education at the Hebrew University, Jerusalem.

VIBEKE GRØVER is Professor of Education in the Department of Education at the University of Oslo.

EVA TEUBAL is Professor Emerita of Early Childhood Education at the David Yellin Academic College of Education, Jerusalem.

Children's Peer Talk

Learning from Each Other

Edited by

Asta Cekaite, Shoshana Blum-Kulka,
Vibeke Grøver and Eva Teubal

CAMBRIDGE
UNIVERSITY PRESS

University Printing House, Cambridge CB2 8BS, United Kingdom

Cambridge University Press is part of the University of Cambridge.

It furthers the University's mission by disseminating knowledge in the pursuit of education, learning and research at the highest international levels of excellence.

www.cambridge.org
Information on this title: www.cambridge.org/9781316644904

© Cambridge University Press 2014

This publication is in copyright. Subject to statutory exception and to the provisions of relevant collective licensing agreements, no reproduction of any part may take place without the written permission of Cambridge University Press.

First published 2014
First paperback edition 2016

A catalogue record for this publication is available from the British Library

ISBN 978-1-107-01764-1 Hardback
ISBN 978-1-316-64490-4 Paperback

Cambridge University Press has no responsibility for the persistence or accuracy of URLs for external or third-party internet websites referred to in this publication, and does not guarantee that any content on such websites is, or will remain, accurate or appropriate.

Contents

List of figures   *page* vii
List of tables   viii
List of contributors   ix
Preface   xi

Part I Introduction   1

1 Children's peer talk and learning: uniting discursive, social, and cultural facets of peer interactions: editors' introduction   3
ASTA CEKAITE, SHOSHANA BLUM-KULKA,
VIBEKE GRØVER AND EVA TEUBAL

Part II Children's peer talk and extended discourse   21

2 "Now I said that Danny becomes Danny again": a multifaceted view of kindergarten children's peer argumentative discourse   23
SARA ZADUNAISKY EHRLICH AND SHOSHANA BLUM-KULKA

3 Narrative performance, peer group culture, and narrative development in a preschool classroom   42
AGELIKI NICOLOPOULOU, CAROLYN BROCKMEYER CATES,
ALINE DE SÁ AND HANDE ILGAZ

4 "Let's pretend you're the wolf!": the literate character of pretend-play discourse in the wake of a story   63
ESTHER VARDI-RATH, EVA TEUBAL,
HADASSAH AILLENBERG AND TERESA LEWIN

5 Explanatory discourse and historical reasoning in children's talk: an experience of small group activity   87
CAMILLA MONACO AND CLOTILDE PONTECORVO

6 Evaluation in pre-teenagers' informal language
  practices around texts from popular culture 107
  JANET MAYBIN

Part III Children's peer talk and second language learning **127**

7 Peer interaction, framing, and literacy in preschool
  bilingual pretend play 129
  AMY KYRATZIS

8 Metasociolinguistic stance taking and the appropriation of
  bilingual identities in everyday peer language practices 149
  ANN-CARITA EVALDSSON AND FRITJOF SAHLSTRÖM

9 "Say princess": the challenges and affordances of
  young Hebrew L2 novices' interaction with their peers 169
  SHOSHANA BLUM-KULKA AND NAOMI GORBATT

10 Language play, peer group improvisations, and L2 learning 194
   ASTA CEKAITE AND KARIN ARONSSON

11 The potentials and challenges of learning words
   from peers in preschool: a longitudinal study of
   second language learners in Norway 214
   VESLEMØY RYDLAND, VIBEKE GRØVER AND
   JOSHUA LAWRENCE

Part IV Conclusion **235**

12 What, when, and how do children learn from talking
   with peers? 237
   KATHERINE NELSON

References 251
Index 272

Figures

4.1	Coding scheme: in-frame and out-of-frame discourse (based on 5875 coded turns)	*page* 70
4.2	In-frame and out-of-frame discourse (based on 5875 coded turns)	70
4.3	Coding scheme: attitude towards text (based on 5875 coded turns)	76
4.4	Children's attitude towards the OST (5875 turns)	76
9.1	Sindy: what's going on here?	173
9.2	Sindy: what's going on here?	174
9.3	Interactional failures	175
9.4	Rough and tender	176
9.5	Rough and tender	176
9.6	Bilingual socialization	180
9.7	Bilingual socialization	180
9.8	Rachel "reading" to novices	182
9.9	"Say wall"	187
9.10	Who likes to eat x?	187
10.1	Continuum between old and new elements	197
11.1	Prototypical trajectories of two children	223

Tables

3.1	Means or mean percentages (and standard deviations) of narrative dimensions for the first and last stories told by children who attended this class from the beginning of the school year	*page* 50
9.1	Nonverbal and verbal strategies of communication	184
11.1	Target children's PPVT-III raw scores	219
11.2	Tokens and types per minute for target children and peers (in play) and teacher-led talk (in circle time)	220
11.3	Intercorrelations between PPVT, tokens and types per minute for target children and peers (in play), teacher-led talk (in circle time) and maternal education	221
11.4	Results of fitting a taxonomy of multi-level models for change predicting raw vocabulary scores	222

Contributors

HADASSAH AILLENBERG, Ph.D., Head of Music Department, Kaye College of Education, Beer-Sheva, Israel.

KARIN ARONSSON, Ph.D., Professor, Department of Child and Youth Studies, Stockholm University, Sweden.

SHOSHANA BLUM-KULKA (1936–June 10, 2013), Ph.D., Professor Emerita, Department of Communication, Hebrew University, Israel.

CAROLYN BROCKMEYER CATES, Ph.D., Assistant Professor, Director of the Bellevue Project for Early Language, Literacy and Education Success, New York University School of Medicine, New York, USA.

ASTA CEKAITE, Ph.D., Professor, Child Studies, Department of Thematic Research, Linköping University, Sweden.

ALINE DE SÁ BARBOSA, Ph.D., Research Psychologist, Instituto Alfa e Beto, Rio de Janeiro, Brazil.

ANN-CARITA EVALDSSON, Ph.D., Professor, Department of Education, Uppsala University, Sweden.

NAOMI GORBATT, Ph.D., Director of Literacy and Language Arts Department, CET – The Center for Educational Technology, Tel-Aviv, Israel.

VIBEKE GRØVER, Ph.D., Professor, Department of Education, University of Oslo, Norway.

HANDE ILGAZ, Ph.D., Assistant Professor of Psychology, Bilkent University, Ankara, Turkey.

AMY KYRATZIS, Ph.D., Professor of Education, Gevirtz Graduate School of Education, University of California, Santa Barbara, USA.

JOSHUA LAWRENCE, Ed.D., Assistant Professor of Language, Literacy and Technology, School of Education, University of California Irvine, USA.

TERESA LEWIN, Ph.D., Head of Curriculum and Teacher Training, Kaye College of Education, Beer-Sheva, Israel.

JANET MAYBIN, Ph.D., Senior Lecturer, Faculty of Education and Language Studies, The Open University, Milton Keynes, UK.

CAMILLA MONACO, Ph.D. Researcher, Department of Educational and Developmental Psychology, University of Rome "Sapienza," Italy.

KATHERINE NELSON, Ph.D., Professor Emerita, The Graduate Center, Psychology, The City University of New York, USA.

AGELIKI NICOLOPOULOU, Professor of Psychology and Global Studies, Director of Social Science Research Center (SSRC), Department of Psychology, Lehigh University, Bethlehem, USA.

CLOTILDE PONTECORVO, Ph.D., Professor Emerita, Department of Educational and Developmental Psychology, University of Rome "Sapienza," Italy.

VESLEMØY RYDLAND, Ph.D., Researcher, Department of Education, University of Oslo, Norway.

FRITJOF SAHLSTRÖM, Ph.D., Senior Lecturer, Institute of Behavioral Sciences, University of Helsinki, Finland.

EVA TEUBAL, Ph.D., Professor Emerita, David Yellin Teachers' College, Jerusalem, Israel.

ESTHER VARDI-RATH, Ph.D., Head of the Department of Early Childhood Education, Kaye College of Education, Beer-Sheva, Israel.

SARA ZADUNAISKY EHRLICH, Ph.D., Lecturer, Beit Berl Academic College, Israel.

Preface: in memory of Shoshana Blum-Kulka

It was with deep sorrow we received the news that Shoshana Blum-Kulka died in Jerusalem on June 10, 2013, just when this book had been completed and was ready to be sent off to the publisher. Shoshana was crucially important to the production of this book and we are saddened that she never saw it published. The idea for a book on children's peer talk and its importance to learning was hers, and throughout the editorial process she played a significant role in conceptualizing the book, recruiting authors, co-authoring chapters, and reviewing contributions. This book would never have appeared without Shoshana's contribution.

At the time of her death, Shoshana was Professor Emerita at the Hebrew University of Jerusalem. With a background in linguistics, she published numerous books and articles on translation, cross-cultural communication, family discourse and media discourse. To understand the phenomena that she explored, she built on both micro- and macro-oriented disciplines, understanding human interaction within power relations and societal theories. Particularly important was her work on pragmatic language development in children, drawing on and contributing to linguistic anthropology, cross-cultural and developmental psychology and education. Examples of her work include *Dinner Talk: Cultural Patterns of Sociability and Socialization in Family Discourse* (Lawrence Erlbaum, 1997) and *Talking to Adults: The Contribution of Multiparty Discourse to Language Acquisition* with Catherine Snow (Lawrence Erlbaum, 2002). By directing attention to the significance of naturally occurring multi-party, intergenerational talk, these books were major contributions to the study of children's pragmatic socialization. Through her teaching and her supportive guidance of students she built a pioneering interdisciplinary research agenda on discursive pragmatics.

In all her writing Shoshana demonstrated sensitive understanding of young children and their way of communicating and expressing themselves. She was always fascinated by the fine nuances of human interaction, such as the way we direct others, formulate requests, and express politeness. When examining the impact of young children's peer talk on their learning and thinking, she demonstrated ways in which peer talk offers opportunities for children's construction of childhood cultures as well as for individual development; both perspectives were captured in her conceptualization of the "double opportunity space."

What stands out is the originality of her thinking, her creativity, and her willingness to cross disciplinary borders. Up to the very last days of her life she continued to wonder at children's peer cultures and how children learn from each other through talking. She was a rare mixture of intellectual power and integrity, of commitment and involvement in social-educational issues. Shoshana displayed a unique human and academic generosity and willingness to acknowledge the contribution of others. We feel deeply privileged to have collaborated with her and give thanks for her life and work.

Asta Cekaite
Vibeke Grøver
Eva Teubal

Part I

Introduction

1 Children's peer talk and learning: uniting discursive, social, and cultural facets of peer interactions: editors' introduction

Asta Cekaite, Shoshana Blum-Kulka,
Vibeke Grøver and Eva Teubal

In school and out of school, both in traditional and modern societies, children of all ages spend extended periods of time in dyadic, multi-party, mixed-age or same-age interactions with their peers. While there is a long history of research on children's peer relations and friendships and their impact on child development (Ladd 2009), the study of peer talk from language and discursive perspectives, with a focus on peers as a discourse community, is relatively new (Ervin-Tripp and Mitchell-Kernan 1977; McTear 1985; Goodwin 1990; Grøver Aukrust 2001; Kyratzis 2004). The present book deploys a specific kind of lens to examine what is happening in naturally occurring peer talk and the potential impact of such talk on socialization and learning. One of its basic premises is the understanding that children's language and pragmatic development is a socioculturally, spatially and temporally situated process in which the child is not alone but is part of a communicative community, that is, a community of practice (Wenger 1998; Nelson, this volume).

The current perspective synthesizes insights from earlier contextually sensitive approaches to children's language and pragmatic development (primarily in adult–child encounters) and explores the learning potentials that characterize children's peer group interactions. A long tradition of research on adult–child interactions has yielded a wealth of information on the effects of this discourse on language learning within the domains of words and grammar (e.g., Nelson 1973; Bates, Bretherton, Snyder 1988), children's development of pragmatic skills (Ochs and Shieffelin 1979; Schiefelbusch and Pickar 1984; Ninio and Snow 1996), conceptual development (Nelson 2007; Rogoff et al. 1993) and on children's discursive socialization into the cultural practices of the community (Ochs 1988; see also Duranti, Ochs and Shieffelin 2012). The developmental research on both first and second language learning has mostly relied on observational data on dyadic intergenerational interactions (Gallaway and Richards 1994; Ninio and Snow 1996, but see Blum-Kulka and Snow 2002; de León 1998 on multi-party discourse) or controlled experimental data (e.g., Bialystok 2001; Hickmann 2003), tracking children's developmental discursive paths.

Concurrently, linguistic anthropologic studies of children's natural peer talk, being primarily interested in cultural structures rather than the developmental aspects of children's discourse, have unveiled a host of child–culture-specific interactional patterns in a rich gamut of social practices and genres (Heath 1983; Ochs 1988; Schieffelin 1990; Blum-Kulka 1997; Watson-Gegeo and Gegeo 1989).

The present book extends this body of research, arguing that children's peer group activities contribute to their socialization in ways that usefully complement the role of adult–child interactions. It emphasizes the need to account for the role of peer activities, and the importance of the peer group and peer cultures in children's everyday experiences. The interest in analyzing children as a discourse community stems from and aligns with the particular place children have gained as a social and cultural group that deserves attention in its own right (Goodwin 1990; Corsaro 2005). The specific contribution of the book is a theoretical conceptualization of children's peer talk and its facilitative potential for children's language and pragmatic/discursive learning. By focusing on the processes of learning through using language in social practices with peers, it emphasizes the need to account for the role of peer activities, and the importance of peer group cultures in children's activities. The book's focus is mainly on the potentials and processes of learning as these appear on the micro-level within peer interaction. The observational methods used by several authors are geared toward capturing the dynamics of the interactive processes between peers in natural contexts and explicating learning processes and potentials by closely following children's discursive collaboration in situ, in a wide range of social and play activities. Hence the book's main emphasis is on the learning potentials and processes associated with language use in social practices with peers rather than on the outcome of such processes (for a discussion of the difference between process- and learning-outcome-oriented research, see Nelson, this volume).

The present volume builds on Blum-Kulka's theoretical view of peer talk as a "double-opportunity space" serving both as a locus for the co-construction of children's social worlds and peer cultures through interactional displays, and as an arena for the development of pragmatic skills in the first and second language (Blum-Kulka 2005a; Zadunaisky Ehrlich and Blum-Kulka 2010). From this perspective, the original notion of "opportunity space" (Ochs et al. 1989) is 'doubled' to promote a dialogue between diverse intellectual traditions by advancing the notion that peer talk functions simultaneously on two discursive planes. The first, mostly identified with the sociological/anthropological approach, is created *within* the social peer trajectory. On this plane, children dynamically negotiate meanings and relationships related to their local peer culture. On the second plane, mostly identified with the psycholinguistic, developmental approach, peer talk is viewed as a locus in which the dynamics of participation in various discursive events can create rich contextual opportunities for language and pragmatic development.

This book develops an interdisciplinary approach to childhood discourse and culture by drawing on educational, psycholinguistic, sociolinguistic and anthropological perspectives: children, both young preschoolers and preadolescents, are viewed as making sense of the world and co-constructing their unique child culture in the present of their childhood, while simultaneously engaging in interactional practices that can provide some of the stepping stones for discursive, social and cognitive development. Importantly, children's discursive activities are embedded within, and informed by, the communicative practices of the wider sociocultural community (including older peers, adults and institutional discourses).

From a discursive developmental perspective, peer talk is also characterized by a relatively egalitarian participation structure that is generally unavailable in adult–child discourse (e.g., Piaget 1995), and that thus allows for particular types of peer collaboration and discursive genres. For children, becoming full-fledged members of society, in which peer group interactions constitute a daily feature of life, necessarily entails engaging with a variety of interlocutors, taking on a wide range of communicative roles, and developing competences in a variety of conversational and discursive genres. It is because peer group interactions (within families, neighborhoods and classrooms) and their communicative practices (such as play frame negotiations, dispute and arguments, language play, story telling and explanations) constitute talk-based childhood cultures that becoming and acting as a member of a peer group involves becoming and acting as a competent member of these particular language communities.

The goal of the chapters in this volume is to describe a number of specific cases across a variety of cultural and educational settings – examining what participation in children's peer talk looks like, children's discursive practices, and the ways in which children can learn from them – and to promote a deeper understanding of how children can gain communicative, cognitive and social skills in various domains as they grow in the present of their childhood within the realm of their peer cultures. The chapters cover the domains of children's first language and extended discourse (literacy, argumentative, narrative events), as well as bilingual and second language encounters (L2 vocabulary acquisition, language play), highlighting the multifaceted learning affordances and possible drawbacks of these experiences. Several chapters examine in detail children's discursive practices and learning processes in peer group activities, while some adopt a longitudinal perspective, documenting the learning outcomes of peer discourse. We will now briefly introduce the theoretical and empirical underpinnings of the present approach and preface some of the issues that emerge.

Theoretical underpinnings

Peer childhood cultures

A significant feature of peer talk is its co-constitutive relation to the shared worlds of childhood culture, which serves as a major resource in cultural and relational work. Our approach to peer interactions and peer cultures builds on and is consistent with new sociologically informed theoretical approaches that have directed attention to children, their social worlds and talk, and peer cultures as being worth studying in their own right (Corsaro 2005, 2012). This interest in children's peer cultures is geared toward understanding the processes of cultural (re-)production in childhood from an emic point of view, namely, approximating as much as possible the children's own perspective. From this perspective, peer cultures are conceptualized as "a stable set of activities or routines, artifacts, values, and concerns that children produced and share in interaction with their peers" (Corsaro 2012: 10). Culture is seen as constituting and constitutive of interactional processes and social practices. Peer cultures, the unfolding childhood habitus, are shaped in and through children's participation in shared, discursively based, practices, that is, their common cultural and communicative landscape. However, to argue that children produce their own cultures is not meant to suggest that children's cultures are separate from the wider societal processes, adult practices (Corsaro 2005) and discursive resources. Rather, there is a dialectic, mutually informing, relation between children's and adults' cultures: it is through the process of "creative appropriation," "interpretive reproduction" and even "secondary adjustments" (e.g., subversive practices, Goffman 1967, cf. Blum-Kulka et al. 2004) that children explore, are socialized, and take their own stance on adult practices, and that they, over time, become part of a dynamically shaped adult culture, acquiring or transforming adult-like communicative competences and resources. Children in peer activities can be seen to both appropriate and reinterpret adult practices and resources in ways that make them peer specific (Zadunaisky Ehrlich and Blum-Kulka; Cekaite and Aronsson this volume).

Children's peer discursive practices and socialization in peer group interactions

One of the theoretical assumptions of the book is that peer culture has its own unique social routines, frames of interpretation and linguistic codes. As demonstrated by several chapters, peer-talk affordances are deeply embedded in relevant sociocultural structures of childhood, and they are tied to the shared discourse worlds of children in given age groups. Practices (symbolic play, cultural narratives such as stories, folktales) in cultural environments common to the preschool years carry developmental potentials by contributing to young children's "narrative consciousness," which is viewed as a discursive path to becoming members of cultural (adults' and children's) communicative communities (Nelson 2007: 212). For preadolescents, peer group sub-culture valued resources, such as sociolinguistic and affective contextualization cues, allow them to adopt and display desirable social, gender and ethnic identities (Evaldsson and Sahlström, this volume). Children thus rely on a variety of semiotic resources in their environment, verbal and non-verbal alike, to co-construct the sociocultural habitus unique to their social group; this habitus is created with the aid of children's deep involvement in the topics and flow of the ongoing discourse. Children's discursive activities are embedded within the constraints imposed by their level of linguistic-pragmatic development, owing to their age or their status as second language learners. Some of the discursive genres children engage in, like symbolic play, are typified by age-related specific formats, while others, like conversational story telling or argumentative discourse, partly echo adult-like discursive genres (Blum-Kulka 2005a; Blum-Kulka and Hamo, forthcoming).

Linguistic ethnography studies have demonstrated children's deep involvement in their shared worlds of childhood culture and their discursive socialization of each other into the social and moral orders (e.g., Goodwin 1990; Kyratzis 2004) through, for instance, calibrating gender-specific directives (see Goodwin 1990 on American, and Kyratzis and Guo 2001 on American and Chinese contexts) and through intricate play access routines (Cromdal 2001; Mor 2010). Among the wealth of peer genres, fantasy play, narratives, disputes and arguments have a solid place in young children's communicative and cultural landscapes (Danby and Theobald 2012). For example, in fantasy play, which is characterized by the joint construction of imaginary worlds, children embellish adult models of social life to fit their concerns and values through a process of "collaborative emergence" (Sawyer 1997, 2002). Collaborative emergence involves a certain amount of collaborative improvisation, that is, engagement with the "imaginative function of language" in their creation of distant, hypothetical, and connected fantasy worlds (Harris 2000), as well as their sensitivity to and expansion of each other's contributions and attuned poetic performance (see Sawyer 1997, 2002; Cekaite and Aronsson, this volume; Vardi-Rath et al., this volume). Importantly, such fine-tuned participation assumes and draws on children's close familiarity with the material, visual and verbal manifestations of childhood genres (Opie and Opie 1959), including adult-activity-based play 'scripts' such as 'shopping,' 'family,' or 'party' (see Sylva, Bruner and Genova 1976; Nelson 2007; also Kyratzis, this volume), as well as with the popular media textual resources that are widely distributed in society (Nicolopoulou et al., this volume). Children's talk is full of references to and repetitions and (subversive) recyclings of vernacular texts, songs, TV films and other popular media (Dyson 2003; Rampton 2006; Maybin 2006, this volume), as well as recyclings of institutional and adult-related activities and talk (Aronsson and Thorell 2002; Kyratzis 2007).

Thus, close studies of peer talk (such as those collected here) trace and demonstrate some of the ways in which young children's cultural resources and modes of interpretation can differ from those of adults. For instance, young children have their specific linguistic codes (like past tense verbs) to mark transition to the world of pretense (Blum-Kulka et al. 2004), they rely on a shared pool of resources, some loosely connected to scripts and characters prominent in popular culture and cultural narratives (e.g., book stories), to establish the thread of a collaboratively constructed pretend play (Vardi-Rath et al., this volume). Similarly, they can collaborate in complicated negotiations around various topics, like the commitment embedded in making a promise, the justification for sharing toys or artifacts of popular culture, or the proper way of enacting a character from a story, based on a set of shared knowledge and moral values (Zadunaisky Ehrlich and Blum-Kulka, this volume). It is this familiarity and children's shared evaluative stances (Du Bois 2007) that promote the achievement of intrinsic motivation and children's intersubjective engagement. Several studies in the book show the complex discursive practices through which the children attempt to overcome social and interactional constraints, preserving sociality despite overt disagreements and language difficulties (Cekaite and Aronsson; Monaco and Pontecorvo; Rydland, Grøver and Lawrence; Zadunaisky Ehrlich and Blum-Kulka, this volume).

Children's peer cultures are thereby inextricably related to their language-mediated socialization into particular kinds of culturally authorized evaluative practices and judgments about how to be and act in the world (Maybin 2006; Goodwin and Kyratzis 2012). These orientations and values in their turn guide and shape children's social positioning, identities and learning opportunities in everyday encounters.

The contribution of social interaction to children's development and learning

The theoretical underpinnings of the present approach to children's peer talk include developmental theories that acknowledge the importance of social interaction as a facilitating factor in children's development. Both Vygotsky's and Piaget's ideas are important in understanding this process. But while they both acknowledged social interaction, Vygotsky and Piaget made different assumptions about interactions with peers and with adults as frameworks for development.

Piaget (1995) viewed children's peer interaction as a fruitful social site for development because peer interactions are not hindered by the power and cognitive asymmetries of adult–child relations and because they allow for dialog and discussion. Owing to their more egalitarian characteristics, peer interactions promote and even maximize cognitive and conceptual conflict, which leads to cognitive change and a higher level of understanding, i.e., re-establishment of equilibrium (Blum-Kulka and Dvir 2010; Tartas, Baucal and Perret-Clermont 2010; Monaco and Pontecorvo, this volume).

In Vygotsky's view, it is through task-related verbal interaction with a cognitively and socially more competent actor that children appropriate skills – skills that later become internalized (Vygotsky 1986). The sociocultural perspective has also been evoked to explain the gains of peer interactions. The conceptualization of knowledge and skills as dynamic and situated provides for the flexible and relational character of expert–novice interactions. In this view, children can learn from each other, fluidly switching between expert and novice roles, because they operate within one another's proximal zones of development (Rogoff 2003; Bodrova and Leong 2007; Blum-Kulka and Dvir 2010; see also Monaco and Pontecorvo, this volume).

Sociocultural perspectives also emphasize the situatedness of learning and teaching encounters within the socially structured practices of peer groups, classrooms and families, all of which are interwoven in larger institutional and cultural frameworks (see Brofenbrenner and Ceci 1994; Hedegaard et al. 2012). The central position is that culture, linguistic discourse, narrative, conceptual knowledge and human cognition intersect and work together in children's participation in community life (Nelson 2007: 212), allowing for multiple developmental gains (e.g., perspective taking, social memory) as well as language and discursive learning. Understanding the outcomes of learning exchanges is therefore dependent on systematic consideration of the larger sociocultural context, societal ideologies and values within which interactions are embedded, and which inevitably structure their nature, meaning and impact, shaping both the participation structures and the availability of learning/teaching interactions. In this view, the benefits of peer discourse depend on multiple contextual factors, including children's age, gender, social class and ethnicity, and are inextricable from the ongoing construction of social positions and identities (Snow 1984; Willet 1995; Cekaite 2012).

The differential roles of peers and adults in interaction

The features that characterize adult–child and children's peer interactions are significant for our understanding of peer talk as an environment for development generally, and for children's language and discursive skills in particular. One of the core aspects of children's interactions with adults is the asymmetry in power, skills and knowledge, and children's interactions with peers might require different strategies of talk management compared with children's talk with adults, (cf. Grøver Aukrust 2004). When adults interact with young children, they tend to do most of the work, initiating and sustaining interaction and repairing breakdowns (Snow 1984; Ninio and Snow 1996). For instance, in family interactions, adults tend to elicit children's explanations and accounts, to support stories with prompts to get started, and to continue, clarify and explicate necessary background knowledge, in this way scaffolding children's talk toward the normative features of adult-like performance (Ochs et al. 1989; Grøver Aukrust and Snow 1998; Blum-Kulka 1997; Sterponi 2009). By way of contrast, peers might provide less support for conversations than adults do (McTear 1985), and in multi-party peer talk, children may need to work hard conversationally to get and keep their turns and speaker roles, thereby meeting the increasing demands of on-line planning (Blum-Kulka and Snow 2002). For instance, when children participate in pretense play, explanatory talk or narratives with peers (who may offer less conversational support and fewer interactional slots to fill in), they may volunteer and set themselves up as explainers or narrators (Grøver Aukrust 2004), using narratives not as factual accounts but as exemplifications and/or justifications for the organization of the emerging play (Küntay and Ervin-Tripp 1997).

In sum, adult–child conversations may offer conversational support and serve as models for adult-like pragmatic development and communicative participation, providing guidelines for culturally and cognitively appropriate conversational performance. However, adult scaffolding may also have a constraining effect on children's discourse: by making the communicative task easier, it may constrain children's investment in the communicative exchange (especially in genres characteristic of children's peer cultures, Pellegrini 2009). Moreover, the interactional ecology that children experience in their daily encounters with adults in formal/educational settings is characterized by marked asymmetry regarding the amount and character of talk. As demonstrated in a study of adult questioning in preschool settings in Great Britain, 94.5 percent of all questions asked were "closed questions that required a recall of fact, decision between a limited selection of choices, or no response at all," and only 5.5 percent were open-ended questions that exhibited a potential for sustained (shared) thinking and talk (Siraj-Blatchford and Mani 2008: 5). These findings reveal the need for an ecologically valid examination of the roles of peers and adults in children's discursive development, motivating socioculturally sensitive explorations of the learning affordances that characterize the conversational genres of children's peer cultures.

Children's discursive literacy and extended discourse in first language interactions

According to the present approach, peer talk may provide children with opportunities for gaining expertise in a wide range of discourse types, by, for instance, offering sites for collaborative social conversations, language play and literate discourse. Several chapters in the book show that young children's peer talk exhibits both oral and literate features and therefore may be considered to occupy an interesting position on the oral–literate continuum. One of the hallmarks of oral cultures is associated with performance – "competence in performance" (Briggs 1988) is part and parcel of the verbal art skills required of storytellers from oral cultures. Young children's peer talk echoes several features of oral performance, in narratives, symbolic play, as well as in other genres (de León 2007). Such features, including playful and ritualized recycling of words and phrases, sound play, formulaic chunks, shifts in intonation and rhythmic variation, have long been noted as typifying preschool children's conversations (e.g., Garvey 1977; Kirschenblatt-Gimblet 1979). For L2 learners, a rich gamut of such poetic-playful uses of language serves as a major resource for entertaining, intrinsically motivating peer discourse and social interaction (Blum-Kulka and Gorbatt, this volume; Cekaite and Aronsson, this volume; Bushnell 2008).

Yet, concurrently, young children's discourse is in many ways literate. One of the impacts of the interface between oral and written cultures throughout history was the development of a literate style in oral language. Indices of a literate style in oral language may include extended stretches of coherent discourse, structures that allow for distancing and decontextualization (like nominalizations) and a precise vocabulary (Scollon and Scollon 1981; Olson 1996). Children in modern societies thus grow up in a sociocultural context deeply embedded in literate traditions and texts involving *discursive literacy* practices (manifest typically but not exclusively by genres of extended discourse; Blum-Kulka 2004: 195). From a holistic perspective on literacy, conceptualized as situated and aimed at meaning-making (Snow 2004), connected discourse about non-current events, tuned to the audience's presumed state of knowledge, is at the heart of "literate" or "decontextualized" genres (Ninio and Snow 1996). From this perspective, we suggest that children's peer group activities (including children's pretend play) represent a fruitful site for pragmatic development and discursive literacy (e.g., Harris 2000; Pellegrini 2009). Conceptual links between pretend play and early literacy are demonstrated through the similarity of the "design features of the language used in social pretend" play and school-based literacy (Pellegrini 2009: 175). Language-mediated participation in pretend play involves the ability to initiate and maintain pretense with peers and requires (as well as allows one to practice) a considerable amount of social cognitive as well as verbal facility. The ambiguity inherent in pretend play – "where there is little correspondence between the meaning of an object or a role in play and its real practice" and where children move in and out of pretense – necessitates that children utilize their perspective-taking ability, enlisting their linguistic skills to explicate the meaning of their play themes in pursuit of intersubjectivity (Pellegrini 2009: 175). In children's multi-party talk, the multiple actors' contributions give rise to the necessity to "juggle multiple perspectives," which, as suggested, constitutes a key capacity in understanding written texts and contributes to the acquisition of academically mediated language skills.

In addition to extended discourse, a characteristic feature of pretend play is speech representation, that is, 'in character' speech that gives children opportunities to perfect their skills in enacting different registers, and to rely on register-specific resources to build extended play events (Sawyer 1997; Aronsson and Thorell 2002), thus contributing to children's (literacy-relevant) high level of coherent performance (Blum-Kulka 2005a). Several chapters in the book examine discursive practices associated with children's discursive literacy, such as distancing and textual coherence in arguments (Zadunaisky Ehrlich and Blum-Kulka, this volume), macro-structure in narratives (Nicolopoulou, this volume), as well as different forms of reflexivity, namely explorations in the way language is used and exhibited in meta-talk related to pretend play (Kyratzis, this volume; Vardi-Rath et al., this volume).

In older children's (e.g., preadolescents') school-based literacy practices, there is a close linkage and cross-fertilization between academic and nonacademic textual (popular culture) resources. Children's social and academic purposes intersect, and a range of language-mediated cultural and textual materials from popular culture (such as various utterance types, words and phrases, Dyson 2003) may constitute the building blocks of both children's social worlds and their language/pragmatic skills (see also Maybin, this volume).

The approach taken, however, does not consider peer discourse (e.g., pretend play and other types of peer discourse) as the sole source of children's discursive learning. Rather, a view taken from the current perspective conceptualizes children's discourse as one of the matrixes for learning (complementary to the learning potentials of adult-based, family and educational practices).

Peer talk and second language learning

Potentials and drawbacks of peer interactions

Since the emergence of interactionist theories of second language (henceforth L2) acquisition, the potential benefits and drawbacks of peer interaction for L2 acquisition have been a focus of interest (Wong-Fillmore 1979, 1991; Ervin-Tripp 1986). Benefits are clearly present when peer interaction provides opportunities for learners to interact with native speakers. These interactions constitute additional (and qualitatively distinct) sources of exposure to the target language beyond that provided by adults/teachers. In educational settings, informal talk with peers in L2 may constitute less anxiety-provoking situations of language use, as compared to formal interactions with adults/teachers, who ask for public displays of formal L2 knowledge (Fassler 1998). It is in peer interactions that children have opportunities to engage in intrinsically motivating discursive genres and use forms of language that are unlikely in interactions with adults/teachers: negotiations, arguments, explanations and questioning, etc. In preschools, where adult–child interactions may be relatively short and infrequent, peers may provide crucial forms of L2 exposure and opportunities for language practice (Karrebœck 2008; Blum-Kulka and Gorbatt, this volume). The teaching potentials of such peer interactions are realized primarily implicitly, rather than as explicit, meta-level educational strategies. In addition to facilitating the broadening of children's communicative repertoires in L2, children's participation in play and related discursive genres (explanatory talk, out-of-frame negotiations) may enhance non-native speakers' academic language skills (receptive vocabulary and word definition skills) in L2 (Grøver Aukrust 2004), and children's participation in fairly complex explanations and out-of-frame negotiations in preschool has an impact on their oral literacy skills in first grade (Rydland 2009).

As noted earlier, the factors related to children's social and cognitive development, communicative practices and social relations all converge in shaping children's language experiences (as potentially different from adults); here, age and context both make a difference in the purposes of language use, the provision and character of conversational feedback (e.g., corrections), and its uptake (Philp et al. 2008; Oliver and Grote 2010). When older children participate in language-education-oriented settings, such as dual-language programs, peer teaching and learning strategies during educational activities (group work) have been found to include practicing by repetition, paraphrasing, translating, clarifying and scaffolding with cues, code-switching, and the use of formulaic language (Angelova et al. 2006; Philp and Duchesne 2008).

Peer interactions in L2 settings may also have drawbacks. The presence of native-language-speaking peers (or proficient non-native speakers of L2) does not automatically lead to beneficial peer interaction and language learning. The indexical relation between the speaker's language proficiency and social identity has been shown to be of significance for the organization of social order and the communicative practices of peer groups: gaining social acceptance from peers (competent language speakers) might pose a challenge to beginner L2 learners or even peer group members who have spent considerable time in the preschool group, and they may be treated as socially irrelevant members of the class/group (Tabors 1997; Fassler 1998; Cekaite and Björk-Willén 2013). Novices thus have to pass a certain communicative threshold before gaining acceptance in verbal interactions with linguistically competent peers (Blum-Kulka and Gorbatt this volume). Detailed longitudinal and context-sensitive studies are therefore significant in painting a nuanced picture of L2 acquisition as inextricable from the learning opportunities generated in various participation frameworks.

Some of the recurrent interactional ecologies for second language learners do not involve possibilities for extensive or wide-ranging interactions with native speakers. In fact, due partly to immigration patterns, segregation, and the complexities of school systems, such interactions are rather limited (Fassler 1998: 381; Cekaite 2012). Across a wide range of settings – including early childhood and primary school classrooms, characterized by a predominance of second language learners from a wide mix of language backgrounds – language learners frequently and increasingly serve as each other's interactional partners. While several studies have demonstrated that, in such environments, children's sociability and evolving social relationships may serve as an impetus for talk in the second language (English; Swedish) (Ervin-Tripp 1986; Cekaite 2007), thus constituting conditions for engaging in productive L2 learning, we need to advance our knowledge about peer talk and learning in particular linguistic ecologies.

Learning about language codes and varieties through peer talk

Peer talk in bilingual and multilingual settings constitutes a significant locus for children's learning about language varieties and new languages, as well as children's adult-unsupervised exploration of societal, educational and local language ideologies. Linguistic ethnographies have convincingly demonstrated the impact of peer (siblings and friends) interactions on language preservation or language shift (Rindstedt and Aronsson 2002; Kyratzis, Reynolds and Evaldsson 2010; Paugh 2012). The sociolinguistic properties of talk (codes, registers and varieties) serve as relevant markers of children's identity and social positioning in children's local peer cultures. In multilingual groups of immigrant children, numerous languages, target language proficiencies and variants may be represented, creating ground for children's attention to correct/incorrect language use and their language awareness, as exercised through, for instance, language corrective practices (Cekaite and Björk-Willén 2013). Code-switching might be used as an interactional resource to organize the social order of the peer group (Cromdal 2004; Kyratzis, this volume), simultaneously allowing for the exploration and/or subversion, as well as cultural (re-)production, of adult-based societal language ideologies and norms. Children's orientations to the valued language varieties or their native language proficiency may account for the differential positioning of L2 speakers and the difficulties they encounter in the process of becoming accepted/ratified and valued members of target-language-speaking peer groups. Peer talk in the first and second language inevitably involves the negotiation of children's social positioning and identity work (Björk-Willén 2007; Blum-Kulka and Gorbatt, this volume; Rydland et al., this volume). Context-sensitive approaches to learning thus call attention to the diversity of social interactions, participant constellations and relations, including the diverse modes of mutual support, collaboration, or exclusion between peers.

The book at hand

As noted at the beginning of this introductory chapter, studies on children's peer discourse have shown increasing interest in the contribution of such discourse to children's language and pragmatic development. However, no extensive systematic effort has been made to synthesize this work and to provide empirical foundations for this theoretical view. The present volume represents such an effort by bringing together a group of scholars who examine peer discourse and discuss its potentials for learning. We believe that the volume benefits from our choice to cover a wide spectrum of contexts of language use, languages and age groups as well as analytical and methodological approaches to children's peer talk, which has allowed us to lay a detailed and well-informed ground for future investigation. The analysis of peer talk is conducted using an array of discourse, pragmatic and conversation analyses and both qualitative and quantitative tools. The chapters report on studies involving children in the age range from early childhood (3 years) to preadolescence (12 years), documenting children's everyday talk and educational practices and focusing on their engagement in peer group communities inside and outside formal educational contexts (preschools, primary schools) during play, group work and recess activities. The studies all present in-depth investigations of small samples, although they range in size from qualitative case studies to larger samples that allow statistical treatment of individual growth. Sample characteristics vary across studies, from children recruited primarily from low-income families to samples reflecting a broad range of socioeconomic backgrounds. The studies comprise ethnographic approaches that rely on video- or audio-recordings or field notes of children's conversations, in some chapters combined with interview data. Moreover, the studies range from extensive analysis of peer talk over a short period, focusing on a particular type of experience or exposure, to those that analyze the potentials (and outcomes) of peer talk from a longitudinal perspective. They have been carried out in a variety of social and cultural contexts: the languages and cultural communities in focus include children speaking Hebrew, English, Spanish, Turkish, Norwegian, Swedish, Finnish, Arabic and Italian.

While this volume's chapters cover multiple analytical and methodological perspectives, they share a constructivist view on child socialization (Corsaro 2005), as well as a sociocultural perspective on learning as a social, interactionally anchored endeavor. The children are engaged in discursive practices in the domains of literacy-related, explanatory and metapragmatic discourse, narrative and argumentative moves, and bilingual language use.

As we have mentioned above, one important goal of this collection of articles is to stimulate our understanding of children's peer discourse as well as to direct future research into some of the themes presented here. There are, inevitably, many areas of child peer interactions not covered in this volume. Children's dyadic – "best friend" – interactions are characteristics of participant constellations in children's everyday life and deserve additional treatment in empirical research, as does children's later pragmatic development (Berman 2004; Blum-Kulka et al. 2004). With regard to the social and cultural embeddedness of children's peer group activities, research needs to consider the differential specificities of peer discourse in a broader range of cultural contexts. Particular attention needs to be paid to non-Western peer cultures (the majority of the world), thus contributing to a view on children's peer learning that is sensitive to cultural and historical transformations. Concerning children's peer interactions and second language learning, further longitudinal and ethnographic research is required to take account of the social and linguistic aspects and outcomes of interactional practices. Finally, as children's lives become increasingly entangled with media and new technologies, we have to pay careful attention to how these resources shape children's practices and interactional engagements with multiple languages (e.g., global English) and novel semiotic/textual materials (Crookal 2007). Below we present a synopsis of the studies collected in this book.

The structure of this book

In this introductory chapter, a comprehensive overview of the research field is provided that discusses a sociocultural and interactive perspective on pragmatic development and on peer talk as a "double opportunity learning space." The merits and drawbacks of children's peer talk in relation to earlier pragmatic, sociolinguistic, anthropological and developmental research on children are highlighted.

Part II (Children's peer talk and extended discourse) focuses on children's peer group interactions in first-language settings. The goal of this section is to distinguish peer talk as a significant locus for recurrent and varied genres of extended discourse, illustrating the ways in which peer talk (narratives, explanations, arguments and pretend play produced together with, and for, a multiparty audience) may enhance the development of a full gamut of discursive literacy skills.

In the first chapter, Sara Zadunaisky Ehrlich and Shoshana Blum-Kulka present the concept of the "double opportunity space" and explore, within this framework, children's argumentative discourse in preschool peer group interactions. The authors examine its multilayered learning affordances and demonstrate that children established and negotiated their social order, co-constructed their peer-culture practices and values, while they simultaneously – at the discursive literacy learning level and through the production of complex linguistic acts – constructed literacy-relevant features of textuality and distancing. In a longitudinal study, Ageliki Nicolopoulou, Caroline Brockmeyer Cates, Aline de Sá and Hande Ilgaz document the emergence and development of shared narrative themes in the story-telling and story-acting practices of preschool children. The authors show that this multi-party activity comprised individual creativity and peer collaboration, in a long-term perspective offering children both resources and motivations for narrative activity and narrative development. Next, Esther Vardi-Rath, Eva Teubal, Hadassah Aillenberg and Teresa Lewin examine the characteristics of children's pretend play in the wake of story reading, considering the influence of literary text on the occurrence of literacy-relevant features (high register vocabulary, decontextualized language, sequence and structure) in preschool play discourse. Camilla Monaco and Clotilde Pontecorvo examine the characteristics of 8- to 9-year-old children's explanatory talk during a small group educational activity aimed at discursive historical reasoning, demonstrating how this activity was instrumental in the children's active exploration of knowledge by allowing them (depending on the social characteristics of the group) to engage in argumentative discourse: to express, negotiate and modify ideas. Finally, Janet Maybin's chapter explores preadolescent girls' affective evaluations in talk. By examining girls' collaborative recyclings and transformations of popular media texts, the author shows how they served as resources in the co-construction of peer group communicative genres and shared evaluative stances, and constituted affordances for their collaborative exploration of social values.

In all, the first set of studies seeks to contribute to a deeper understanding of particular peer group discursive activities by documenting and exemplifying the diverse ways in which peer talk affords the opportunity to negotiate sense-making on discursive and social planes.

In Part III of the book (Peer talk and second language learning), empirical studies examine children's interactions in a second language. By considering multiple participant constellations in which second language learners use peer talk, the authors investigate the conditions under which peers' talk provides a fruitful locus for practicing and learning a second language. All studies provide a complex picture of children's L2 interactions, showing that peer talk inextricably involves socialization into normatively appropriate language use and negotiated access to desirable and valued cultural and peer identities (including the potential drawbacks and negative effects of peer exclusion).

In the first chapter, bilingual children's pretend play and their use of a range of contextualization cues (code-switching, explicit statements, material artifacts) in a Spanish–English preschool are explored by Amy Kyratzis. The study illustrates how the children collaboratively established the framing of a pretend scene as they accomplished social alignments and, through the use of decontextualized language, engaged in literacy-relevant discursive practices. Next, Ann-Carita Evaldsson and Fritjof Sahlström explore children's language alternation practices in multilingual peer group talk. In a case study of an immigrant girl's attempts to learn Finnish in different language and cultural communities (Finland and Sweden), they document the peer group's metasociolinguistic stances taken towards majority/minority languages and highlight the importance of power and control as well as the agency of second language learners (in learning processes).

Several studies conducted detailed contextualized, longitudinal analyses of peer contributions to the process of learning a second language. Shoshana Blum-Kulka and Naomi Gorbatt, in a language socialization study, consider the interactional accomplishments and failures of Hebrew L2 novices with their Hebrew-speaking peers in preschool and school interactions over time. Through a detailed tracking of children's interactions, an intimate link between children's access to L1-speaking peers, their negotiation of intercultural identities and learning affordances are revealed: while immigrant children strived to acquire membership in the new communities of practice by constantly repositioning themselves socially and culturally, the facilitative role of peer interactions was not available as long as they did not master at least rudimentary modes of communication in the new (majority) language. Asta Cekaite and Karin Aronsson present an ethnographic examination of spontaneous peer-language play in a Swedish language immersion classroom, highlighting how metalinguistic and metapragmatic reflexivity were actively exploited in children's collaborative ludic interactions, generating opportunities for talk, as well as sensitizing children to second language structure and pragmatic conventions. In a longitudinal study of peer talk in preschool and school with Turkish children learners of Norwegian (conducted by Veslemøy Rydland, Vibeke Grøver and Joshua Lawrence), the productive link between peer play talk and second language and vocabulary skills is documented. The authors assess the potential long-term impact of peer talk during playtime in preschool and provide quantitative and qualitative results on the relation between the quality of peer play talk and children's short- and long-term L2 vocabulary development.

Finally, the concluding chapter by Katherine Nelson tracks the historical development of socially oriented child language research and discusses the overall discursive features of peer interactions.

Concluding observations

The present volume synthesizes a range of theoretical perspectives and empirical research and presents a collection of up-to-date empirical research on the affordances of peer interactions, thus contributing to and extending the insights gained through ethnographic, sociolinguistic and developmental studies of peer interaction. Distinguishing the ways in which children's conversations (in and out of school) serve as dynamic social sites for social-relational work, cultural (re-)production and discursive learning, the book strives to contribute to a more holistic understanding of children's peer talk. Our hope is that while bringing together a rich collection of issues related to peer discourse, the story that emerges will provide a multifaceted and coherent view on children's talk as a productive matrix of social, cognitive and discursive development. Though certainly not limited to the areas covered, we envisage continued investigations into the specificity of peer talk in different age, social and cultural groups and context-sensitive pedagogical practices that take account of, and productively use, the social and discursive potentials of peer discourse.

Part II

Children's peer talk and extended discourse

2   "Now I said that Danny becomes Danny again": a multifaceted view of kindergarten children's peer argumentative discourse

Sara Zadunaisky Ehrlich and Shoshana Blum-Kulka

Introduction

"Now I said that Danny becomes Danny again." Is the speaker telling an imaginary story or is he or she engaged in an ongoing pretend play between peers? The speaker in this case is Rafael, a six-year-old boy, arguing with Danny, his mate, playing at the computer. In this event, documented at preschool, Rafael and another boy previously tried to undermine Danny's status by turning him into a sweet potato. Thus, at this point in the event, the utterance signals Rafael's intent of reconciliation with his mate Danny. During the event, both children turn each other into sweet potatoes and become children again, illustrating how children employ a metaphor in a short narrative that serves opposing argumentative goals, showing one of the varied means preschool children make use of to cope with events of an argumentative character. Argumentation constitutes a significant feature of all human interaction. The present study set out to explore the argumentative discourse of children with peers.

We consider young children's conversations as a unique linguistic, social and cultural phenomenon. Our approach to argumentative discourse draws on viewing children's peer talk as a *double opportunity space*: from this double perspective, peer talk serves simultaneously as an arena for meaning-making within childhood culture, as well as a springboard for the mastering of social, cognitive and discursive skills (Blum-Kulka, Huck-Taglicht and Avni 2004). Through peer talk children participate at any given moment in a process of meaning-making unique to their given community of practice, co-constructing at different age levels the discursive, social and cultural worlds of childhood. This joint, moment by moment process of the creation of childhood peer culture is a central feature of childhood. Yet, as will be demonstrated here for argumentative discourse, the concurrent collective creation of fictive and non-fictive realities in space and time offers varied opportunities for individual, social, cognitive and discursive developmental gains.

The speech events children are engaged in are rich in developmental *affordances*.[1] The term is used here to refer to those aspects of given contextual and textual occasions which are geared to children's abilities to allow for reciprocal linguistic and social socialization, presumably serving as a nursery for gaining experience in and elaboration of a gamut of discursive and social skills (Blum-Kulka 2010a). Accordingly, peer-talk speech events embody two concepts of time – time *in* childhood and the time *of* childhood. Time *in* childhood is the passage of time as subjectively experienced by the children in the present of their childhood; the time *of* childhood is the objective chronological passage of time that keeps moving forward, its movement carrying developmental consequences (Blum-Kulka, Huck-Taglicht and Avni 2004; Blum-Kulka 2005a; Blum-Kulka and Hamo 2010).

Viewing these two processes as simultaneous requires a balanced methodological view, one that considers the cultural and developmental as complementary aspects of every peer-talk speech event, for the children as much as for the researcher. Indeed, in our former work on argumentative discourse, we have explored children's argumentative discourse in natural peer interactions at preschool from such a double perspective, integrating the cultural and a developmental approach within one model of peer-talk discursive events. We pinpointed – on the plane of childhood culture – the ways argumentative events maintain and transform the social order and display features of children's culture; and on the developmental plane, we showed how children's discursive strategies incorporate innovative child-unique strategies, as well as strategies which echo discursive conventions from the adult culture (Zadunaisky Ehrlich and Blum-Kulka 2010).

In this chapter, our goal is to pinpoint the social, cultural and discursive affordances and gains of argumentative discourse, thereby enhancing the need for a multifaceted view of peer talk at large. As will be shown, although the social and cultural affordances are strongly associated with the 'on-line' co-construction of childhood culture, and discursive affordances tie in more with language socialization, each of these dimensions also carries within it the potential for gains on the other plane.

Research on children's argumentative discourse has been carried out from multiple perspectives that are not necessarily aware of each other. Roughly speaking, these studies are associated with two main traditions that parallel the two planes of the double opportunity space: a developmental tradition and a socio-cultural one. The former tended in recent years to highlight the role of conflicts as occasions for the learning of social skills, for refining the separation of self and other, for gaining emotional understanding, for foreseeing the outcome of specific behaviors and for the refinement of social argumentative skills towards more mature adult-like forms (see for instance, Dunn 1999; Stein and Albro 2001). The latter refers to argumentative events between peers as a site of enculturation in which children cultivate their own culture while adopting and having their own reading of the cultural pattern of the society at large (Goodwin and Kyratzis 2007; Kampf and Blum-Kulka 2011). The present work draws on both traditions, unveiling a double perspective in the study of argumentative discourse in natural peer talk, both socio-cultural and developmental. The novelty of our approach resides in our attempt to demonstrate that the affordances of argumentative discourse go beyond social learning and include opportunities for cultural and discursive literacy gains. It is in this way that we ascribe to argumentative events between peers in particular, and to peer talk, in general, a double opportunity space that allows for children's active co-construction of their social world and culture in the present of their childhood, and provides simultaneously a wide gamut of occasions for children's overall development.

Defining argumentative events in peer talk

Defining argumentation is controversial (Plantin 2002). Some definitions emphasize reasonableness and coherent justifications as the very core of the argumentative activity (see, for instance, Govier 2001), while others consider argumentation as mainly a social interaction aimed at conflict expression, in which the role of emotions needs to be taken into consideration (Weigand 2006).[2] We adopt a linguistic-discursive approach to argumentation that emphasizes its dialogic dimension. Based on Hymes' notion of speech event,[3] we define an argumentative event as a contextually situated form of social practice, in which at least two parties take alternative positions on the same issue and develop adversative positions in various ways by providing justifications, grounds, support, explanations, stories, and so on. This definition comprises instances that range from discussions to disputes. Discussions are usually identified with a notion of rationality and the application of coherent thinking tools, and disputes are perceived as being governed by extra-rational and affective factors (Dascal 2000). However, we maintain that this pre-demarcation depends on the orientation adopted (whether logical, interactional or goal oriented) and on the perspective taken (whether an etic or emic viewpoint). We adopt a participant's emic view that does not impose an a priori clear-cut demarcation between discussions and disputes, since they can be intertwined within one single argumentative event: a dispute can evolve dynamically into a discussion and vice versa.

Participants and data gathering

The children who participated in this study (4;3 to 6;5 years old) all attended preschool at the secular education stream in Israel and had Hebrew as their native language. The entire sample was taken from a socially mixed parental background presenting a broad distribution of professions and years of education. The children were recorded during free-play time, interacting in a variety of participation structures in three different settings: (1) individual audio recordings of children wearing lapel microphones connected to a tape recorder in a small pouch; (2) setting-focused audio recordings taped by a small tape recorder placed at the center of some activity (e.g., the drawing table); and (3) setting-focused video recordings. An observer was present for all interactions, taking extended field notes that included a detailed description of participants, situations and actions that were later integrated into the transcripts of the audio. The materials recorded were transcribed using an amended version of the Jeffersonian Conversational Analytic transcription system (see transcription conventions at the end of the chapter). The children were recorded for relatively extended periods, from one and a half to two hours. After a first screening and listening to the material gathered, a partial transliteration of the tapes that combined field notes with the audio data was used as a basis for segment selection for transcription, 20 minutes per child. In the next stage, we identified stretches of talk in the transcripts as *argumentative discursive events*,[4] according to the definition above, and they served as our basic unit of analysis. Our analysis, informed by a discourse analysis approach, portrays a rich picture of peer talk, showing the social, cultural and discursive literacy *socialization affordances* of argumentative events to children's development, as will be shown in the following illustrative examples.

Co-constructing the peer group socio-cultural habitat

Social affordances

Sociality is a basic driving force of human interaction. In Enfield and Levinson's formulation, "At the heart of the uniquely human way of life is our peculiarly intense, mentally mediated, and highly structured way of interacting with one another" (Enfield and Levinson 2002: 1). In Levinson's view, human interaction is driven by an "interaction engine" based on cooperative modes of behavior (linguistic and otherwise) unique in the animal world (Levinson 2002). Sociality is hence at the heart of language development; it creates – both personally and socio-culturally – the basis on which children develop not only understanding of intentionality, as crucial for human understanding, but also the ability to create joint attention and shared intentions with the other (Tomasello 2002). The study of children's peer culture strongly confirms the degree to which sociality is of prime value in human interaction at large and in children's worlds in particular. Children rely on all available semiotic resources in their environment to co-construct and enrich the social and cultural habitat of their peer group; it is a habitat built on the intense involvement of its participants, which is also subject to the discursive and pragmatic developmental constraints of the given age group. The need to compensate for such constraints gives rise to a gamut of age-related discursive strategies (Blum-Kulka 2005a; Blum-Kulka and Hamo 2010).

Argumentative events are adversative by nature. However, as will be shown, they are managed by the children – in play and out of play – in ways that do not necessarily threaten sociality. Corsaro (1985) argues that children's efforts to collaborate in play are tied to their concept of friendship: one needs to develop stable relations with several playmates to maximize opportunities for play, conflicts pose a threat to play and to friendship and hence the effort to avoid conflicts. Yet Corsaro also noted that comparative research of kids' cultures shows that conflicts can contribute to the development and strengthening of friendship bonds (Corsaro 2003). We concur with the latter claim.

We view collaboration between peers in argumentative events as tied to the children's general commitment to sociality, which in turn can give rise to the formation of close friendship ties even in preschool. It is this commitment that may override all other considerations even in adversative contexts, in and out of play, and among children with varying degrees of friendship ties (Kampf and Blum-Kulka 2007, 2011; Zadunaisky Ehrlich and Blum-Kulka 2010). Here we show how sociality comes into play when children sustain underlying cooperation even in an event of adversative nature (Excerpt 1), and when children draw on the world of fantasy to avoid entering a conflict (Excerpt 2).

In the first excerpt, a group of children are drawing. Two of them are sitting by the drawing table while others are waiting for their turn to draw. During the entire event, the children mostly disagree about how to draw things and show a real concern regarding who is copying what from whom. At some point, the children reach a compromise that avoids entering into new conflictive sequences, by stipulating role division (who is doing what and with whom).

Ex. 1: "You'll do also what I do?"

Date: 24 February 2000. Galit kindergarten, Jerusalem.
Participants: Amit (m., 4;8), Yuval (m., 4;7), Yaron (m., 4;6) and Golan (m., 5;2) are sitting at a small table drawing.

4.	AMIT: °kodem ani ose ge:za° (…)	AMIT: First I do the (trunk) (…)
5.	YUVAL: LO! (1.5) k, ki ata ose ma she-ani ose, (2.5) tamid carix la'asot rishon.	YUVAL: NO! (1.5) 'cause, because you do what I do, (2.5) you always must do first.
		((turns omitted in which the children kept drawing))
25.	YARON: >ze bidiyuk oto ha-davar kmo she (…) ani ose laxem,< (…) shte- shteynu na'ase oto davar kemo shelahe:m?	YARON: >It's exactly the same as (…) I do for you,< (…) we both will do the same they do?
26.	GOLAN: naxon, ani ya'ase ma she-ata ose.	GOLAN: Ok, I'll do what you do.

27.	YUVAL: ata ta'ase gam ma sheani ose, yaron?	YUVAL: You'll do also what I do, Yaron?
28.	GOLAN: ani, ani gam ya'ase ma she-shtexem osim.	GOLAN: I, I will do also what you both do.
29.	YUVAL: ata ta'ase gam ma she-<u>ani</u> ose?	YUVAL: And also what <u>I</u> do?
30.	GOLAN: ke:::::n.	GOLAN: Ye:::::s.

In this small segment, it is notable how children maintain topical continuity (see the wording of the verb *do*), building cross-turn cohesion that leads to high textual density (see turns 26, 27, 28 and 29). This density in turn, indicates a high level of conversational cooperation which is at odds with the clearly oppositional nature of the exchange. Concurrently, the argument requires close attentiveness to each other's contribution and hence indirectly contributes to the development of *dialogic skills* (such as the Gricean pragmatic rules of conversation, Hamo and Blum-Kulka 2007).

Ex. 2: "Batman the new"

Date: 28 February 2000. Rachel kindergarten, Ashdod.
Participants: Yoni (m., 4;5) and Shon (m., 4;5) are impersonating superheroes.

93.	YONI: ANI, BA↑TME::N!	YONI: I AM, BA↑TME::N!
94.	SHON: en lexa glima.	SHON: You don't have a cape.
95.	YONI: (2.5) l↑o, carix glima yesh li Knefa↑yim.	YONI: (2.5) N↑o, there is no need for a cape. I have wi↑ngs.
96.	SHON: (2.0) ata batman a-<u>xa↑dash</u>.	SHON: (2.0) You are Batman the <u>new</u>↑.
97.	YONI: (0.8) na↑xon.	YONI: (0.8) Ri↑ght.

In this short fragment, Shon pre-empts the development of further conflict that might have arisen in the discussion about what Batman should look like. Shon modifies the concept of Batman when he states that Batman 'the new' is a batman without cape and with wings. Here, the children 'stretch' the limits of the fantasy world to pre-empt a conflictive situation (see also Vardi-Rath et al., this volume), and in keeping the social relations in good standing, they allowed the play to go on. The creative solution offered here was specific to the current situation but the process of flexing the norms of fiction to find ways of solving or managing conflicts is reminiscent of young children's general tendency of learning by *exploring* a wide range of possibilities rather than by step-by-step goal-oriented progress (Gopnik 2009). The next example also shows that the exploration of distanced worlds is especially salient in pretend play. In Gopnik's formulation, especially in such play, "Our young selves get to freely explore both this world, and all possible counterfactual worlds, without worrying about which of the worlds will turn out as inhabitable" (Gopnik 2009: 71).

Ex. 3: "Tinki Winki is the driver"

Date: 30 December 2000. Galit kindergarten, Jerusalem.
Participants: Amit (m., 5;6), Ariel (m., 5;5), Yaron (m., 5;4), Yoav (m., 5;2) and Erez (m., 6;8). The children are playing impersonating Teletubbies characters.

93.	AMIT: >ku↑lam le'i↑kanes le-yad a-(…),< le:::↑-dik°si°	AMIT: >Every↑boy, en↑ter. by the-(…),< to:::↑-dik°si°
94.	YARON: (4.0) °u axi gadol°.	YARON: (4.0) °He is the biggest°.
95.	AMIT: DIKSI, A-NA'AG,	AMIT: DIKSI, THE DRIVER,
96.	YARON: >ani ve-amit, na'a↑g°nu.°< na'ag?	YARON: >I, and-Amit, dro↑° ve°< drove?
97.	AMIT: >LO,< atem, e, tamid Tinki Winki no::e↑g.	AMIT: >NO,< you, e, always Tinki Winki dri::↑ves
98.	YARON: °gam PO ani noeg°.	YARON: °also HERE I drive°.
99.	AMIT: lo naxon, TA↑mid, Tinki Winki no'e↑g.	AMIT: Wrong, AL↑ways, Tinki Winki dri↑ves.
100.	YARON: °lo°.	YARON: ° No°.
101.	AMIT: #ken naxon#.	AMIT: #Yes ((it is)) right#.
102.	YARON: °lama?°	YARON: °Why?°
103.	AMIT: ani, yode'a. (1.1) she-a'iti, ben, shalos ra'iti, (1.2) seret, she- (0.6) >kol pa'am,< she-a↑-teletabiz racu, liso↑'a::, em em amr'r:u le- le-Tinki Winki, ve-az u esi'a otam. [(…)]	AMIT: I know. (1.1) when I was three years old I saw, (1.2) a movie which – (0.6) >every time,< that -the↑-Teletubbies wanted to dri↑ve::, they they said, to- to-Tinki Winki, and then he took them on a ride [(…)]
104.	YARON: [ani] yode'a gam ani raiti az gam ani [itxa].	YARON: [I] know I also saw it, so I'm with [you too].
105.	AMIT: [ve-ani,] Tinki Winki, az ani mesi'a otxa.	AMIT: [and –I,] Tinki Winki, so I take you on a ride.

In this example, the children impersonate Teletubbies characters and discuss who should be the driver in a scene of entering a car. First, Yaron maintains that Diksi is supposed to be the driver since he is the biggest, but Amit insists that it is Tinki Winki's job (turns 97 and 99). This discussion arises in the realm of the children's pretend world anchored in the media (a TV show). However, in order to make their points, the children mix the actual and fictional worlds by recalling a real event (I saw it in a movie) in which they witnessed a fictional instance (in the movie the Teletubbies wanted to go for a ride and asked Tinki Winki to be the driver) to build 'evidence-based' explanations. This combined evidence was also witnessed by Yaron, who aligns himself with Amit and seconds Amit's position by stating explicitly "I saw it so I'm with you too." This illustrates that although children have a solid grasp of division between reality and fantasy (Harris 2000), they can choose to ignore it in order to sustain the social necessities that arise in their play.

Thus, in events of argumentative character during spontaneous and natural play, it seems that children import from all the above-mentioned worlds so as to pre-empt or solve adversative or potential conflictive situations and keep playing. Specifically, in the example above, the children were able to keep playing since they implicitly agreed to accept the mixed reality-fiction explanation as evidence.

In the argumentative events illustrated above, disagreements arise, but the sharing of common make-believes allows children to lean on them and employ them for the pre-emption or attenuation of conflicts. Children's implicit agreement regarding their 'co-constructed world' is based on the fact that, on the one hand, their fantasy world is unlimited (so you can put a spell on one squirrel in a book and you get two), but on the other hand, you must look for 'evidences' that exist 'for real' about the same fantasy world (you saw it in a TV show). This unique mixture makes the solutions plausible and even reasonable for the children. In this way, the social ground for playing is re-nourished, and though disagreements occur, children approach them in ways that enable friendship to be sustained and the activity at hand to be continued.

Following this line of thought, once conflicts arise, children can avoid direct confrontation by displaying strategies that prevent their escalation. For instance, on one occasion, two boys, Amir and Gadi, were trading Pokemon stickers (stickers based on cartoon characters) (for a full analysis see Kampf and Blum-Kulka 2011; Zadunaisky Ehrlich and Blum-Kulka 2010). One of the children employed various strategies to avoid overt and direct refusals to give up or trade a valued sticker: first, he provided a justification ("but I have only six"), then, he enlisted the aid of his audience by speaking about his opponent in the third person ("He WANTS me to give him such a Pokeball sticker"), and finally, he evoked the voice of his older sister, an authoritative third party, to completely avoid the possibility of compliance with his opponent's request ("my sister will scream at me that I gave one for free"). This brings to mind, in a sense, adults' practices in business negotiations, whereby participants avoid direct moves of refusal and try to manage disagreement without displaying it too overtly.

Based on all the examples above, we can see that while negotiating over stickers or over their participation in different activities, children also negotiate their social relations. Though not all children's disputes manifest the strategies of pre-empting or mitigation, on the whole, it appears that children seem oriented to cooperation and face concerns. Due to the children's commitment to sociality, they express clearly opposing acts, but do so in a conversationally cooperative way, relying on face-saving indirect moves and a shared leaning on a common fantasy world. It is the children's social co-constructed world in the present of childhood which is most responsible for young children's modes of conflict resolution (Kampf and Blum-Kulka 2011). In this way, children

Kindergarten children's argumentative discourse

cultivate and renew their own culture, while simultaneously acquiring social skills of conflict management as well as discursive skills.

Cultural affordances

Through their participation in cultural routines, children creatively appropriate information from the adult world to produce their own peer culture (Corsaro 1992). The cultural habitat of young children's peer groups is constantly reshaped by the children themselves; in the process they draw on those aspects that speak to them from the cultural capital of the adult world and on the norms and conventions that constitute the 'institutional culture' of their preschools or kindergartens. At the same time, they are also engaged in negotiating and creating local cultural norms and conventions specific to their age group, sometimes at odds with those of the adult world. For example, telling a friend to "stand in line" in a game or echoing the teacher's directive to tidy up evoke adult norms, while declaring being in a state of "sholem" (peace) after a fight is performing an Israeli cultural ritual of preschoolers (Blum-Kulka and Hamo 2010). The following examples show, for instance, the development of local conventions geared to the momentary needs of the children's peer group society and culture.

Ex. 4: "Today I'll be a boy"

Date: 1 May 2000. Rachel kindergarten, Ashdod.
Participants: Ben (m., 4;1) and Idit (f., 4;7). The children are on their way to washing their hands. The two basins and toilets were assigned by the children as belonging to boys or girls.

50.	BEN: ZE SHEL A-BAN- at ben?	BEN: THIS IS FOR THE-BOY (BOYS)-are you a boy?
51.	IDIT: °day. ani lo bat ve-ben, az ani kan. (2.2) ani lo bat ve ben. °	IDIT: °Stop it. I'm not a girl and a boy, so I'm here. (2.2) I'm not a girl and a boy.°
52.	BEN: MA?	BEN: What?
53.	IDIT: ° [(ani gam ben ve-ani gam bat.)] °	IDIT: ° [(I'm a boy and also a girl)] °
54.	CH1: <[anaxnu banot].>	CH1: <[We are girls].>
55.	BEN: >at,< axshav at- ayom at be::n?	BEN: > You,< now, are you today a bo::y?
56.	IDIT: °>ken<°.	IDIT: °>Yes<°.
57.	BEN: ve-maxar m:a ti'i?	BEN: And tomorrow wha:t will you be?
58.	IDIT: °>bat<. maxar ani eye bat, °a-yom ani-ye ben.°	IDIT: °A girl. Tomorrow I'll be a girl,°today, I'll be a boy°.
59.	BEN: ve::: axarey maxa:r?	BEN: A:::nd after tomo:rrow?
60.	IDIT: (1.4) ani:ye bat.	IDIT: (1.4) I'll be a girl.

In this example, Idit approached one of the basins but Ben stopped her by saying firmly that the basin was for the boys. Idit initially appealed as not being either (turn 51), while subsequently maintaining that she was both a boy and a girl (turn 53), indicating that she was ready to negotiate flexibly the boundaries of the category of gender to achieve her local goal of reaching a specific basin. Moreover, when upon Ben's query (turn 55) she is asked to resolve the gender issue she decides that today she is a boy, thereby gaining access to the basin she was attempting to reach. The question of 'gender consistency,' namely, whether and when gender is a fixed characteristic that is not altered by external transformations in appearance or activities, has been investigated in children from a cognitive perspective, but the age at which children accomplish complete gender constancy remains to be resolved (Ruble, Martin and Berenbaum 2006). It was generally found that children achieve gender constancy at about age 6–7 years, after a period at preschool and kindergarten in which they negatively evaluate gender role violations (such as wearing opposite-sex-typed clothing). Interestingly, appearance violations tend to be judged as particularly serious for boys in comparison to girls. It seems that the consequences of norm violations for girls in terms of activities are more tolerable, possibly because boys' activities are often seen as more desirable (Zosuls, Lurye and Ruble 2008). Against this background, our interest here is in how the category of gender is socially constructed in the process of interaction (Butler 1990). Gender is an important resource for people, both as an inference-rich way of categorizing people and as feature of grammar that helps to relate initial and subsequent references to the same person (Logan Kelin 2011: 66). Society, through language, furnishes children with terms related to gender as boys–girls, he–she and so on, for referring and categorizing each other. In this segment, it is notable how children approached a conflictive event related to gender in a way that seems to be unique to childhood: Ben not only recognized Idit's self-reference as a boy (turn 55) but he also enabled Idit to produce a subsequent and future self-reference, changing again and becoming a girl the day after even if today she is a boy. By continuing the conversational sequence ("and the day after tomorrow?"), not only did Ben not repair Idit's statement but he also implicitly confirmed that the flexibility in gender attribution and categorization was also shared by him and responded to the children's ongoing goals. Thus this way of managing the argumentative sequence as a moment-to-moment construction of shared meaning, in which children may modify ("violate") norms related to gender definition and constancy, illustrates a specific moment in the co-construction of childhood culture in the setting of their own norms and conventions.

Discursive literacy affordances

Last, we argue that argumentative events between peers afford opportunities for learning as well as for practicing 'discursive literacy' skills. By 'discursive literacy' skills we mean children's underlying competence that allows the production and interpretation of 'literate' uses of language in both oral and written discourse. At large, over the centuries, literate uses of language in oral discourse have been associated with the impact of writing on cognition and culture (Olson 1994). In the study of child discourse, such uses have been alternatively identified as manifest in children's 'decontextualized' or 'extended' discourse[5] (see also Kyratzis, this volume). In our conceptualization, discursive literacy incorporates, but is not limited to, extended discourse. We view discursive literacy as "the ability to process and produce a rich repertoire of texts in different modalities (e.g., speech and writing), in a variety of discourse words, registers and genres" (Blum-Kulka 2010a: 24). Discursively literate texts are typified – in different combinations and to different degrees – by a relatively high level of explicitness, clearly marked textual cohesion and coherence, context sensitivity, lexical preciseness and syntactic complexity. To be discursively literate is further associated with varying levels of reflexivity, namely the ability to reflect on and repair language use (Blum-Kulka 2010a). In the following argumentative segments, we discuss and show illustrative examples of two main principles associated with discursive literacy: the principle of *textuality* and the principle of *distancing*. The former refers here to the ability of one speaker/writer stringing sentences together in a cohesive and coherent sequence that has a clear textual fabric and internal logic within one (or several) extended turn(s) in conversation or a given passage in writing. The latter is highly associated with the ability to fine-tune the text's level of explicitness to the participants' assumed level of familiarity with its underlying assumptions (Blum-Kulka 2002, 2010a). Both principles are commonly evident in genres of extended discourse, that is, in children's production of coherent, relatively autonomous and sequentially constructed texts that fit genre conventions. However, we argue that they can also emerge in different language configurations as in the form of a phrase that is unexpected in its precision, abstractedness, generality or remoteness in children's argumentative events, as shown below.

Applying the principle of textuality

The ability to build a consistent and continuous sequence that has a coherent internal logic, in multi-party events of argumentative character at preschool, depends not only on children's experience in text construction but also on their skill in holding extended turns of talk. This is not an easy task to accomplish, in particular when the events are emotionally charged exchanges of adversative character. While arguing, children not only need to possess sufficient pragmatic knowledge to get their right to speak, but they also need to know how to hold the floor and gain time in order to build a relatively long sequence in which they can advance or expose their arguments. This may explain why we do not have an abundance of extended turns in our database.

Nevertheless, we have found a few examples that illustrate children's ability to sequentially build good arguments and hold extended turns of talk. On one occasion, two children, Oren and Dani, were impersonating Pokemon characters (for an additional analysis, see also Blum-Kulka 2005a). At some point, Dani accused Oren of having killed a Pokemon character and Oren countered him by building a coherent argument. He claimed in a dramatic tone as if telling an old secret tale: *The Dentils disguised themselves, one Dentil disguised ((himself)) as me, because he- because he- he wanted you to think that I did it. He simply had an accurate disguise because of his simulating device.* In this extended turn, we note an evidence-based explanation that is sequentially organized in a coherent way. Oren provides an alternative explanation (it was someone else), a chain of intentions and motives for another entity to be responsible for the act of killing a Pokemon, and additional evidence to back up his point (the entity had an accurate simulating device that misled Dani). This extended turn also illustrates how 'theory of mind' works in a natural setting. Theory of mind goes hand in hand with the concept of pretense and it refers to the ability of a person to attribute mental states to self and to others and to predict behavior on the basis of such states (Premack and Woodruff 1978). Here, mental and intentional states are attributed to three different imaginary characters (present and non-present): it was the non-present Dentil character who wanted you (in your present guise as another character) to think that I (in my guise as Pikachu) did it (Blum-Kulka 2004: 282).

This short fragment is, in a sense, reminiscent of a natural version of one of the false-belief tasks traditionally tested in the study of theory of mind, in which reality and belief diverge and actions depend on the beliefs rather than on the real situation (Wellman, Cross and Watson 2001). Namely, Oren puts himself in Dani's reality of *seeing* him doing something wrong. He explains to Dani that a third party is responsible for this act (the Dentil) and causes Dani to *believe* him though it contradicts what he actually saw. No doubt the backing evidence (the Dentil's simulating device that misled Dani) sounds convincing (in the next scene, the children started looking for the bad one). Oren, in fact, captures the fact that "the emotional impact of a situation depends not on its objective features but on the beliefs that are brought to it" (Harris et al. 1989: 379).

In another sequence, two children (Gadi and Amir) engaged in a long argumentative sequence when trading a Pokeball sticker (see also Kampf and Blum-Kulka 2011). Amir agreed to concede Gadi eleven cards to get the specific sticker he wanted. However, since Gadi kept refusing to trade, Amir explained the profitability and fairness of the deal and argued: *But eleven (…), so it's not that bad that you don't have one (that you'll have one less) sticker of Pokeball. If you had one (only) you wouldn't have given it, that's all right, and I would have (bought), Five, five, you will be left with five, not one, five! (3.0) It's not so bad if you'll give me only one sticker.* It is notable how this extended turn is embedded in and contributes to the socio-cultural habitat of the peer group, namely, to the only world in which commodities like Pokemon stickers have such a high value.

Although such examples were not frequent in our data, they illustrate that in argumentative events in which social issues and activity goals come into play, children are also capable of holding extended turns, stringing ideas coherently and building textually well-constructed and logical arguments.

Acts of distancing in children's argumentative events: evoking a speech act

The principle of distancing comes into play when people refer to language in reflective ways; for instance, when people display meta-pragmatic awareness in language use, representing language's own structure and use to embed acts of language use within other acts of language use (Silverstein 1993) or to the language user's conceptualization of linguistic behavior while engaged in it (Verschueren 2004). In the following segment, children reflect on language by making meta-pragmatic comments that explicitly refer to a speech act.

Ex. 5: "You promise and you do not keep your word"

Date: 31 May 2000. Rachel kindergarten, Ashdod.
Participants: Noam (m., 4;7), Revital (f., 4;10), Merav (f., 4;4), Idit (f., 4;10), Shirli (f., 4;0), Itamar (m., 4;6) and Child (unidentified child).
The teacher sends everybody to wash their hands, and the children play with the water and soap. Then the teacher calls the children to come back and have their lunch.

18.	NOAM :titni↑ li anavim	NOAM : Give↑ me grapes
19.	REVITAL: lo. ani oxal et ku↑lam.	REVITAL: no. I will eat them all↑
20.	NOAM: lama? (2.9) biglala-at- aval at lo [mekayemet]. ((turns 21–24 Noam keeps asking and Revital keeps refusing))	NOAM: Why? (2.9) 'cause of her but you don't [keep your word].
25.	NOAM: ani brogez*. at mavtixa ve-lo mekayemet. (6.1) at lo mekayemet. (4.9) lo mekayemet. (0.5) °at lo mekayemet.° ((turns 26–29 Revital explains why she does not want to share and Noam becomes angry))	NOAM: I'm *brogez** (mad). You promise and you do not keep your word. (6.1) You don't keep your word (4.9). You don't. (0.5) °You don't.°
30.	REVITAL: Noam gam ata mavtiax ve-lo mekayem	REVITAL: Noam you promise too and you don't keep your word. ((three turns skipped))
33.	REVITAL: =pa'am shamati she-amarta she-'ta tavi anavim↑ ve- lo eveta anavim.	Once I heard that you said that you'll bring grapes↑ you didn't bring grapes.

34.	NOAM: naxon↑ ve-lo eveti anavim. Em pa'am pa'am pa'am ma at roca↓ at roca be-(... ...) lo hayiti po.	NOAM: Right↑ and I didn't bring grapes. Em once once once what do you want↓ do you want and-(... ...) I wasn't here.

The argumentative sequence above occurs during lunchtime, and the issue being discussed is an apparent promise of sharing grapes that Revital gave to Noam. Revital tries to justify not sharing the grapes. As she keeps refusing the discussion is 'detached' from the actual action of sharing or getting grapes and moves into the plane of dealing with promises or broken promises, by referring explicitly to the speech act of promising (turns 25, 30, 33). Though promising is considered a relatively late-developed speech act (Ninio and Snow 1996), children recognize a promise as a commitment, as more than just something you say you will do (Maas and Abbeduto 2001). The act of talking about a speech act is an instance of reflexivity, which refers to the language user's reflexive awareness of what is involved in a usage event (Verschueren, Östman and Blommaert 1995). As such, it is considered a manifestation of discursive literacy since it is an act of distancing the talk from the here-and-now. Promising, like any other speech act, depends on intra-cultural social conventions (Sperber and Wilson 1995), and hence simultaneously the children are setting the ground for negotiating the moral order of their culture. Here we can see very much the 'on-line' process by which the adult expectation that promises should be kept is appropriated and elevated to the status of a norm also in childhood culture.

Distancing means: talking about abstract issues

Developmentally speaking, by kindergarten, differences in opinions and beliefs become an issue of interest during argumentative events (Chen et al. 2001). This reflects the children's growing ability to focus on others' ideas or attitudes (Dunn 1999). These differences in opinions and beliefs include topics related to social behavior, conventions (Corsaro and Rizzo 1990; Kyratzis and Guo 2001) or game rules (Cobb-Moore et al. 2009; Goodwin 2006), but much less is known about topics associated with socially remote spheres (for exceptions, see examples in discussion about ethnicity in Hamo and Blum-Kulka 2007 or in Grøver Aukrust and Rydland 2009). In the following two consecutive examples, children discuss such distant and abstract topics as whether a country can die and God's existence.[6] Both segments were part of a long talk that evolved near Independence Day in Israel in a period of terrorist attacks. The conversation started when the children made reference to a recent terrorist attack that had happened a couple of days before. In the first sequence, the subject matter of the conversation triggered the topic of whether it is possible for a country to die. At some point, one of the children assumed that if someone can kill God, it is also possible to kill a country. From that point, God's

Kindergarten children's argumentative discourse

existence turned to be the topic of conversation in the second sequence of the same argumentative event.

Ex. 6: "The country will never die"

Date: 17 March 2002. Dana kindergarten, Kfar Sava.
Participants: Roy (m., 5;10), Gal (f., 6;2), Tom (m., 5;8) and Child (unidentified child).

19.	ROY: a, (.) ani'yodea ani yodea she she im yearsu ota.	ROY: a, (.) I know I know if they will destroy it. ((the country))
20.	TOM: a-medina[a-medina af paam lo-]	TOM: The country [the country will never -]
21.	ROY: [she-tiye gdola], (0.2) v'az, she te she te, she-thyie bat mea ve-eser.	ROY: [When it will be big], (0.2) then, when it will be one hundred and ten years old.
22.	GAL: #hi af paam lo tamut#	GAL: #It will never die# ((in an assertive tone))
23.	ROY: im hi tiye [bat]	ROY: and if it will be [years old]
24.	GAL: [>hi] af pam lo tamut<	GAL: [>It] will never die<
25.	ROY: im hi tyie bat-	ROY: and if it will be – (years old)
26.	GAL: >hi af pam lo tamut<	GAL: >It will never die <
27.	ROY: im hi tiye bat tshameot ve-tesha?	ROY: and if it will be nine hundred and nine years old?
30.	GAL: hi adayn lo ta ((tamut))	GAL: It still will not di ((die))
31.	TOM: HI AF PAAM LO TAMUT	TOM: IT WILL NEVER DIE ((losing his patience))
32.	ROY: #ma ze?#	ROY: #How is it? # ((surprised)) ((turn omitted)
34.	GAL: hi adayin lo tamut	GAL: It still won't die.
35.	CLI: °ani lo mevina pashut°	CLI: °I simply don't understand°
36.	ROY: im hi tiye bat elef?	ROY: If it will be one thousands years old? ((turn omitted))
38.	GAL: lo tamut.	GAL: It won't die.
39.	ROY: #ma ze?# lolam (le-olam) lo tamut?	ROY: #How is it? #It will never (never ever) die? ((as surprised))
40.	TOM: hi lo (…) oto	TOM: It won't (…) him
41.	CHI: […	CHI: […
42.	ROY: she sh'im (she-im) ya'argu t'kol-a-anashim hi tamut?	ROY: that that if (if) all the people will be killed, will it die?

This segment centers on the children's testing of the hypothesis that a country can die and it progressively evolves as the children make the testing conditions 'more extreme' by raising the age of the country. The children deal with a hypothetical situation, namely, they think about alternatives to the way the world is believed to be, under changing conditions – 'what would happen if...' Hypothetical thinking demands the recruiting of imagination, making inferences about the imagined states and interpreting the consequences of the states imagined (Harris and Kavanaugh 1993). Research has shown that even young children correctly answer future hypothetical or counterfactual questions (Robinson and Beck 2000; Gopnik 2009). Here, the children imagine alternatives as they generate different questions (what will happen when the country is 110 years old? 900 or 1,000 years old? and so on). Still, the interpretation of the results of the imagined situations was not immediately grasped by the children. This was manifest on the one hand, as Roy kept asking additional questions and Gal kept answering in a quasi-automatic manner ("it won't die," turns 22, 24, 26, 30, 34 and 38). On the other hand, Tom (turn 31) lost his patience and made an attempt to stop the questioning sequence by formulating a general statement, as if saying "no matter how much you raise the age of the country, IT WILL NEVER DIE." From another angle, it is possible to explain this same conversational format not on the basis of children's difficulties in counterfactual thinking, but as a sort of call–response format that intensifies the argumentative experience. The 'call–response' format (Roy asks repetitively and Gal automatically responds) has its roots in music (Gregorian chant) and is characterized by a singing leader who is imitated by a chorus of followers. This format, whether verbal or not, is also closely associated with African oral culture and music (Sale 1992), with children's aptitude in rhythmic word play (Hamo and Blum-Kulka 2007) and with conversational play with songs and music (see Maybin, this volume). Here, note how the exchanges between Roy and Gal resemble the 'call–response' format, as both children were mutually tuned in rhythm and repetition of phrases, displaying conversational cooperation.

Later on, in the same argumentative sequence, Tom argues across many turns that it is impossible to reach a conclusion about God's existence. First, he provides a justification for why it is impossible to kill God (nobody can see him). Then he relates God's existence to the creation (you can't know who created us), under the assumption that if we knew who created 'us,' we would know something about God's existence. Finally, in an extended turn, he advances his main argument, describing in a playful tone and rhythm the degree of recursiveness of the discussion: *and who gave birth to her (your mom)? Her grandma e her mom, and who gave birth to her? her grandma, and who gave birth to her her mom, and who gave birth to her? Her grandma and… it doesn't matter.*

In the two sequences above, on top of the fact that children discuss abstract and distant topics clearly associated with discursive literacy, they also become agents of their own potential learning by hypothesizing, justifying and arriving at conclusions, gaining practice in the use of rational modes of argumentation.

Summary and conclusions

By definition, the oppositional nature of the argumentative sequences provides children with opportunities of finding grounds, explanations and counter-examples to support their own claims or opinions or undermine those of the others. However, we have found that argumentative events among children are complex and display multiple facets at the same time. These findings have led us to adopt a more comprehensive view of these argumentative events. We have shown that the various affordances of argumentative events in peer talk function as cultural events and offer developmental opportunities through moments of intense meaning-making in children's worlds. Explicating the actual discursive processes through which children attend to each other's arguments allowed us to highlight the learning potential of such events. Our illustrative examples of argumentative events between children in adult-free, naturally occurring peer interactions reveal that argumentative discourse operates simultaneously on several interwoven levels: (a) At the social level, argumentative events assist children in establishing their own social order. In spite of their adversative nature, children establish an underlying cooperation to keep friendship values, a cooperation that is also conversationally accomplished. (b) At the cultural level, while participating in argumentative events, children actively co-construct moment-to-moment transient worlds of childhood, drawing on a rich repertoire of strategies, some unique to child culture and some echoing adult norms and conventions. Children's cultural habitat partly echoes 'Culture with a capital C,' namely the norms and conventions of the adult culture, as perceived and interpreted by the children, and is partly unique to the children's age-group culture. (c) At the discursive literacy level, literacy-related skills come into play in argumentative discourse through children's acts of constructing textuality and distancing in complex linguistic ways.

Children construct a community that shares norms and beliefs and develops common processes of meaning-making and a shared view of the world. This function of building shared-world concepts is central to the children's argumentative activity. However, children also extend and elaborate their own peer culture by transforming information and resources from the adult world to meet the concerns of their peer world. The aforementioned affordances at the different levels reflect the fact that argumentative events between peers become an arena in which children's co-constructed social and cultural world evolves, but at the same time, they serve children as a springboard that enables them to develop and refine discursive argumentative practices towards developed and even grown-up discourse conventions.

This view of argumentative events as providing children with a double opportunity space is rooted in constructivist approaches to childhood, which call for a new appreciation of children's self-constructed social, cultural and moral worlds as a vital and necessary complementary addition to the more traditional developmental psychological approaches (Blum-Kulka 2005a; Hamo and Blum-Kulka 2007; Cromdal 2009).

From a broader perspective, we think our study of argumentative discourse illustrates the affordances of peer talk in general. Children's peer talk has recently emerged as a major area for understanding how a range of discourse skills is developed during peer interactions and how childhood culture is created by children's distinctive practices (Blum-Kulka and Snow 2004). We think peer talk deserves more attention than it usually gets, especially from psychologists, because through it we can gain access to inner processes of meaning-making in children's worlds, as well as to observable processes of learning and development. Arguably, we can better understand how children gain communicative, cognitive and social skills in various domains as they grow, by paying close attention to the ways in which they enlist all their resources for meaning-making moment to moment in the present of their childhood.

TRANSCRIPTION CONVENTIONS

[words]	overlapping talk
=	overlatch
(0.5)	timed intervals
(.)	interval of less than 0.2 seconds
(…)	incomprehensible words
(words)	transcription doubt
.	a falling intonation at the end of an utterance
,	a continuing rising intonation
?	a rising intonation at the end of an utterance
↑	a sharp rise in pitch
↓	a sharp fall in pitch
WORD	high volume
°word°	low volume
word	emphasis
wo::rd	sound stretch
wor-	cut off
>words<	fast rhythm
<words>	slow rhythm
{word}	unusual pronunciation
#words#	unusual tone, indicated in a comment
word/word/word	rhythmic pronunciation
((comment))	transcriber's comments

NOTES

1 Originally referring to ecological affordances, namely the possibilities for action offered by conditions in the environment to specific creatures (Gibson 1982).

2 Alternative terms proposed for the study of the same or similar phenomena include "conversational arguing" (Muntigl and Turnbull 1998), "conflict talk" (Grimshaw 1990), "polemical exchanges" (Dascal 2000), "oppositional argument" (Schiffrin 1985) and "agonism" or "ritualized adversativeness" (Tannen 2002).
3 Speech events are those "activities or aspects of activities that are directly governed by rules or norms for the use of speech" (Hymes 1974: 52).
4 The data set of argumentative events was drawn from the mapping of all peer interactions by genre. All peer interactions during the first year (age 5) and third year (age 7) were divided into discursive events and coded for primary genre. The salience of argumentative events emerged by comparison to other genres: the first-year argumentative events comprised 22.5% of all events, second only to *instrumental talk events* (25%) and in a similar proportion to *pretend play events* (21%) (n=111) (Blum-Kulka 2010b).
5 Alternative terms, with similar but not necessarily the same conceptualization, include "decontextualized language" (Ninio and Snow 1996), "literate style" (Scollon and Scollon 1981), "extended discourse" (Wells 1985), "linguistic literacy" (Ravid and Tolchinsky 2002) and "literate" language (Kyratzis, this volume).
6 These two examples were taken from a doctoral thesis, "Argumentative discourse in kindergarten children: a comparison between peer talk and teacher-children talk," that was carried out and supervised by the authors of the present chapter (SZE and SBK, respectively). The thesis analyzed data from peer talk presented in this chapter as well as data collected by SZE. Specifically, the two examples were documented at an additional kindergarten (in Kfar Saba, Israel) characterized by the same demographic features as those referred to in the present chapter. In the specific examples that follow, though the general conversation was initiated by the teacher as a topic related to Independence Day, the topics whether a country can die and whether God exists were raised and discussed by the children themselves.

3 Narrative performance, peer group culture, and narrative development in a preschool classroom

Ageliki Nicolopoulou, Carolyn Brockmeyer Cates, Aline de Sá and Hande Ilgaz

Introduction

This chapter uses the analysis of a preschool storytelling and story-acting practice to explore some of the ways that peer-oriented symbolic activities and peer group culture can serve as valuable contexts for promoting young children's narrative development. In the process, it suggests the need to rethink, refine, and broaden the conceptions of the "social context" of development now used by most research in language socialization and development.

There is a substantial and growing body of work on the role of social context in language development (Hoff 2006). In practice, most research on this subject has focused on delineating and analyzing various forms of adult–child interaction, usually dyadic, in which an adult caregiver transmits information, provides cultural models, and in other ways instructs, guides, corrects, and "scaffolds" the efforts of the less capable child. By comparison, research on the complementary role of peers in socialization and development has been, as Blum-Kulka and Snow (2004: 292) put it, relatively "peripheral and noncumulative." As the present volume helps to demonstrate, that situation has gradually been changing. But with some notable exceptions, the perspectives informing peer-oriented developmental research often remain limited in important respects. Even when interaction between children is studied, it is usually assimilated to the one-way expert–novice model, with an older sibling or other peer taking on the "expert" role. And both adult-oriented and peer-oriented research tend to reduce the social context of development, explicitly or in effect, to interactions between individuals and their direct consequences.

Interactions between unequals obviously play a very important role in children's development, education, and socialization. But an overly narrow focus on the model of expert–novice interaction obscures or neglects other crucial dimensions of social context. The role of peers is not limited to one-way transmission or facilitation, but also includes modes of genuine peer *collaboration* (Rogoff 1998). Furthermore, the contexts and outcomes of such collaboration are not restricted to dyadic (or even multi-party) interaction between individuals. Children, like adults, also create, maintain, and participate in *fields of shared activity* that provide resources, motivations, and affordances for development, including narrative development. To borrow a useful formulation from Ochs et al. (1989: 238–239), these constitute *opportunity spaces*, collectively defined and maintained, that enable and promote certain forms of activity and development (for a similar perspective, see Blum-Kulka et al. 2004). This chapter seeks to offer one concrete illustration of such processes.

To avoid any possible misunderstanding, the point is not to minimize the significance of interaction. But socially situated research needs to overcome its prevailing temptation to *reduce* the social context of development, conceptually and/or methodologically, exclusively to interactions between individuals. The social world of the child includes, for example, not only individual peers but also the peer *group* and peer culture, whose structure and dynamics have their own emergent properties and effects (emphasized, e.g., by Maccoby 2002). Interactions are themselves embedded in – and simultaneously help to constitute and maintain – various types of sociocultural context that enable and constrain them, and that structure their nature, meaning, and impact. At the most intimate or immediate level, these contexts include families, peer groups, classroom minicultures, and socially structured practices and activity systems – for example, the shared symbolic space of the play-world. And those are in turn enmeshed in larger institutional and cultural frameworks ranging from organizations and communities to culturally elaborated images of identity, conceptual tools, and systems of meaning. These sociocultural contexts, both small and large scale, have to be understood as genuinely *collective* realities that, in manifold ways, shape the actions and experiences of those who participate in them. An effective approach to understanding development requires that we pay systematic attention to the ongoing interplay between three dimensions of the human world that are at once analytically distinct and mutually interpenetrating: individual, interactional or relational, and collective. (For some elaboration see Nicolopoulou 1996, 2002; Nicolopoulou and Weintraub 1998.)

A peer-oriented narrative practice as a matrix for development

The research reported here is one offshoot of a long-term project by the first author and associates that has examined the operation and effects of a storytelling/story-acting practice pioneered by the teacher/researcher Vivian Paley (1990) and widely used in preschool and kindergarten classrooms in the United States and abroad (e.g., McNamee 1987; Nicolopoulou 1996, 1997, 2002; Cooper 2009). Although this practice is conducted with variations in different contexts, its main outlines are fairly consistent. At a certain period during each day (usually during "choice time" activities), any child who wishes can dictate a story to a designated teacher or teacher's aide, who writes down the story as the child tells it. These are usually fictional or imaginary stories, rather than "factual" accounts of personal experience characteristic of "show and tell" or "sharing time." Later that day, each of these stories is read aloud to the entire class by the teacher, while the child/author and other children, whom he or she chooses, act out the story.

This is an apparently simple activity with complex and powerful effects. Several features are especially worth noting. Although this is a structured and teacher-facilitated activity, the children's storytelling is voluntary, self-initiated, and relatively spontaneous. Their stories are neither solicited directly by adults nor channeled by props, story-stems, or suggested topics. Because this practice runs through the entire school year and the children control their own participation in storytelling, it provides them with the opportunity to work over, refine, and elaborate their narratives and to use them for their own diverse purposes – cognitive, symbolic, expressive, and social-relational. Furthermore, the way that this practice combines story*telling* with story-*acting* has several important implications. Children typically enjoy storytelling for its own sake, but the prospect of having their story acted out, together with other children whom they choose, offers them a powerful additional motivation to compose and dictate stories. To a certain degree, this practice also combines two aspects of children's narrative activity which are too often treated in mutual isolation: the discursive exposition of narratives in storytelling and the enactment of narratives in pretend play. And perhaps most important, one result of having the stories read to and dramatized for the entire class at group time is that the children tell their stories not only to adults, but primarily to *each other*; they do so not in one-to-one interaction, but in a shared public setting. When this practice is established as a regular part of the classroom activities, all children typically participate over time in three interrelated roles: (1) composing and dictating stories; (2) taking part in the group enactment of stories (their own and those of other children); and (3) listening to and watching the performance of the stories of other children. Thus, the children's storytelling and story-acting are embedded in the ongoing context of the classroom miniculture and the children's everyday group life.

There is strong evidence that these conditions lead children to produce narratives that are richer, more ambitious, and more illuminating than when they compose them in isolation from their everyday social contexts and in response to agendas shaped directly by adults (Sutton-Smith 1986; Nicolopoulou 1996). And, indeed, previous studies have suggested that preschoolers' participation in this storytelling/story-acting practice can significantly promote the development of narrative and related oral-language skills for children from middle-class (Nicolopoulou 1996) and from low-income and otherwise disadvantaged backgrounds (Nicolopoulou 2002).

Adults certainly play a significant role in this practice, but their role is more facilitative than directive. Their key contribution is to help establish and facilitate a predominantly child-driven and peer-oriented activity that develops its own autonomous dynamics, within which children themselves can take an active role in their own socialization and development. As we have already suggested, it seems clear that the public *performance* of the children's narratives plays a critical role in these processes. It does so in several ways, but above all by helping to generate and maintain a *shared public arena* for narrative performance, experimentation, collaboration, and cross-fertilization. Even in a small class of children from similar backgrounds, different children come with distinctive experiences, knowledge, skills, concerns, and personal styles. The story-acting component of this practice allows these skills, perspectives, and other elements to be transformed into shared and publicly available narrative resources that each child can try to appropriate and develop, and to which he or she can contribute, in his or her own way. To borrow a telling formulation from Paley (1986: xv), this public arena offers children an "experimental theater" in which they can reciprocally try out, elaborate, and refine their own narrative efforts while getting the responses of an engaged and emotionally significant peer group audience. The fact that each child is at different times an author, a performer, and part of the audience further enhances the impact and developmental potential of this storytelling/story-acting practice.

Narrative performance, narrative development, and the uses of narrative activity: an introductory overview

This chapter focuses on the dynamics and consequences of this storytelling/ story-acting practice in one preschool classroom during the 2006–07 school year. However, to establish some necessary background we will first outline, very schematically, some findings from previous and ongoing studies of this activity.

Over the past two decades, the first author and associates have studied the use of this storytelling/story-acting practice as a regular part of the curriculum in twenty preschool classrooms differing by geography and social-class composition. Eleven were in preschools in California and Massachusetts serving children from middle-class backgrounds; the other nine were in programs serving children from poor and otherwise disadvantaged backgrounds, including two Head Start classes, one in Massachusetts and one in Pennsylvania, and seven classes in a preschool/childcare program in Pennsylvania studied from 2005–07. Collection and analysis of the children's stories was complemented by ethnographic observations of the classroom activities, friendship patterns, and group life of the children involved.

In certain respects, the patterns have been strikingly consistent across all the classrooms studied, though every classroom also has its unique features. In all cases, children became enthusiastically involved in this storytelling/

story-acting practice and brought considerable energy and creativity to it. As the school year progressed, children's stories became more complex and sophisticated, manifesting significant advances in both narrative competence and cognitive abilities. But along with these broad similarities, it is also worth noting some systematic differences between the predominantly middle-class preschools and those serving low-income and otherwise disadvantaged children – whose backgrounds also included higher degrees of family disorganization and instability. In the latter, children tended to begin the year with weaker oral language skills, including narrative skills (as one would expect from, e.g., Peterson 1994; Hart and Risley 1995; Hoff 2006), and less familiarity with the basic conventions for constructing free-standing, self-contextualizing fictional narratives (for some elaboration, see Nicolopoulou 2002:128–129, 139–141). Thus, by comparison with the middle-class preschoolers, they were much more in the position of building up the basic foundations for their participation in this narrative activity from scratch, rather than simply applying and expanding narrative skills they had already mastered.

In constructing their narratives, the children drew themes, characters, images, plots, and other elements from a wide range of sources including fairy tales, children's books, popular culture (especially via electronic media like TV and computer games), and their own experience; they also drew elements from each other's stories. However, they did not simply imitate other children's stories, nor did they just passively absorb messages from adults and the larger culture. It is clear that, even at this early age, they were able to appropriate these elements *selectively*, and to *use* and rework them for their own purposes. These processes of active and selective appropriation and narrative cross-fertilization became increasingly conspicuous as the children achieved greater mastery of narrative skills. So they took off more rapidly in the middle-class preschool classes, but in the long run they flourished in the low-income preschool classes as well.

This was also true for one striking manifestation of this active and selective appropriation: the emergence of systematic gender differences in the children's storytelling, linked to the formation of two gendered peer group subcultures within the classroom that defined themselves, to a considerable extent, against each other (see Nicolopoulou et al. 1994; Nicolopoulou 1997; Nicolopoulou and Richner 2004; Richner and Nicolopoulou 2001). This was initially an unexpected finding, since all the preschools involved made strong and deliberate efforts to create an egalitarian, non-sexist atmosphere, and one goal in using this storytelling/story-acting practice was to help generate greater cohesion and a common culture within the classroom group. The children did indeed use their narrative activities to help build up a common culture; but they also consistently used them to help build up gendered subcultures within this common culture. Intriguingly enough, this gendered narrative polarization emerged more quickly and sharply in the middle-class than in the low-income preschools. That difference may seem counterintuitive, but at least part of the explanation is probably that middle-class preschoolers usually began the school year with greater mastery of the relevant narrative skills and a greater ability to use them effectively and flexibly for their own purposes. In the long run, however, broadly similar tendencies appear in both types of preschool classes.

The gender-related dimensions of children's storytelling in the low-income preschool classes still require further examination (both Nicolopoulou 2002 and the present chapter make some preliminary efforts along those lines). But these gender differences have emerged strongly and unambiguously in all the middle-class preschool classes we have studied, so we will begin by sketching out some of the patterns there. Although the stories were shared with the entire group every day, analysis has demonstrated that they divided consistently and increasingly along gender lines. They were dominated by two highly distinctive gender-related *narrative styles*, differing in both form and content, that embodied different approaches to the symbolic management of order and disorder, different underlying images of social relationships and the social world, and different images of the self. The girls' stories, for example, typically portrayed characters (or at least a group of core characters) embedded in networks of stable and harmonious relationships, whose activities were located in specified physical settings. One common genre revolved around the family group (including pets) and its activities, centered topographically on the home. In contrast, the boys' stories were characteristically marked by conflict, movement, and disruption, and often by associative chains of extravagant imagery. One genre often favored by the boys might be termed "heroic-agonistic," since it centered on conflict between individuals or, in some cases, rival teams. While the girls tended to supplement their depictions of family life by drawing on fairy-tale characters such as kings and queens or princes and princesses, boys were especially fond of powerful and frightening characters such as large animals, cartoon action heroes, and so on. Each of these narrative styles can be seen as a *generative framework* for further development, characterized by different themes and concerns, different narrative possibilities, and different formal problems (for elaboration, see Richner and Nicolopoulou 2001).

Furthermore, this narrative polarization was one aspect of a larger process by which two distinct gendered subcultures were actively built up and maintained by the children themselves. These subcultures were marked by the convergence of gendered styles in the children's narratives, gender differentiation in their group life, and increasingly self-conscious gender identity in the children involved. At the same time, the crystallization of these subcultures within the microcosm of the classroom provided a framework for the further appropriation, enactment, and reproduction of crucial dimensions of personal identity as defined by the larger society, including gender.

These findings suggest some broad conclusions that go beyond the specific subject of gender. The narrative construction of reality is not a purely individual process but a sociocultural one, whose cognitive significance is inextricably linked to the building up of group life and the formation of both individual and collective identities. Children participate – by way of narrative practices – in the process of their own socialization and development, and they do not do this *only* through the individual appropriation of elements from the larger culture. They also help to construct some of the key sociocultural contexts that shape (and promote) their own socialization and development.

The current study

The study reported here sought to reconstruct and analyze these processes as they unfolded over the course of a school year in a preschool class of low-income and otherwise disadvantaged children. A key orienting concern was to examine the complex interplay between the emergence and transformations of the classroom peer culture and the development of the children's narrative activity, with careful attention to the mediating role of the storytelling/story-acting practice, especially its story-enactment component. For reasons suggested above, there were grounds to expect that analyzing this interplay in the context of a low-income preschool class not only could help broaden our understanding of the operation, effects, and potential benefits of this storytelling/story-acting practice, but also might bring out some of the most basic developmental dynamics in especially illuminating ways.

Method: participants, data, and procedures

This preschool class was included in a recent project that examined whether this storytelling/story-acting practice could be used effectively as a school-readiness program to promote the development of oral language (including narrative), emergent literacy, and social competence. During 2005–07 the storytelling/story-acting practice was introduced for an entire school year into six experimental classrooms in a preschool/childcare program in Pennsylvania; seven classrooms served as controls. This chapter focuses on one of the experimental classrooms during the 2006–07 school year and follows the children's narrative activities and development, as well as the evolving peer group culture in the classroom, over the course of the year.

Participants

The sample consisted of eighteen children who attended this preschool class. In September the class comprised fifteen children, eight girls and seven boys, most of whom were four-year-olds (age range 3;10 to 5;0). If we set 4;4 as a convenient dividing line between younger and older children, two of the girls were younger (3;10–4;4) and six older (4;5–5;0), whereas four boys were younger (3:10–4:4) and three older. There was some turnover during the year. Two children, a girl and a boy, left around the middle of the year, at the end of January and February, respectively. They were replaced by three new children, one girl and two boys, who were transferred from a nursery class in the same building when they turned four. Thus, the stories analyzed in this study were generated by the eighteen children who spent all or a significant part of the year in this classroom. (A few other children were officially enrolled at one point or another, but since they were in the classroom for short periods and told almost no stories, they were not included in the analysis.) The children came from low-income and working-class families, and 28% were Head Start eligible (very poor). Most (61%) were European-American, 28% were Hispanic, and 11% African-American; all spoke English as their first or only language. A majority (56%) lived with a single parent, usually their mother.

Procedure

The storytelling/story-acting practice was conducted from the middle of October through the middle of May. During the storytelling phase, usually during morning choice activities, any child who wanted could dictate a story to a designated teacher or to a research assistant who helped take down the stories. This storytaker wrote down the story in a classroom composition book as the child told it with minimal intervention, usually asking only for clarifications that would be critical for the story-acting phase later the same day. In the enactment phase, each story dictated during the day was read aloud to the entire class by the teacher during large-group time, while the child/author and other children acted out the story. The selection of actors was carried out by the child/author immediately after dictating the story. The author first chose a role for himself or herself and then picked other children to be specific characters in the story performance.

The activity took place two days per week, with three or four stories recorded each day. (In the middle-class preschool classes we have studied, this practice took place almost every day. But in those classrooms it was already well established as part of the regular curriculum.) If other children wanted to tell a story when the daily quota was filled, they were placed on a waiting list for the next time. At the end of the year, we collected the storybooks for analysis.

Coding and analysis

The analysis is based on a total of 210 stories generated and collected during the 2006–07 school year, which included stories from all eighteen children in the sample. The stories were analyzed in two stages. First, to conduct a baseline test of whether narrative development occurred over the course of the year, we focused on the fifteen children who began the class in the fall and coded each child's first and last story using five standard measures of narrative development (Table 3.1).

Table 3.1 *Means or mean percentages (and standard deviations) of narrative dimensions for the first and last stories told by children who attended this class from the beginning of the school year*

	First story (N = 15)	Last story (N = 15)	F and *p* values
Length (# of clauses)	7.13 (3.42)	16.60 (5.33)	F (1, 14) = 34.36, *p* < 0.001
% of clauses in the past tense[a]	55.21% (44.57)	78.33% (27.55)	F (1, 14) = 4.49, *p* = < .05
Temporal & causal connectivity[b]	1.67 (0.98)	2.60 (1.12)	F (1, 14) = 7.34, *p* < 0.05
Narrative voice[c]	1st person: 53% (N = 8) 3rd person: 47% (N = 7) 1.47 (0.52)	1st person: 6.7% (N = 1) 3rd person: 93.3% (N = 14) 1.93 (0.26)	F (1, 14) = 12.25, *p* < 0.01
Standard opening & ending[d]	20% (N = 3) 0.53 (0.83)	73% (N = 11) 1.60 (0.74)	F (1, 14) = 16.00, *p* = 0.001

[a] Mean proportions.
[b] It is based on a 0–5 system: 0 = none, 1 = conjunctions, 2–3 = temporal only, 4–5 = plus causal per story.
[c] These are Means and (Standard Deviations) based on a 3-point system per story: 1 = 1st person, 2 = mixed, 3 = 3rd person.
[d] Percentages indicate stories with both standard opening and closing. It is based on a 0–2 system: 0 = none, 1 = any one, 2 = both.

Second, we analyzed the complete set of stories using a systematic interpretive analysis directed by the first author. In addition to basic quantitative measures such as length and number of characters, stories were coded in terms of themes, level of coherence (high, medium, low), story voice (first- or third-person), and tone (neutral, scary, or humorous). We also tabulated general and specific elements shared with other stories by the same child and between different children. Two other sources of information were consulted: (a) field notes by two research assistants who visited the classroom twice per week and by the third author, who coordinated the intervention in this classroom, and (b) focused observations of children's classroom interactions (e.g., play and self-regulation) conducted three times per year (October, March, and May).

Results and discussion

Narrative development from children's first to last story

As Table 3.1 indicates, the children's narratives improved significantly over the course of the year on all measures. Children's stories got longer, were told more consistently in the third person and past tense, used more complex temporal and connective language, and included a higher number of conventional openings and endings. Having established this basic pattern of narrative improvement, we moved to a more detailed examination of the processes through which these and other developments occurred.

Narrative cross-fertilization and narrative development in the context of an evolving classroom peer culture: three phases delineated

This section reconstructs and explores the interplay between the evolving patterns of narrative cross-fertilization in the classroom peer culture and the development of the children's storytelling. Over the course of the school year, this process went through three broad phases. During the initial phase, many of the children were still struggling to master the ability to construct even the simplest kinds of coherent, free-standing fictional narratives. And their participation in the storytelling/story-acting practice generated only a limited amount of mutual sharing and creative appropriation of narrative elements. The main exceptions on both counts, to a certain degree, were among the older girls, most of whom shared a fictional family genre.

During the second and third phases, the children's stories became longer, more complex, and eventually more coherent. However, their developmental trajectories were far from simple, uniform, or unilinear – partly, we would suggest, because the children were pursuing several ultimately complementary but sometimes competing agendas in their narrative activity. At the same time, the children made increasingly active and effective use of the possibilities afforded by the shared public arena of narrative enactment. Analysis of their narratives indicates that the children became increasingly attentive to each other's stories as they listened to them being performed or participated in their enactment, and in constructing their stories they also took increasing account of their peers as an audience and of the broader patterns and dynamics of peer group life in the classroom. Furthermore, the third phase was marked by the emergence of a widely shared fictional genre among the boys in the class, based on Power Rangers cartoons, that served as a generative framework for narrative cross-fertilization, elaboration, and development.

Phase 1. Setting the stage: idiosyncratic first-person narratives and the beginnings of a family genre

During the first month-and-a-half of the storytelling/story-acting practice (from mid-October through November), the children composed and enacted a total of fifty-one stories, including some very rudimentary proto-stories. All the children told at least one story, though some were considerably less active than others. The great majority of stories fell into one of two categories: 39 percent were first-person "factual" accounts of personal experiences and 33 percent were third-person fictional stories organized around the family and its activities. These categories shared some features, since most of the first-person stories included family members (overwhelmingly parents) and some stories in the family genre lapsed into the first person and/or included the storyteller either explicitly or in thinly fictionalized form. The other 28 percent were fictional stories of miscellaneous types, including 18 percent based on characters and themes drawn from TV cartoons, video games, and other electronic media sources (e.g., Thomas the Tank Engine, Cars, SpongeBob SquarePants, PowerPuff Girls) and 10 percent that drew on themes from various other sources.

The distribution of stories in the two main genres was linked to age and gender differences. The first-person accounts of personal experiences were almost all composed by younger children (4;4 or younger at the beginning of the school year), specifically by three of the four younger boys and one of the younger girls. These first-person narratives tended to be brief and simple; they were typically a few sentences long and contained few actions. Children often repeated the themes in their stories and rarely borrowed from other children's stories, so one could quickly recognize stories by particular children. For example, one boy liked to talk about the foods his mom made for him, while another described the special outings (which may have been real or wishful) that he took with one or both parents.

My mommy and I went to McDonald's and my daddy picked me up at McDonald's. My mommy and I went to the park and my daddy picked me up at the park and I went home. (Kayleb, October 23, 2006)[1]

On the other hand, almost all of the stories in the (largely) third-person explicitly fictional family genre were told by older girls (4;5–5;0), and four of the older girls (4;8–5;0) told stories predominantly in this genre. This pattern is not surprising, since in most preschool classrooms where this activity has been studied the family genre was disproportionately and characteristically a girl's genre – and increasingly so as the children developed greater mastery of narrative skills (e.g., Nicolopoulou 1997, 2002; Richner and Nicolopoulou 2001; for one instructive exception, see Nicolopoulou 2002:147). Children who compose family-genre stories typically attempt to achieve relational completeness in their picture of the family group, making sure to include at least a mother, father, brother, and sister (or, in the fairy-tale versions that were rare but not entirely absent in this particular classroom, a king, queen, prince, and princess), and sometimes a baby as well. Animals may also be integrated into the family group as pets. In this classroom, the family stories during the first phase were not always relationally complete, but they tended in that direction. These stories were longer than the first-person narratives and often included several episodes. Here is an example:

My story is about little girls. Once upon a time there was two little girls walking. They were so cute they had a doggie and a cat. And they had a mommy and a brother and a sister. And there was a little little boat for the dog. And the dog was riding the boat, and the mommy and daddy took a shower with the dog. They were gone for 3 days and they didn't know how to get home because they were lost in the woods. The end. (Tanya, November 8, 2006)

In this phase, the use of this family genre remained largely restricted to the subgroup of older girls (though toward the end of November two boys told stories that included royal families); and even within that subgroup, the sharing of more specific narrative elements was fairly minimal. Each girl's family stories had distinctive features that gave them a recognizable personal flavor – for example, Maxi's stories often included a baby; Tanya's often included a scary or frightening element, as in the example just quoted; and Ruby often inserted herself, her family, and/or her friends into her stories. None of those specific features was picked up, adapted, and elaborated by any of the other girls. And the other categories of stories showed even less evidence of narrative sharing and cross-fertilization. During this initial phase, it would appear, the children's energies were largely tied up in constructing this shared narrative activity, mastering its operation, and familiarizing themselves with its possibilities. During the next phase they began to exploit these potentialities more extensively and creatively.

Phase 2. Playful experimentation, peer group cross-fertilization, and the search for narrative coherence

By the end of November this practice had become solidly established in the classroom, and during December and January the children's storytelling entered a transitional phase whose features are not easy to summarize neatly or completely. There was a notable increase in narrative sharing and cross-fertilization, along with other indications that the children were listening more attentively to each other's stories and were increasingly willing and able to draw on them effectively. The children's stories were more ambitious, diverse, and eclectic than during the first phase. They became longer, included more characters and episodes, and incorporated a wider variety of themes. First-person narratives about real or alleged personal experiences also became less frequent, though one boy persisted with them until mid-March. (For a similar shift from first- to third-person narratives in another low-income preschool class, see Nicolopoulou et al. 2006.) However, the development of the children's storytelling did not proceed in a straightforward, uniform, or unilinear manner. Different aspects of their narratives changed at different rates and in different combinations for different children, with occasional plateaus and reversals for specific characteristics. And in many cases the children's stories actually became less coherent and more fragmented than during the first phase. The overall pattern that marks this second phase is that the children were attempting to include a wider range of elements in their stories and to use their storytelling in more flexible and ambitious ways, but were still struggling to integrate these elements successfully into coherent and satisfying narratives.

The complexity and unevenness of these developmental rhythms should not be entirely surprising, but their salience during this phase of the children's storytelling was especially striking. At this point, we can offer only a tentative and preliminary explanation, but our analysis in this and previous studies suggests that this pattern resulted, at least in part, from the interplay of several distinct and sometimes competing agendas being pursued in the children's storytelling. In the long run, these agendas are complementary and can help promote children's narrative development in mutually supportive ways; but in the short run, they may operate in tension, with uneven and centrifugal effects on the developmental trajectories and coherence of the children's narratives, until the children are able to balance and integrate them successfully.

Most generally, children's narrative activity in this storytelling/story-acting practice appears to be shaped and driven, to a considerable extent, by the interplay of two analytically distinct but ultimately interrelated types of motivating concerns (see Nicolopoulou 1996: 383–387). Each of these sets of concerns is influenced by, and at the same time helps to sustain, the sociocultural context of the children's narrative activity. And the different ways that children manage this interplay help generate a range of distinctive trajectories of narrative development. On the one hand, it is clear that children's storytelling is guided, to varying degrees, by what might be termed *intrinsically narrative concerns* – cognitive, symbolic, expressive, and formal – including the mastery of narrative form for its own sake. Certain children seem especially preoccupied with developing a greater control of characters and their interrelations, attaining more coherent plot structure, achieving more powerful or satisfying symbolic effects, and so on. On the other hand, children are also motivated by *social-relational concerns*, including various pragmatic functions of their narrative discourse that go beyond those inherent in direct conversational interaction. In the context of this practice, these are linked directly or indirectly to its story-acting portion, which mediates between the storyteller and the evolving classroom peer culture. These social-relational concerns affect the character of stories in a number of ways, two of which are especially worth mentioning.

First, children can use their narratives as vehicles for seeking or expressing friendship, group affiliation, and prestige. This is especially true since the author of a story chooses the other children to help perform it – and children visibly enjoy the feelings of power and influence involved in the selection process. In composing stories, a child may be inclined to include specific characters that his or her friends like to act out, as well as using themes that will appeal to them or that mark the subgroup to which he or she belongs. In addition to encouraging closer attention to the narrative preferences of other children, these concerns may also promote the inclusion of larger numbers of characters in a story. Everything else being equal, multiplying the number of characters allows children to include all their friends, as well as potential friends and playmates who will then owe them a favor in return. And, indeed, between the first and second phases the average number of characters per story increased from about four to about seven. But children often included more characters in a story than they could manage effectively – naming characters, for example, without giving them actions to perform – and some stories even swallowed up all the children in the class, leaving none to serve as the audience. Second, during this phase, the children's storytelling manifested greater awareness of their audience and its responses. This increased attentiveness could motivate children to construct more effective, interesting, and satisfying narratives, but it could also tempt children to include popular themes and other elements before they were fully capable of integrating them in their stories.

Among both the boys and girls, these dynamics were further complicated by an increased tendency for playful, even exuberant, experimentation in their storytelling. Children often spiced up their stories by adding elements that were scary (e.g., monsters, vampires, ghosts, skeletons), humorous, or silly. A number of stories, especially by boys, included powerful or frightening animals (e.g., lions, bears, tigers, crocodiles). Children were also increasingly likely to draw characters and images from cartoons or video games. Animating inanimate objects (e.g., walking socks, singing cars, talking pencils) was one device that often drew laughs from the audience. Here, for example, one of the older girls begins by outlining the basic framework for a family story and then moves on to describe the comical adventures of a walking sock.

There was a <u>baby</u>. And the baby and the <u>mom</u> and the <u>dad</u> and the <u>sister</u> and the <u>brother</u>, and they were pushing the baby to McDonald's. And then I went somewhere else and we went to Chucky Cheese and a lot of houses and then we went to Grandma's house and then we went to Daddy's house and then we went to Mommy's house and then something peeked out of the room. And then a sock came, peeking out of the room and then the sock started to walk. And then the sock went into the brother's room and the sock bit the brother's heiny. And then the sock went into the sister's room and bit the sister's butt. And the sock went into daddy's room and bit Daddy's butt. And the sock went into mommy's room and bit the mommy's butt. (Maxi, December 6, 2006)

This particular story actually hangs together fairly well. But in many cases disparate elements were simply added on to the story without really being integrated, resulting in a string of loosely connected or even disconnected characters and episodes.

For several of the boys, an additional factor was at work. During this phase, as noted earlier, children who had been composing first-person narratives of personal experiences (real or alleged) began to shift away from them toward third-person fictional stories. From a long-term perspective, that could be regarded as an advance. But one ironic side-effect of this shift, in the short run, was the loss of some formal advantages of the earlier narrative genre. Like the family genre favored by the older girls, the younger children's first-person genre provided an interrelated set of characters that ran through the story, and the brevity and simplicity of their first-person stories made it easier to maintain their continuity and coherence. Now these children faced the challenge of finding and mastering an alternative narrative genre that would allow them to construct third-person fictional stories with more characters, greater complexity, and a wider range of themes. In the meantime, their narrative ambitions often overloaded their narrative abilities, and their stories were often thematically scattered, jumbled, and fragmented.

Phase 3. The emergence of a dominant shared storyline: the Power Rangers genre

The final phase, running from February through the end of the storytelling/story-acting practice in the middle of May, was marked by two notable developments. It commenced with a significant shake-up in the classroom peer group. Ruby, a popular older girl who was also one of the most capable storytellers, left the class at the end of January, and one of the boys left later in February. Three new children, who had just turned four, entered the class together. An older girl, Denise, who had been part of the original class in September and October but then had attended only intermittently for several months, began attending regularly again (along with her younger sister, who was one of the new girls). The new children were integrated into the classroom peer culture over time, but some after-effects of this disruption were apparent through the end of the school year. However, the more striking feature of this phase, beginning around the end of February, was the emergence and consolidation of a shared narrative genre, based on the Power Rangers cartoons, that came to be dominant among the boys and affected the classroom peer culture as a whole.

The new children quickly began to participate in the storytelling/story-acting practice, both as storytellers and as actors, and their participation clearly helped integrate them into the class. On the other hand, their storytelling skills were limited. Unlike the younger children in the fall, they did not go through a period of telling first-person stories about personal experiences, but for some time their efforts to construct fictional stories were rudimentary. Often, in fact, they did little more than list disconnected characters, with minimal or non-existent descriptions of actions for the characters to perform; instead, they used much of their storytelling time to indicate which children would take which roles in the story enactment. At the beginning, their concerns with the social-relational aspects of the storytelling/story-acting practice seemed to take priority over the mastery of narrative skills, and it took some time for their narrative efforts to develop beyond these primitive proto-stories.

Narrative performance and peer group culture

The other children in the class continued their ongoing process of narrative experimentation and cross-fertilization, and at the end of February a cluster of them began to converge on a shared story paradigm that could serve as a framework for constructing relatively coherent multi-episode stories. This genre centered on the Power Rangers, a team of cartoon characters who were also familiar to the children as toy figurines. The crystallization of this genre involved both continuities and discontinuities with previous tendencies. As mentioned earlier, the children's stories had increasingly drawn characters and other elements from cartoons, and since December this had sometimes included putting one or more Power Rangers into stories with a different focus. But it was not until the end of February that children began to compose stories that used the Power Rangers and their actions, chiefly fighting monsters and other bad guys, as an organizing framework. It is also worth noting that although elements of violence and conflict were present in some stories from the beginning, the boys in this class had not developed a storytelling genre with a heroic-agonistic focus. Now, with the emergence of the Power Rangers genre, they did so.

The initial crystallization and diffusion of the Power Rangers storyline emerged from a process of collaboration, mediated by the storytelling/story-acting practice, between three boys who had been in the class from the beginning of the school year. On February 28, Taylor dictated a proto-story that essentially listed the Wild Force Power Ranger characters without assigning them any actions. Later that day, Theo told a coherent fictional story with a multi-episode plot involving a series of conflicts between Power Rangers and some monsters.

Once upon a time there was a <u>red Power Ranger</u> and then there was a <u>blue Power Ranger</u> and then they killed the <u>monsters</u> and then they were done and then the monsters were dead because the Power Rangers fought them. And then the Power Rangers changed back into people. There was a <u>yellow Power Ranger</u> too and the yellow Power Ranger was a girl, and then there was the <u>white Power Ranger</u> and they changed back too. And then they eat food, and they went out to see if there were monsters outside and there were. So they changed back into Power Rangers and then the Power Rangers fighted them and then they were done. The end. (Theo, February 28, 2007)

Theo himself did not immediately return to the Power Rangers theme, but during March, the Power Rangers storyline was taken up and re-used, with variations and elaborations, by Taylor and another boy, Tobi. At the beginning of April, Theo told another Power Rangers story, and thereafter all the rest of his stories were in this genre. By April, in fact, this storyline was consolidated as the dominant narrative model among the full-year boys, and in April and May four of the boys told stories exclusively in this genre. Furthermore, this storyline became a shared point of reference even for many stories of other types, including stories by some of the full-year girls and narrative efforts by the new children. In February only 13 percent of all stories in the class included some mention of Power Rangers, even in a peripheral or inconsequential manner. This proportion increased to 22 percent in March, 47 percent in April, and 48 percent in May. In short, this story paradigm became the common property of the classroom peer group, and Power Ranger elements became widely diffused in the children's storytelling.

Nevertheless, this genre remained clearly and distinctively a boys' genre, and was recognized as such by the classroom peer culture. Almost all of the fully developed stories in the Power Rangers genre, as distinct from stories that merely mentioned Power Rangers or included Power Rangers themes in other frameworks, were told by full-year boys. The exceptions were three stories that Grace, one of the most ambitious and prolific storytellers in the class, told in April and May. And even then, her Power Rangers stories suggested a lack of full enthusiasm for this genre, or even some ambivalence about it. This story, for example, begins with a nicely compact presentation of a typical Power Rangers scenario, but then veers off into themes more characteristic of the girls' preferred storylines, including family life, babies, and romance.

Once upon a time the Power Rangers fight the monsters. The monsters just dead. There were more monsters and then the Power Rangers said "Power up" and swung back up. And then they just cut the monsters. And they come back out and they looked fat. The Power Rangers had a gingerbread baby and they put him to sleep and gave him a good night kiss and they told him a story and they rocked him to sleep. And the pink Power Ranger said "You're a nice boy" to the red Power Ranger. The green Power Ranger says "You're a nice one" to the pink Ranger. The yellow Power Ranger says "You're a nice one" to the green Power Ranger. The end. (Grace, April 16, 2007)

One feature of the Power Rangers story framework, and the way that the children made use of it in the storytelling/story-acting practice, helped to link it even more firmly to the structures of peer group life in the classroom. The Power Rangers characters are distinguished by color and gender: the red, blue, green, white, and black Power Rangers are identified as boys and the pink, yellow, and purple Power Rangers as girls. In assigning roles for story enactments, different Power Rangers were always matched with actors of the same gender. What was more unusual was that the Power Ranger roles treated as central in the children's stories, red and blue, were consistently reserved for two specific boys, even if another child was telling the story. The red Power Ranger was always acted by Tobi and the blue Power Ranger by Taylor. For example, in the story just quoted, Grace assigned the role of red Power Ranger to Tobi and named herself the pink Power Ranger. The roles of monsters and bad guys were almost always given to younger boys or girls, who tended to be less choosy about which characters they portrayed. Thus, the enactment of the Power Ranger stories could be used to symbolically mark, and perhaps help to construct and consolidate, the evolving social boundaries and relational structures within the classroom peer culture. In this respect, it appears that one function of this storytelling/story-acting practice was to do social-relational work in the classroom.

Why did the Power Rangers genre, in particular, take hold so strongly among the boys in this class? Most likely there is no definitive answer to that question, but at least part of the appeal of this story paradigm for the boys was probably that it offered them an effective and readily usable generative framework for their storytelling that allowed them to construct increasingly complex, coherent, and satisfying narratives informed by themes that especially interested and engaged them – including, of course, violent and competitive (that is, agonistic) conflict. In our previous studies of young children's spontaneous storytelling we have often found that when boys begin to move beyond disconnected individual conflicts, they are often drawn to teams or coalitions of cartoon heroes (Power Rangers, Teenage Mutant Ninja Turtles, Batman and Robin, etc.). These teams or coalitions provide a set of interconnected characters that can run through the story and help give it coherence, but the theme of conflict remains dominant. The possibility of repeated conflicts between good guys and bad guys can also help to structure the plot and maintain temporal coherence across various episodes. At all events, as the Power Rangers genre became consolidated as a shared framework for storytelling and for narrative cross-fertilization, the boys' stories became (on the whole) stronger, more complex, and more sophisticated. The boys also composed stories more frequently than before, and the overall proportion of stories by boys increased.

It may not be surprising that the girls were less eager than the boys to adopt the Power Rangers genre. But why did they fail to develop or maintain an equally strong shared narrative genre of their own? The fact that they did not is especially puzzling given that from October through January their storytelling was generally stronger, more ambitious, and more sophisticated than the boys'. And as early as the first phase the older girls had introduced a family genre that might have served, as it has in other preschool classes, as a powerful generative framework for further narrative collaboration, cross-fertilization, and development. But rather than being further enriched and elaborated, the girls' family genre largely faded away during the third phase, no shared genre emerged to replace it, and – if we overlook the proto-narrative gropings of the new children who entered the class in February – the frequency of storytelling by most of the girls actually tended to decline. At this stage of the analysis, we can only speculate about possible reasons for this outcome. It seems likely that at least part of the explanation is linked to the social dynamics of the classroom peer culture. The girls' peer group seems to have been more disrupted than the boys' by the population turnover in February, and thereafter the girls never managed to achieve as much cohesion and solidarity within their subgroup as the boys. This weakened their capacities for narrative sharing and collaboration – which, in turn, made it harder for them to use their narrative activities to help consolidate and strengthen their collective identity and group life.

Conclusions and reflections

The study reported in this chapter, which built on and extended a long-term line of research, explored the operation and effects of a narrative practice combining spontaneous storytelling and group story-acting in a preschool class of children from low-income and otherwise disadvantaged backgrounds. By comparison with children in middle-class preschools we have studied, these children began the school year with weaker narrative skills and less familiarity with the conventions and narrative resources for constructing free-standing fictional stories. But over the course of the year, the quality of their stories, as well as their narrative and narrative-related skills, improved significantly. Without recapitulating our analysis of the processes by which this occurred, we will highlight some of the theoretical and practical implications.

This storytelling/story-acting practice, which integrates individual spontaneity with peer group collaboration and mutual support, provides a concrete example of how a peer-oriented narrative practice can serve as an effective matrix for promoting children's narrative development – not through expert–novice interactions between individuals but by serving as a socially structured *opportunity space* that offers participants both resources and motivations for narrative activity and development. And the public *performance* of the children's narratives in the story-enactment component of this practice plays a critical role in that process, not least because it helps to generate and maintain a *shared public arena* for narrative communication, appropriation, experimentation, collaboration, and cross-fertilization. At the same time, it helps to enmesh the storytelling/story-acting practice in the sociocultural fabric of the children's everyday peer relations and group life. On the one hand, this practice helps to form and sustain a common culture in the classroom (while also facilitating the expression and articulation of differences within this common culture); and, reciprocally, this practice is shaped, supported, and energized by its embeddedness in that peer group culture. There is thus a complex ongoing interplay between the evolution of the classroom peer culture and the transformation of the children's storytelling.

In the process, the children become increasingly attentive to each other's stories and influence each other extensively – in ways that are mediated by friendship ties, subgroup formation, gender, and so on. But the potential for fruitful narrative collaboration and cross-fertilization between them is itself a developmental achievement that children need to master. Through their participation in this storytelling/story-acting practice, the children are helping to constitute and enrich this field of shared activity as a context for their own socialization and development and, at the same time, are building up the skills and orientations that enable them to benefit most fully and effectively from their participation.

This chapter argues against a one-sided focus on the role of adult–child relations and other expert–novice interactions in children's socialization and development, but of course it would also be foolishly one-sided to overlook their importance. Even with respect to predominantly peer-oriented activities like this storytelling/story-acting practice, adults can make important contributions – not only through their direct role in facilitating the practice itself, but also by helping provide resources and foundations for the children's narrative activity in various indirect ways. For example, one notable feature of the children's stories in this classroom was that they became increasingly infused, not only with characters and other specific elements drawn from cartoons, but with a more general cartoon sensibility – emphasizing strings of disconnected actions and startling images, often humorous or destructive, at the expense of continuity and coherent plot development. What was rare, by contrast with corresponding middle-class preschool classrooms, was the presence of characters, plotlines, and other influences drawn from children's books. This conspicuous absence was probably linked to the fact that low-income children usually enter preschool with dramatically less experience of bookreading by parents and other caregivers than middle-class children (Nicolopoulou 2002: 140). And although there was some bookreading in this classroom, it was too infrequent to overcome this gap effectively. There are good reasons to expect that if children are provided with extensive background experience of interactive bookreading, to supplement the elements of popular culture they get from electronic media, that could significantly strengthen and enrich their narrative activity in this storytelling/story-acting practice and enhance its benefits for those involved.

This study adds further support to an accumulating body of research which argues that children's peer interactions and peer group activities can contribute to their socialization and development in ways that usefully complement – without displacing – the role of adult–child interactions. Both narrative research and educational practice should recognize the significance of peer group life as a developmental matrix of prime importance, rich complexity, and great potential.

Acknowledgment

The research reported here was supported by a grant (NIH/NICHD R21 24–0795445) to the first author. The rest of the authors are listed alphabetically as they contributed equally to the research and analyses.

NOTES

1 Pseudonyms have been assigned to the children. Characters acted in the stories are marked by underlining.

4 "Let's pretend you're the wolf!": the literate character of pretend-play discourse in the wake of a story

Esther Vardi-Rath, Eva Teubal, Hadassah Aillenberg and Teresa Lewin

Introduction

The pervasive view today is that literacy constitutes one of the major factors in the promotion of economic development and prosperity (Barton 2007). Numerous literacy programs have been sponsored by various organizations and foundations but with no satisfactory results. Universal discontent with poor levels of literacy achievement has led governments to make literacy skills a compulsory component of early education curricula.

This new emphasis on literacy and numeracy skills is generating activities in early childhood settings that have the characteristics of formal schooling and are pursued at the expense of play (OECD 2006). This poses a threat to what was formerly considered by Western early childhood educators to be the *kindergarten tradition*.

As a reaction to this state of affairs, researchers have begun to investigate the positive relationship between pretend play and literacy. Since the 1970s, it has been believed that this connection has the potential to bridge the gap between play and academic achievement (Pellegrini 2009; Roskos et al. 2010).

This connection derives fundamentally from Piaget's (1962) and Vygotsky's (1978) theories, which point to symbolic capacity as a salient feature of both pretend-play (also called *symbolic play*) transformations and written language. Given that symbolization is involved in both domains, the connection between pretend play and literacy has been taken for granted by many authors, who have not conducted empirical studies demonstrating the existence of transfer or relations between the two contexts. However, in light of the substantial research findings,[1] and in order to adopt adequate intervention principles and sound educational policy, it is imperative that we deal with the still existing "problem of defining the salient characteristics of play influential in literacy learning" (Smith 2005).

The aim of the present study is to look for the relation between specific features of social pretend play, namely, the characteristics of peer interaction, and their potential link to literacy features that are manifested in children's discourse. Our focus is on a specific discourse emerging in the process of play and discursive *literacy skills*, such as use of decontextualized language and high register language (Blum-Kulka 2004; Zadunaisky Ehrlich and Blum-Kulka, this volume), rather than those related to print and grapho-phonemic aspects.

The study explored the links between the main features of a particular type of pretend play, namely *pretend play in the wake of story reading* (PPWS), and specific literacy-related aspects of children's behavior during that play. We chose to address this issue by means of an ethnographic study using discourse analysis of young children during PPWS. Our analysis focused on those aspects of discursive literacy competence that were manifested in the discourse produced by children while pretend-playing a story that had just been read to them, here called the original story text (OST). Thus, the activity dealt with here constituted an instance of participation in peer group interaction – mediated both by the OST and by the accessible illustrated children's storybook from which it was read. We assumed that the activity affords spontaneous learning opportunities (characterized as incidental learning) rather than learning opportunities resulting from systematic instruction. Before the presentation and detailed analysis of the activity, we will clarify the concepts of literacy and pretend play as adopted in this chapter.

Defining literacy, play and pretend play

Literacy

There is a wide spectrum of approaches to literacy. Our stance derives from those views influenced by multidisciplinary approaches that have led to a reconceptualization of literacy in cognitive, linguistic, social and cultural terms (Wagner, Venezky and Street 1999; Barton 2007; Olson 2009). These include both written and oral modes in a wide range of registers and genres, which thereby serve various social functions in several social contexts (Blum-Kulka 2004, 2010a; Olson 2009; Ravid and Tolchinsky 2002). The mutual influence between literacy competence and linguistic knowledge throughout the course of development is underscored by Ravid and Tolchinsky (2002). They consider: (a) the contribution of metalanguage to language development to be a defining process of linguistic literacy, and (b) familiarity with written language to be a register, and written language to be a notational system. Blum-Kulka's notion of discursive literacy includes the use of autonomous, decontextualized language in a variety of oral and written genres, as well as the ability to construct textually cohesive and coherent stretches of discourse. In the present study, we focused on Blum-Kulka's notion of discursive literacy (2010a) and on Ravid and Tolchinsky's (2002) concept of written language as a register, as potentially emerging in the oral discourse of children during PPWS.

Play

Play is a particularly elusive term to define (Sutton-Smith 1998; Pellegrini 2009). Our view is based on a consensus that has emerged among numerous researchers. From a dynamic perspective on development, play is not an end state (Brofenbrenner and Ceci 1994), but is rather a process characterized by certain salient features, such as intrinsic motivation (means-over-ends orientation, and play for the sake of play). Play is characterized by behavior that is not functional in its immediate environment, by the benefits related to creativity and novelty, positive affect, non-literality, flexibility, and autonomy (Rubin, Fein and Vandenberg 1983; Smith and Vollstedt 1985; Pellegrini 2010), and by freedom from all but personally imposed rules, which are changed at will (Bettelheim 1987). Pellegrini (2010) differentiates between *play* and *games*: games, unlike play, are developed later in childhood; they are goal oriented and governed by rules. Regarding this distinction, the activity used in the present study can be seen as 'play,' while more rule-structured pretend activities are 'games.' This distinction is of great importance, in our view. In the next section, we will see the particular relevance of this issue in the realm of pretend play.

Pretend play

Pretend play (PP) is the activity by means of which an alternative reality is superimposed on the actual reality in which the players are embedded (Lillard 2011). Children create this alternative reality through their talk, gestures, prosody and transformative manipulation of objects (Sawyer 1997). They behave as if they were in this imaginary reality, while remaining conscious of their actual surroundings. This may lead to multiple transitions back and forth from present reality to the made-up imaginary world. These multiple transitions are akin to the "literate capacity" mentioned by Harris (2000) – the cognitive processes characteristic of skilled readers, as they move back and forth between reality and the world of the text.

Children engage in PP in diverse settings that vary in terms of the interaction dimension: *adult–child play*, characteristic of infant–mother play in middle-class Western societies (Lillard 2011), *single-child play*, e.g., making (small) toy figures that interact within an individually created imaginary realm (Ilgaz and Aksu-Koc, 2005), or *social PP*, involving interaction between peers (Sawyer 1997), as was the case in our study. In social PP, for the play to take place, the group needs to share a co-constructed interactional frame: the play frame. This involves negotiation and shifts in definition as the participants interact either by speaking as their play character ("in frame"), or speaking as themselves ("out of frame"). The terms "in frame" (i.e., "within the pretend play frame") refer to the imaginary world and "out of frame" (i.e., "outside the pretend play frame") refer to the real context (Sawyer 1997). The frequency of in-frame–out-of-frame transitions grows when pretend play is based on the enactment of an OST: the text constraints and distancing factors bring about an increased need for out-of-frame discourse.

In research on literacy development focusing on PP, Roskos et al. (2010) found two alternative models had been adopted by the surveyed studies: *environmental design* or *instructional design*. Environmental design studies involve environmental manipulation in which thematic props (toys such as miniature farm animals) and/or theme-related literacy materials (such as menus and order pads in a restaurant-themed area) are added to play settings. These studies focus on a variety of outcome variables such as oral language, story comprehension and literacy activity during play of the kind referred to by Ravid and Tolchinsky (2002, see above) as the notational aspects of written language. Instructional design studies are more tightly structured: a storybook is read to children and an adult then guides the children to re-enact the story while props (i.e., environmental manipulation) are usually kept to a minimum. These studies focus on story comprehension and narrative skills. Neither environmental nor instructional design includes totally spontaneous and free PP such as that described by Sawyer (1997) and Corsaro (1993).

The activity in our study was somewhat similar to the instructional design studies, although there was a difference in the degrees of freedom enjoyed by the children. The guidance characteristic of instructional studies was absent from our play activity: the children were totally independent while playing the story. The degrees of freedom were limited only by the OST, which, however, the children were free to modify as they saw fit. We view the degrees of freedom children have to construct and negotiate their own script as one of the main characteristics of PP activity: we assume this affords a beneficial environment for practicing discursive literacy skills (Blum-Kulka 2004, 2010a; Zadunaisky Ehrlich and Blum-Kulka 2010). From this perspective, the amount and type of adult involvement affects the degrees of freedom in play: the less adult involvement, the more degrees of freedom for peer interaction, which results in children jointly co-constructing and negotiating the play frame. The difference between games and play (indicated above) essentially consists of the degrees of freedom afforded by the activity. Therefore, the more constraints imposed by the script behind children's PP and the more governed by rules it is, the less it is 'play' as opposed to a 'game.' This would be the case when children are taught to play scripts that they are not at liberty to modify.

The specific topics dealt with in this chapter stem from (a) the children's need to construct the play frame while departing from the OST and the impact of this need upon their ability to behave alternately in two contexts: the reality in which they are embedded and the imaginary situation created by their pretense (in-frame and out-of-frame mobility), and (b) the impact the OST read to the children has on the discourse produced during their enactment of it.

Participants and data gathering

A total of thirty transcripts (5875 turns) were analyzed. These came from play sessions of preschoolers, kindergarteners, and first- and second-graders in Israeli educational institutions. The PPWS method employed was developed by the authors in the course of tutoring our students. It was adopted by the educational institutions where the students were training, so that the children were familiar with it by the time our research took place. A fairy tale was read by a student teacher to a group of four or five children. The stories read were fantasy tales rather than realistic stories, so as to stimulate the children's ability to detach themselves from the here and now, which is essential to discursive literacy.

The story was read without pauses, enabling the children to experience the story as a whole. Immediately after the reading, the student asked the children to go and play the story and supplied neutral artifacts for the children to use as they wished. The children received no further adult guidance during their play session, which lasted about twenty minutes.

During the story-playing session, two student teachers (the one who read the story and another in charge of the videotape) sat near the group. The first wrote down the children's speech and actions, as well as descriptions of play objects and props, while the second made sure the videotape stand was adequately placed to capture the children as they moved around. After the session, they produced a transcript that combined information from the written notes and videotapes.

The children in the sample were from four preschools, four kindergartens, four 1st-grade and two 2nd-grade classes. The children's ages ranged from 3.5 to 7.0 years. The majority (about 70%) of the children came from low-income and working-class families. Below we will present the picture obtained through analysis of the transcripts of the children's play sessions.

Characteristics of children's discourse during PPWS

While enacting their pretend story, the children processed the OST in an active, multi-modal way. On the one hand, the OST was a source of information and language structures that enriched the children's repertoire. Awareness of the *book language* characteristic of the OST became a lever with which the children enhanced their spoken language. On the other hand, the OST was a constraining factor, which limited their degrees of freedom as they produced their enactment. The features characteristic of PPWS involved a number of transitions from the original to the enacted story. We shall address these transitions below.

1. From written language to spoken language

The children created a new, oral narrative text based on their interpretation of the OST. The language in this new text was a combination of the children's own everyday language and the book language.

2. From listening to doing

This transition took place when the children enacted the characters from the OST: rather than talking about the characters, they enacted them. At times, they did so by transforming objects: by representing an item from the story through a chosen object, or by using various props in their surroundings to represent the scenery or background (e.g., a forest, the sea, darkness).

3. From free play to play within the constraints of a given story

The OST created a starting point for the children's negotiation of the imaginary frame. This negotiation can be considered in relation to two aspects:

(a) The text was a constraining factor impacting on play: PPWS offered the children multiple degrees of freedom, while at the same time demanding that the OST be taken into consideration. The OST became a backbone for the children's activity, requiring them to play according to its content and structure. This constraint led the children to active collaboration in order to solve problems, thus stimulating their capacity to improvise. The combination of the OST and PP can be seen as encouraging the children's verbal creativity, interpretive reproduction and metacognitive references to the play (e.g., Sawyer 2001, 2002).

(b) The text served as a distancing factor in the children's discourse: the OST transported the children to a more distant, imaginary, OST-based play world, far from the here and now. This process can be seen as beneficial for fostering decontextualized discourse, which is essential to children's literacy development (Blum-Kulka 2010a; Pellegrini 2009). During the OST-based play, the children were required to use distanced discourse: to adjust the degree of explicitness and abstraction according to the presumed knowledge level of their interlocutors.

Pretend play as an arena for in-frame and out-of-frame mobility

Our analysis of the transcripts revealed several types of discourse that the children produced to create the play frame.

Out-of-frame discourse

We noted two types of out-of-frame discourse: (a) *metaplay* discourse and (b) *here-and-now* discourse, which are detailed below.

Metaplay discourse

Pellegrini and Galda (1998) have characterized metaplay discourse as involving metatalk – talk about linguistic (e.g., 'you are saying it wrong') and mental (e.g., 'he's all mixed up') states. They singled out metatalk as a crucial aspect of literate language that can predict school-based literacy learning. This is apparently related to the decentering and perspective-taking opportunity it affords children. In the present study, the children planned and directed their pretend play in metaplay discourse (Sawyer 1997), taking into account both the OST and the constraints set by their present reality. Metaplay discourse included children's talk about their play and the stipulation of the imaginary frame (Harris 2000). During this discourse, the children acted out of character, as outside observers of their PP, speaking with their own voices about the characters they played.

Here-and-now discourse

The children discussed the immediate reality in which their play took place, sometimes without relating it to the play frame, while at other times incorporating real-world daily experiences. At times, the children's here-and-now discourse was elicited by the surrounding context, and at others, it originated in their own world.

In-frame discourse

During the children's in-frame discourse, which followed the OST, they enacted one or more characters, showing varying degrees of adherence to the OST. In-frame discourse sometimes deviated from the plot and characters: for example, the children extended the story, added characters and changed the place or time. The children entered their characters and talked through them, using the first person and adopting the characters' dominant characteristics, including posture, movements, gestures and vocalizations.

Figure 4.1 displays the coding scheme of the categories that emerged from analysis of the transcripts (described above).

Figure 4.2 graphically represents the relative quantities in which the different categories (described above) appeared in the children's discourse produced during the analyzed portion of their PPWS.

We have seen that a major part of the discourse occurring during PPWS is out of frame (71%). Analysis of the out-of-frame discourse occurring during

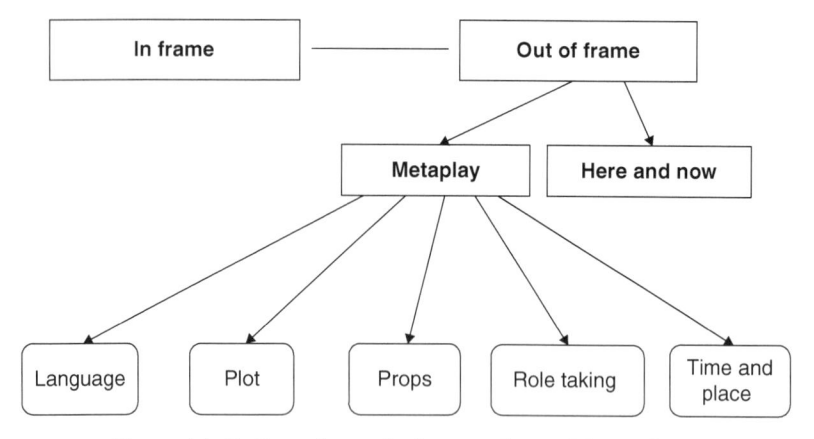

Figure 4.1 Coding scheme: in-frame and out-of-frame discourse (based on 5875 coded turns)

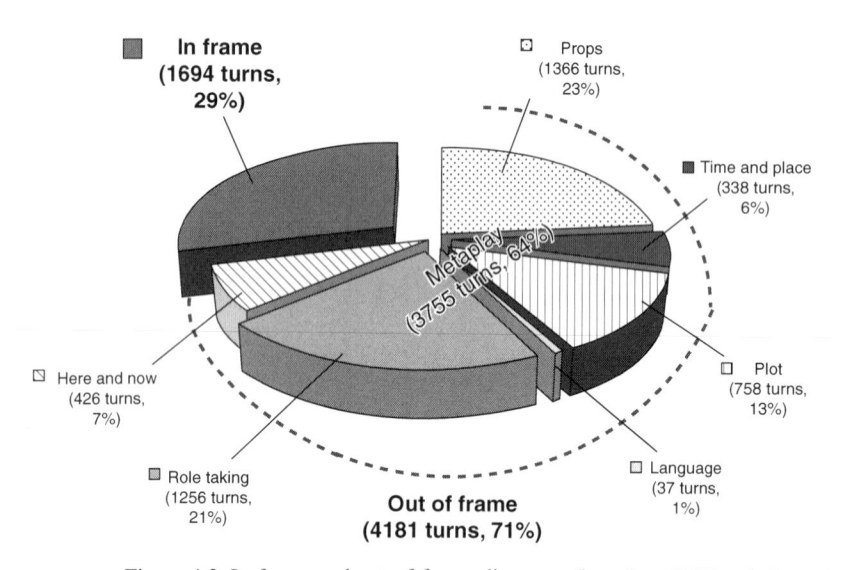

Figure 4.2 In-frame and out-of-frame discourse (based on 5875 coded turns)

PPWS shows that metaplay discourse was a major element (64%), while here-and-now discourse was far less apparent (7%). Metaplay discourse consisted of negotiations about props (23%), roles (21%), plot (13%), time and place (6%) and discourse about language (1%).

Below we present two examples of PPWS that followed the reading of "Little Red Riding Hood." The examples illustrate the children's mobility between in-frame and out-of-frame discourse, as well as the discourse characteristics mentioned in the above coding scheme (Figure 4.2). Ex.1 shows how the metaplay discourse evolves in a way that can beneficial to fostering children's discursive literacy and social skills. It includes planning and setting up the pretend play, while referring back to the text for role allocation, the characters' appearance, and, above all, making sure the children's acting ability is good enough for them to enact their roles. It also shows that there were many degrees of freedom during PPWS peer interaction, with the children taking it upon themselves to expand and change the story when the need arose.

Ex. 1: Out-of-frame role negotiation within metaplay (following "Little Red Riding Hood" by the Brothers Grimm)[2]

Date: 25.1.06. Kindergarten, Beer Sheva.
Participants: Tal (m., 5.2), Yuval (f., 5.5), Lior (f., 5.1), Noam (f., 5.8).

116.	Lior: mi ha-ze'ev kan? ke'ilu mi, mi, mi yaxol la'asot kol shel ze'ev? ve-ledaber iti kmo ze'ev?	Lior: Who is the wolf here? Like who, who, who can make the sound of a wolf? And talk to me like a wolf?
117.	Yuval: lo 'ani.	Yuval: Not me.
118.	Noam: lo 'ani.	Noam: Not me.
119.	Lior: ata yaxol la'asot kol shel ze'ev? [to Tal]	Lior: Can you make the sound of a wolf? [to Tal]
120.	Tal: aval … aval …	Tal: But … But …
121.	Lior: az eyn lanu ze'ev! ve-az i efshar la'asot et ha-misxak ha-ze.	Lior: So we don't have a wolf! Then [we] can't play this [literally, do this play, the verb "do" being then echoed by Tal].
122.	Tal: aval, aval yesh li ra'ayon ma na'ase.	Tal: But, but I have an idea what we can do.
123.	Lior: ma yihiye a-ze'ev? navi buba ze'ev?	Lior: What would be the wolf? Shall we bring a doll wolf?
124.	Tal: xaki … anaxnu …	Tal: Wait … we …
125.	Lior: az ta'ase ke'ilu ata ha-ze'ev, ke'ilu dimyomi.	Lior: So you make like a wolf, pretend (ke'ilu), imaginary.
126.	Tal: lo! ha-ze'ev lo haya shama, hu haya kodem kol ahh …	Tal: No! The wolf was not there, he was first of all mmmm.
127.	Lior: naxon, ke'ilu ani avarti ba-shvil ve-ata ke`ilu bata elay, ke'ilu hayita ha-ze'ev ve-gam ha-cayad ve-asita rrr … rr [sitting on all fours and making the sound of a wolf].	Lior: Yes, pretend I passed on the path and you came to me as if you were the wolf and the hunter and you went rrr … rr … [sitting on all fours and making the sound of a wolf].
128.	Tal: aval, ani menase laxshov ma anaxnu osim.	Tal: But, I'm trying to think what we're doing.
129.	Lior: tal takshiv li [shows him the book]! naxon siparnu axshav et ha-sipur shel kipa aduma? naxon haya ze'ev?	Lior: Tal, Listen to me [shows him the book]! Didn't we just tell the story of Little Red Riding Hood? Right, was there a wolf there?
130.	Tal: ken.	Tal: Yes.

131.	Lior: ata carix lihiyot gam ha-ze'ev ve-gam ha-cayad.	Lior: You have to be both the wolf and hunter.
132.	Tal: aval ma im ani eheye gam ze'ev ve-gam cayad, ani gam axtox oto ve-gam ikra li la-mita?	Tal: But if I'm both the wolf and the hunter, I'll cut him and he'll also call me to bed?
133.	Lior: ke'ilu, ke'ilu, ke- 'i- lu! ata yode'a ma ze ke'ilu?	Lior: Pretend, pretend, pre–tend! Do you know what pretend means?
134.	Tal: ma ze? lema at mitkavenet?	Tal: What is it? What do you mean?
135.	Yuval: ani asbir lexa, ata carix lihiyot …	Yuval: I'll tell you, you should be …
136.	Lior: tasbiri lo at, kashe li lehasbir lo, hu lo yode'a kol kax tov.	Lior: You tell him, I can't tell him, he doesn't know so well.
137.	Yuval: ata racita lihiyot ha-cayad, Lior racta lihiyot kipa aduma, gam ani raciti, aval vitarti al ze. ani ha-ima ve-no'am hi ha-savta. aval en od mishtatef she-haya ha- ze'ev.	Yuval: You wanted to be a hunter, Lior wanted to be Little Red Riding Hood, I also wanted to, but I let Lior be her, I'm the mother and Noam is Grandma. But we have nobody to be the wolf.
138.	Lior: az ata tihiye ha-ze'ev ve-gam ha-cayad.	Lior: So you'll be the wolf and the hunter.
139.	Tal: aval …	Tal: But …
140.	Lior: aval, ma?!	Lior: But, but what?!
141.	Noam: [repeating Lior] aval, aval ma [laughs].	Noam: [repeating Lior] But, but what [laughs].
142.	Tal: az, az lama lo hizminu od exad?	Tal: So, why didn't they invite another person?
143.	Lior: ki kaxa ze, kaxa ha- kvuca racta.	Lior: That's how it is, that's what the group wanted.
144.	Yuval: Eti, lama lo mazminim od exad? [turns to the student]	Yuval: Eti, can't we invite another one? [turns to the student]

The example starts with the children's negotiation of role allocation, the children considering the presence of the other players, their needs (e.g., "Not me," *lo 'ani*, turn 117) and their real-life skills ("Can you make the sound of a wolf?", *ata yaxol la'asot kol shel ze'ev?*, turn 119). The negotiators were faced with a reality-based problem, as there were fewer children than characters to be enacted, a constraint that compelled one of the children to play two roles. None of the children wanted to take on the wolf's role, thus making the situation even more problematic.

Lior tried to convince Tal to be both the wolf and the hunter (see turns 121, 125, 127) by frequently using the word "pretend" (*keyilu*) (turns 125, 127, 133). The word, used in the children's metaplay, created an expanded, decontextualized discourse that took their interlocutors into account. Lior's explicit use of the word "pretend" became a discourse marker for the other children to enter the imaginary frame and made it easier for them to contend with the various constraints posed by reality and by the story.

As good and creative as they were, Lior's ideas could only be implemented if Tal agreed to them, and he did not do so readily. Their negotiation underscored

Lior's capacity to improvise (Sawyer 2001) as well as the importance of cooperation in social PP. This is also a good example of the contribution of the questioning child to the development of the group members' literacy skills. Tal, the questioning child, was the one who raised queries, expressed doubt, and did not understand or agree with what was happening (see turns 120, 122, 126, 128, 132, 134, 139).

Were it not for Tal's reservations and questioning, the group discussion, which led to an expansion of the discourse, might not have taken place. His questions forced his peers to explain and interpret what had previously seemed obvious to them.

While in formal settings children rarely express their reservations or lack of understanding, PP provides a comfortable setting, inviting natural reactions such as objection, disapproval and even emphatic expression of a lack of understanding. The following example, from the same enactment (plus one child), illustrates both in-frame and out-of-frame discourse.

Ex. 2: In-frame and out-of-frame mobility (following the story "Little Red Riding Hood" by the Brothers Grimm)

Date: 25.1.06. Kindergarten, Beer Sheva.
Participants: Tal (m., 5.2), Yuval (f., 5.5), Lior (f., 5.1), Noam (f., 5.8).

144.	Yuval: kipa aduma kxi et ze [red robe] al terdi me-ha-shvil ve-al tedabri im zarim. *(in frame)*	Yuval: Little Red Riding Hood, take this [red robe], don't get off the path, and don't talk to strangers. *(in frame)*
145.	Lior: ken ima *(in frame)*. at shaxaxt mila axat [putting on the robe] *(out of frame)*. at crixa lehagid li yaldati ha-metuka, at crixa latet le-sevta et ha-sal ha-ta'im ha-ze she-hi tavri. *(Quote – outside frame)*	Lior: Yes Mommy *(in frame)*. You forgot one word [putting on the robe] *(out of frame)*. You have to tell me "My sweet child, you have given this tasty basket to Grandma to make her better" *(Quote – outside frame)*
146.	Yuval: xaki, anaxnu …	Yuval: Wait, we …
147.	Lior: ani holexet le-beyta shel savta. *(in frame – book language high register)*	Lior: I'm going to Grandmother's house. *(in frame – book language high register)*
148.	Yuval: al tishti, kxi et ha-oxel le-savta [She gives the bag to Lior] al terdi me-ha-shvil, al tedabri im zarim, al tesaxki maxbo'im ve-al ta'acri. *(in frame)*	Yuval: Don't drink, take the food to Granny [she gives the bag to Lior], don't get off the path, don't talk to strangers, don't play hide and seek, and don't stop. *(in frame)*
149.	Lior: tov ima, yalla! [starts to walk in the room]	Lior: OK Mommy, Yalla! [Arabic for "let's go!" or "come on!"] [starts to walk in the room]
150.	Tal: hey, yalda, le-an at holexet? [changing his voice]	Tal: Hey, girl, where are you going? [changing his voice]
151.	Lior: le-savta.	Lior: To Granny's.

152.	Tal: az lama lo hevet la praxim? *(out of frame)* [indicated by tone of voice]	Tal: So why didn't you bring her flowers? *(out of frame)* [indicated by tone of voice]
153.	Lior: ani mamash axshav bati lakaxat la praxim. *(out of frame)*	Lior: I was just going to take flowers for her right now. *(out of frame)*
154.	Tal: beseder.	Tal: All right.
155.	Lior: tov, bye [puts the bag down]. shit, lama lo heveti praxim, yesh shama [pointing to the kindergarten's household corner]. *(out of frame)*	Lior: Bye [puts the bag down]. Oh, why didn't I bring flowers, there's some there [pointing to the kindergarten's household corner]. *(out of frame)*

The children appropriated the story "Little Red Riding Hood," while interweaving elements from their own culture (Corsaro 2005). A further characteristic of out-of-frame discourse is its relation to the present reality (here and now). Reality sometimes intruded into the framework of the PP without disrupting the natural progression of events in the enactment. The children were aware of the context of the OST, yet they still added personal associations to their enactment.

Ex. 3: Out-of-frame discourse incorporating here-and-now elements (following the story "Hansel and Gretel" by the Brothers Grimm)

Date: 5.1.04. First grade, Beer Sheva.
Participants: Noy (f., 6.3), Raz (f., 6.7), Ben (m., 6.2), Tal (m., 6.5).

161.	Raz: tov, ata ha-xatul sheal henzel ve-gretel, bo.	Raz: OK, you're Hansel and Gretel's cat. Come on.
162.	Ben: eyfo ani eshev?	Ben: Where do I sit?
163.	Raz: ba-xeder, po. bo tihiye ha-xatul.	Raz: In the room, here. Come be a cat.
164.	Ben: ah ... [on all fours]	Ben: Oh ... [on all fours]
165.	Tal: noy, tivdeki im yesh lo karciyot. [laughs]	Tal: Noy, see if he has ticks. [laughs]
166.	Raz: tivdeki im yesh lo kinim. [to Noy about Ben]	Raz: See if he has lice. [to Noy about Ben]
167.	Noy: etmol ha-mora amra she-yesh le-Ben ve-le-Tal kinim.	Noy: Yesterday the teacher said Ben and Tal have lice.
168.	Ben: ma pit'om! eyn li kinim! ima sheli menaka li kol shavu'a.	Ben: No way! I don't have lice! My Mom cleans me every week.
169.	Noy: nu. day.	Noy: OK. Enough.
170.	Tal: aba, carix lishlo'ax et ha-yeladim la-ya'yr ve-lehash'ir otam shama.	Tal: Father, we've gotta send the kids to the forest and leave them there.
171.	Noy: aval im hem yihiyu re'evim?	Noy: But what if they're hungry?
172.	Tal: lo nora, nikax otam la-ya'ar ve-nash'ir otam shama.	Tal: Never mind, we take them to the forest and leave them there.
173.	Ben: ma im ha-karciyot sheli?	Ben: What about my ticks?

174.	Raz: tavo axaray [he follows her on all fours] tov, lo lehagzim.	Raz: Follow me [he follows her on all fours]. C'mon, don't overdo it.
175.	Ben: lama lo menakim li ta-karciyot?	Ben: Why don't they clean my ticks?
176.	Raz: nidbak lexa karciyot, ani yoda'at.	Raz: The ticks got stuck on you, I know.

Note that there is no cat in the original story. However, the story does refer to a table inside the witch's candy house "with legs like those of a cat," which may be the origin of this reference. Perhaps Tal's active imagination led him to create the cat's character, and then personal associations caused him to bring up the ticks. Raz pursued this further to include the lice on Ben's head. Thus, they both transferred the enactment to the here and now, using humor and teasing. Pretend play, mirroring reality, can thus lead to jests and humor.

The OST as scaffold for the enhancement of discursive literacy skills

We found that when children engaged in PPWS they re-created the OST. The PPWS involved a process of negotiation somewhat similar to the process that takes place between a reader and the written text: the reader re-creates the text. Our focus was on the interaction that took place between the children and the OST. Transcript analysis showed that the enactment that followed the OST gave the children an opportunity to practice and experience discursive literacy skills by using language of a higher register, referred to as the *written register* by Ravid and Tolchinsky (2002) and *book language* by us. The latter concept makes salient the impact that the children's interaction with the book had on our activity: the children turned to the book as a source of authority and engaged in interpretive reproduction of the text while maintaining the OST structure and sequence. At times, it was possible to discern the children's metacognitive approaches to the text.

The coding scheme below represents the different types of interaction between the children and the OST.

The qualitative aspects of the different categories (Figures 4.3 and 4.4) are described and detailed below.

Lack of awareness of the OST

Lack of awareness of the OST (14%) refers to the element of the children's discourse that disregarded the OST during the supposed enactment. This might have been due to associations arising as the children played or their difficulty in recalling the story: for example, during an enactment following the story "Snow White and the Seven Dwarves," the children enacted "Gulliver's Travels in the Country of the Dwarves." It can be assumed that lacking awareness of

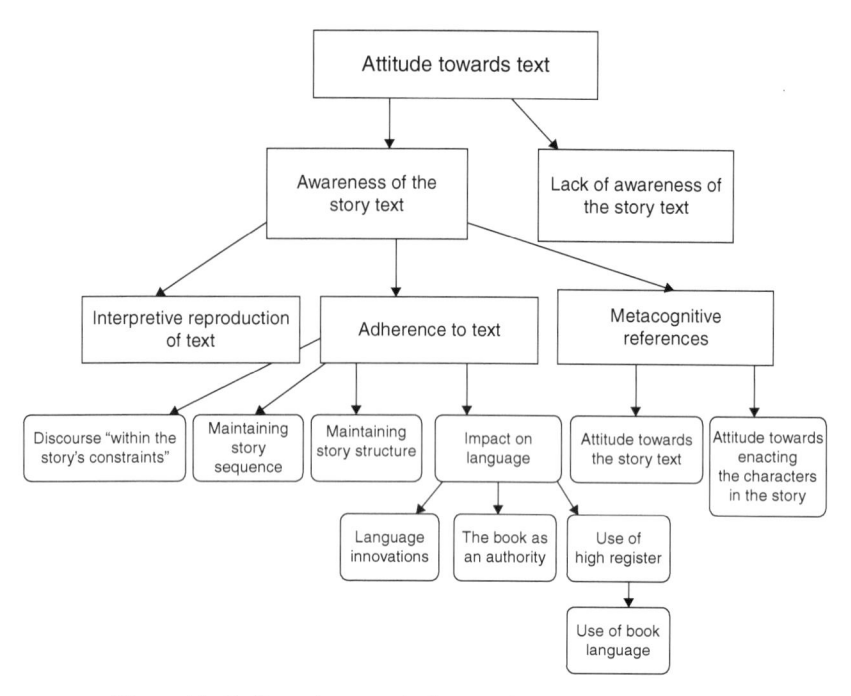

Figure 4.3 Coding scheme: attitude towards text (based on 5875 coded turns)

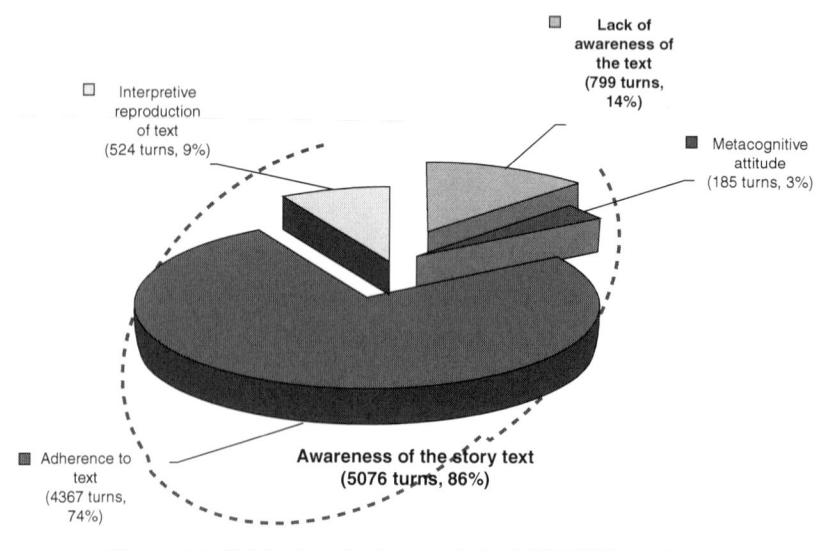

Figure 4.4 Children's attitude towards the OST (5875 turns)
Note: When coding, we have dealt with categories as though they were mutually exclusive: in the few cases in which an utterance could have been included in more than one category, the most salient one was chosen.

The literate character of pretend-play discourse 77

other parts of the story, the children allowed the characters of the dwarves to wander naturally from one story to the other. Lack of awareness of the text also includes out-of-frame discourse that refers to the child's immediate, contemporary reality (e.g., one child describes a program he saw on TV the previous day).

Awareness of the OST

Awareness of the OST (86%) refers to the children's ability to base their enactment on the OST. This includes turns in which the children changed the text while maintaining the story structure.

As can be seen in the scheme, awareness of the text is manifested in three different ways:

- **Adherence to text** (74%): adhering to the OST, without changes or additions.
- **Interpretive reproduction** (9%): the children were aware of the text without adhering to it. They expanded and changed it, while interacting with each other in response to their OST-related interaction.
- **Metacognitive reference to the text** (3%): the children's critical attitude towards the text, taken from a position external to the text itself.

The following is an example that illustrates many of the characteristics discussed above. It follows the story "Apartment to Let" by Leah Goldberg, which tells about a vacant apartment for let in a building whose tenants are different animals. The tale has a recurrent pattern of stanzas, in each of which a different animal character enquires about the apartment. One after the other, each potential tenant denigrates one of the neighbors, stating that neighbor's negative quality as the reason for not renting the apartment. In the last stanza, the pigeon who decides to rent the apartment does so because, despite the apartment's drawbacks, she finds a good quality in each and every neighbor.

Ex. 4: Various forms of awareness of the text (following the story "Apartment to Let" by Leah Goldberg)

Date: 9.1.05. First grade, Beer Sheva.
Participants: Lidor (m., 6.1), Aynav (f., 6.5), Yochai (m., 6.3).

49.	Lidor: li kor'im dag. [leaving the book and holding a fish in hand]	Lidor: My name is Fish. [leaving the book and holding a fish in hand]
50.	Aynav: shalom dag nexmad.	Aynav: Hello nice fish.
51.	Lidor: axshav tish'ali al ha-bayit.	Lidor: Now ask about the house.
52.	Aynav: ata roce lagur ba-bayit ha-xadash? ata roce lehikanes la-bayit?	Aynav: Do you want to live in the new house? Do you want to come into the house?

53.	Lidor: lo, tagidi ha-na'e ha-bayit?		Lidor: No, you have to say "Do you consider this house pleasant?"
54.	Aynav: ma ze na'e?		Aynav: What's "pleasant?"
55.	Lidor: yafe.		Lidor: Nice.
56.	Aynav: ha-na'e ha-bayit?		Aynav: Is the house pleasant?
57.	Lidor: ani lo roce lagur im arnav kaze shamen she-kofec kol ha-zman, ani lo ohev arnavim kofcim.		Lidor: I don't want to live with that kind of fat rabbit who keeps hopping, I don't like hopping rabbits.
58.	Aynav: shalom ani xili ha-xilazon. roce la-gur ba-bayit? [yelling]		Aynav: Hello, I'm Snelly the Snail. Do you want to live in the house? [yelling]
59.	Yochai: yafe ha-bayit bishvilex?		Yochai: Do you think it's a nice house?
60.	Aynav: na'e ha-bayit.		Aynav: A pleasant house.
61.	Aynav: roce lagur iti?		Aynav: Want to live with me?
62.	Yochai: lama she-ani yagur im xili xilaxon she-mash'ir rir ve-ani edabek?		Yochai: Why should I live with Snelly the snail who leaves goo that I'll stick to?

The above example shows the interaction between the children and the OST. The enactment provided for the children's active involvement, through which the text became the basis for group interaction: the children taught each other new words, using a higher linguistic register, and interpretively reproduced the text, while simultaneously maintaining the story structure.

Adherence to the text

Olson (1994) has made salient the fact that texts became much easier to adhere to after the appearance of written language. Written texts are readily available because they are represented on accessible surfaces. This allows for distancing from the context in which they were produced. Written texts afford decontextualization and distancing and thus are an essential element for the development of discursive literacy.

In the present study, adherence to the text (74%) indicates the players' degree of commitment to the OST. During the enactment, the children tended, on the whole, to take the OST as the basis for their negotiated re-creation. Physical exposure to the written text appears to have had a substantial contribution to this effect. The following are features that show the children's adherence to the text:

1. Discourse taking place within the OST constraints

This refers to the children's general enactment behavior regarding the OST: children talked the story while enacting it (see turns 52 and 61 in Ex. 4).

2. Maintenance of the OST structure

The transcript analysis showed that, while engaged in PPWS, the children behaved according to the OST organization scheme, based upon a sequence of events and usually also upon causal relations (Dressler and de Beaugrande 1981). By story structure (in this case the OST structure) we mean the sequence of events, real or imaginary episodes, in which the characters were involved (Segal 2008).

PPWS involves children's interpretive reconstruction of the OST and can therefore constitute a potential arena for the development of children's narrative abilities. The children are aware of the OST, but at the same time allow themselves changes based on both their world and the immediate reality surrounding the play.

Our study showed that the pragmatic-communicative needs of the children participating in PPWS affected their interpretation of the OST: the story emerging from their play depended not only on the OST, but also on their immediate context, needs of the moment and interaction with their surroundings. In Ex. 4, we saw that the children adhered to the recurrent pattern of the OST and applied it to the structure of their co-constructed, emergent story, while at the same time adding characters that did not exist in the original story – such as the fish, the rabbit and the snail. When Lidor said: "I don't want to live with that kind of fat rabbit who keeps hopping, I don't like hopping rabbits" (*ani lo roce lagur im arnav kaze shamen she-kofec kol ha-zman, ani lo ohev arnavim kofcim*, turn 57), he was applying a pattern recurring in the OST: referring to a negative quality ("a fat rabbit that keeps hopping," *arnav kaze shamen she-kofec kol ha-zman*) and explaining it ("I don't like hopping rabbits," *ani lo ohev arnavim kofcim*).

3. Maintenance of the OST sequence

Maintaining the story structure requires that one respect the sequence of events. PPWS provides an opportunity for children to plan, reconstruct and reorganize activities according to the original events sequence of the story. These are literacy skills, contingent upon memory, comprehension and awareness of context. As a rule, one of the children took on the role of sequence keeper. In the above example, when saying "now ask about the house" (*axshav tish'ali al ha-bayit*, turn 51), Lidor was indicating to the other participants that there was a narrative sequence to adhere to.

4. Impact of the story text on children's language

Linguistic innovations This refers to self-made independent linguistic expressions that show evidence of linguistic creativity: original words, mispronounced words, invented verbs that are not part of the conventional lexicon, and use of words derived from morphologically based patterns (Segal 2011). All of these are based on linguistic knowledge and grammar rules already mastered by children, which grow and develop with their increased literacy skills. These linguistic innovations are usually created when children lack a word they need while playing and use interesting declensions or morphemes derived from familiar words which undergo transformations according to the playing context. In the example taken from "Apartment to Let," we saw Aynav create a nickname for the snail, "Snelly" (*xili*, turn 58), derived from the noun, and then Yochai, while adhering to the narrative structure, picked up her linguistic innovation and explained his dislike of the snail by referring to a reality-based trait of snails (turn 62).

We found another example of the above that involved the PPWS of three first-graders enacting "The Emperor's New Clothes" by the Brothers Grimm. Two of them tried to impose the role of the scoundrel upon the third. The third child rejected the role on the grounds that he had never *scoundreled (naxalti)*, by which he meant he had never behaved like a scoundrel. He turned a noun (not necessarily familiar to him, *a scoundrel*), into a verb *scoundreled* – conjugating it as he would other regular verbs (for example, *cheat – cheated*, *bike – biked*, and therefore *scoundrel – scoundreled*).

Using a high register We found that PPWS provided children with an opportunity to vary linguistic registers and genres. They sometimes used the story language as it was, at other times they imitated grown-up language, and on other occasions they used their natural language, affected by the book's presence. Below we present one aspect of high register language use: the use of children's storybook language.

Use of children' storybook language Occasionally when enacting a narrative text, the children appeared to enjoy the use of language that was not part of their everyday repertoire. The OST was one of the factors that inspired them to use a higher register. In Ex. 4, following the story "Apartment to Let," Lidor demonstrated metalinguistic knowledge when he taught Aynav the use of the word "pleasant" (*na'e*, turn 53). Lidor was aware both of the meaning of the synonym and of the literary choice of the word "pleasant" (taken from the book) instead of "nice" (*yafe*, which is common in children's language).[3] It is interesting to note that Aynav demonstrated her eagerness to learn by subsequently using the word: she replied to Yochai's question "do you think that's a *nice* house?" (*yafe ha-bayit bishvilex?*, low register, turn 59) by saying "a *pleasant* house" (*na'e ha-bayit*, high register, turn 60). One can assume that motivation played a decisive role here. Aynav's willingness to ask her peers was salient, as was Lidor's eagerness to teach them a new word because of his social need to keep the play activity close to the book's refrain.

Turning to the book as a source of authority This occurred when the children were required to choose, or had doubts about, a detail in the story. They frequently addressed the book in order to solve problems that arose while playing, such as the appearance of a certain character or the right items of clothing. In the absence of an adult authority figure, the book became the authoritative resource the children turned to. They were observed referring to both the written text and the accompanying illustrations when having to make decisions.

Ex. 5: Turning to the book as a source of authority (following the story "Hansel and Gretel" by the Brothers Grimm)

Date 2.3.05. Kindergarten, Beer Sheva.
Participants: Nadav (m., 5), Or (m., 6), Komashi (f., 5.8).

33.	Nadav: ani mitxapes le-mashehu axer.	Nadav: I'm dressing up as something else.
34.	Or: le-barvaz.	Or: A duck.
35.	Komashi: aval barvaz hu lo ose kolot, hu raq soxe ba-yam.	Komashi: But a duck – a duck doesn't make any sounds, he just swims in the sea.
36.	Nadav: aval ra'iti ba-sipur.	Nadav: But I saw the storybook.
37.	Komashi: bo nivdoq ba-sefer. [looking at the illustrations in the book]	Komashi: Let's check the storybook. [looking at the illustrations in the book]
38.	Nadav: be'emet ani lo meshaker.	Nadav: Really, I'm not lying.

Turning to the book gave the children a sense of security, the book being a neutral authority and external body that could help them decide when doubts arose. Observation of many enactments showed that first- and second-graders, as well as preschoolers, turned to the book for assistance, but whereas the former, who had already acquired reading, were able to browse the text for corroboration of needed details, the latter tended to look for illustrations that would support them.

Interpretive reproduction
This refers to the children's ability to interpret and reproduce the narrative text creatively, appropriate it and enact it from their own point of view (Corsaro 1997, 2005). When engaged in enactment following a story, the children constructed and re-created peer culture through an interpretive process that was a result of negotiations within the group as well as with the text. They actually constructed something new that took into account the original text, the immediate enactment context and the peer culture.

In Ex. 4, we found two manifestations of interpretive reproduction: (a) the invention of new characters who acted and responded according to the original narrative structure (the fish, the fat rabbit and the gooey snail) and (b) argumentation based on the new neighbor's reality-based unpleasant trait – the type of argumentation required by the narrative structure: the rabbit "hops all the time" (*kofec kol ha-zman*, turn 57) and the snail is "gooey" (*mash'ir rir*, turn 62).

A further example of interpretive reproduction was observed during an enactment of "Little Red Riding Hood" by four first-graders. The lack of a *red* riding hood drove them to change the protagonist's name to "Little *White* Riding Hood."

Ex. 6: Interpretive reproduction (following the story "Little Red Riding Hood" by the Brothers Grimm)

Date: 21.4.04. First grade, Beer Sheva.
Participants: Mor (f., 6.2), May (f., 6.6), Danny (m., 7), Yuval (m., 6.3).

33.	Mor: nu may, at kipa aduma ve-lo kipa levana. [to May who is wearing a white scarf on her head, a white scarf around her neck, and white striped shirt]	Mor: Come on, May, you're Little Red Riding Hood, not Little White Riding Hood. [to May, who is wearing a white scarf on her head, a white scarf around her neck, and white striped shirt]
34.	May: aval eyn li po mashehu lilbosh adom ve-ani lo sama et ha-kova ha-megoxax ha-ze.	May: But I have nothing to wear in red here, and I'm not putting [on] this ridiculous hat.
35.	Danny: axshav at tihi ha … ani ecba otax be-ceva adom. [35 turns omitted]	Danny: Now you'll be the … I'll paint you red.
70.	Mor: shalom lax, eyx kor'im lax? [to Yuval]	Mor: Hello there, what's your name? [to Yuval]
71.	Yuval: ani ima shel kipa aduma.	Yuval: I am Little Red Riding Hood's Mother.
72.	Mor: toda ima shel kipa levana! [leading Yuval to the middle of the room] Tistaxavi, ima. [as if introducing her]	Mor: Thank you, Little *White* Riding Hood's Mother! [leading Yuval to the middle of the room] Bow, Mother. [as if introducing her]
73.	Yuval: kipa levana holexet le-savta.	Yuval: Little White Riding Hood is going to Granny.

The children all agreed that the heroine's name derived from what she wore. Mor carefully enforced the use of her proposed name throughout the enactment. When Yuval continued using the customary "Red Riding Hood" (*kipa aduma*), she insisted on her implicit metacommunicative use of "White Riding Hood" (Sawyer 1997, 2002): "thank you, Little White Riding Hood's Mother" (*toda ima shel kipa levana!*, turn 72). Yuval's response ("Little White Riding Hood is going to Granny," *kipa levana holexet le-savta*) indicated that he had indeed picked up her adaptation and adopted it.

Metacognitive reference to the text

Metacognitive discourse refers to thinking about thinking while maintaining an internal or external reflexive process (Astington 1993). We observed two distinct types of metacognitive references made by the children: (a) metacognitive references to the OST and (b) metacognitive references to enacting the characters in the story.

1. Metacognitive attitudes towards the OST

The following example is from the enactment following the story "Scram!" by Hannah Goldberg. The story tells of an abandoned cat and a lonely girl who has just moved into a new apartment. During the enactment, the children added more and more cats to the original story, until the cats actually took over the enactment and became the only characters present. Tal, who found this state of affairs unacceptable, complained about it.

Ex. 7: Metacognitive attitudes (following the story "Scram!" by Hannah Goldberg)

Date: 24.3.04. First grade, Beer Sheva.
Participants: Tal (m., 6.5), Paz (f., 6.8), Asil (f., 7.0), Sahar (m., 6.5).

273.	Tal: lo, ze kef she-yesh lefaxot ben adam exad, ze lo kef she-kulam xatulim.	Tal: No, it's fun to have at least one human being; it's no fun that everyone's a cat.
274.	Paz: az shtey klavim ve-shtey xatulim?	Paz: So, two dogs and two cats?
275.	Tal: lo! ben adam, ben adam ani roce!	Tal: No! A human being, a human being's is what I want!
276.	Paz: ah, ben adam.	Paz: Oh, a human being.
277.	Asil: at ben adam, nu! [to Paz]	Asil: You're the human being, come on! [to Paz]
278.	Paz: lo roca kvar lihyot ben adam.	Paz: I don't want to be a human being any more.

Tal may have been trying to tell his peers that the enactment had strayed too far from the original story. It is also possible that he was worried that an enactment without a human character would not be as interesting. He was most insistent and wouldn't even accept Paz's suggestion of two dogs and two cats.

2. Metacognitive attitudes towards enacting the characters in the story

Children's disagreements about the assignment of characters during PPWS teaches us about their attitudes towards the characters. The elicited negotiations constitute an occasion for argumentative discourse that enhances discursive literacy learning (see Zadunaisky Ehrlich and Blum-Kulka, this volume). The following example shows Itay expressing and explaining his refusal to play the wolf.

Ex. 8: Metacognitive argumentative discourse (following the story "The Wolf and the Seven Kids" by the Brothers Grimm)

Date: 27.02.06. First Grade, Beer Sheva.
Participants: Ronnie (m., 6.3), Itay (m., 6), Nathaniel (m., 5.8), Ella (f., 6.2).

18.	Ronnie: ata tihiye ha-ze'ev. [to Itay]	Ronnie: You'll be the wolf. [to Itay]
19.	Itay: lama ani carix lihiyot ha-ze'ev? ani lo roce! [to Ronnie, angrily]	Itay: Why do I have to be the wolf? I don't want to! [to Ronnie, angrily]
20.	Ronnie: ki kaxa ata carix lihiyot ha-ze'ev. [to Itay]	Ronnie: Because. You have to be the wolf. [to Itay]
21.	Itay: lo roce lihiyot ha-ze'ev ha-ra. [to Ronnie]	Itay: I don't want to be the bad wolf. [to Ronnie]
22.	Nathaniel: ani eheya ha-ze'ev. ani ohev lihiyot ra. [putting on gloves and raising his hands joyfully]	Nathaniel: I'll be the wolf. I like being bad. [putting on gloves and raising his hands joyfully]
23.	Ella: ani axshav holexet le-kniyot, naxon ze ba-sipur?	Ella: I'm going shopping now. Right, that's in the story?

This example shows refusal to play a character perceived as negative (the wolf). Itay explained his reasons: "Why do I have to be the wolf? I don't want to!" (*lama ani carix lihiyot ha-ze'ev? ani lo roce!*, turn 19). Nathaniel presented a different perspective: he volunteered to be the wolf, explaining, "I like being bad" (*ani ohev lihiyot ra*, turn 22). Group members could interpret Nathaniel's action from two possible perspectives: either he is going to be bad because he is playing the bad character, or, by volunteering to enact the negative character, he is being the good boy, thereby facilitating the enactment.

Summary and discussion

The present study focused on a special kind of peer interaction: children's social pretend play in the wake of a story just read to them out of a children's storybook (PPWS). The aim of the study was to look for the interaction during the enactment of the OST, and the resulting discourse elicited in the process as manifesting discursive literacy skills, such as the use of decontextualized and high register language.

We found that the OST constrained the children's enactment while simultaneously allowing them multiple degrees of freedom. The main characteristic of the children's discourse was the major role of metaplay discourse. This may indicate the high level of awareness of the OST underlying their enactment. The constraints inherent in the enactment of a given OST provided possibilities for fostering the ability to create alternative realities while intensifying the process of mobility between in-frame and out-of-frame interaction: the children suspended their enactment (in-frame interaction) in order to plan, talk about, explore options and consider alternatives (out-of-frame interaction), and then returned to enacting. These cognitive processes are characteristic of skilled readers as they move back and forth between reality and the world of the text (Harris 2000).

In light of the analysis presented above, we can suggest that the OST and its subsequent enactment exhibit the potential to foster discursive literacy. The children engaged in pragmatically appropriate use of spoken language, they used a high register inspired by the storybook language and decontextualized language, and they demonstrated linguistic innovativeness and interpretive reproduction of the text. In particular, the analysis suggests that a conflict between participants can serve as a springboard for the development of argumentative skills (see Zadunaisky Ehrlich and Blum-Kulka, this volume; Monaco and Pontecorvo, this volume). Coping with peer conflict without adult interference can be seen to create possibilities for the children themselves to engage in negotiations, problem-solving, persuading and supporting their positions with appropriate arguments. In sum, PPWS apparently allowed the children to reconstruct the OST through an interpretive process that included negotiations about the various meanings derived from the story. Thus, demanding adherence to the OST affords a very special kind of constraining factor: it is likely to drive children to generate problem-solving strategies and creative interpretations.

In light of the above analysis, we suggest that PPWS can be seen as having the potential to foster discursive literacy skills. Given that the cluster of characteristics of the discourse emerging during children's PPWS is related to the discursive features that afford children's development of discursive literacy, this type of activity appears promising for the realization of a fruitful play–literacy connection in which children *actually play* and *learning opportunities are incidental*. In educational settings nowadays, children are frequently engaged in highly structured situations that are very often conceived of as play. We have argued in this chapter that rule-based games do not afford children the degrees of freedom essential to the assumed beneficial role of play in children's development, those benefits being positive affect, flexibility and autonomy. PPWS is quite different from activities in which play has become a kind of fig leaf for explicit teaching.

NOTES

1 See, for example, Pellegrini (2009) and Roskos et al. (2010), who review studies that served as the basis for what is called *evidence-based* educational policy.
2 All the examples we present are translated verbatim from Hebrew. Brackets are used to mark the children's non-verbal responses.
3 The register gap for these words is greater in Hebrew than it is in English.

5 Explanatory discourse and historical reasoning in children's talk: an experience of small group activity

Camilla Monaco and Clotilde Pontecorvo

Introduction

Small group work is generally assumed to facilitate "exploratory talk" (Barnes 1976). In this study we hypothesized that it would also facilitate the exploratory development of "historical thinking" in primary school children. Our main aim was to investigate the effect of social and discursive aspects of small group interaction on the development of historical reasoning.[1]

As far as teachers' and educationalists' intentions are concerned, history teaching should aim, among other things, at developing the skill to give more adequate and articulate explanations for events and actions concerning people and protagonists of the past, capturing them in their space and time settings, within the society and the culture in which they lived. In a word, the aim of history teaching should be to develop the ability to locate phenomena and people within temporal and contextual frameworks. (Girardet 1991: 201, our translation)

History teaching should be based on what Girardet defines as "learning to explain historically" (1991). This capacity is grounded outside the school, in children's everyday efforts to try to explain their own and others' behavior. Starting at a very young age, children are able to construct explanations concerning their deviant behavior (Pontecorvo and Sterponi 2002): it is rather common to observe how young toddlers, for instance, are able to give good reasons for having refused a requested action (Pontecorvo and Sterponi 2006; Zadunaisky Ehrlich and Blum-Kulka 2010, this volume). Studies on historical reasoning development show that such a skill improves together with cognitive development and with the accumulation of life experiences (Fasulo et al. 1998; Girardet 1991). Within this developmental process, peer interaction plays a decisive role: "explaining is a social activity: one explains something to someone else in order to obtain a change in the audience's view" (Girardet 1991: 202). If one sees historical reasoning as a socially mediated ability, school is undeniably one of the best settings for its development and learning. In particular, social interaction is one of the more appropriate contexts for stimulating and promoting children's and youngsters' explanatory skills (Muller Mirza and Perret-Clermont 2009; Pontecorvo and Arcidiacono 2010; Goldberg, Schwarz and Porat 2011).

Pupils' main activity, starting from their entrance in school, is to speak to schoolmates and teachers: all educational relationships are based on communication and discourse. Although we cannot reduce all psycho-educational activities to a sociolinguistic dimension, it is undeniable that discourse is the main tool of any communication that is developed within an educational setting (Pontecorvo 1999). Language enters the classroom in the guise of a wide range of symbolic tools that constitute a relevant part of the semiotic mediation offered by formal schooling. Written texts, narratives, books and figurative materials are all cultural artifacts that transmit relevant socio-cultural dimensions. Classroom discourse, and the related language, can be considered the meeting point of many social and cognitive processes (Pontecorvo 1991).

Beginning in the 1970s, and thanks to the contribution of sociolinguistics and ethnography of communication, the study of school discourse has evolved steadily, both at a theoretical and applied level. These new perspectives have contributed to seeing the classroom setting as an important framework in which we can to try to understand the influence of cultural factors on instructional practices and results (Cazden et al. 1972). From this perspective, school can be considered "a meaningful social institution, where teachers' discursive practices aim at attributing power to students and at building, or not building, their autonomous initiative, even as regards gender diversity" (Fasulo and Pontecorvo 1999: 71, our translation).

Working within small groups: cooperation, opposition and conflict

The idea of learning as a linear, individual and mental transmission – an idea that still characterizes most of school ideology – has been seriously called into question by the socio-constructivist model of distributed cognition (Mercer 1992; Pontecorvo 1999; Pontecorvo and Girardet 1993). As a matter of fact, there are many alternative ways in which the school could help children to develop a more critical and explorative way of facing the world of knowledge. One of these ways is represented by *small group activity*: it is a tool that makes the active appropriation of knowledge easier and it is also an important element of children's socio-cognitive development.

Some teachers' resistance to this type of schoolwork is perhaps due to an implicit theory of learning, according to which the dyadic adult–child interaction is the ideal context for new knowledge acquisition (Kyratzis, this volume): it is taken for granted that only an expert and competent teacher is able to offer to children all the new and complete information they need (Pontecorvo 1999). However, peer interaction represents a relevant tool for learning and development processes, even beyond the school setting, because children often discuss among themselves various "facts and opinions" (Genishi and Di Paolo 1982) while they are playing (Garvey 1990).

Small group work can present two relevant dimensions of knowledge construction and organization: on the one hand, there is the symmetrical feature of the interactional exchange, and on the other hand, there is the open and dynamic nature of the task. Children are motivated "to explore links and to figure out alternative solutions: in so doing it is necessary to mobilize their knowledge resources and to make room for logical processes of a diverse type" (Fasulo and Pontecorvo 1999: 81–82). When situations of misunderstanding and opposition occur, children show they are dissatisfied with not understanding: they do not easily accept statements they do not agree with and, what is more relevant, they feel authorized to express incomplete or provisional ideas and opinions. In peer interaction, the relationships that students establish with the objects of study also take on new meaning: as students discover they can be handled, modified and used to oppose and persuade someone else, finally those contents become tools – and not only objects – of knowledge.

As Fasulo and Pontecorvo (1999) state, the cooperative aspect may be regarded as the flipside of the oppositional one: opposition is productive when it is based on sharing the activity aims (Vardi-Rath et al., this volume). Thus, cooperation and opposition represent two main aspects of learning that can be carried out in the small group setting. When we speak about collaboration in learning, we are referring to two complementary aspects of collaboration: the consensual aspect, when there is a substantial convergence of points of view, and the oppositional one, when a divergence of opinions has to be faced and solved. In fact, it is truly in the discursive opposition that the teacher's role in peer interaction is less important, because students are often able to "collaborate" in managing their disputes without needing an adult's support and mediation. This is an opposition that we can define as "constructive," because it represents a stimulus to look for new solutions, to negotiate new meanings and to find new agreements.

According to Barnes (1976), peer interaction in small group work should facilitate the development of a discursive mode, which is particularly fruitful in promoting effective learning. We are dealing with so-called "exploratory talk," which is characterized by suppositions, long-range hypotheses and attempts to verify different opinions by referring them to virtual situations. All participants can express their own opinions without fear of being mistaken and, from a discursive point of view, each turn is linked to a previous one and is the basis for the subsequent ones.

It is also important to consider the socio-affective dimension of a situation colored by a strong social interaction between peers. The audience within the small group assumes particularly meaningful features from both a cognitive and an emotional perspective. Students are aware that they are addressing peers who are all at the same level, that is, "they do not yet know," and for this reason they do not have the authority to give evaluations or definitive judgments. This awareness allows for affective involvement and facilitates the activity of "thinking together," because it reduces the anxiety and fear of being mistaken, while increasing the general emotional charge aimed at reaching a common solution (Pontecorvo and Pontecorvo 1986; Pontecorvo and Girardet 1993). The result is that each pupil feels authorized to think and contribute only a small piece of the discourse, which can be discussed and processed by the others in a collaborative way as well as used in the construction of the subsequent piece of reasoning.

It is important to underline, however, that small group work does not always imply only a collaborative mode of interaction and meaning construction (which may be either cooperative or oppositional). It sometimes happens that a high level of conflict characterizes the interactional dynamics, so that the collaborative activity does not take off. It is thus important to clarify the terminological distinction between the concepts of conflict and opposition. Whereas the latter refers to a particular form of collaborative interaction – predicating on a divergence of opinions that requires a "constructive" solution – the former indicates a "breaking" of the discursive exchange. Conflict is therefore considered a "non-constructive" interactional mode, which hinders the conversational flow and leads to a condition we have defined as "stalemate."

Empirical investigation

This study is part of a national Italian research effort, carried out in the context of a COFIN project directed by Clotilde Pontecorvo, for the Department of Developmental, Social and Educational Psychology of "Sapienza," University of Rome: the general object was the classroom verbal interaction as an instrument of learning mediation. The research was based on a specific theoretical presupposition: because small group work facilitates "exploratory talk" (Barnes 1976), we hypothesized that it would also facilitate the exploratory development of "historical thinking" in primary school children.

The study involved two fourth-grade classes of a state school in southern Italy: there were forty-two child participants, aged between 8 and 9 (Monaco 2007). In particular, we aimed at analyzing three different aspects:

- organization and management of discursive and interactional roles, that is the possibility of discerning the presence of one or more "leaders" within each group;
- the establishment of a collaborative (either as cooperation or opposition) versus a conflict-based interactional mode;
- the presence of "historical talk" even in primary school children's discourse.

Concerning the research issues and conditions, the two classes were somewhat different: whereas in Class 1 pupils already had some familiarity with small group activity, in Class 2, at the time of data collection, the children had no experience with this work mode.

Work procedures: iconographic documents as investigation tools

In order to promote the small group work, we chose five images that reproduced as many sections of the famous Bayeux Tapestry, an embroidered cloth, 70 meters long and 50 centimeters wide, which illustrates the conquest of England by Norman people. In a series of pictures supported by a written commentary, the tapestry tells the story of the events of 1064–1066 culminating in the Battle of Hastings. The two main protagonists are Harold Godwinson, recently crowned King of England, leading the Anglo-Saxon English, and William, Duke of Normandy, leading a mainly Norman army, sometimes called the companions of William the Conqueror.[2] The tapestry consists of some fifty scenes with Latin *tituli* (captions), embroidered on linen with colored woolen yarns.

The features of this visual document seemed to us potentially useful for the co-construction of new meanings through peer interaction. According to Barthes (1980), visual documents – both images and photographs – can include valuable features for symbolic communication. In particular (Fasulo et al. 1998):

- any description of an iconographic document requires the passage from a simultaneous mode to a sequential one, which is typical of language and discourse;
- the description and explanation of the images' content require a proper linguistic translation, because images are in themselves "mute resources."

As Fasulo et al. (1998) state, images are problematic when we consider them as documents. Goodwin (1994) studied the way in which vision is affected by cultural practices: he spoke about "apprenticeship to vision," stating that even color recognition needs a certain practice and a continuous re-adaptation of recognition criteria. Knowledge acquisition – even at a visual level – does not depend on the development of abstraction skills, but on the invention of concrete and specific codes, through procedures that are strongly affected by contextual aspects (Pontecorvo 1985). In our study, we used images both as symbolic objects and as historical sources, considering the interpretation of an iconographic document as a specific knowledge domain, characterized by peculiar methodological procedures and discursive practices.

As Di Cori states (1999: 56), history is not only made up of events, protagonists, diachronic factors, sources, archives and documents: the ways in which historians construe history are a part of history itself, as are the different "modes by which the historian's discourse is composed in certain contexts (where and how one speaks and writes about, who is doing it, and which audience is being addressed)." History, in fact, is not only made up of those events and materials that historians study, but it is also the product of "their invention, creation, and construction" (1999).

In our study, each image corresponded to a letter of the alphabet (from A to E) and was accompanied by a list of a few questions. The first and last questions were common to all the images we used, while other questions referred to the specific features of each picture. In both classes, five groups were formed: each of them received an image (a part of the tapestry), with the related questions.

In your opinion, who are the characters represented here and what are they doing?
In your opinion, what means of transportation were used?
In your opinion, what arms were used in the war?
How were they dressed?
Does the image suggest any other ideas?

The groups were organized spontaneously (only in a few cases did the teachers modify the spontaneous composition, owing to specific relational considerations). Some children advanced the proposal – immediately accepted by all – to attribute a name to each group and to choose it within the category of "animals."

The researcher presented the activity to both classes as "Let's play at being historians": each child, together with his or her group mates, could do what historians have been doing for a long time by looking at images. "An image, in fact, can tell us many things. To each group I will give an image, with some questions written down. You will pretend to be historians, discuss within your group and agree on what to write down. You will write down only what you agree upon" (these instructions were given to all children). After this introduction to the group work, some general information was given about the Bayeux Tapestry, and it was suggested that each group would be free to choose how to write the answers: they could choose a child as the "scribe" or could take turns in writing, perhaps by using pencils of different colors.

We consider it relevant to underline that their answers should be regarded as hypotheses that they could verify with books or with the teachers' words or by comparing the answers of different groups at a subsequent collective meeting.[3] Each group received an audiotape recorder that the children had to use autonomously after a short familiarization. The researcher's recommendation was to turn off the audio recorder only when the children thought it was absolutely necessary. The activity was accepted with much interest and enthusiasm, and the possibility of using the audio recorder autonomously gave rise to much curiosity, and perhaps increased the motivation to complete the task. In addition to the audio-recording, the work of two groups was also video-recorded.

The audio-recording, and the video-recording of two groups, provided the initial data for the present study. The first step of analysis was transcription of the audio and video data, using the AC-Jeffersonian system (Sacks et al. 1974; Schegloff et al. 1977).[4] The transcripts were analyzed according to the main principles of discourse analysis (DA), in order to study interaction and discourse between pupils. We chose this approach because it regards language as social action and analyzes its use, regardless of production form: discourse itself becomes the object of study. DA is therefore an analytical procedure that examines how participants construct, make relevant or invoke any kind of external meanings of mental contents in any form of discourse (Potter and Wetherell 1987; Edwards and Potter 1992; Edwards 1993, 1997).

Participants

The two classes that took part in our research were composed of 24 (Class 1) and 18 (Class 2) students, respectively,[5] whose parents had given their informed consent. In each class we had five groups (of between 3 and 5 members).[6] As soon as each group received the image and the papers containing the tasks to be done, the children turned on their audio recorders and began the observational and discursive activity. By the end of the work, after having delivered the papers with the answers, most pupils declared they had very much enjoyed pretending "to be historians." The organizing features and the interactional modes were personal and even idiosyncratic within the group and were dependent on specific relational dynamics.

Analysis and results

As mentioned above, small group work was promoted in this study, based on the assumption of its relevance and usefulness in children's socio-cognitive development. In fact, this kind of activity is an effective tool in "mediating and facilitating" the process of knowledge construction in peer interaction (Pontecorvo 1999; Zadunaisky Ehrlich and Blum-Kulka 2010).

In both classes, the analysis of discursive structures and interactional dynamics confirmed that peer interaction operates as an "activator" for the talk type that Barnes (1976) defines as "hypothetical or exploratory." In most cases, pupils showed their involvement in the activity of reaching a common solution through comparison, cooperation and, sometimes, also through opposition. They had a shared aim, which was to observe and discuss an iconographical historical document, and they tried to reach it together, by freely expressing their ideas, by formulating hypotheses and by trying them out through negotiation with their mates. In several cases, the small group work elicited the participation of those children who, in the traditional setting, spoke rather rarely and who were defined by teachers as "less collaborative."

The organization of discursive and interactional roles: three types of leadership

Within the ten groups, we could identify one or more participants who played a relevant role concerning some aspects of interaction and meaning negotiation. Because this was an exploratory study based on observation, which aimed at analyzing knowledge co-construction within small groups, the results we are going to show should be considered as a starting point for further research analyses rather than as findings that are generalizable.

We know that studies on leadership within a small group concern mostly adults or adolescents (Gergen and Gergen 1990). For instance, Fielder (1978) proposes two main types of leadership: one is oriented to the task, while the other one is oriented to the relationship. Task-oriented leadership appears to be very helpful when the social situation is characterized by very high – or very low – levels of control. In contrast, relationship-oriented leadership is particularly effective when the social situation shows a balanced level of control (Fielder 1978).

Readapting these studies to an interactional situation where children are the main participants would be a very complex – and a bit audacious – operation. For these reasons, we chose to observe what actually happened within our ten groups in order to see which types of leadership occurred more frequently.

The qualitative analysis of our interactional data pointed to three different types of leadership (Monaco 2007):

- *Opinion leadership*: one of the participants played a prominent role concerning the most important contents of discussion and answers negotiation; the opinion leader tended to affect and guide the whole interaction in relation to topic selection and answer co-construction. An example of discursive action typically belonging to an "opinion leader" (who guides the others' observation) was: "OK, but according to you, did they use only lances?"
- *Organizing leadership*: one of the participants performed a directive and charismatic function regarding the organizational aspects of the task. This participant worked as leader, whether from a discursive-conversational point of view or regarding activity management. Discursive actions such as "So, we all must agree. Do we agree?" or "Please, speak with a louder voice, since she *(referring to the researcher)* needs to hear" or again "Now let's put it in the middle of the table *(referring to the image)*" are all examples that can effectively describe this type of leadership.
- *Stylistic-expressive leadership*: one of the participants held a prominent role concerning the management of some formal and expressive aspects of the

task, mostly linked to the moment of writing answers. A typical stylistic-expressive leader took care in rectifying her mates' answers from a formal and stylistic point of view, before writing them on the sheet. In a group, for instance, at a certain moment, one pupil suggested writing "Some vessels are *drakkar* (a typical Norman vessel)" and immediately another child disagreed with him: "Part of *(the vessels)*! We have already written 'some'."

We think it is important to highlight that, while in some cases the leader took on a clearly democratic role, in others it was possible to identify more elements of a certain authoritativeness. In particular, it seems that, where the interactional dynamics were centered on conflict (seen as a "non-constructive" opposition that leads to a "stalemate") more than on cooperation and constructive opposition, it was possible to observe a lower presence of any kind of leadership. The intervention of the teacher is not required when children are opposing reciprocally (Orsolini and Pontecorvo 1992).[7]

Such evidence could have some relevant operational consequences in the educational context: whether or not it is true that the presence of a leader within a small group is somehow linked to the initiation of collaborative modalities of interaction, teachers could take this phenomenon into consideration when they propose a small group activity. In fact, the promotion of interaction between children who have different interactional competences – in terms of knowledge, organizational skills and stylistic-expressive abilities – could be a successful educational action in order to facilitate collaboration, both in terms of cooperation and constructive opposition.

Even though the small group activity between "peers" is commonly considered a *symmetrical* form of interaction, our data suggested making a relevant distinction: on the one hand, we have interactional symmetry (all pupils have the same *status* within the discussion, because no individual may be officially considered "more expert and competent" than another), but on the other hand, the equality that derives from the condition of being the same age and belonging to the same class does not necessarily imply a homogeneity of communicative, cognitive, organizational and stylistic-expressive competences. In other words, although this kind of interactional exchange is basically symmetrical (Barnes 1976; Fasulo and Pontecorvo 1999), it is also possible to find features of "non-symmetrical" forms of interaction and collaboration, for instance, when one or more pupils have specific competences that allow them to play the leader role.

This last reflection concerns gender differences as regards the distribution of the three types of leadership we observed: our data indicated that in both classes, while the opinion leader could be either a boy or a girl, both the organizing leader and the stylistic-expressive one were more likely to be a girl. Owing to the small number of participants and the exploratory nature of our study, these reflections on gender differences should be regarded as a starting point for further hypotheses that should be investigated more deeply and carefully.

The interaction within small groups: between collaboration and conflict

In the small group interaction studied in this research, knowledge co-construction was never an easily achieved aim, especially in cases where some kind of "interactional tuning" between group members seemed to be almost absent. This fact shows, once again, how emotional aspects are relevant to the processes of knowledge co-construction and meaning negotiation (Pontecorvo and Pontecorvo 1986).

By comparing the different interactional dynamics within our ten groups, it is quite clear that each of them was characterized by its own way of establishing and managing conversation and discussion. We can make a general preliminary distinction between the seven groups in which collaboration was the most important aspect (four groups in Class 1 and three groups in Class 2) and the last three, where, for several reasons, collaboration seemed to be a very difficult objective to attain (one group in Class 1 and two groups in Class 2). Because there are several ways to collaborate and to cooperatively interact, as well as to be in opposition with someone else, it may be useful to focus for a while on the social features of the different groups in relation to this specific aspect of the interaction.

Only two groups (Class 2) out of ten were characterized by a nearly total absence of either collaboration (seen as cooperation but also as constructive opposition) or conflict. In both cases, indeed, the group's activity was mostly based on itemizing the acceptable answers and immediately accepting those that seemed to be more suitable, without any kind of proper negotiation, even during the writing phase. As it was a situation of small group activity, it is evident that children's work is based on a complex system of exchanges and interactions. However, we chose to regard collaboration and conflict as being "absent" here, because in these two groups pupils tended to accept individual proposals, without really getting engaged in discussion or comparing ideas.

In contrast, within two groups (one from each class) collaboration had the features of cooperation – or opposition – mostly concerning stylistic-expressive aspects (e.g., formal decisions regarding the operation of writing the shared answers). In C group (Class 1), for instance, while a boy was writing the answer related to the last question, a girl pointed out: "You must write 'un albero' (i.e., "a tree") without the apostrophe because it is masculine." In Italian language, with the indefinite masculine article the apostrophe is not necessary. Also, within J group (Class 2) the writing operations took longer than the discussion, and the situation was characterized by a wider presence of collaborative dynamics: all pupils contributed to constructing a satisfactory answer. Although in some cases formal changes were for the worse (e.g., the Italian word for "knight," *cavalieri*, was at a certain point transformed into *cavaglieri*, a misspelling), the outcome of discursive actions was in any case significant from an interactional and communicative point of view. In fact, before deciding that it was necessary "to correct" something and establishing how to do it, the children were engaged in a serious and complex negotiation activity, where everyone's opinions were relevant.

Moreover, by comparing the activity of the ten groups, it is possible to observe only one situation in which conflict had a prevalent role during the whole interaction (E group, Class 1). In this case, it was particularly evident that the children had not developed a sense of "group identity" and, also because of that, it was very difficult for them to "work together" in order to achieve a shared purpose. The high level of conflict and the low grade of tuning were made clear by one member's negative statement: "I regret ending up in this group!" as is seen in the next excerpt.

Ex. 1: E group, Class 1

76.	Luigi:	oh! we are not getting anywhere, I am telling you, eh!
77.	Dalila:	but you haven't said anything, really!
78.	Luigi:	I regret ending up in this group!
79.	Gabriele:	me too!
80.	Marcella:	me too!

Finally, in the remaining five groups (three groups in Class 1 and two groups in Class 2) we wish to underline the presence of complex and very refined forms of collaboration (both as cooperation and constructive opposition), not only regarding the stylistic-expressive features of the task, but also in the negotiation of new meanings.

To address this aim, we use an excerpt drawn from D group's activity (Class 1), as we would like to give a clearer and more detailed explanation of the process of collaboration oriented to knowledge construction that occurred through hypothesis formulation and their discussion within the group. Here we can observe that there is a strong interest among all participants to reach a real agreement:

Ex. 2: D group, Class 1

11.	Aurora:	so, to me (0.2) to me it seems that they are at war
12.	(2.0)	
13.	Children:	no!

14.	Francesco B.:	no!
15.	Giuliano:	to me it seems that they are
16.	Francesco B.:	they are preparing
17.	Giuliano:	that they are cutting down the <u>trees</u>
18.	Francesco M.:	eh!
19.	Giuliano:	because they do have the hatchet
20.	(2.5)	
21.	Francesco B.:	they are doing some of their activities
22.	Francesco M.:	ah yes OK! they are construct-
23.	Aurora:	°yes, but don't shout° *((she lowers her voice))*
24.	Francesco M.:	they are constructing vessels and sailing *((he lowers his voice))*
25.	Francesco B.:	because- what? vessels and sailing?
26.	Francesco M.:	at least yes they do (0.2) the boats!
27.	Children:	(boats!) no vessels!
28.	Aurora:	they are doing some of their activities
29.	Francesco M.:	and what kind of activity (0.5) sailors and pirates (1.0) sailors.
30.	(2.5)	*((Aurora reads the question again))*
31.	Francesco M.:	Norman people eh (0.5) Norman people that are constructing some boats
32.	Aurora:	so, (0.2) before writing all of us we must agree. (.) do we agree?
33.	(5.0)	*((in turn the children state their agreement))*

After some important contributions (turns 11–19), Francesco B. tried to formulate a first generic answer (turn 21), which started an interesting interactional exchange (turns 22–29) in which the group tried to specify which activities the characters were engaged in. At a certain point, Aurora read the question again (turn 30), allowing Francesco M. to reformulate his hypothesis in a more structured way (turn 31). It is interesting to note that the conclusion of the excerpt (turns 32 and 33) was characterized by Aurora's clarification of the need to reach a shared agreement throughout her mates' different answers.

This kind of interactional modality was maintained during the whole discussion activity in the D group, where we can observe several moments of cooperation. In addition, it often happened that the pupils explicitly referred to the opportunity of "agreeing" and their contributions were oriented to the co-construction of a shared solution.

Even though this concerned a limited number of participants and, of course, an equally small number of groups, we think it would be interesting to compare the two classes in an attempt to understand *how* collaboration – or its absence – characterized the activity that we called "Let's play at being historians." Particularly, by focusing our attention on Class 1, we can see that four groups out of five showed the presence of some form of collaboration (cooperation or constructive opposition), while only the fifth one (E) was characterized by an interaction that was mainly based on a kind of conflict that aimed at obstructing discussion and the co-construction of meaning. On the contrary, in Class 2 three groups out of five displayed collaborative ways of interacting, while the remaining two groups distinguished themselves by not showing either collaboration or conflict.

The reasons for this situation could be manifold: for instance, some groups might not have felt particularly motivated and/or interested in the task, or their attitude might have been linked to their teacher's educational style. We should remember, indeed, that there was a relevant difference between the two classes as regards small group activity: while in Class 1 pupils were used to this kind of work, in Class 2 our study was the first experience of this type.

Actually, it is not possible to establish *whether* and *how* the children's familiarity with small group activity affected interactional and discursive dynamics within the ten groups. However, it is quite evident that collaboration – meant both as cooperation and constructive opposition – was more strongly present in the class with pupils who had already worked in small groups before. The condition of working together on the same task, without any adult intervention (except initial instructions), permitted the children to "think together in historical terms" and to reach an agreement through the comparison of and exchange between individual contributions. The procedures used to obtain this result were, from time to time, different and strictly linked to all those factors and characteristics that distinguished each group from the others.

Thinking together in historical terms: *"historical discourse" is viable in primary school*

As regards the last objective of the research, an interesting piece of evidence is that, in most cases, the discussion activity within a small group effectively facilitated the process of negotiating historical meanings. In fact, the children's discourses often dealt with some key points of historical methodology, such as the *reliability of the historical source, its precise interpretations,* the *possibility of generalization* and the *comparison between past events and present time* (Fasulo et al. 1998).

The following excerpt shows how, within a small group, the exploratory procedure of reasoning and, specifically, the "historical thinking" developed:

Ex. 3: A group, Class 1

341.	Nico:	excuse me, they went to war, I think with (0.5) with things of war, isn't it?
342.	Veronica:	with things that- the, eh, what do you call them? wait
343.	(2.5)	
344.	Nico:	with knight's things ohm
345.	Veronica:	eh!
346.	Gloria:	what do you call them?
347.	Felicia:	they are written also in our book

348.		(1.0)
349.	Veronica:	with (0.5) the armor, the armor!
350.	Felicia:	oh yes the armor!
351.	Gloria:	the armor!
352.	Veronica:	yes but here, eh but here they are different
353.	Nico:	yes well, but she *((referring to the researcher))* she said that we can put- that we can make a hypothesis!
354.		(0.5)
355.	Felicia:	maybe they could be armors, but they are made from iron
356.		(1.5)
357.	Veronica:	yes well, but con- consider that this is an embroidery!
358.	Nico:	so, let's do-
359.	Veronica:	this is an embroidery!
360.	Felicia:	armors I think!

In turns 341–351, the pupils, who were trying to answer to the question "How were they dressed?" (the characters in the image), exchanged ideas and opinions, and they collaborated to identify the right term for indicating "the things of war." The noun that the members of the group were looking for was "armor," but initially they were not able to bring it to mind (turns 342–348). At a certain point, Felicia (turn 347) directly referred to their school book ("They are written also in our book") in an attempt to facilitate collective remembering and, effectively, after a one-second pause (turn 348), Veronica pronounced the expected term (turn 349). Her turn immediately met with Felicia's and Gloria's approval (turns 350 and 351).

Turn 353, where Nico claimed the right "to hypothesize," represented a metacognitive consideration that proved to be very useful in spurring the discussion within the group. Concerning *historical thinking*, Veronica's turn 357 ("Yes well, but consider that this is an embroidery") was particularly interesting because through it the girl invited Felicia to consider the material conditions of the document at hand. Veronica's reflection was, at the same time, a clear reference to the problem of the reliability of the source – from a material point of view – which represents one of the key points of the historical methodology (Fasulo et al. 1998). In fact, when Felicia was trying to establish "from what material armors are made" (turn 355), Veronica called the group's attention to a specific fact: the image they were analyzing was the reproduction of an embroidery which, in turn, reproduced a suit of armor. At this point, Nico made an attempt at organizing (turn 358), but he was immediately interrupted by Veronica (turn 359), who repeated her opinion ("This is an embroidery!"). The excerpt (but also the discussion on this topic) closed with Felicia (turn 360), who abandoned the purpose to establish whether the armor was made from iron and stated "Armors I think!"

Excerpt 4, which follows, is another interesting example of the development of "historical thinking" within a small group activity:

Ex. 4: B group, Class 1

154.	Matteo:	some of them are eating
155.	(1.0)	
156.	Francesca:	some are eating and some others-
157.	Matteo:	and some others (0.5) some are doing
158.	Francesca:	so, wait!
159.	Tonio:	and some others-
160.	Lorenzo P.:	according to me,
161.	Matteo:	and some others are doing with the sword
162.	Lorenzo P.:	according to me, eh some characters represented here are Norman people.
163.	(1.0)	
164.	Matteo:	yes well, it is quite clear that they are Norman people
165.	Lorenzo P.:	ohm but she asks that, doesn't she? ((referring to researcher's question))
166.	(1.0)	
167.	Lorenzo P.:	Norman people
168.	Francesca:	eh!
169.	Lorenzo P.:	some of them are eating, (0.5) and what are they doing? according to me they are celebrating something.
170.	(0.5)	
171.	Tonio:	yes well, but from where do you understand it?
172.	Lorenzo P.:	why not?
173.	Tonio:	from where do you understand that they are celebrating something?
174.	Lorenzo P.:	yes well, because at a banquet you celebrate aft-
175.	Francesca:	this one, not this one!
176.	Lorenzo P.:	usually you celebrate after a war
177.	Matteo:	and look here ((speaking to Francesca))
178.	Matteo:	what are you saying. after the war!
179.	Tonio:	what are you saying! also for a birthday, also when you get home you eat (0.5) you don't need-
180.	Matteo:	yes well to eat no!
181.	Francesca:	yes well, let us say that some of them are eating and some-
182.	Matteo:	some are eating, some others are cooking
183.	Francesca:	and some,
184.	Matteo:	some are eating you see? here ((he points to the image))
185.	Lorenzo P.:	yes
186.	Lorenzo P.:	some are cooking
187.	Matteo:	some, (0.2) some are playing an instrument
188.	Lorenzo P.:	no they are not playing
189.	Francesca:	they are playing, cooking,
190.	Matteo:	you see? there is also the violin!
191.	Francesca:	what are they doing?
192.	Tonio:	those there are working.
193.	Francesca:	the violin? (0.5) it didn't exist, the violin, at all!

In turns 154–180, the pupils were discussing the characters' activities and comparing opinions concerning possible answers (they are eating, "doing with the sword," celebrating something, etc.). In particular, when at turn 162 Lorenzo re-examined the characters' identity ("According to me some characters represented here are Norman people"), Matteo answered that "It is quite clear that they are Norman people," implicitly referring to a previous discussion. Lorenzo accounted for his contribution by reminding the others of the researcher's instructions (turn 165) and, after a one-second pause, reaffirmed that the characters are Norman people. The boy met with Francesca's immediate approval (turn 168). After this short discursive exchange with Matteo regarding the opportunity of repeating "who are" the characters, Lorenzo (turn 169) proposed his own hypothesis about the activity they were engaged in: "they are celebrating something."

At this point we can see Tonio's intervention, through which the boy, as quite often happened, turned Lorenzo's statement into a problem (turns 171 and 173). From Tonio's second question ("From where do you understand that they are celebrating something?") arose an exchange of opinions that involved the whole group (turns 174–180), where the pupils tried to come to an agreement about the "celebration hypothesis." Tonio usually represented the constructively oppositional voice of the group and, in this particular case, owing to the absence of agreement on the association between food and celebration, he stressed that "Also when you get home you eat" (turn 179). Lorenzo's inferences – according to which the characters were eating and thus this was a banquet (turn 174) and moreover "Usually you celebrate after a war" (turn 176) – were not approved by Matteo either (turns 178 and 180). But, unlike Tonio, Matteo did not offer any reason for his own dissent.

Francesca's turn 181 could be considered an attempt at mediating between Tonio's and Lorenzo's positions, but the girl was not able to end her speech, because Matteo proposed his conclusion (turn 182). The last turns of this excerpt (183–193) were a further under-sequence of discourse co-construction, through the formulation of hypotheses and the related expression of opinions by each member of the group.

Excerpt 4 was also an interesting example of "how" *historical reasoning* can develop throughout the "exploratory talk" (Barnes 1976), which is typical of the interaction within a small group. If "historical thinking" is primarily based on the ability to search and identify *explanations* for events and behaviors, this excerpt becomes particularly significant. For instance, Tonio's reiterated use of expressions such as "From where do you understand it?" led the other group members to account for what they had said up to that moment, thus facilitating discussion and negotiation. Moreover, we saw that in some cases (turn 179) Tonio did not accept the proposals of explanation offered by his mates, spurring a return to an exploratory way of reasoning (turns 180–193) until a satisfactory and shared solution could be reached.

Finally, regarding the process of "history making," Francesca's turn 193 ("The violin? It didn't exist, the violin, at all!") – with which she responds to Matteo's previous proposal (turn 190) – demonstrated the presence, even within discourses of 8- to 9-year-old children, of another key point of historical methodology, that is, the necessity of historically contextualizing past events, by comparing them with the present time (Fasulo et al. 1998). We can also see this kind of process in Excerpt 5, where pupils are looking at their image and reasoning about "how people were dressed":

Ex. 5: I group, Class 2

441.	Vincenzo:	Bermudas!
442.	Andrea G.:	they were dressed in Bermudas: (0.5) what are the Bermudas?
443.	Vincenzo:	this thing *((pointing to the image))*
444.	Andrea G.:	what?
445.	Alessandra:	*((while she is writing))* they were dressed with-
446.	Federica:	Bermudas! the short trousers!
447.	Alessandra:	Ber-mu-das, Berdamudas *((she makes a linguistic mistake))*
448.	Children:	*((they laugh))*
449.	Vincenzo:	trousers,
450.	Andrea G.:	yeah, jeans! do they go to the disco? *((ironical intonation))*
451.	Children:	*((they laugh))*
452.	Vincenzo:	trousers!
453.	(1.0)	*((some pupils speak in loud voices, while Alessandra goes on writing))*
454.	Vincenzo:	trousers, shoes, (0.5) and skirts.
455.	Alessandra:	and skirt?
456.	Vincenzo:	skirt!

At turn 441, Vincenzo formulated a hypothesis that provoked a certain difficulty of understanding in his mates (turns 442–448) and, afterwards, their hearty laughter (turn 448). In this case, the contextualization of past events passed through their comparison with the present time (see Excerpt 3) ironically used by Andrea ("Yeah, jeans! Do they go to the disco?", turn 450) when he answers Vincenzo's consideration ("Trousers," turn 449). Andrea's consideration caused his mates' hilarity (turn 451), but it was not taken into consideration within the discussion, because the children eventually put "trousers" on their list of clothes.

These brief discursive fragments show how a small group can be stimulated – through collective interpretation of an iconographical document – to produce historical reasoning. A good example is to be found in B group, where we could observe Tonio's frequent insistence (e.g., "From where do you understand it?") concerning the visual source we submitted to their attention (see Excerpt 4). In Excerpt 2, moreover, the pupils tried to move beyond the evidence at hand and inferred the purpose of the activity represented in the image (the cutting down of trees), namely the construction of "boats": the hypothesis concerning the creation of "vessels" was almost immediately rejected, perhaps because they regarded "vessels" as being closer to modern sailing equipment.

Finally, by comparing Excerpts 4 and 5, we notice that present experience was often used by the children as a source of comparison both for the analogies (e.g., Tonio's turn 179 in Excerpt 4: "Also when you get home you eat") and for the differences (e.g., Francesca's turn 193 in Excerpt 4: "The violin? It didn't exist, the violin, at all!" or also Andrea's turn 450 in Excerpt 5: "Yeah, jeans! Do they go to the disco?").

Conclusions

Our study aimed at observing the discursive interaction between peers during small group activity, as this makes room for collaboration – intended both as cooperation and opposition – and facilitates the development of "exploratory talk" (Barnes 1976). In particular, we wanted to investigate the importance of social and discursive interaction for the development of historical reasoning, within ten small self-directed groups of 8- to 9-year-old children.

As regards the first aspect we analyzed – that is, the children's organization and management of the interactional and discursive roles, including leadership structure – we identified three different types of leadership, related to *opinions*, *organizing matters* and *stylistic-expressive choices*. Our data showed that, although on the one hand, the exchange and discussion between "peers" had a symmetrical nature from an interactional point of view (all pupils had the same *status*), on the other hand, the "equality" that derived from the condition of being the same age and belonging to the same class did not necessarily imply homogeneity of communicative, cognitive, organizing and stylistic-expressive competences. With regard to this aspect, it would be interesting to further investigate the possible gender differences in the distribution of the three typologies of leadership (from our data it seems that the organizing and stylistic-expressive types are more often acted out by a girl than by a boy).

Concerning the interactional procedures used by the children within the small group, our research highlighted that, in most cases, *peer interaction* proved to be an important "activator" for so-called "exploratory talk." We know that explanatory discourse is a crucial factor in the development of historical reasoning. Moreover, historical reasoning is based on explanatory processes that can be supported and facilitated by the small group activity, as this kind of interactional situation can elicit the production of alternative solutions.

In our study, the opportunity to "work together" in order to meet a shared objective allowed the pupils to discuss, to collaborate, and sometimes also to argue, without paying too much attention to the formal aspects of the exchange. The activity of discussion within a small group enabled the children "to think together," to make hypotheses and to verify and negotiate old and new meanings. The processes of comparing ideas and peer collaboration could play out more easily within an interaction that left out the presence of "experts" who could evaluate and judge what the children said: the children felt "authorized" to freely express their own opinions and were more motivated to compare them with their mates' ideas. In only one case did we find a situation that we defined as conflict-oriented, where the opposition between pupils had non-constructive features and provoked a stalemate, obstructing discussion and negotiation. In general terms, it is important to note that the collaborative activity was stronger in Class 1, where children had some familiarity with small group work.

The last aspect that we investigated concerns *historical thinking*, i.e., the possibility of discovering – in 8- to 9-year-old pupils – the presence of historical discourse reasoning. Our study showed that, in most cases, the small group discussion effectively facilitated the process of negotiating historical meaning. In fact, the children's discourses touched on some key points of historical methodology, such as the *reliability of the historical source*, its precise *interpretation*, the *possibility of generalization* and the *comparison between past events and present time* (Fasulo et al. 1998).

In the course of an activity such as "Let's play at being historians," the pupils were not satisfied with hypotheses that would appear reasonable and acceptable: in many cases, they felt the need to contextualize, to compare, to justify and to argue – in a precise and detailed way – their inferences within the group. In general terms, data analysis confirmed that, in both classes, this type of interactional situation often favored the process of historical learning-reasoning, based on collaboration and negotiation, which developed within an atmosphere of collective intersubjectivity. In fact, the procedures and styles used by the pupils differed according to the situation and were strictly linked to the contextual communicative, interactional and discursive features of every group.

In conclusion, our research represents a further confirmation of the importance of the small group as an interactional context that is particularly suitable for a concrete and dynamic realization of the process of knowledge co-construction. For these reasons, this kind of activity could – or even should – become a commonly used educational practice among younger pupils too.

TRANSCRIPTION CONVENTIONS

Conversational data are transcribed using a modified version of the Jeffersonian system (Sacks, Schegloff and Jefferson 1974).

-     indicates a cut-off in sound
- [a left bracket marks the onset of overlapping speech
- (0.4) indicates silent pauses expressed in tenths of a second

:	colon indicates elongation of preceding sound
(xxx)	indicate indecipherable talk
ital	words in italics indicate intonational stress
CAPS	capital letters mark increased volume
.	full stop indicates a strong fall of intonation
,	comma indicates a light fall of intonation (such as within a list)
°xxx°	indicates talk uttered in a low voice
xxx	underlining indicates emphatic talk
((xxx))	nonverbal actions

NOTES

1 We use the concepts of "historical reasoning" and "historical thinking" interchangeably because of the awareness that human thinking can be considered as the interiorization of human external discourse that develops within a collective reasoning process (Vygotskij 1934; Arendt 1977).
2 It is said that the tapestry was embroidered by Countess Matilda, William's wife, while she waited for her husband to return from the war.
3 This last activity (that we will present elsewhere) would have allowed a "pooling" of the news coming from the different groups, with the aim of getting richer and more articulated answers.
4 See the transcription conventions above.
5 For reasons of privacy, the children's names are fictitious.
6 Every group has been assigned a different letter of the alphabet.
7 Orsolini and Pontecorvo 1992.

6 Evaluation in pre-teenagers' informal language practices around texts from popular culture

Janet Maybin

Introduction

Children's use of evaluative language, in other words the expression of their views and feelings towards what they are talking about (Hunston and Thompson 2000), is significant both in terms of what it reveals about their emotions, judgements and tastes, and in what it suggests about the ways in which these are being shaped. This chapter examines the emergence of ten- and eleven-year-olds' evaluative language stimulated by texts from popular culture, which provides children of this age with an important resource of emotionally and morally loaded imaginary scenarios. I draw on linguistic ethnographic research to build up a "thick description" (Geertz 1973) of the ways in which children collaboratively appreciate and interrogate these texts in the course of ongoing conversations with peers across the school day. The analysis is informed by a sociocultural approach to children's learning and development (Vygotsky 1978), where talk among peers is seen to serve as a kind of collective thinking (Mercer 2004).

Children's conversations about popular culture provide a field of shared experience and activity, a naturally occurring opportunity space where children both co-construct peer culture and also learn how to express judgements about behaviours, events and aesthetic dimensions of texts. In this introduction I start by defining evaluative language in terms of affect, judgement and appreciation, and suggest that shared texts of various kinds provide rich evaluative reference points for children of different ages.

From a linguistic perspective, Martin (2000) suggests that affect is the most basic evaluative semiotic resource which becomes socially configured and institutionalised through social practice into judgement (rules and regulations concerning ethics and morality) and appreciation (social criteria organising taste and value directing the appreciation of texts, objects and performances). Painter (2003), investigating the emergence of evaluative language in children under five years old, suggests that they move developmentally from expressing emotion into judgement and appreciation. She argues that the motivation to share feelings, in the context of pursuing various functional goals, is an important driver in children's early development of a semiotic system and that emotionally loaded topics are particularly important sites for cognitive development.

While Painter surveyed a wide range of young children's naturalistic oral language, she also found that, even at this early age, engagements with texts were evaluatively significant. In particular, she suggests that the shared reading of picture books provides a rich context for young children to name the emotions of third parties and express judgements about their actions and, furthermore, enables them to learn about the visual representations of affect and its construal in story-telling. Young children's engagement with hypothetical scenarios and beings in picture books can thus be seen to contribute to their development of "social referencing" skills used to monitor and understand other people's affective displays, which are crucial to their social and cognitive development and continue to be important for sociability, for instance, in the development of friendships (Ochs and Schieffelin 1989).

Throughout childhood, texts of various kinds continue to provide significant cultural resources for the organisation of expressions of evaluation and associated social learning. Schools of course provide curriculum texts and, in addition, the opportunity for a substantial amount of informal talk among children themselves which is full of references to songs, television and other kinds of popular media (Maybin 2006; Rampton 2006). These texts provide the focus for evaluative conversations among older children which often continue intermittently alongside the margins of official classroom activities. In this chapter, I suggest that while evaluation may appear fleeting and fragmentary in the ten- and eleven-year-old children's individual spontaneous exchanges, the dialogic connections generated across ongoing conversations throughout the school day produce a rich resource of cumulative interactive evaluative activity, which children can use to inform future individual evaluative behaviour (Vygotsky 1978).

Ten- and eleven-year-olds, at the transition between childhood and adolescence, are at a particularly interesting stage in terms of their evaluative practices. These children still orientate to some extent towards the world of childhood, of which they are now experienced members, but they are also anticipating and practising new kinds of evaluation, which signify a more teenager-like identity. Becoming the "I" for a pre-teenager involves discovering a new "we" in peers of a similar age and gender, and recognising the self through the eyes of those people who seem most similar to the child themselves (de Singly 2007 in Monnot 2010). This makes the peer social world an increasingly important site for evaluative practices (Evaldsson 2002, 2007; Goodwin 2006). Within this context, where children still have limited first-hand experience of teenage and adult social practices, popular culture provides an important source of shared imaginary experience, a rich resource for judgement and speculation.

In the discussion below, I apply the description of evaluative language which has been developed within systemic functional linguistics. This brings together affect, judgement and appreciation within an appraisal system construing interpersonal meaning (Martin 2000; Martin and White 2005). More specifically,

Affect construes emotional reactions, for instance, expressions of horror, happiness, sadness or disgust;
Judgement involves assessing people's behaviour according to social norms, for instance, as fair or unjust, kind or cruel;
Appreciation construes the value of things, for example, the aesthetic value or effectiveness of texts, processes or natural phenomena.

These three kinds of evaluative meanings are interrelated in various ways in the children's talk I recorded. For instance, evaluation may combine affect with judgement in an expression of disgust at someone's behaviour, or it may combine affect with appreciation in an expression of pleasure at the line of a song. These evaluations can be graded by speakers through intensifiers, repetition and so on, and their expression can be more or less monoglossic or heteroglossic, depending on how far the speaker acknowledges other opinions and positions. While much research has focused on the lexical and grammatical inscription of evaluation, it is also acknowledged that paralinguistic and contextual cues play a crucial role (Hunston and Thompson 2000; Martin and White 2005). This suggests that analysis should include attention to children's local situated practices. Furthermore, in addition to its sensitivity to the immediate context, evaluative language also indexes and reproduces broader cultural beliefs and values. For example, narrative evaluation is part of the ongoing negotiation of reflective judgement which is central to children's enculturation as well as to their story-telling (Coupland, Garrett and Williams 2005). Similarly, popular songs embody values embedded within broader discourses of popular culture, and their performance by children implies ethical agreement, to some degree, with a particular way of making sense of the world (Frith 1996). These factors suggest a need for analytic attention to both the local and also the broader sociocultural context (cf. Nicolopoulou et al., this volume).

In the discussion below, I look first at children's ongoing informal talk across one morning in school about a particularly dramatic episode of the UK television soap opera *EastEnders*, which many pupils had viewed at home the previous evening. I then discuss children's performance of, and talk around, musical fragments from films including *Titanic* and *Mama Mia*, and a rhythm and blues song by Rihanna: "Unfaithful." Overall, these examples illustrate the dynamic interconnections between affect, judgement and appreciation in children's talk, and their calibration through peer interaction. I shall suggest that while children's performances enact dominant cultural values, thus inducting them into conventional discourses, their exchanges with peers and their revoicings (Bakhtin 1981, 1984; Voloshinov 1973) of characters and singers also provide evidence of experimentation and play with different evaluative positions and different degrees of commitment. Despite public anxiety in Britain about the potentially negative influence of popular culture on children (the Bailey Review, Department for Education 2011), the data suggests that in their informal talk and performances around texts, as in other areas of peer group talk (Kyratzis 2004), children are not passively absorbing textual messages but are actively creating meanings and at times playfully subverting dominant representations.

Methodological approach and data

My analysis draws on ongoing ethnographic research into pre-teenagers' use of informal language and literacy practices to construct knowledge and identities. The data discussed below come from recordings of ten- and eleven-year-old children's continuous spoken language experience across the school day over two weeks in the spring term in two Year 6 classes in a predominantly working-class, multiethnic English primary school. A small voice recorder carried in a belt pouch and attached to a lapel microphone pinned to the top of the child's shirt was alternated across two girls and two boys (one to four days recording for each child). Four talkative children of average ability were identified by the teacher and permission for the recordings obtained from their parents and from the children themselves. Permission was also obtained from all the parents and children in the two Year 6 classes for a second recorder to be moved around the classroom to collect additional data and to capture different perspectives on the events recorded by the lapel microphone. During these two weeks, I sat at the back of the classroom or observed from the edges of the playground at break and lunchtime. Two months later, I returned to the school and recorded informal semi-structured interviews with forty-seven children in friendship pairs or trios, where I asked them about issues cropping up in the continuous recordings.

Overall, recordings include fifty hours of children's ongoing talk and eight hours of interviews. Linguistic analysis of these is informed by ethnographic observations of children's activities and interactions supplemented by collections of texts and photographs, by children's explanations of their activities and interests in the interviews and by contextual knowledge about the educational and local environment. A significant aspect of the analysis below derives from the longitudinal nature of the audio recordings I collected via the lapel microphones worn by children. These recordings included children's talk in corridors, cloakrooms and the playground as well as in the classroom. Using these longitudinal recordings of children's continuous talk across the school day, I was able to track topics which reoccurred at different points and in different contexts, and to identify various evaluative threads which continued across their ongoing conversations. Thus, I could examine cumulative and interlinked processes of evaluation as children returned a number of times to the topics and texts in which they were most interested.

Evaluation could be explicitly expressed (e.g., "I hate Archie") and was also conveyed more indirectly through the tone of a child's voice, or projected through their stylised reproduction of the voices of media characters and singers. I use "stylised" here to mean a voice reproduced as if it were one's own but with "a slight shadow of objectification" (Bakhtin 1984: 189). Evaluation was also signalled through prosody and paralinguistic cues; for example, I have represented a sound conveying disgust as "eu:" (see transcription conventions at the end of the chapter). I focus below on data collected via the lapel mic worn by two girls, Jess and her close friend Mel. These girls were average ability, talkative eleven-year-olds. Jess was lively, effervescent and popular, while Mel had a reputation among her circle of girlfriends for being independent-minded and amusing. Both were active and athletic, taking part in the daily informal mixed-gender football games organised by children at break and lunchtime. Mel played in the school netball team which won a regional school tournament on the evening before the final day of recording. While Jess's father was from West Africa and the girls' friendship group included children from diverse ethnic backgrounds, they were all native or fluent English speakers. Mel's parents were both white British.

Talk around popular drama: the interplay between affect, judgement and appreciation

The children's talk about an incident in a recent *EastEnders* episode, which I discuss in this section, is similar in a number of ways to children's and young people's oral narratives of personal experience, which are a key site for the articulation and negotiation of social judgement and evaluation (Goodwin 1990; Evaldsson 2002; Coupland et al. 2005; Maybin 2006). As in talk about personal experience, children re-create scenarios from films and television, partly through reproducing the voices of the people involved, and comment in various ways on the characters and events. Researchers analysing evaluation in narratives of personal experience have drawn on Labov's (1972) classic account of evaluation as the significance of the events for the speaker and the whole point of narrating them in a story. Labov suggests that evaluation may be conveyed through an external aside by the narrator, a judgement embedded in the speech of a character and the use of intensifiers and comparisons. Recently there has been increasing interest in the interactional dynamics of story-telling, which were somewhat neglected in Labov's model (Koven 2002; Georgakopoulou 2007). For instance, Koven points out that oral narratives are multi-voiced and involve a more complex orchestration of different evaluative stances than Labov suggests. She examines the interweaving of the evaluative positions of interlocutor (in the current interaction where the story is told), narrator (of the story) and character (within the story) in her analysis of narratives from interview data.

In talk around film and television drama, however, rather than reflecting directly on events in their own lives, children orientate together towards the experience of imaginary third parties, in the context of their knowledge about particular genres. Evaluation is, as Koven suggests, complex and multi-voiced, as children orchestrate the perspectives emanating from their interactional position in the ongoing conversation, their position as narrator and the positions of the characters they revoice. However, in comparison with narratives about their own personal experience, there is also an additional narrative layer when children talk about a shared fictional text. A film or television soap opera is not only treated by children as a slice of real life containing people whom they love or hate, and whose actions they can judge, but also as a fiction created by actors and producers. Thus, talk about a story from a popular soap opera like *EastEnders* can provide an opportunity not only to express affect and develop judgement, but also to begin to articulate aesthetic appreciation.

Rather than narrating the plot of a film or television episode, when this was assumed to be shared knowledge, children tended to focus on a climactic moment, often performing and embroidering the dialogue between characters at a crucial point in the plot. Performances of these narrative fragments are semiotically very rich, serving to simultaneously replay the climax of a story, index the relevant plotline and represent and comment on a central evaluative point. Over the Friday before the mid-term break, Mel was particularly preoccupied by the death of a teenage female character, Danielle, in an episode of *EastEnders* broadcast the previous evening. This was a pivotal episode, much publicised in the media and watched by an estimated 11.5 million people (*Mail Online* 2009). Just as nineteen-year-old Danielle is about to be reunited with her long-lost birth mother, Ronnie, she is accidentally run over by a car driven by another character, Janine. Ronnie's father, Archie, had previously tried to prevent Ronnie finding out that Danielle was her daughter, as this would reveal Archie's earlier lie that Danielle had died as a baby. Ronnie initially rejected Danielle but finally believes her. The episode ends as Danielle lies dying in her mother's arms, surrounded by horrified neighbours, including Ronnie's sister, Roxy. Mel first refers to this episode at around 10.00am on Friday, as the children discuss the various DVDs they have brought into school for class viewing later in the day. Mel's emotional response to another child's reference to the DVD *My Girl*, where a young boy dies after being stung by bees, prompts her reference to *EastEnders*.

Ex. 1

1.	Mel	[ah, that is so: sca-, and then he's next to the bumble bee hive and he goes allergic to bumble bees. Ah that was such a fab film when I watched it. *(exaggerated sad voice)* Felt like crying
2.	Emily	I <u>did</u> cry the first time I watched it
3.	Mel	me too. Just like it made me cry watching EastEnders last night
4.	Emily	I know
5.	Mel	I actually did cry. My eyes were watering I was just like
6.	Emily	d'you know what (xxx) TV video=
7.	Mel	=wish you could freeze it when Danielle was just so close to it. (…) I'm going to push her out of the way he he (.) Ronnie must be <u>very</u> upset. Archie's going to be like *(nonchalant voice)* "Sorry, I'm getting the train, bye"

Mel and Emily's recalling of tearful responses to *My Girl* (turns 1–2) cues Mel's reference to her similar emotional response to *EastEnders*, which Emily then shares (turn 4). In turn 7, Mel then imagines a deus ex machina role where she stops the action and projects herself inside the story in a last-minute rescue of Danielle: "Wish you could freeze it when Danielle was just so close to it. (…) I'm going to push her out of the way he he." Her short laugh signals that this suggestion is a fanciful fiction, but she then goes on to refer to the feelings of Danielle's mother and grandfather, as if they were real people, adopting a serious tone for "Ronnie must be <u>very</u> upset" whereas "Archie's going to be like *(nonchalant voice)* 'Sorry, I'm getting the train, bye'" (turn 7). Here, we can see Mel shifting from recalling her own emotional response to imagining the emotions of the characters. She also conveys judgements about them: her sympathy with Ronnie comes across through the tone of her voice in the recording, the intensifier "very", and the alignment of Ronnie's feelings with those of Mel and Emily. Mel's disapproval of Archie's lack of feeling over his granddaughter's death is conveyed through her production of his nonchalance directly after her reference to Ronnie's distress *within* the narrative and in the context of Mel and Emily's talk *about* their own responses to the episode. Thus evaluation may involve the dialogic resonance of a reproduced voice both in relation to the position of other characters and in relation to the positions of Mel and Emily as interlocutors. While evaluation in Extract 1 emerges through the interaction between Mel and Emily in their ongoing conversation, through the contrast between Ronnie and Archie's reactions and through the ways in which Mel as creator reproduces and positions their voices, it also emerges through links across these levels, which create a more complex dialogic web of meaning.

The children's talk moved on to other matters, then fifteen minutes later they returned to the topic of *EastEnders* in Extract 2, below, which includes

114 J. Maybin

further animations of dialogue from the scene of the accident, comments about characters, and an extended argument about whether Danielle is actually dead. There is also recognition of *EastEnders* as a fictional text. As the children are finishing off their work, Mel asks "Who watched *EastEnders* last night?" and when several children confirm that they did, she exclaims "Oh my god, I felt like crying" and repeats her wish to freeze the action and save Danielle. Other children confirm similar feelings and mention their mothers and sisters crying over the episode. Mel then re-creates exaggerated plaintive voices for Danielle's and Ronnie's interaction at the death scene.

Ex. 2

128.	Mel	(*plaintive voice*) "I'm your baby, aby", and then Ronnie's there and she's like turned her back on her and she's like "baby?" She's like "baby?" and then, I wish I just could <u>freeze</u> it when Janine was that close and then push her out of the way and then pu- play it=
129.	p	=well what did you [expect
130.	Mel	[I know but that is so cruel for them to do that=
131.	p	=(…) I recorded it and I've got to watch it (.) I'm going to watch it today (xxx)
132.	Mel	how could you not watch the wedding?
133.	p	I was out, it wasn't my fault=
134.	p	=I wish Archie wasn't in it any more, I hate Archie
135.	p	exactly
136.	Mel	he's evil, Danielle would still be alive if it weren't for him
137.	p	do you think she's do you think she's going to survive? That's what Ann said
138.	p	she ain't, she's dead you idiot
		(…) (*sounds of pupils arguing about whether Danielle is dead or not, and a pupil humming the opening of the signature tune "de de de" which Mel picks up:*)
149.	Mel	dum dum de de de de no she's like (*exasperated*) "don't just stand there" and then she sits there going "A ha ha" (*horrified gasps*)
150.	p	(… "Janine" …) and they're all crying (…)
151.	p	she could still be alive
152.	Mel	and then she goes "My ba::by" and then it goes dum dum de de de de (*signature tune*)
153.	p	I think she's going to survive though
154.	p	I think she might
155.	p	why would she shout like (*exaggerated high voice*) "she's dead!"
156.	Mel	maybe she's unconscious
157.	p	Exactly
158.	Mel	she might be
159.	p	maybe she's unconscious
160.	Mel	I'm just trying to find a happy (*turns to the picture she is drawing*) he he d'you want to see? d'you want to see? HE HE HE
161.	p	(xxx) then you've got to write GA (*her initials*) or something on the top
162.	Mel	HE HE HE sorry he he he I'm just going to write Newforest (*name of school*)

Pre-teenagers' informal evaluative language 115

163.	P	I hate Archie
164.	Mel	Danielle would still be alive if it weren't for him. I wish I could pause it
165.	P	she might not be dead
166.	Mel	I know that's what I said to them, I said she could be unconscious. I wish, when Janine was that close, I pulled the TV, jump into the TV, push Danielle away, come back in and play it. Don't you wish that was so sad, though. *Ma mia (high voice)* "you're my mother". Why is Archie such an idiot? (...) *(talk about netball match and how many goals individuals scored, then back to the argument about whether Danielle has died)*
203.	Mel	she could be unconscious you never know
204.	P	exactly (xxx)
205.	Mel	cause, because they did that in Hollyoaks once, they said she was dead and she was actually unconscious *(argument continues)*

The common practice of viewing *EastEnders*, which makes it an important shared resource for children's evaluative talk, is confirmed by a pupil having to account for her failure to watch this pivotal episode which featured Archie's wedding as well as Danielle's fatal accident (turn 133). Here, the debate about whether Danielle is dead or only unconscious involves children drawing on evidence not only from within the episode: "Why would she shout like *(exaggerated high voice)* 'she's dead!'" (turn 155), but also from the comparison with another popular television soap opera, *Hollyoaks*: "cause, because they did that in Hollyoaks once, they said she was dead and she was actually unconscious" (turn 205). This comparison involves recognition of generic similarity (it is valid to compare *EastEnders* and *Hollyoaks*) and of director-level decisions: "they did that." While children know that tragedies are typical of *EastEnders*: "well what did you expect" (turn 129), Mel still objects to the producers' decision to kill Danielle: "I know but that is so cruel for them to do that" (turn 130). (Her subsequent references to the producers in later extracts below confirm them as the referent here). And Mel suggests that her argument that Danielle could be just unconscious relates to her wish to have a happy ending (turn 160). These responses to the episode as an artful text are both emotional and judgemental (the producers are cruel) and are also appreciative of generic choices (a character who seems to be dead can turn out to have been merely unconscious).

While illustrating the children's responsive engagement with the production of the episode, Extract 2, like Extract 1, shows children expressing their own feelings towards the characters, which can then prompt judgements of their actions. For instance, when a child comments: "I wish Archie wasn't in it any more, I hate Archie" (134), Mel responds "he's evil, Danielle would still be alive if it weren't for him" (136). This exchange is partially echoed in turns 163–4. Mel's judgement emerges initially in turn 136 partly in response to a previous comment in the current ongoing conversation. Evaluation is also conveyed, as in Extract 1, both through Mel's re-creation of characters' evaluative positions and through her representation of these, as narrator. Here, she seems to enter into the poignant intensity of Danielle's death scene (with a hint of objectification) through her enactment of Danielle's final exchange with her mother: "'I'm your baby, aby', and then Ronnie's there and she's like turned her back on her and she's like 'baby?' She's like 'baby?'" (turn 128). In fact, in the original television episode, Ronnie calls "Baby" to Danielle, who doesn't speak but runs towards her and is then knocked down by the car. Mel's refashioned dialogue, however, with the double meaning of "baby" as a term of endearment and also a reference to Danielle's relationship to Ronnie, is indexically rich. "Baby" brings together the beginning of Danielle's story, when she was removed as a baby from Ronnie, with their eventual loving reunion just seconds before she dies. The poignancy is increased by viewers' experience of the long lead-up to Danielle revealing her true identity to her mother, despite Archie's efforts to prevent her from doing this and Ronnie's initial rejection. A fragment of their final exchange is repeated again in turn 152, with a further echo in turn 166 which also creates a link with a film popular among the children, *Mama Mia* (also about seeking for a long-lost parent): "'Ma mia *(high voice)* you're my mother'." Mel seems to taste and retaste Ronnie and Danielle's emotions, momentarily experiencing their anguish but slightly distancing herself through the hyper-stylisation. The tension of their final interaction is heightened by the distinctive rhythmic beats of the signature tune (turn 149).

So far, while recognising that *EastEnders* is a constructed fiction, the children have also appeared very involved in the characters' feelings, caring strongly about whether Danielle is alive or dead, hating Archie, and wishing for a happy ending. Emotional responses to characters and events drive comments about narrative direction, e.g., "I wish Archie wasn't in it any more" (turn 134), "she could be unconscious" (turn 203). Five minutes later, however, when Mel and Jess go into the girls' toilets on their way to morning break, they produce a much more playful, parodic re-enactment of Ronnie's distress (turns 242–3) and her sister Roxy's horrified reaction, which Jess embellishes with high-pitched screams:

Ex. 3

242.	Mel	"don't just stand there" I need go toilet
243.	Jess	"don't just stand there" go "AH:" *(screams)* he he
244.	Mel	he he
245.	Jess	and then when she when she closes her eyes yea, Roxy goes over to her and she's like "AH::::"
246.	Mel	I know [he he he
247.	Jess	["AH::::, AH:::"

248.	Mel	AH:: he he he go toilet *(sound of running)* he he he. She's lying on the floor, *(to Jess)* pretend to be Roxy he he
249.	Jess	"AH::::"
250.	Mel	he he he I know, but that's how she really said. Why can't she be unconscious, they only just found out o::: I hate the bloody producers
251.	Jess	eu: there's pee on the toilet seat
252.	Mel	he he. It's so annoying though, oh my go:d

Here, there is a sense of mockery as well as mimicry (Sutton-Smith 2001), in what Blum-Kulka et al. (2004) term a "mocking-subversive keying" of Ronnie and Roxy's interaction (see also Cekaite and Aronsson, this volume). The more exaggerated hyper-stylisation of their voices suggests that Mel and Jess are further distancing themselves from the raw emotions that they are re-enacting, in exaggerated form. The child-like playacting and high hilarity appear to offer a release from the heavy emotional tone of their earlier discussion. Mel, however, also repeats her frustration at the producer's decision to kill Danielle at this point, when Ronnie has only just "found out" (turn 250): "I hate the bloody producers" (turn 250), "It's so annoying though, oh my go:d" (turn 252). Following this interaction, Mel does not raise the subject of Danielle's death again until around an hour later as she sits colouring with Jess while they watch *Home Alone 2*, when the girls again comment on the producers' decision, adding speculation about the motives of the actor who plays Danielle. Mel remarks "I can't wait to watch EastEnders tomorrow. I hope Danielle's not dead." Jess complains "They only just found out" and Mel responds "Exactly, the producers are well mean." Jess then suggests "She might want to leave and she might want to make it good before she left" but Mel replies "Stupid producer. Come in like a month or two and then go just away like that *(exaggerated sad voice)* and make me cry."

The children's emotional responses to Danielle's death are an important driver across the various, linked conversations about *EastEnders*. Children identify the emotions of characters ("Ronnie must be very upset") and express their own emotional response to characters as if they were real people (e.g., "I hate Archie"). In replaying and voicing these responses, children appear to vicariously experience the emotions almost as if they were their own, but with a hint of distancing in the stylisation which is increased in the toilet conversation. They also signal their evaluation of the characters' positions, through the ways in which they re-create and frame their voices (Voloshinov 1973). For instance, Mel in narrator position uses the emotional force of reconstructed dialogue to convey the tragedy of Danielle's death (Extract 2 turn 128), and in interlocutor position a pupil revoices a character to prove a point: "Why would she shout like *(exaggerated high voice)* 'she's dead!'"(turn 155). There is also an evaluative shift from Mel's relatively sympathetic reproduction of Ronnie and Danielle's emotions in Extract 2 turn 128, to Mel and Jess's playful parody of Ronnie and Roxy in Extract 3. Affect and judgement are closely intertwined here, as in the children's reactions to the producers (e.g., "well what did you expect", "I hate the bloody producers", "that is so cruel", "the producers are well mean", "why can't she be unconscious").

These comments about the producers, and about the actor playing Danielle ("She might want to leave and she might want to make it good before she left"), also point to emergent appreciation of *EastEnders* as dramatic television, which, it might be argued, is also signalled through the children's savouring and subsequent parodying of the dialogue at the climax of the episode, and their reproduction of the signature tune. In addition to the children's own position as narrator when they reproduce characters' voices and replay their interactions, they are also here responding to the producers and actors as the original "narrators" of the episode. While individual children exhibit the buds of development rather than clearly identifiable critical competencies in aesthetic appreciation and critique, their conversations across the morning provide an array of evaluative resources which are now available for children to internalise and work into individual development (Vygotsky 1978).

Film and popular music: the entrainment of emotions among friends

While I focused in the last section mainly on children's emotional engagement, judgements and appreciation of the *EastEnders* characters and plot, children's responses were also being calibrated in important ways through their interactions with each other, which confirmed individual tearful reactions, sympathy with Ronnie, hatred of Archie and so on as generally shared, leading to judgements of particular kinds of actions as ethically acceptable or despicable. This kind of calibration and mutual alignment of evaluative reactions contributes to children's moral and aesthetic development, and also simultaneously expresses and confirms social relations. Friends may be drawn to each other because of similar values, and they may also, at this impressionable stage of early adolescence, moderate their own judgements as part of affiliation with another child or peer group. In this section, I now examine more closely how emotional, judgemental and aesthetic responses to texts are mediated through children's interactions and sociability.

The way in which children use the *EastEnders* signature tune to simultaneously index emotional suspense and plot structuring is one example of the semiotically rich functions which music performs in the children's talk. Across their conversations in general they reproduced a wide variety of musical references, particularly in connection with film. While earlier research (e.g., Livingstone 2002; Rampton 2006) suggested that children watch less film than television, their increasing access to the web (Livingstone and Bober 2004) may account for the frequency of references in my data to feature films along with their sound tracks, and to the videos produced by popular singers as well as to their songs. All except one of the forty-seven children I interviewed had access to the internet at home. Almost all homes also had a DVD player, and over two-thirds of the children mentioned having a personal DVD player in their bedroom. Many children seemed very familiar indeed with the films produced for class viewing on the final day before the school break, often indicating that they had already watched them a number of times, comparing their preferences of sequels and prequels and recalling favourite sequences.

As in the talk around *EastEnders*, children frequently expressed strong emotional reactions to films and they often aligned their emotions with each other, repeating or rephrasing other children's utterances (as Mel and Emily did in turns 2–5 in Extract 1). This tendency towards mutual alignment was particularly the case among close friends, even if they initially expressed rather different positions. In Extract 4 below, Mel and Jess are talking together in their literacy class on Wednesday afternoon while making up puzzles for the younger children who will visit on the following day. The two girls are looking at an old picture of Leonardo DiCaprio in a magazine and Mel says "He is so he he he but he's quite old now, he's quite old and disgusting but I loved him then. Ahh, if this was his knee, I'd be like *(sound of panting)*." She starts humming and announces "I've got that song stuck in my head, you know the Titanic one" and she sings the line "I see you, I hear you, I need you." Three minutes later, as the children are preparing to leave the classroom at the end of the session, she starts singing again:

Ex. 4

9.	Mel	*(xxx) my heart will go on* ah: I love The Titanic, it's becoming one of my favourite films now. I just <u>love</u> it so <u>much</u>, now
10.	Jess	I don't really <u>watch</u> it very much
11.	Mel	me neither but I just love it
12.	Jess	I like it when it's flooding the room's flooding=
13.	Mel	=yea=
14.	Jess	=and big (xxx) that's one of my favourite bits of all=
15.	Mel	=my favourite bit is when Jack's holding Rose against, that bit, and then they're like and then they kiss. Hm: that was me!

Mel's recalling of *Titanic* through a musical link, then expressing strong, intensified, emotional appreciation, "I just <u>love</u> it so <u>much</u>, now" (turn 9), and the girls' identification of favourite scenes (the flooding room, turn 12; the kiss, turn 15), is a typical sequence of moves in their talk about films. As in the discussion of Danielle's death, Mel imaginatively inserts herself into the experiences and emotions of a character, identifying with Rose as she kisses Leonardo DiCaprio, "Hm: that was me!" (turn 15). Rather than confirm an immediate shared reaction, however, as Mel and Emily did when talking about *My Girl* and *EastEnders* in Extract 1, in Extract 4 Mel and Jess negotiate a mutual alignment over turns 10–12, moving from Jess's initial lack of enthusiasm in turn 10 ("I don't really watch it very much") through Mel's realignment ("me neither") but subsequent repetition of her own position ("but I just love it") in turn 11 to Jess's shift to acknowledging "liking" a specific sequence (turn 12), then intensifying her response "that's one of my favourite bits of all" (turn 14). Mel then starts the next turn by echoing Jess's phrase "my favourite bit…" This kind of negotiated shared positioning, where children check and calibrate expressions of affect and appreciation among themselves, consolidates friendships and at the same time produces an entrainment of emotions and appreciation around particular value positions and ways of feeling expressed in texts.

A similar kind of entrainment appeared when children synchronised rhythm, pitch, body stance and movement in their shared singing of popular songs. As Mel and Jess are queuing up at the end of break to return to class, they produce a conflation of the first lines of two Abba songs, "Honey, honey" and "Money, money, money" from the film *Mama Mia*. Here, their rhythmic passing backwards and forwards of the line "Honey, honey honey", sung to the tune of "Money, money, money" (turns 2–6), perfectly expresses their alignment as close friends.

Ex. 5

1.	Mel	Emily's got that word stuck in my head. *honey, honey, honey, hon* (xxx) I don't know if she's saying "Honey, honey, honey" or "hooley, hooley, hooley"
2.	Jess	it's "honey" (American accent) *"honey, honey, honey"*
3.	Mel	*(American accent) honey, honey, honey (xxx)* he he (xxx) as long as you don't say it like "hoo hoo:"
4.	Jess	*honey, honey, honey*
5.	Mel	*honey, honey, honey*
6.	Jess	*honey, honey, honey*
7.	Mel	stuck on (xxx) medal he he I got this in silver and gold now *(pointing to her netball medal)*
8.	Jess	*honey, honey, honey, you are very funny* (xxx)
9.	Mel	he he I got this in silver and gold now
10.	Jess	[ah:: *(kissing sound) (xxx)*
11.	Mel	[except that's the time (xxx)
		(…)
18.	Jess	(xxx) when we leave school I'm definitely (…) >I'm not going to let go of you I'll be like that superglue=
19.	Mel	=I'm going to be like um:::: I'll never let go=
20.	Jess	=every five seconds I'll be like=
21.	Mel	=I'll be like, I'll be like holding onto you every day [I'll be like, get superglue
22.	Jess	[I'll be like yea
23.	Mel	ah I'm going to so have to come to Highton with you now<

In Extract 5, Mel and Jess echo back each other's words and phrases: *honey, honey, honey*, "I'll be like" (in turns 18–22), "superglue" (turns 18 and 21). Their additional close rhythmic alignment in turns 4–6 is echoed in turns 18–23 where the girls mirror each other's rapid rate of speech, as well as declarations of mutual attachment, in anticipation of their imminent separation when they have to move on to different secondary schools. After this exchange, they then go on to compare their hands and arms, each claiming that theirs are the most hairy. As they move into class, Mel echoes the tune of *Honey, honey, honey* in a playful reversioning as *hairy, hairy, hairy*:

Ex. 6

33.	Mel	look at my arms
34.	Jess	they're not that hairy
35.	Mel	(.) hairymania. *hairy, hairy, hairy*
36.	Jess	are you saying they're hairier than this? Not really (.) [he he
37.	Mel	[he he
38.	Jess	we're two gorillas he he *(they move into class)*

Here, the girls' friendship, expressed partly through the pleasurable repetition and echoing of musical phrases, provides a safe context for sharing anxieties, mutual reassurance and the transformation of a commonly negatively marked feminine body feature into a symbol of togetherness, "we're two gorillas he he", turn 38. In Extracts 5 and 6, their rhythmic, synchronised singing plays an important part in Mel and Jess's expressions of mutual attachment. A number of scholars have noted the holistic nature of musical experience, where sensation and emotion take precedence over symbolic meaning as people "absorb songs into ... lives and rhythm into ... bodies" (Frith 1996: 121). Turino (2008) suggests that the power of music to invoke sensual perception, feeling and movement in combination with symbolic thought produces a pleasurable integration of the physical, emotional and rational self. In what Turino terms participatory music, as when Mel and her friends sing together, he suggests that this holistic individual experience is combined with a sense of deep connection with others, making the girls' shared reproduction of a popular song a particularly powerful site for aligning emotions, appreciation and judgement.

During Friday, interspersed with their discussions of *EastEnders*, Mel and her friends also repeatedly hummed or sang snatches from rhythm and blues singer Rihanna's "Unfaithful", a song focusing on the singer's ambivalent feelings about her sexual infidelity. The most sustained performance of the song occurs in the literacy class as the girls finish off their written work. The teacher is tolerating quite a high level of noise and their singing merges with the general clatter.

Ex. 7

1.	Mel	(nasal singing voice) and I know that he knows that, and I killed him inside da da da da happy with somebody else. I can see which one is she=
2.	ps	=the story of my life, searching for the right, but it keeps avoiding me
3.	Emily	sorrow in my soul
4.	Mel	(nasal singing voice) something something wrong (xxx) me
5.	ps	(xxx) and this is more than love, and this is why the sky is blue
6.	Mel	he he (humming)
7.	ps	and he knows I'm unfaithful and it kills him inside, to know that I am happy with some other guy
8.	Mel	I can see him dying
9.	ps	I don't wanna do this anymore, I don't wanna be the reason why, Everytime I walk out the door, I see him die a little more inside, I don't wanna hurt him anymore, I don't wanna take away his life, I don't wanna be…A murderer:: I feel it in the air, while I'm doing my hair (xxx)
10.	Emily	I like it where em (singing) I said I won't be long=
11.	ps	=just hanging with my girls
12.	Emily	that's my favourite bit, I love that bit
		(…)
17.	Mel	(nasal singing voice) the sky is blue he he (Mel continues to hum)

While Mel starts out distancing herself from the song through the nasal quality of her rendition, as it catches on and spreads among her group of friends, she takes on the voice of the singer with them more directly (by turn 7). The alternation of turns 1–8 between Mel, Emily and the three or four girls is clearly unplanned but the song draws them into an improvised interactional synchrony (Sawyer 2005), which enhances social bonding (Turino 2008). By turn 9, the girls' chorus has become a fully fledged performance, where they appear to have entered unreservedly into the singer's feelings. So closely attuned are they that, when Emily identifies her favourite place (turn 10), the other girls rhythmically link directly with her in singing the next line (turn 11). After merging her voice more or less completely with the evaluative expression of the song in the middle section, Mel's resumption of her nasal voice at the end and her short laugh (turn 17) suggest a withdrawal to a more self-conscious stance.

Mel continues to hum snatches of "Unfaithful" throughout the day, and has a short discussion at break time about which is the boyfriend and which is "the other man" in Rihanna's video performance of the song. This video includes highly sexualised stances and gestures and it has been argued that pre-teen girls' fascination with popular singers inducts them into a precocious sexuality linked with submission to dominant heterosexual visual and aesthetic codes of consumption (e.g., Monnot 2010). However, while Mel and her friends often appeared to take on and enjoy the emotional tenor of songs they reproduced, there was also evidence that they sometimes distanced themselves from the stance of the singer or appropriated the tune for their own purposes. For example, Mel's nasal voice at the beginning and end of "Unfaithful" suggests a lack of complete commitment, and her playful reversioning of "Honey, honey, honey" as "Hairy, hairy, hairy" transforms a rather anodyne phrase indexing heterosexual romance into an ironic, perhaps even oppositional, expression of female solidarity. Furthermore, role models available in popular culture are no longer so monolithically heterosexual. Over the three days she was being recorded, as well as referring to Leonardo DiCaprio's attractions, Mel also played "lesbian nurses" at lunchtime with friends (possibly prompted by a popular Catherine Tate television sketch), talked about a character in *Hollyoaks* who might be lesbian, and said her sister was a lesbian. Lesbianism appeared to be a target for play and humour, rather than explicitly negatively evaluated by Mel and her friends, as they explored and tried out various sexual identities from the popular media. The borrowing of singers' voices, as in children's re-enactments of characters from *EastEnders*, enables them to momentarily experience, empathise with and inhabit possible future selves while retaining the option to also play with and distance themselves from the emotions and judgements involved.

Conclusion

I have argued that emotionally loaded popular texts provide a rich shared repository of representations of social experience for ten- and eleven-year-olds on the brink of adolescence, and they are an important resource for the development of evaluative language. The children I studied frequently recycled snatches of popular texts within their conversations, re-enacting the emotions and judgements of teenage and adult characters and discursively connecting these with their own responses to fictional scenarios. In the context of their ongoing, intermittent conversations, I have suggested that children's re-creation and reconfiguring of the voices of characters and popular songs is particularly significant for their exploration and calibration of evaluative positions. It enables them both to take on and vicariously experience particular emotions and judgements and also to express varying degrees of mitigation and commitment towards these evaluations. This is done through stylisation, for example, in Mel and Jess's exaggeration of Ronnie and Roxy's reactions in Extract 3 and Mel's nasal voice in Extract 7. Children also express and explore their own evaluative perspectives through articulating dialogic connections between the voiced positions of characters, narrators and interlocutors, for instance in the contrasting of Ronnie and Archie's responses in Extract 1.

While children's evaluations in individual exchanges may appear fleeting and fragmentary, analysis of the longitudinal recordings suggests that there is an interconnected accumulation of expressions of affect, judgement and appreciation in ongoing conversations across the school day. This web of dialogically connected emergent evaluations produces a shared discursive resource of knowledge which is available for individuals to draw and reflect on in relation to their future evaluative behaviour (Vygotsky 1978). In this sense, children's collaborative identifications and reproduction of fictional characters' affective displays, and the judgements exchanged about their actions, can be seen to contribute to the development of individual social referencing skills. Children's evaluative discursive activity also generates and confirms understandings about what counts as acceptable or reprehensible social behaviour and knowledge about how to "do" family relationships and heterosexual romance.

At the same time, the mixing and overlapping of appreciation, subversion and critique, as pupils shift between identification and mockery, maintains a certain degree of heteroglossic openness, where shock and distress can be parodied as well as emulated and sexuality is not yet entirely pinned down under the available labels.

Within the dynamic interlinking of expressions of affect, judgement and appreciation, feelings spark off judgements and both of these prompt and are implicated in the emergent aesthetic appreciation expressed in comments about producers, actors, plotlines and generic connections. Children are becoming familiar with generic representations of affect and judgement and their construal in particular kinds of narrative. They engage with the hypothetical scenarios not only as vicarious slices of life, but also as aesthetic texts which have been constructed and produced in particular ways. This double-layered reading suggests emergent possibilities for critical media literacy and for the development of more general knowledge about how to engage with fictional texts.

There seems to be a distinctive difference between the explicit expression of affect and judgement around *EastEnders* and children's interactive, performative responses to song where appreciation is expressed by entry into and appropriation of rhythmic and melodic forms, often strongly emotionally imbued. While children negotiated and calibrated their responses to all the texts within peer group interaction, their shared appreciation of popular song appeared to be the most intensely holistic interactive practice, where the mixing and mutual alignment of voices, words, tunes, rhythms and body movement melded together personal experience, a deep shared connection between friends and the social and expressive values of popular culture. However, I have suggested that children did not always unreservedly enter into the positions provided in popular songs, and on occasion distanced themselves from the stances they are reproducing, as they did in the talk about *EastEnders*. Overall, in their talk about popular texts, alongside the frequent interactive entrainment of evaluation among friends, individual differences, as well as similarities, were logged. While children's engagement with popular culture undoubtedly mediates their induction into particular conventional ways of construing evaluation, their individual differences contribute to the production, between peers, of a dynamic, heteroglossic resource of discursive expressions of affect, judgement and appreciation which can be revisited, revised, or even abandoned, in the future.

TRANSCRIPTION CONVENTIONS

Names have been changed. Some punctuation relating to intonation patterns has been inserted to aid comprehension. Speaking turns are numbered within stretches of talk relating to a particular text from popular culture.

p/ps	unidentified pupil/s
=	latching
[	overlap
<u>annoying</u>	emphasis
li::fe	stretched sound
honey, honey	singing or rhythmic, musical expression
CAPS	louder than surrounding talk
(.)	pause of under a second
(xxx)	unable to transcribe
> <	quicker pace than surrounding talk
he	indicates laughter (number of tokens indicates duration)

Comments in italics and parentheses clarify prosodic or paralinguistic features, e.g., *(exaggerated sad voice) (short laugh)* or provide additional notes, e.g., *(Mel continues to hum)*.

Part III

Children's peer talk and second language learning

7 Peer interaction, framing, and literacy in preschool bilingual pretend play

Amy Kyratzis

Children's social pretend play as a foundation for literacy

Many researchers have noted that "children's acquisition of narrative [and extended discourse] skills in their preschool years is an important foundation of emergent literacy" (Nicolopoulou, McDowell and Brockmeyer 2006: 125; see also Blum-Kulka, Huck-Taglicht and Avni 2004; Dickinson 2001; Nicolopoulou, Cates, de Sá and Ilgaz, this volume; Snow 1999). Dramatic narratives of pretense (Heath 1986; Kyratzis 1999; Blum-Kulka 2005b) are one type or genre of extended discourse in which young children engage; others include explanations and definitions (Blum-Kulka et al. 2004).

Researchers of child development and education have noted a relationship between children's pretend play and their literate behavior, particularly their use of decontextualized language, that is, "language convey[ing] meaning textually" (Pellegrini 1985: 109; see also Wells 1985; Nicolopoulou, McDowell and Brockmeyer 2006). As Pellegrini notes, "decontextualized language conveys meaning ... by the language itself. Using decontextualized language to convey meaning is contrasted with relying on shared knowledge between interlocutors or contextual cues to convey meaning" (Pellegrini 1985: 109). Decontextualized language is necessary in pretend play because relying on shared knowledge is not always possible, since fantasy involves transformations of the physically present context (Pellegrini 1985; Vygotsky 1978). Along similar lines, Snow (1999) argued that beyond the "pragmatic skills of the conversationalist," the pragmatic tasks that are unique to "literate discourse" are those that "require recognizing the reality (or maintaining the fiction) that (1) one's audience is distant, unknown, and nonresponsive; (2) one cannot presume shared background knowledge with the audience; and (3) the goal full comprehension of explicit information by the audience" (Snow 1999: 145).

According to Catherine Snow, literate discourse and decontextualized language skills also involve the ability to "construct extended discourses autonomously" (Snow 1999: 146). To do this, children must develop "certain formal aspects of the linguistic system," which include past and future tenses, subjunctive mood, and general "devices for establishing relationships across utterances"

(1999: 147). This marking of relationships across utterances to which Snow refers may have to do with what Pellegrini views as another feature of literate behavior often seen in pretend play, "narrative competence." "Narrative competence involves the construction of story schema, or mental representations of story structure (Mandler and Johnson, 1977) ... An important part of narrative competence is knowing story characters' prototypical behavior and knowing that characters' plans and acts are temporally and causally motivated" (Pellegrini, 1985: 109). According to Pellegrini, "children use such character knowledge while enacting roles in symbolic play" (1985: 109).

When children enact narratives of pretense, they evidence the first of these literate qualities that Snow and Pellegrini refer to, that of not assuming shared background knowledge with an audience. As noted by Goldman, "establishing and maintaining pretense contexts makes demands on co-players ... in terms of the way they conduct their talk. Sustaining such play sequences requires children to coordinate their discourse" (Goldman 1998: 142). For example, through what Goldman terms "underscorings," "statements which verbally foreground definitions of specific actions or states of being ... 'I'm doing X'" (Goldman 1998: 119), young narrators "alert a present or imagined overhearing audience to the development of the enacted fantasy script" (Goldman 1998: 119). In collaborative play, the players must signal for one another the projected imaginary scene that they are orienting to (Goodwin 1993), and if they are to play together, must achieve some level of agreement on this scene. For this reason, according to Goldman, in pretend play "players place undue stress on verbalizing their performance or play states" and monitor their joint understanding of the scene by using such announcements, as well as through using repetitions (123).

Heath (1986) has also noted the need for verbal explicitness in children's pretend play. She noted children's use of "eventcasts" or verbal announcements of the type that are uniquely produced during dramatic play, where "baskets become baby beds, or cats become tigers" (Heath 1986: 89), (e.g., "this is milk"; "you're the mom"). Like Snow, Heath also underscored the need for marking connections among events: "within such eventcasts, children must include subordination as well as some indication of hypothetical connectedness – from actions to results – as well as coordination (see Galda and Pellegrini 1985)" (Heath 1986: 89). Zadunaisky Ehrlich and Blum-Kulka (this volume) characterizing "discursively literate texts" similarly remark on their typical features of having "a relatively high level of explicitness" and "clearly marked textual cohesion and coherence" (see also Cekaite, Blum-Kulka, Grøver and Teubal, this volume). As Goldman (1998), Heath (1986), and Goodwin (1993) point out, signaling, monitoring and achieving a shared understanding of what the reimagined scene and set of people and objects are during collaborative pretend play requires a great deal of verbal work (explicit announcements of actions, props, and roles) on the part of young players.

When we talk about signaling, monitoring, and achieving a joint understanding of a scene among participants, we are talking about social-interactive phenomena. For a fuller understanding of these processes, it is helpful to turn to theoretical constructs from sociolinguistics and conversation analysis, particularly to the notions of "framing" (Goffman 1974), "footing" (Goffman 1981a), "contextualization" (Gumperz 1982), and "participation" (Goodwin and Goodwin 2004). These constructs are reviewed in the section which follows.

Children's "framing," "contextualization," and "participation" during pretend play

Goodwin argued that Goffman's "frame analysis" (Goffman 1974) provided a way of understanding how, in pretend play, children frame the interaction and signal for one another "what it is that they are doing now, displaying for others what constitutes the common scene in front of them" (Goodwin 1993: 160). Goodwin further argues that "endeavoring to sustain the definition of the situation as play ... is accomplished through skillful managing of staged identities, artful uses of a repertoire of voices, and careful attention to the framing of interaction" (1993: 160).

Speakers accomplish these different kinds of signaling and mutual understandings of the scene in front of them and of the characters whom they animate within that scene through what Gumperz (1982, 1996) termed "contextualization" cues (1982). For example, a child player can signal that they are the (adult) mother speaking to a child by using an explicit formulaic announcement to that effect ("I am the mother"). Alternatively, they can use implicit or paralinguistic cues of contextualization (Gumperz 1982, 1996), for example, signaling that they are speaking in the role of a mother speaking to a child by speaking in a pitch that is higher than their own and by using distinctive address terms (e.g., "mija" or "my child") or directive forms. Cook-Gumperz and Gumperz (1978) argued that among children pretending together, when switches of context are signaled "through the use of cues both semantic and intonational but not supported by any formulated comments [this] is ... very different from what we would expect in adult–child and adult–adult interactions" (Cook-Gumperz and Gumperz 1978: 17–18).

In addition to participants endeavoring to "dis[play] for others what constitutes the common scene in front of them" (Goodwin 1993: 160), Goffman also saw participants as actively endeavoring to display for one another the "footing" (Goffman 1981a) or alignment they take to the utterances they produce within that scene. This alignment may be in terms of how they position themselves and others in the "participation framework," which refers to "whether a recipient is addressed or not, and whether s/he is cast as ratified or non-ratified participant" (Cromdal and Aronsson 2000: 435; see also Goffman 1981a: 131–137), as well as in terms of the "production format" of the utterance. Goffman (1974, 1981a) described how participants report or animate the speech of others in replays of conversations, story-tellings, and other performances. "Production format" refers to different types of speaker roles; the animator who reports the speech of another, the author who speaks the words that are reported, and the principal, the person or group "whose beliefs have been told" by the words spoken by the author (Goffman 1981a: 144–147). These switches in alignment or footing can be signaled through the use of explicit announcements. However, as argued by C. Goodwin (1984) and Goodwin and Goodwin (2004), verbal means should not be privileged "over other forms of embodied practice that might also be constitutive of participation in talk" (Goodwin and Goodwin 2004: 225). These include pointing, gesture, movements of the body through space, and paralinguistic cues, as well as one type of paralinguistic cue implicated by Goffman but not strongly associated with his writing (Cromdal and Aronsson 2000), that of code-switching (Goffman 1981a).

Footing ultimately has to do with the regulation of "participation," that is, "actions demonstrating forms of involvement performed by parties within evolving structures of talk" (Goodwin and Goodwin 2004: 222). Goodwin and Goodwin (2004) argue that there are limitations to "the analytic approach to participation offered" in Goffman's (1981a) notion of footing. These include that "speakers and hearers inhabit separate worlds" and that "no resources are provided for looking at exactly how speakers and hearers might take each other into account as part of the process of building an utterance" (Goodwin and Goodwin 2004: 225). Goodwin and Goodwin argued that participation should be studied within "an analytic framework that includes not only the speaker and her talk, but also the forms of embodiment and social organization through which multiple parties build the actions implicated in a strip of talk in concert with each other" (Goodwin and Goodwin 2004: 223), with speakers attending to hearers "as active coparticipants and systematically modify[ing] their talk as it is emerging so as to take into account what their hearers are doing" (Goodwin and Goodwin 2004: 222). Incorporating this model of participation entails consideration of the embodied displays through which all participants, including hearers, express and modify their stances, so as to capture "the ways in which these stories constitute relevant social action by members of a community" (Goodwin and Goodwin 2004: 237).

Goffman's (1981b) and the other analysts' work on framing, footing, and reported speech can be applied to understanding children's contextualization of scenes and voicing of characters during story-telling and pretend play.

Children have been observed manipulating the footings that they take to their utterances during pretend play to accomplish different forms of participation and social organization; for example, they may speak in a character voice (e.g., that of a mother) to a peer (e.g., in the role of a child) in order to distance themselves from an utterance which insults, scolds, or otherwise differentiates the peer in the interaction (Goodwin 1990, 1993; Kyratzis 2007; Tetreault 2009). Moreover, a particular frame of play that children establish, such as family play, can itself align the children to one another in particular ways in the interaction (Berentzen 1984; Sheldon 1996; Kyratzis 2004; Goodwin and Kyratzis 2007, 2012). The peers in turn can ratify or not ratify the role identity or framing of a scene projected by a speaker (Goodwin 1990). In summary, the studies and theoretical accounts reviewed in this section emphasize the mutual signaling of the emerging frames, speaker roles (production formats), and participation frameworks to which participants (speakers and hearers both) orient during story-telling and pretend play and how this signaling can be accomplished through both explicit verbal statements as well as through embodied and paralinguistic means, including code-switching.

The study

How these interactive processes – of framing and contextualization – play out in bilingual preschool children's peer pretend play interactions is the focus of the present study. The children attended a bilingual Spanish–English preschool serving families, predominantly of Mexican heritage, in a community in California. In this bilingual setting, what kinds of resources and signaling devices do children use? Do the children make use of bilingual resources for signaling shifts in frame, footing, and alignment, as predicted by Goffman (1981a) and as found by subsequent researchers, mostly working with older children (Zentella 1997; Ervin-Tripp and Reyes 2005; Gumperz and Cook-Gumperz 2005; Kyratzis, Tang and Köymen 2009) and outside of the context of pretend play? Moreover, the relationship of bilingual children's pretend play interactions to "literate behavior" as understood in the child development research reviewed earlier will also be examined.

Research setting and methodology

The excerpts selected come from a single (extended) play episode. This episode was drawn from an ethnographic study of children's free-play peer interactions conducted at a bilingual Head Start program serving families of (predominantly) Mexican heritage in California. Two classrooms were followed over two years, with a different cohort of children enrolled in the classrooms each of the two years. The children were videotaped in spontaneous play in their friendship groups twice weekly over each academic year of the study. The classes were mixed-age, with children (three to five-and-a-half years old) both one and two years from attending kindergarten.

The data were collected several years after passage of Proposition 227 in California (1998), which ended bilingual education in most public elementary and secondary schools in the state. It requires that immigrant children in public schools, after a transitional period (one year) of receiving English as a second language (English immersion) instruction, receive instruction which is conducted entirely in English.

The bilingual preschool center serves economically disadvantaged families. For the majority (80–90%) of the families of the children at this preschool center, Spanish is the language spoken in the home. In the preschool, the children's family language is supported, and the curriculum is bilingual. Both Spanish and English are used during instructional activities, and they are also allowed during free play. However, in order to support children who will be going on to English-only kindergarten classrooms the following year, it is recommended to teachers that they use mainly English towards the end of the school year in small group work with those children.

Ethnographic background on the friendship group

The extended activity of pretend play to be analyzed in this paper involves a friendship group of six girls. One group member, Gaby,[1] was a monolingual English speaker. With the exception of a few Spanish loan words, we did not observe her using Spanish in the recordings made of her friendship group. The other group members, Norma, Tracy, Frances, Gloria, and Erika, spoke both Spanish and English. (Most of these girls had stronger competencies in Spanish than English, although Tracy had about equal competencies in both languages.) Gaby and Norma maintained leadership roles in the group, while Tracy, Frances, Erika, and Gloria were more peripheral members.

Data analysis

Ethnographic methods combined with analysis of talk-in-interaction were used to analyze naturally occurring peer group interactions (Goodwin 1990, 2006; Evaldsson 2005; Kyratzis 2007). Segments of play in which children were orienting to a common thematic frame (e.g., house/family play) were selected and analyzed for how child speakers were "framing" (Goffman 1974, 1981b; Goodwin 1993) or "contextualizing" (Gumperz 1982) or signaling that common frame for one another, using the frameworks of Goffman, Goodwin and Goodwin, and Gumperz, referred to earlier.

Signaling orientation to a frame of birthday

The detailed analysis of the girls' pretend play shows that through various categorization devices and contextualization cues (e.g., event and prop mentions; paralinguistic cues signaling in-role speech of a mother, child, or excited party-goer; explicit verbalizations of actions being taken), the children constitute their play as that of birthday party (Butler and Weatherall 2006: 451; Kyratzis 2007; Sacks 1992). Moreover, group members orient to different sub-frames within the broader birthday party frame: one as a birthday party involving acts such as shopping for the party, calling people and inviting them, and entertainment (showing movies, dancing at the party), organized mostly in English by Gaby and Tracy; and another one as food preparation for the birthday party (organized in Spanish by Norma and involving also Frances and Erika). In this bilingual setting, bilingual resources (hybrid Spanish–English utterances, code-switching) are central to the children's framing of play and management of shifting alignments to the two possible sub-frames of birthday party play. Particularly notable also are the efforts exerted by the girls for the continued framing and upkeep of the birthday party frame and for the upkeep of the extended type of co-constructed discourse created within their birthday party play, sustained across several physical displacements in the preschool space and separations of the players. In the text which follows, I will demonstrate the multiple contextualization cues the girls use when signaling and negotiating their orientation to a birthday party frame.

The play begins as the girls put on white party dresses which are available in the house play area. Early in the play, one of the girls, Gaby, asks another, Erika, "are you gonna come to our party?" This question is no doubt triggered by physical props, the party dresses, which all the girls except Erika have been donning. Gaby refers to the party frame a second time a few turns later, asking "is there a party, are-are you guys having a party over there?" as she is brushing Tracy's hair, as well as a third time when she mentions something about needing some dresses, and asks "who's coming to this party?" Several of the girls are still on the other side of the room, donning the dresses. The birthday party frame finally gets taken up by the group, however, when, several turns later, Tracy announces "I'm gonna go to the party" as she takes a plastic toy credit card that is lying on a table to the side of the main table in the house area. This is an underscoring (Goldman 1998) that announces her own activity but also displays her shared orientation to the party frame that Gaby has introduced, and Gaby, in turn, builds on this. After Gaby and Tracy struggle over the credit cards, and Gaby tells Tracy that "I'm having these two cards," Tracy walks away from the central table of the house area where they have been talking. Possibly as a means of getting her to come back to the central table, Gaby calls Tracy back and offers her the credit cards ("Okay Tracy, Tracy. Tracy here.

Here"). It is after this point that the first extended segment of birthday party play occurs, featured in Example 1A below.

Ex. 1A: Birthday party preparation

1.	Gaby:	Okay Tracy. Tracy. (0.1) Tracy here. Here. ((hands her toy credit card)) Tracy here's your credit cards. Credit cards. ((places credit card on table)) Credit card. ((hands her a credit card)) Are-are you going right now?
2.	Tracy:	Yeah. I'm gonna go to the party now. ((turns to Gaby, returns to table))
3.	Gaby:	Okay bye. I-I-I will call you when I'm coming okay?
4.	Tracy:	Okay.
5.	Gaby:	Call me when it's going to start.

In line 1, Gaby shows continued orientation to the birthday party frame by asking "are you going right now?" In response, Tracy turns to face Gaby, returns to the table, and ties to the format (Goodwin 1990, 2006) of Gaby's question, responding "I'm gonna go to the party now" in line 2. Even though Tracy does not use a statement that makes the frame fully explicit (as in saying "Pretend we're going to a birthday party"), by using this "underscoring" statement (Goldman 1998) describing her own activity and mentioning "party," a word that Gaby had used earlier, Tracy displays a shared orientation to the birthday party frame. In line 3, Gaby displays her orientation to a role consistent with birthday party, that of being a party-goer and invitee, as she calls out another act consistent with the frame, her plan to call the hostess to inform her of her own (as one of the party guests') imminent arrival ("I will call you when I'm coming okay?"). With this statement, she also projects Tracy as being in the hostess role. She also projects an act appropriate for Tracy's role, "call me when it's going to start" (line 5). Through these announcements of actions categorically related to parties (calling people to coordinate arrival) and through role-appropriate speech acts (Gaby's promise to call Tracy as the hostess about her arrival time), the girls establish and display to one another their joint orientation to a frame of birthday party play.

After this beginning, another girl who had been donning the dresses, Norma, gets drawn into the frame of play. She picks up a broom and begins sweeping near Gaby and Tracy, announcing "I clean," which is an activity semantically tied with or "programmatically relevant" (Sacks 1992) to the frame of getting ready for a party which Gaby and Tracy had been displaying orientation to.

To orient to Tracy and especially Gaby, Norma uses English in Example 1B. However, in the middle of the interaction, Tracy proposes that there be "dancing" at the party. Norma, however, protests this invasion of a new act into the birthday party frame, and code-switches to Spanish to shift the frame and launch her own sub-frame of play.

Ex. 1B: Birthday party preparation

[Gaby and Norma are by the kitchen table in the house area, dusting, sweeping, and talking to a boy. Shortly thereafter, Tracy appears. Later in the example, Norma leaves the table to go to the play sink in the corner, and Gaby and Tracy run to an area across the classroom to watch a "movie."]

1.	Gaby:	I said to go play outside cuz we have to get the party ready. ((to boy))
2.	Norma:	=Yeah and we're cleaning. ((sweeping))
3.	Gaby:	Yeah. ((Gaby grasps cloth, "dusts" stack of cots))
4.	Norma:	It's a mess, at the house. ((raises arm up, flips it, grasps broom and sweeps again))
5.	Gaby:	We don't _need_ the socks. ((stuffs socks between cots))
6.	Norma:	Yeah! ((flips arm inward and up, continues sweeping))
7.	Tracy:	Okay. Let's dance now= ((Tracy arrives at table))
8.	Norma:	=No way, it starts! ((Norma flips her arm, leaves center of house area and goes to corner with sink))
9.	Gaby:	Yeah. You could go dance but we're trying to clean the house. ((to Tracy, as tries close cookie box top))
10.	Tracy:	Mommy. I'm tired. ((stands, facing Gaby, uses plaintive pitch. Gaby doesn't look at her))
11.	Gaby:	Go to bed. I bet it's under here. ((points under table)) But you can't go. Your bed is over there. ((points to other side of room))
12.	Tracy:	Okay. ((goes away from table, out of camera range))
13.	Tracy:	Who clean up this mess máma? ((returns, stands looking at Gaby)) Mommy-mommy who cleaned up (xxxxxx) in my room-of my room máma? ((faces Gaby, who looks up; uses slow cadence, plaintive voice))
14.	Gaby:	Your room is over there, where your party is going to be. ((points to pillows on far side of room, Tracy goes))
15.	Tracy:	Um um my my room is gonna be started.= ((Tracy returns to table))
16.	Gaby:	=Okay. We go do- come on. ((Gaby, Tracy run to pillows across room))
17.	Tracy:	Yeah I'm (xxx) every body is going to be there. Everybody is going to be there this time and it's gonna be and we're gonna see the movie of Shark Tale and= ((Tracy sits on pillows, faces wall, Gaby arranges pillows))
18.	Gaby:	=Shark Tale?
19.	Tracy:	Yeah! ((flings back against cushion)). Come here.
20.	Gaby:	=(xxx) before your party. ((still arranges pillows))
21.	Norma:	=Hay que ir al dentista! ((calling from sink, as Frances walks past pillows, heading towards her)) =_We have to go to the dentist!_

In the beginning of this excerpt, Norma and Gaby are cleaning together. Gaby says to a boy who comes by that he should "go play outside," "cuz we need to get the party ready" (line 1). Through a directive with a justification, Gaby orients to the boy in a way that is consistent with the frame of a family getting ready for a birthday party and with her role as a mother who can order him to go play outside (even though no real-world outside play is occurring or is even allowable in the preschool at this time of the day). As noted by Pellegrini, "An important part of narrative competence is … knowing that characters' plans and acts are temporally and causally motivated" (Pellegrini 1985: 109), and Gaby's justification shows an understanding of the reasons that would motivate a mother or other adult to order a child to go play outdoors at a time of getting ready for a birthday party.

Norma ties to Gaby's statement, first, by tying to the code-selection of English, and second, by affirming and expanding it. Cleaning is an act semantically tied to the event of getting ready for a birthday party, and Norma capitalizes upon that association; she says "yeah and we're cleaning" (line 2) to show orientation to the birthday party play the two other girls, Gaby and Tracy, had been organizing. She then, in line 4, ties semantically to Gaby's and her own utterances about cleaning for the party by providing a reason, saying "it's a mess at the house" (line 4), accompanied by a dramatic gesture, and Gaby further aligns with the suggestion of cleaning by proposing to put some socks away (line 5). Across lines 1 through 6, Gaby and Norma display a shared alignment to one another and to cleaning as their shared activity. When Tracy arrives in line 7, after being away from the scene, and displays orientation to a different birthday act, suggesting "let's dance now," Norma (in line 8) opposes this ("no way, it starts"). Her word "starts" ties to Gaby's utterance in the previous excerpt (Example 1A, line 5), in which Gaby had asked Tracy to "call me when it's going to start." The girls constantly display to one another their shared alignment to the birthday party frame through verbally referring to actions consistent with the frame (cleaning, putting socks away, party starting). Their "format tying" to acts previously mentioned by themselves or other players illustrates the quality of repetition in children's pretend play noted by Goldman (1998).

In line 9, Gaby goes along with the cleaning continuing, saying to Tracy "you could go dance but we're trying to clean the house." Despite Gaby's support of the idea of continuing the cleaning, Norma displays a stance of opposition to Tracy's suggestion of dancing. In addition to saying "no way, it starts!" she shows her disalignment by physically walking away from the table (line 8) towards the corner of the room, where there is a play sink. At the sink, she is off camera but, according to field notes, she is engaged in solitary pretend food preparation.

In lines 10–14, after Norma leaves, Tracy changes her footing and engages in in-character speech as a child. She uses particular directive forms, vocatives, and prosodic features and makes complaints ("I'm tired") of Gaby, in which she uses the vocatives "mommy" and "mama," that project Gaby as being in the role of her mother. She also uses information requests that frame the "mommy" as being in a more knowledgeable position than she is (Goodwin

1990). She also uses a slow cadence and plaintive pitch, which further index her status of being less knowledgeable and in the role of a child. Gaby in turn orients to Tracy as her mother; she uses commands ("go to bed") and instructs Tracy ("your bed is over there"). These forms align the participants Gaby and Tracy in a hierarchical way in the interaction (Goodwin 1993), but also create a positive alignment between them (Hoyle 1998).

To Tracy's information request, Gaby responds that the party is going to take place on the far side of the classroom and points there. In line 15, Tracy, like Norma had done, ties to Gaby's earlier utterance, "call me when it starts" (Example 1A), by saying "my room is gonna be started," but she mentions an inanimate object, "room," rather than an event, "party." As a three-year-old, Tracy may have difficulty in fully matching the format of Gaby's earlier utterance, "call me when it starts," because she may not know what kinds of subjects (events rather than things) can be "started." Nonetheless, partially tying to Gaby's utterance gives the younger peer practice in approximating the complex grammatical construction (Goodwin 2006) that Gaby had used, and lends cohesion to the text that the girls are building together as well as displaying her continued alignment to the birthday party frame. In line 16, Gaby orients to the party starting as well ("okay we go do- come on") and both girls run away from the house area to a cozy area on the other side of the room set up with large pillows. Here, they proceed to display an orientation to the birthday party by saying things a party-goer might say, projecting excitement at lots of people being at the party and watching movies there.

Sitting on the pillows looking at a blank wall (as though a movie is being shown), Tracy says, "Everybody is going to be there this time and it's gonna be and we're gonna see the movie of Shark Tale and=". She also makes an embodied display of appropriate affect, that of excitement (e.g., flinging her back against the pillows – line 19), while Gaby, continuing to orient to her role as a mother, stands by and arranges the pillows in the area. The children's bodily alignment and the things they are saying display their orientation, and their characters' orientation, to watching an animated cartoon movie, *Shark Tale*, that was popular at the time. Their design and representation of the speech of characters qualifies as a "form of reflexivity" and therefore of literate discourse (Cekaite, Blum-Kulka, Grøver and Teubal, this volume).

Even though their orientation to the birthday party frame is partially signaled through non-verbal, multi-modal means (e.g., through code-switching, slapping of the back against a pillow to express excitement, physical props, movements of the body towards and away from particular areas of play), verbal announcements are still salient (Heath 1986; Goldman 1998), seen in their use of underscorings such as "we're gonna see the movie of Shark Tale" (Tracy) and "and we're cleaning" (Norma), as well as other event and state descriptions ("it starts," "everybody's going to be there"; "you could go dance but we're trying to clean the house"). As noted by Goldman (1998) and M. H. Goodwin, in order to achieve agreement on "what constitutes the common scene" (Goodwin 1993: 160) among the players, a certain degree of verbal explicitness is necessary. Moreover, the girls make use of format tying and repetition; proposals are explicitly tied to (and justified in terms of) the overall frame of play, seen in the causal, adversative, and locative statements with connectives which the girls use throughout (e.g., "you could go dance but we're trying to clean the house," "I said to go play outside cuz we have to get the party ready," "yeah and we're cleaning; it's a mess, at the house"; "Your room is over there, where your party is going to be"). This acknowledging of one another's suggestions and tying of them to the overall frame of play may be related to the "participation frameworks" (Goffman 1981b) and "forms of social organization" (Goodwin and Goodwin 2004) which the girls are building through their play narrative; the girls go to great lengths to display their alignment to the overall frame of birthday party, and through that, their alignment to one another (Hoyle 1998). This entails them using literate features – a considerable degree of verbal explicitness (e.g., underscorings) and devices of textual cohesion (repetition, connectives) in their play.

After Gaby's and Tracy's departure from the house area, Norma, who has been playing by herself at the table off to the side, makes a bid to organize her own activity. It is here that we begin to see the children using bilingual resources to organize their play. In line 21, she shifts to Spanish and calls out "hay que ir al dentista!", a suggestion possibly evoked by a toy plastic drill that is in the vicinity of the children. She calls this out loudly, so that she can be overheard by a Spanish-speaking girl, Frances, who has just walked past the pillow area and is heading towards the sink where Norma is. This announcement is an "outloud," an utterance that is not directed to any particular participant but is stated so that it is available for all co-present participants (Goffman 1978: 796). Regarding her shift to Spanish, Norma is using a code-switch here to shift the frame of play (Goffman 1981b), setting it off from the footing or orientation that the girls had been taking to the activity up to this point. As noted by Cromdal (2004), "divergence from the language spoken previously is a way of ... showing her disalignment" (204: 38) with the previous activity or frame.

In Example 1C, Frances orients to the new play frame that Norma ushers in with her outloud "hay que ir al dentist," and the two girls eventually become engaged in cooking play in Spanish.

Ex. 1C: Birthday party preparation

[Norma and Frances, the principal players in this example, are off camera at the sink in the corner.]

Peer interaction and framing in bilingual play   141

1.	Norma:	=Hay que ir al dentista!
		=*We have to go to the dentist!*
2.	Frances:	Quítale esto. Allí está la comida.
		Take that away. There is the food.
3.	Norma:	Estamos cocinando. Primero hay que cocinar sí? Mientras vienen=
		We are cooking. First we have to cook yes? Before they come.
4.	Frances:	=COMI:DA! NORMA LA COMI:DA!
		=*FOOD! NORMA THE FO:OD!*

As noted, Norma switches into Spanish in line 1 to index a shift in her alignment, both to the frame, and to the participation framework of players. In line 2, Frances displays orientation to participating in an activity with Norma, but turns the activity into cooking play by suggesting the category set of food, "Allí está la comida" (*there is the food*) instead of something related to the dentist. In line 3, Norma also displays orientation to food, suggesting an activity semantically tied to and involving food, cooking, saying "estamos cocinando." In other words, by saying "hay que cocinar," she ties to the semantic shape of Frances's utterance and to the syntactic shape of her own earlier utterance from line 1 ("hay que ir"). With these format ties (Goodwin 1990, 2006), the girls display their shared alignment to a theme, and by mentioning activities and props that are "programmatically relevant" to the theme (Sacks 1992) of cooking, construct their play as such.

However, in line 3, Norma also ties the frame that the two girls are contextualizing at the moment to the frame to which the other girls and Norma had been orienting earlier, in Example 1B, getting ready for the party. She does this through using the temporal phrase "Primero hay que cocinar sí? mientras vienen" *(First we must cook, yes? before they come)*. With this temporal construction, Norma is filling Frances (and possibly Tracy and Gaby, who are within earshot) in on the fact that the cooking play that they are framing at the moment is relevant to the other scenario that was begun together with the other girls, Gaby and Tracy, and to the activity that Gaby and Tracy are engaged in now, birthday party play. In other words, Norma makes an effort to frame the new activity as a side-activity of the larger birthday party play. It is notable how her efforts to display alignment to Gaby and Tracy lead her to deploy cohesion devices. In addition to the temporal construction with "mientras," the word "vienen" is a semantic tie to the birthday party frame because it suggests an event to which people will come and its plural marking ("en") invokes Gaby and Tracy in the present cooking frame.

In the next example, 1D, Gaby returns to the central table and shortly thereafter Norma and Tracy return there as well. Norma finds Gaby embroiled in a conflict with another peer, Gloria. Norma shifts back into English and attempts to return the play to birthday party, and when she is not effective in ending the conflict between Gaby and Gloria, she leaves and renders an outloud to shift the frame back to "comida" play with Frances.

Ex. 1D: Birthday party preparation

1.	Gloria:	Aw that hurts. ((to Gaby; Tracy and Norma arrive at table))
2.	Norma:	Okay! ((Norma at table, standing, looks at Gaby; Tracy also arrives at table and sits, doesn't speak in this example))
3.	Gaby:	(Don't, don't) be her friend. Be my friend ((looking at Norma))
4.	Norma:	OKAY! I'M GONNA PART THE COMIDA AND START (blip!) ((Gaby looks down, cleaning)) ((Norma walks away from Gaby toward corner, flipping her arms))
5.	Gaby:	S-Stop! ((to Gloria, as conflict between Gaby and Gloria continues))
6.	Norma:	QUI:ÉN QUI:ERE VINO? ((off camera, calls out from corner)) *who wants wine?*

After arriving back at the table, at a pause in the conflict between Gaby and Gloria, Norma (line 2) uses an expression ("Okay!") with falling intonation. The discourse marker "okay" marks resumption of activity (Kyratzis 1993), and Norma seems to use it here to mark resumption of the frame of preparing for the birthday party. When she is not effective in dispelling the conflict between Gaby and Gloria (line 3), she seems to give up the attempt and starts walking back towards the sink area (line 4) where she and Frances had been playing "comida" earlier. As she goes, she calls out something out loud in both Spanish and English, possibly indexing that although she is leaving their table, what she is going to do still relates to Gaby's and Tracy's activity. In line 4, she calls out "OKAY! I'M GONNA PART THE COMIDA AND START (blip!)"

This utterance is "heteroglossic" (Bakhtin 1981; Kyratzis, Reynolds and Evaldsson 2010), capitalizing on the bilingual children's Spanish and English resources. The word "part" suggests that Norma may be referring to the Spanish verb "repartir" (meaning "distribute," as in distributing food). Although she uses an underscoring (Goldman 1998) to talk about her own activity ("OKAY! I'M GONNA PART THE COMIDA AND START (blip!)", she designs her announcement in such a way that it is relevant to Gaby and Tracy's activity by speaking partly in English. By using a heteroglossic utterance and stating it as an "outloud" (Goffman 1978: 796), that is, in a way that it is made audible and available to all co-present participants (see also Szymanski 1999), Norma is displaying orientation to both frames simultaneously, the larger birthday party frame that had involved Tracy, Gaby, and herself earlier (Example 1B), and the "comida" play that had involved her and Frances in the corner (Example 1C), an area towards which Norma is now walking. By using English and Spanish language resources in a single utterance, she also makes a "bilingual knowledge display" (Evaldsson and Sahlström, this volume), thereby marking her affiliation with a bilingual peer group (Rampton 1995; Zentella 1997). Moreover, she ties to the syntactic shape of Gaby's much earlier utterance using the word "start" in Example 1A ("call me when it it's going to start"), lending cohesion to the play, although, like Tracy, she does not quite accurately provide the arguments of this verb.

At the end of the example (line 6), as she reaches the sink in the corner of the house area where the comida play had been occurring earlier, Norma shifts to Spanish "QUI:ÉN QUI:ERE VINO?", an outloud that indexes a shift to a new sub-frame, serving beverages, and a new participation framework, with Frances and another girl, Erika, who are nearby. Both the shift to Spanish and the category term (Sacks 1992) "vino," as well as the physical location to which she has moved, signal a return to food-related activities (that had been going on in Example 1C). The question format of her utterance signals its function as an offer. She may be voicing an adult character in the birthday party frame, possibly that of host/hostess, demonstrating once gain her narrative competence and knowledge of the types of factors that motivate characters (Pellegrini 1985). "QUI:ÉN QUI:ERE VINO?" is just the sort of thing a host would say to their guests if they were having a party, after they had formulated a plan about serving food, as Norma seemed to do in line 4 with her heteroglossic statement.

Example 1E is from later in the birthday party play, in a segment that occurs after Gaby has returned to the main table of the house area after having been called away by a teacher and has announced a plan: "Okay. I'm-I'm going to sweep the stuff and you have to cook and=". This announcement has brought Norma back from "comida" play and she is now responding to Gaby in English. When Gaby uses an underscoring to announce that she will complete the cleaning so that she can call the party guests, Norma validates this plan with a reason.

Ex. 1E: Birthday party preparation

[All four girls, Gaby, Norma, Tracy, and Gloria are at or next to the table.]

1.	Gaby:	Okay make a cake and you get it ready and I will sweep. ((starts sweeping))
2.	Gaby:	And I'll clean up the room too. ((sweeping))
3.	Norma:	What is this? ((walks to other side of table))
4.	Gaby:	Because I have to call them before they could come. Guess how many people are coming. ((stops sweeping, walks, steps, looks up at the researcher))
5.	Res:	Really=
6.	Norma:	=Yeah because, because, ((Norma also walks over to the researcher))

144 A. Kyratzis

| 7. | Res: | =How many? |
| 8. | Norma: | =Because we're making a party. ((after utterance, walks back towards table)) |

In line 2, Gaby uses an underscoring to announce that she will clean up the room. Then, in line 4, she provides a reason for this plan ("because I have to call them before they could come"); as one of the hosts, she has to finish cleaning so that she can call the guests; they have to be called "before they could come." She marks her reason for finishing cleaning with the connective "because," illustrating once again her narrative competence and knowledge of the factors that motivate characters in a birthday party planning scenario, as well as her competence in building cohesion into her text. She also expresses a host's excitement at a large number of guests being at her party, saying "Guess how many people are coming?" Her peer, Norma, provides a reason why party-givers or planners like herself and Gaby might pose such a question (or expression of affect) and also reaffirms the frame by re-mentioning it, saying excitedly, "Yeah because, because, because we're making a party" (lines 6 and 8). This segment of play shows these young children's literate skill in providing character motives (Pellegrini 1985) and "construct[ing] extended discourses autonomously" (Snow 1999: 146).

Conclusions

These examples illustrate the virtuosity that young children display in framing (Goffman 1974) pretend play and signaling for one another "what constitutes the common scene in front of them" (Goodwin 1993: 160). Children used a range of contextualization devices (Gumperz 1982) to frame the play, and manage shifting frames, voices, and participation frameworks within it. These framing activities enabled the children to sustain play over multiple physical displacements of players and allowed them to display reorientation to participation frameworks (Goffman 1981b; M. H. Goodwin 1990) and frames (Goffman 1974) after they had been disrupted by players leaving the scene or after players became involved in momentary disputes or competing participation frameworks and frames. The children were no doubt guided by event knowledge in "organiz[ing] pretense over an entire verbal interaction" (Seidman, Nelson and Gruendel 1986: 179), but they were also actively involved in building participation, agentively "display[ing] to one another what they are doing and how they expect others to align themselves toward the activity of the moment" (Goodwin and Goodwin 2004: 222).

As noted by Goodwin and Goodwin, the children not only used explicit verbal statements but also made use of "other forms of embodied practice that might also be constitutive of participation in talk" (Goodwin and Goodwin 2004: 225; Goodwin 1984). They signaled their orientation to the birthday party frame through movements of their bodies towards and away from particular areas of play, through slapping of the back against a pillow and facing a wall to express excitement at watching a movie; through plaintive pitch and information requests to signal the voice and footing of a child; through loud volume and discourse markers of resumption ("Okay!"); through physical props such as dresses; through semantic ties (Cook-Gumperz and Gumperz 1978; Sacks 1992), using words like "starts" and "cake," as well as speech acts and expressions ("Everybody is going to be there," "guess how many people are coming?", "I have to call them before they could come") tied to the thematic frame of birthday party, to signal that frame in the interaction and to differentiate it from side-play, a cooking activity, where the girls made use of alternative semantic ties ("vino," "cocinando").

For these bilingual children, code-switching between Spanish and English was a major resource that they used to shift the frame of play and index their shifting orientation to frames and groups of players and to sustain the fantasy narrative over wide expanses of time and space in the preschool classroom. Norma used a code-switch into Spanish to index a shift in her orientation away from the birthday party play of Gaby and Tracy. She used English to reorient to the birthday party play in Example 1D, and when she was not successful in re-engaging Gaby, used a heteroglossic Spanish–English utterance to signal that she was still orienting to Gaby and Tracy's frame even though she was now moving away from them and back towards "comida" play with Frances. She also shifted to English to reorient to Gaby, Tracy, and the main birthday party frame in Example 1E. Frances, who spoke both English and Spanish, used Spanish to show orientation to the side-play of cooking that Norma initiated in Example 1C (and in a segment that followed Example 1D, not shown here). Goffman (1981b) noted long ago that code-switching could be a resource for signaling shifts in frame and footing in interaction; code-switching was an important resource for the children's framing of pretend play in this bilingual setting.

Explicit verbal announcements were highly salient in the children's pretend play (Heath 1986; Goldman 1998). The children made extensive use of underscorings such as "we're gonna see the movie of Shark Tale" (Tracy); "and we're cleaning" (Norma); "OKAY! I'M GONNA PART THE COMIDA AND START (blip!)" (Norma); "Okay make a cake and you get it ready and I will sweep" (Gaby); and "And I'll clean up the room too" (Gaby). They also used other event and state descriptions ("it starts," "everybody's going to be there"; "you could go dance but we're trying to clean the house"). As noted by Goldman (1998) and Heath (1986), in order to achieve agreement on "what constitutes the common scene in front of them" (Goodwin 1993: 160) among the players, a certain degree of verbal explicitness, one of the hallmarks of "literate behavior" and "literate discourse" (Pellegrini 1985; Snow 1999), was necessary. Moreover, proposals were repeated (e.g., the proposals made at several points that the party "starts"), explicitly tied to and justified in terms of the overall frame of play, seen in the extensive use of format tying and repetition, and causal, adversative, temporal, and locative statements with connectives which the girls use throughout (e.g., "you could go dance but we're trying to clean the house," "I said to go play outside cuz we have to get the party ready," "yeah and we're cleaning; it's a mess, at the house"; "Your room is over there, where your party is going to be"; "Primero hay que cocinar sí? Mientras vienen" and "I'll clean up the room too because I have to call them before they could come"). This repetition of, harkening back to, and expansion of one another's proposals also led to the extensive use of connectives and discourse markers like "and" (e.g., in Example 1E) and "Okay" (Examples 1D and 1E). Through their play narrative, through explicitly acknowledging one another's proposals and tying and relating them to the overall frame of birthday party play, the girls build forms of social organization (Goodwin and Goodwin, 2004) among themselves. These practices result in another "literate feature" of their collaboratively produced pretend play texts – "clearly marked textual cohesion and coherence" (Zadunaisky Ehrlich and Blum-Kulka, this volume; see also Heath 1986; Snow 1999).

A final literate feature of the children's collaboratively produced pretend play texts seen in these examples is one noted by Pellegrini: "narrative competence ... knowing that characters' plans and acts are temporally and causally motivated" (Pellegrini 1985: 109). The children displayed this form of literate behavior and narrative competence. In Example 1B, Tracy engaged in in-character speech as a child in which she made information requests of the girl in the role of her mother, Gaby; Gaby, in turn, projected an appropriate footing by issuing commands to Tracy and instructing her. Although it was sometimes unclear in the examples whether the children were assuming a footing of narrator or story character because of their use of first-person reference, throughout the play, they made the excited affective utterances of would-be party-goers (or party-planners), as in Tracy's "Everybody is going to be there this time and it's gonna be and we're gonna see the movie of Shark Tale and=". They expressed speech acts and affect appropriate for party hosts and planners, as in Norma's "QUI:ÉN QUI:ERE VINO?" stated after her plan to prepare food. They also sometimes explained these expressions, as in Gaby's "And I'll clean up the room too; Because I have to call them before they could come." These utterances show an understanding of the perspective of a party-planner, the role they were sometimes assuming in the play, and the concerns that would motivate such a character role (Pellegrini 1985), as well as the feature of "intertextuality" described by Wolf and Hicks (1999).

To summarize, the children make extensive efforts for the continued framing and upkeep of the birthday party frame and for the upkeep of the extended type of co-constructed discourse created within their birthday party play. These efforts can best be understood within Goffman's notion of "participation framework" (1981b) and Goodwin and Goodwin's construct of "participation," "actions demonstrating forms of involvement performed by parties within evolving structures of talk" (Goodwin and Goodwin 2004: 222). The children go to great efforts to display their alignments to the overarching frame of birthday party in order to build their alignments to one another in the interaction (see Nicolopoulou et al., this volume for related processes in story dictation/acting out). These efforts are realized through the children's use of multi-modal resources. In this bilingual context, code-switching was a major resource the children relied upon to display their alignments and disalignments with shifting sub-frames of play and with shifting participation frameworks of players (see also Evaldsson and Sahlström, this volume). Despite their multimodal expression, these efforts also entail the children in using forms of reflexivity and features of "literate discourse," as described in the literature (Cekaite, Blum-Kulka, Grøver and Teubal, this volume; Pellegrini 1985; Snow 1999), including use of explicit verbal statements, and the building of strong cohesive and intertextual ties in their co-constructed texts, seen in the use of format tying and connectives. Although the children do not make fully explicit statements of the scene (e.g., "We're playing birthday party") at every moment of the play, many of the statements the children do use, for example, underscorings, are quite explicit. Children use these statements to keep one another apprised of how they are orienting to the scene moment-to-moment. Moreover, the format tying and language play of the children also provide a space for language learning (Cekaite and Aronsson 2004, this volume; Ervin-Tripp 1991; Evaldsson 2005; Goodwin 2006), as seen in the recyclings of expressions with the verb "start" (which continued beyond Examples 1A–1E) by children of varying ages and competencies in English.

These findings suggest that in order to support bilingual children's emergent literacy, including the use of explicit verbal statements, and the building of strong cohesive and intertextual ties in collaborative pretend play texts, preschool programs should encourage children's peer pretend play by providing toys, props and dedicated classroom areas (e.g., house play area) that support such play, and by allowing time in the classroom day for free play among peers (e.g., Genishi and Dyson 2009). The literate forms encompassed in pretend play could support children in transitioning to the "more literate environment of primary school" (Nelson, this volume). These examples also suggest that preschool programs should allow children to use their bilingual communicative resources as a preparation for schooling. Bilingual resources, among their other resources, would seem to lead the children to have high "levels of control over th[e] pragmatic orientations [required for literacy achievement] in oral contexts" (Snow 1999: 145). These resources and practices could serve as "strengths" (Zentella 2005) and "funds of knowledge" (González, Moll and Amanti 2005) upon which children's command of school-based discourses and forms of decontextualized language and narrative skills (e.g., narratives, explanations, definitions) required in school could build.

TRANSCRIPTION CONVENTIONS

The transcription symbols are as follows:

[	the beginning of overlapping talk
]	the end of overlapping talk
.	falling intonation
?	rising intonation
,	continuing intonation
-	abrupt cut-off
=	talk produced without transition
space	silence
:	prolonged syllable
warm	prominent syllable
YOU'LL	loud speech
(×××)	undecipherable speech
{[ac]}	accelerated speech
(0.5)	pause of designated no. of seconds
((smiling))	transcriber's comments
------	lines omitted from transcript
food	English transl. of Spanish speech

NOTES

1 All names of children used in the examples are pseudonyms. Transcription conventions are given above.

8 Metasociolinguistic stance taking and the appropriation of bilingual identities in everyday peer language practices

Ann-Carita Evaldsson and Fritjof Sahlström

Introduction

In this chapter we explore the accumulation of stances taken in peer-language alternation practices as an emergent feature of children's identity work and socialization to use of language. Our analysis takes its point of departure in the set of stances taken over time by an 'immigrant' girl, whose parents are immigrants from Rwanda, in her transition from one language community (Finland) to another (Sweden). In particular, we focus on how the stances taken by children in peer-language alternation practices are important resources for accomplishing social relations, displaying language competencies and indexing more durable sociolinguistic identities. Jaffe (2009: 17) calls such displays of positions taken toward the assumed connections between language and identity with respect to hierarchies and ideologies a *metasociolinguistic* stance. As will be demonstrated in this chapter, such metasociolinguistic stances are enacted by children in peer group interactions through the use of both implicit and explicit forms of evaluations and social categorizations, affect, knowledge and agency as they orient to others and make claims regarding particular sociolinguistic matters (cf. Kyratzis, Reynolds and Evaldsson 2010; for reviews Goodwin and Kyratzis 2012). For example, how are language choices commented on and evaluated by children? What social consequences do the metasociolinguistic stances taken have, both on the appropriation of sociolinguistic identities and on the ways children organize their peer group participation? These are the questions this chapter aims to answer.

The analysis focuses on trajectories of peer-language alternation practices across the two different linguistic communities. It relies on ethnographic techniques based on video recordings of multilingual peer group practices in which the focal girl is an important participant. We apply a peer-language socialization approach to explore how children's evaluations of the multiple and sometimes conflicting linguistic and cultural resources at their disposal within linguistically diverse peer groups and educational settings provide an important context for linguistic and cultural socialization (cf. Goodwin and Kyratzis 2012; Kyratzis, Reynolds and Evaldsson 2010). In the analysis, we attempt to move away from a view of bilingualism as "the co-existence of two linguistic systems" (cf. Garrett, 2007; Heller, 2007). Instead we focus on how children in multilingual settings, as they comment on language choices, deploy particular sociolinguistic resources, involving the differential use of two or more normatively defined codes (Schieffelin 1994). This also involves learning how metasociolinguistic stances on particular language alternation practices may index specific social categories, statuses and identities (Garrett 2007; Garrett and Baquedano-Lopez 2002; Ochs 1993, 2002).

Of overall interest here is how the children's stance-taking practices are built up over time in courses of activities across peer group encounters and language communities. By focusing on the metasociolinguistic stances taken across trajectories of peer-language alternation practices, we will demonstrate how an individual, in this case the focal child, Sara, accumulates a record of stances, which index a bilingual identity, as she learns how to use language in culturally appropriate ways. The analysis also highlights how differences in the metasociolinguistic stances taken by and attributed to Sara are consequential for her shifting participation status, moving from being a novice within the peer group to becoming a language expert. Further, Sara's capacity for metasociolinguistic stance taking and linguistic creativity in learning how to use language simultaneously draws attention to the agency of language learners and the ways in which children's peer-language practices provide for specific linguistic identities along with the transformations of wider sociolinguistic ideologies.

Stance taking and children's peer language socialization

Du Bois's (2007) theorizing of stance is a starting point for our analysis. Du Bois (2007: 163) defines stance as a "public act by a social actor, achieved dialogically through overt communicative means (language gesture and other symbolic forms), through which social actors simultaneously evaluate objects, position subjects (self and others), and align with other subjects, with respect to any salient dimension of the sociocultural field." The three interrelated key dimensions of stance, concerning the actor's evaluation and assessment, either of certain objects of discourse or of an interlocutor, alignments and positioning, are also focused on here. Central to our understanding is a view of stance as emerging from interaction between participants in dialogic and sequential contexts. It is a public action that is shaped by the talk and stances of other participants in sequentially unfolding turns-at-talk (cf. Du Bois 2007; Goodwin 2007; Jaffe 2009; Kärkkäinen 2006). In Goffman's (1981a) terms, the studied participants display their stance, footing or "projected selves" and the alignments they take up toward themselves and other subjects, and the evaluative target or object of stance. Besides its social relational aspects, here metasociolinguistic stance taking is also associated with particular subject positions, i.e. social categories and identities, including the indexical relationship between talk and sociolinguistic identities (see Harré and Van Langenhoeve 1991; Jaffe 2009 for an overview). The metasociolinguistic stances taken by children in trajectories of language alternation practices toward the languages available can be seen as indexing specific social, cultural and linguistic formations and identities (Garrett 2007; Garrett and Baquedano-Lopez 2002; Ochs 1993, 2002).

As has been demonstrated in peer-language socialization studies in multilingual and linguistically stratified settings, children make use of an array of linguistic practices to evaluate group members and constitute their peer group participation (see Goodwin and Kyratzis 2012, for reviews). As children act to "construct and reconstruct their social organization on an ongoing basis" (Goodwin 1990: 35), they appropriate adult registers, performance genres and language varieties in ways that render their own commentary on normatively defined codes and dominant ideologies (Garrett 2007; Kyratzis 2010; Minks 2010; Paugh 2005; Reynolds 2010). For example, Garrett (2007) demonstrates how children in Morne-Carré transform and resist adults' efforts to socialize younger children to use English. Despite the age-based restrictions on the use of Kwéyòl, the children, particularly as they grow older, draw on both English and Kwéyòl to (re)position themselves in relation to other children. Moreover, Paugh (2005: 80) found that children in code-switching practices in peer–kin groups in Dominica "transform the associations with the languages through using them in their play." Although they were forbidden to speak Patwa (a local French-lexicon Creole), they used it in their role-play to enact adult roles and create imaginary play spaces, possibly supporting the maintenance of indigenous languages in the region. In contrast, in a study of multiethnic peer groups at two schools in Sweden, Evaldsson (2005; see also Evaldsson and Cekaite 2010) shows how children strengthened their within-group alignments by criticizing their peers for limited language proficiency in the majority language, Swedish. However, the criticizing children shifted stances and challenged the very same monolingual norms at other moments, using code-switching and crossing, thereby indexing bilingual identities. In addition, Kyratzis (2010, and this volume) has shown how, through code-switching practices, Mexican-heritage immigrant girls negotiate alignments and position one another while acting upon and exploiting the two languages (i.e., English and Spanish) to construct and reshape the social organization of their (bilingual) peer group.

In this chapter we will use a peer-language socialization approach to explore the ways the cumulative metasociolinguistic stances taken in trajectories of language alternation practices across two different multilingual peer group formations may change an individual child's status from linguistic novice to bilingual expert. As Jaffe (2009: 4) notes, the accumulation of particular linguistic stances taken over time may index more durable aspects of social identity. This makes trajectories of children's stance taking in language alternation practices a crucial point of entry for an analysis of the intricate social process through which individual children, as they learn how to navigate between multiple linguistic codes and the social valences associated with them, simultaneously appropriate a particular sociolinguistic identity that endures over time (cf. Garrett 2007; Paugh 2005).

Attempting to understand how immigrant children appropriate multifaceted identities while acting upon and exploiting multiple languages and language ideologies in educational settings is closely related to a sociocultural view on learning. The basic sociocultural argument is that learning can be seen as "changing participation in the culturally designed settings of everyday life" (Lave and Wenger 1991). A sociocultural approach to the role of peer talk in children's language learning is also taken by Blum-Kulka and Snow (2004) in their work on children's pragmatic development and second language learning, and by Blum-Kulka and Gorbatt in this book (Chapter 9). However, our analysis of children's peer talk focuses primarily on social aspects of language learning; that is, how children, as they comment on and display their communicative competencies in a second language, may appropriate particular sociolinguistic identities (see, for example, Cekaite 2007; Cekaite and Evaldsson 2008; He 2002; Slotte-Lüttge, Pörn and Sahlström 2013). Moreover, we are interested in the ways children, as they accumulate a record of metasociolinguistic stances, act upon and creatively appropriate the often incongruous, sociocultural and linguistic expectations and constraints they encounter in multiethnic settings.

Methodologies for studying children's peer-language socialization

This study draws on methods used within peer-language socialization research (Goodwin and Kyratzis 2012), combining multi-sited ethnography with methodologies for studying talk-in-interaction. The ethnographic work was carried out by the second author (Sahlström) and his research team in Finland (particularly by Hummelstedt 2010). Data draw on ethnographic observations and video recordings of eight focal children's everyday peer interactions in the classroom and on the playground in two urban primary school settings in Finland and Sweden.

The first ethnographic fieldwork was carried out during one semester at a Swedish-medium preschool in Finland when the focal girl, Sara, was seven years old. The second fieldwork was carried out one-and-a-half years later at a different Swedish-language school setting in Sweden, when Sara was eight-and-a-half years old and her family just had moved there. The multi-sited fieldwork provided ethnographic knowledge about the various language, gender and ethnic arrangements across the two different school settings. To obtain information about the children's everyday interactional practices in the two different settings, the researcher spent considerable time observing classroom and peer group activities. Both instances of fieldwork granted access to recording instances of Sara's repeated performances in peer-language alternation practices (between Swedish and Finnish), performed at a high pace at places outside the teachers' supervision.

Video recordings made visible the different forms of features (language, gesture and other symbolic and cultural resources) through which the children organized their participation in the midst of their peer interaction (cf. Goodwin and Kyratzis 2012). The conversation analysis (CA) (cf. Goodwin 2000; Schegloff 2007) attention to how talk is sequentially organized – at a level at which participants are understood as agents actively engaged in procedures for organizing participation and producing a taken-for-granted order in the midst of talk – was critical to the analysis. The methodological approach (ethnography and CA) is combined here with Goffman's (1981b) notion of participation and footing, as developed by C. Goodwin and M. H. Goodwin (2004). We use Goffman's notion of footing to make visible the alignments speakers take up toward themselves and others and the performed actions, demonstrating the complex web of projected sociolinguistic stances displayed toward the normatively defined codes. More specifically, we use the concept of metasociolinguistic stance to examine an immigrant child's emerging peer group participation and appropriation of a social (bilingual) identity in trajectories of language alternation practices across two linguistic communities. In so doing, we rely on Jaffe's (2009: 10) formulation of how to explore the appropriation of social identity and production of ideology in children's stance taking as "the inventory of footings taken in the course of communication."

Attending a Swedish preschool class in Finland

The first set of data was collected when the focal child, Sara, was a newcomer in a Swedish-medium preschool class (a one-year transitory education from kindergarten to first grade) in the Finnish-dominated Helsinki metropolitan area in Finland.[1] Sara, who was born in Finland to parents who were refugees from Rwanda, spent her first years in Finland in a part of the country where Swedish is the dominant language. Because of this, Sara spoke mainly Swedish, and some English, with her parents. Sara spoke almost only Swedish with her siblings, while the parents spoke Kinyarwanda, English or French to each other. When moving to Helsinki, where Finnish dominates, the family continued to rely on Swedish in their contacts with childcare and education, and placed their children, including Sara, in Swedish-medium childcare and education. In this preschool context, Sara's multilingual background differed radically from that of the other children, who were mainly Swedish–Finnish bilingual, meaning that most of the children were competent speakers of at least Swedish and Finnish.

As a consequence of the Finnish-dominated language context in Finland, there was an explicit emphasis among the teachers in the Swedish-medium preschool class that Sara attended to support the children's use of Swedish. According to the teachers, Swedish was regarded as the weaker language for many of the children. Teachers used Swedish in and outside classroom activities. The languages used among the children in the preschool class shifted, depending on situation and social constellations. All children with Swedish–Finnish bilingual backgrounds code-switched on and off to Finnish in the preschool class. Some used Finnish as their common language in peer group interactions, and almost all of them code-switched between Swedish and Finnish, using (certain) lexical terms from Finnish. Thus, language competence in both Swedish and Finnish was expected among the children in peer group interactions, despite the fact that Finnish had not yet been taught as a school subject.

The above description of the ways Sara's multilingual background differed from the other children's Swedish–Finnish bilingual competencies, along with the language ideology at the preschool, is needed in order to keep track of the sociolinguistic features oriented to by the studied children in the subsequent analysis. We will demonstrate that the children themselves, in their metasociolinguistic stances, are oriented to bilingualism as a central feature of peer group participation as well as adhering to the dominant monolingual ideology of the preschool context. We hope the reader's attention to and understanding of the ways the children navigate between doing being bilingual and the normatively defined monolingual code of speaking Swedish is supported rather than predetermined by the information provided.

Contesting linguistic expertise and claiming epistemic authority

In line with Jaffe (2009), as stated above, we understand displays of attitude and positions in relation to language hierarchies and ideologies as metasociolinguistic. Affective and epistemic stances are both socially situated and mutually exclusive resources through which the children evaluate themselves and others, lay claim to identities and establish authority in relation to sociolinguistic aspects. Prior research in similar educational settings to the one focused on in the first data collection (i.e., a Swedish-medium school in a Finnish-dominated area) has shown children's orientation to a monolingual Swedish norm in the classroom, where the speaking of Finnish is frowned upon by both teachers and children (Slotte-Lüttge 2005). In the forthcoming analysis we will focus on the sociolinguistic resources the focal child and her interlocutors rely upon for taking up metasociolinguistic stances in respect to knowing Finnish in peer-language alternation practices. In line with Kärkkäinen (2006: 75), we define epistemic stance as "marking the degree of commitment to what one is saying, or marking attitudes toward knowledge." Moreover, as will be shown, the epistemic stances taken toward sociolinguistic matters are not "affectively neutral" (Jaffe 2009: 3).

The selected transcripts demonstrate a common feature of the entire ethnographic material, in which there are a large number of instances when the children commented and topicalized epistemic claims in relation to language proficiency in Finnish and English (cf. Sahlström 2011; Slotte-Lüttge, Pörn and Sahlström 2013). For example, Sahlström (2011) has shown how the same focal child, Sara, takes part in a number of informal peer events related to learning English, with epistemic topicalization as a salient feature. In addition, Slotte-Lüttge, Pörn and Sahlström (2013) have also demonstrated how Sara learns how to use the Finnish word **tähti** ("star") over the course of a few days, including many instances of topicalizaton of epistemic claims in relation to Finnish. Hence, the linguistic features shown in the selected excerpts can be viewed as examples of recurring practices among the children, whereby metasociolinguistic stance is not only implied and oriented to, but is also made explicit and topicalized in respect to knowing Finnish (cf. Jaffe 2009).

The first excerpt draws on an exchange that emerged from a peer group interaction between Sara and her classmates as the children were standing in line outside, waiting to enter the dining hall. In what follows, one of the boys, Janne, first comments on Sara's social conduct (lines 2–3) and then begins to criticize her bodily appearance. This is followed by an exchange of turns on Sara's assumed mastery of Finnish (lines 7–9). In the transcripts, words in Finnish are shown in bold, in both the original and the English translation. For other transcript issues, please refer to the transcription key at the end of the chapter.

Ex. 1: Contesting linguistic expertise and claiming epistemic authority

1.	Sara:	ö-ö: [:h*u-u: :h*
2.	Janne:	[vafö du (.) **seuraa** vet du ve- du
		[*why are you **following** you know you-*
3.		du ka- kallas i:so nenä
		*you're called **big nose***
		(1.6)
4.	Janne:	huhuh
		(1.5)
5.	Janne:	<**iso nenä**>
		<***big nose***>
6.	Sara:	du e själv
		no you are
7.	Janne:	du vet int va de betydä: e[des
		you don't know what it means e[ven

8.	Sara:	[jå-å stor näsa
		[*ye-eh big nose*
9.	Janne:	m ja:
		m ye:s
		(1.2)
10.	Janne:	öhehe (.) **ISO NENÄ** (.) ja-
		*uhhuh (.) **BIG NOSE** (.) yes-*
11.	Janne:	[((looks at teacher))
12.	Teacher:	[((comes out))

In the above excerpt, claimed and contested epistemic authority in relation to 'knowing Finnish' are important resources for asserting powerful positions and strengthening within-group alignments of more and less proficient Finnish language users. As demonstrated, Janne code-switches on line 2 from Swedish to Finnish, using the word **seuraa** ("follow"), in the midst of his accusatory question to Sara. This is followed by the derogatory expression "you're called **iso nenä**" ("big nose"), with only the derogatory part in Finnish. The insult receives no response. Following a brief pause, Janne laughs and then recycles and intensifies the insult (line 5). The playful and affective framing makes it difficult for Sara to make a counter-attack, as this would put her in a position of acting as someone who insists on taking the racial insult seriously (Goodwin 1990). The emotionally charged negative category depiction within which the actions and physical demeanor of Sara are denigrated makes inferentially available a more general reference to her ethnic identity as deviant (Evaldsson 2005). In what follows, Sara responds with a code-switched counter, effectively turning the insult back on Janne. In doing so, she manages to strengthen her position and also effectively attempts to refuse the use of "**iso nenä**" as a resource for mobilizing a racial categorization.

Sara's counter-move leads to an escalation and is met by another counter from Janne, "you don't know what it means **even**," on line 7, in which he code-switches **edes** ("**even**") to Finnish. Line 7 could possibly be understood as either intensifying the moral and affective content of the accusation (i.e. "big nose" as a racial insult) or providing a shift in the inferred negative category depiction of Sara's limited language proficiency in Finnish. In contesting this double-edged affective and epistemic claim, Sara displays her orientation to the upgraded insult as mainly related to her mastery of Finnish. In overlap with Janne, Sara orients to the propositional content of his prior insult, disclaiming "jå-å" ("ye-eh") on line 8, the authoritative epistemic stance taken toward her limited linguistic competence. Through recycling the lexical format in Swedish, Sara manages to demonstrate her understanding and linguistic knowledge of the Finnish words **iso nenä**. Simultaneously, her notably lowered voice and averted face show evidence of her emotional state concerning the pejorative racialized person description as being humiliating.

The sequentially accomplished unfolding of the events through which Janne forces Sara to, in a stepwise fashion, articulate in Swedish the code-switched negative person descriptor in public displays her subordinate and emotionally vulnerable position in the bilingual peer group. Meanwhile, Janne's recycled insulting indexes his primary right to assess her linguistic competence in Finnish, thus positioning himself as a bilingual Finnish–Swedish expert (cf. Raymond and Heritage 2006, on epistemic authority) while distinguishing himself from the immigrant 'other.' Identity work is thus accomplished, directly via epistemic authority and subordination, as well as by the affective stances taken toward the epistemic claims made. While bilingual expertise emerges as the salient, oriented-to category, it is evident that the evaluations of Sara's different language and ethnic background are a resource for social differentiation and boundary making. The two children's different epistemic rights to assess what counts as appropriate linguistic competence highlights Sara's emotionally vulnerable position and the difficulties inherent in an 'immigrant girl' making claims about knowing Finnish in this bilingual Finnish–Swedish peer group context.

Probing epistemic authority and displaying bilingual expertise

As will be further shown, Sara often code-switches to Finnish and tries to solicit the other children to use Finnish in everyday peer interactions, thereby attempting to change her participation status in the bilingual Finnish–Swedish peer group. In our next excerpt, she is engaged in playing a card game with another girl, Hanna. While Hanna orients to playing the game as their joint activity, Sara makes several attempts to comment on and topicalize her code-switched use of Finnish lexical terms. The ensuing topicalization of the Finnish word **vahaa** ("**wax**") in Excerpt 2 on line 2 can be interpreted as a metasociolinguistic stance taken with respect to the language hierarchies at play within the particular bilingual peer group. As will be demonstrated, the probing of what counts as appropriate Finnish terms provides resources for Sara to change her subordinate participation status in the bilingual group. Moreover, the meta-commentaries serve as a way of locating language as a valuable object for teaching and learning in peer group interaction, and are not related to any aspect of the formal teaching of Finnish as a second language in the school setting.

Ex. 2: Probing epistemic authority and displaying bilingual expertise

1.	Hanna:	då blandar vi igen dom (.) dom igen så här
		then let's mix again them (.) them again like this
2.	Sara:	ja hata att blanda (0.4) mä vaHaa blanda
		I hate to mix (0.4) I *wAx mix

		(1.4)
3.	Hanna:	nå (.) å sen gå[r du
		well (.) and then y[ou go
4.	Sara:	[vet du va e (.) va e **vahaa**
		[*do you know what's (.) what's **wax***
5.	Hanna:	ja by- (.) ja byter [den här
		I cha- (.) I change [this one
6.	Sara:	[Hanna va e **vahaa**
		[*Hanna what's **wax***
7.	Hanna:	ja byter nu färg (.) vicken färg byter du
		I change now colour (.) what colour do you change
8.	Sara:	ja e: ja kan va gul (.) **eiku** nää ja kan va blå
		*I am: I can be yellow (.) **or no** I can be blue*
9.	Hanna:	vi kan göra [(xx)
		we can do [(xx)
10.	Sara:	[Hanna (.) va e- vet du va e **vahaa** på finska
		[*Hanna (.) what's- do you know what's **to wax** in Finnish*
11.	Hanna:	nå
		what
12.	Sara:	hata
		to hate
		(1.5)

On line 2, Sara code-switches to Finnish but does not get the Finnish word right, as she confuses the Finnish word **vahaa** ("**wax**") with **vihaa** ("**hate**"). However, the use of the particular word is clearly audible as an attempt at speaking Finnish. Hanna does not respond to this at all and continues with the card game. On line 4, Sara makes a shift in footing and takes on a metasociolinguistic stance toward the code-switched word by asking what **vahaa** means. Hanna again ignores the question, and Sara also goes along with this at first. Then, she recycles the question on line 10, now probing an epistemic authority in relation to whether Hanna knows what **vahaa** means. Here she receives a response, "what" from Hanna (line 11).

Sara's code-switching to Finnish and the authoritative epistemic stance taken toward the sociolinguistically salient code aligns with the bilingual language competence displayed by the other Swedish–Finnish speaking children in this peer group. However, this alignment also restricts the other girl's possible stance taking, as lexical terms like *wax* and *hate* are presumed to be known by the members of the bilingual peer group. Both Sara and Hanna have mutual access to the well-established and oriented-to fact that Hanna is fully proficient in Finnish, and that she can be expected to know what the word **vahaa** means in Finnish. Hence, Sara's unusual use of the lexical item **vahaa** does not, in this context, necessarily index linguistic incompetence. Rather, it may signal linguistic expertise extending beyond the common use of the Finnish words. It is against this background that Hanna's initial ignoring of the question can be understood. The question is reformulated on line 10, from "what's" to "do you know what". Hanna's response "nå" ("what") conveys that Sara is assumed to have epistemic authority in relation to the question and will provide the answer in the next turn. In the current language situation, this authority is not related to the commonly used epistemic claims in relation to the meaning of **vahaa**. Rather, it orients to Sara's question as a known-answer question, whereby the expected answer is the uncovering of a joke or riddle. In responding with "nå" ("what") on line 11, Hanna, who is fluent in Finnish, allows Sara to claim valued linguistic expertise in Finnish, a language presumed to be known by members of the bilingual Finnish–Swedish community.

In relation to how Sara, in her initial formulation, construes the Finnish word **vahaa** as learnable, it is interesting to note that it is difficult for a novice and less proficient speaker like Sara to ask questions about lexical terms. The fact that the common assumption is that the Finnish language is expected to be known transforms questions about lexical terms into known-answer questions. In the above excerpt, the metasociolinguistic stances taken by and attributed to Sara in respect of her use of Finnish are construed in different ways. First, competence in Finnish is oriented to as valuable, as indicated by Sara's code change on line 2 and the ensuing interaction. Second, it is oriented to as expected knowledge, as indicated by Hanna's responses, particularly on line 11. Third, as a consequence of the first two, learning Finnish is construed as valued and taken for granted. Thus, a difficulty for Sara in taking up a position as learner of Finnish emerges in this educational peer-learning setting. Both Excerpts 1 and 2 demonstrate how the children in the bilingual peer group learn how to navigate between multiple positions, depicting themselves and the other children as either monolingual or bilingual (Cekaite and Evaldsson 2008). Hence, metasociolinguistic stance taking allows the children to position themselves as language novices or experts, monolingual or bilingual speakers, and good or bad friends.

In transition to a monolingual Swedish school in Sweden

A year after the first data-collection period, Sara moved with her family from Finland to Sweden. The second data set was therefore collected at a Swedish school in a multiethnic suburban area, which Sara attended after her family's transition to Sweden. At the time of the second data collection, with one full week of intensive video recordings at its core, Sara has attended the school in Sweden for approximately three months. Sara has grown since the previous excerpts, from seven years old in Excerpts 1 and 2 to eight-and-a-half in Excerpts 3 and 4.

The Swedish school educational policy promotes immigrant children's mastery of the official Swedish language of the nation, government, administration and school. The great emphasis on Swedish in Swedish educational settings is situated within wider societal and political processes that formulate integration as an issue of language competence, that is, as 'proper' mastery of the majority language. Independent of children's ethnic and linguistic backgrounds, classroom instructions are exclusively given in the majority language – Swedish – and there is an explicit emphasis among teachers to support immigrant children's use of Swedish. In addition, all students with immigrant backgrounds are entitled to supplementary instructions in their home language (Sw. *modersmålsundervisning*) for a couple of hours a week. However, the integration of home-language classes is still problematic.

The children in focus in the following excerpts attended the same school class as Sara, with eighteen children (ten boys and eight girls) aged 8–9 years with diverse ethnic backgrounds (mainly from the Middle East and Finland). Finnish also constituted one of the home language classes at the school. A majority of the children with immigrant backgrounds were fluent Swedish speakers; most had spent almost their whole life in Sweden (5–6 years), except Sara, who had recently arrived from Finland. Sara's Rwandan background did not make her stand out in the same way at the Swedish school as at the Finnish one, where she was one of very few students with a non-European background. Instead, as the analysis below will show, the very same resource – proficiency in Finnish – which was questioned as insufficient in the Finnish context, will turn out to be a valuable resource for claiming exclusivity in the multiethnic Swedish peer group.

Affiliative epistemic stances and bilingual knowledge displays

For the children in the multiethnic peer group, Swedish constituted a kind of lingua franca in the school-yard. As noted, the children's use of Swedish as an in-group peer language also existed in a wider school context of ethnic stratification and division, where it was obligatory for pupils to speak Swedish in classrooms, regardless of their ethnic background (Cekaite and Evaldsson 2008). However, children in multilingual peer groups are not only involved in the normatively preferred monolingual language use of Swedish (cf. Evaldsson 2005; Evaldsson and Cekaite 2010). As we will demonstrate, Sara recurrently initiated and engaged in language alternation practices in which she codeswitched to Finnish as a common language in interactions with classmates with Finnish language backgrounds. Intriguingly, then, a child with an immigrant background like Sara may exploit institutionalized monolingual norms of language use to negotiate alignments and thereby position herself as a bilingual (i.e. Swedish–Finnish) speaker.

When we meet Sara in her new school context she is with the peer group of children (Carola, Kristoffer, Anna, Lina), who are walking side by side from a theater performance back to school. At the beginning of the excerpt, Kristoffer (line 1) begins to ask Sara whether she has seen something. This is cut off and then followed by a code-switch to Finnish, in which he asks Sara about the fieldworker. Sara responds in Finnish, **se on suomalainen** (line 2), informing him that the fieldworker **"is Finnish."**

Ex. 3a: Affiliative epistemic stances and bilingual knowledge displays

1.	Kristoffer:	ha du (.) se- **lähteekse huomenna jo** (.) **se**
		have you (.) se- is she leaving tomorrow already (.) that
2.	Sara:	**se on suomalainen**
		she is Finnish

In Excerpt 3a, some aspects are similar to the previous peer group situation at the Swedish-medium school in Finland, when Sara was accused of having a big nose. She is approached by a boy, who begins speaking to her in Swedish and then code-switches to Finnish (line 1). However, here the similarities end.

First (line 1), the code-switch from Swedish to Finnish is used by Kristoffer to affiliate with Sara, by including her in a bilingual community of Swedish–Finnish speakers, of which Kristoffer also is a member. The code-switched turn on line 1 is also subversive and designed to exclude the fieldworker, assuming her and the overhearers' lack of language competence in Finnish. This is accomplished through the cut-off, noticeably ending the initial unit, through the continuation of the turn in Finnish, and through its content, commenting on the fieldworker in the third person. Sara's response also displays her orientation to the subversive nature of the code-switch as she corrects Kristoffer, telling him of the fieldworker's language competence (**"she is Finnish"**) on line 2. She thus indexes her right to assess the language used by the fieldworker and thereby positions herself as a competent bilingual Swedish–Finnish speaker. The choice of code established by Sara in her response in Finnish also provides resources for displaying an affiliative metasociolinguistic stance toward both herself and Janne as competent speakers of Finnish.

Following Excerpt 3a, Sara and Kristoffer continue to exchange a few turns in Finnish, in which they expand on the issue of both of them being part of the research project. Toward the end of their dialogue, Sara begins to say **mut**, (**"but"**) in Finnish (Excerpt 3b, line 3), followed by a hesitation, **ää**, and a 2.9-second silence. She then code-switches back to Swedish. As shown in Excerpt 3b, Sara's hesitant move and code-switching to Swedish opens up a change in footing toward both the language used and Sara's and Kristoffer's respective Finnish language knowledge. The metasociolinguistic stance taking is initiated (line 6) by a girl in the peer group, Carola, who has taken notice of Sara and Kristoffer's language choice.

Ex. 3b: Affiliative epistemic stances and bilingual knowledge displays

3.	Sara:	mut ää (2.9) me int- när ja ska hem de ska int filma
		but uh (2.9) but no- when I go home they don't film
4.		mig då när jag är hemma (.) hela tiden.
		me when I am home (.) all the time.
5.		(2.0)
6.	Carola:	talar ni finska med varandra
		do you speak Finnish with each other
7.	Sara:	a:
		yeah:
8.		(4.7)
9.	Carola:	förstår ni va ni säger
		do you understand what you say
10.	Sara:	[jå
		[*yes*
11.	Kristoffer:	[ekse tienny vai
		[*didn't she know or*
12.	Sara:	mitä
		what
13.	Kristoffer:	no vaan et me puhutaan suomee
		well just that we speak Finnish
14.	Sara:	joo kyl mä tiesin että sä osaat puhuu suomee
		yeah she knew yeah that you can speak Finnish

When Carola asks Sara and Kristoffer if they "speak Finnish" on line 6, she also comments on and topicalizes their use of Finnish as a separate and different language. Through the evaluative stance taken toward the two children's use of Finnish, Carola also casts the children in the peer group as belonging to contrastive categories of Finnish-speaking and Swedish-speaking children. Sara can be seen to confirm the claimed bilingual identity as she immediately responds with "yeah" (line 7). Following an extended silence, Carola then recycles her evaluative stance questioning the children's understanding of what they say (line 9). Thereby she also displays her own lack of knowledge about Finnish, as well as evaluates the language used as almost incomprehensible, meaning that the children themselves might not even know how to speak it. This in turn provides a warrant for Sara and Kristoffer to change the topic into their language proficiency in Finnish.

The affective stance taken toward the two children's language choice and competence is firmly responded to, with "yes" by Sara (line 10). In overlap, Kristoffer then code-switches to Finnish and makes a metalinguistic comment on their language choice, asking Sara whether she (Carola) did not know about their knowledge of Finnish (line 11). In what follows, Sara code-switches to Finnish as well (line 12). The language alternation is not noticed or topicalized by the two children, who in this particular instance, through their epistemic and affective stances toward Finnish, collaboratively constitute themselves as 'bilingual peers.' Following a repair initiation, **mitä** ("**what**"), by Sara on line 12 and the ensuing repair by Kristoffer on line 13, Sara makes an epistemic claim and affectively complex account that she (probably referring to Carola) knew that Kristoffer knows Finnish (line 14). In so doing, the two children manage to navigate a form of bilingual self-identification that distinguishes them from the other children and indexes shared cultural experiences.

As can be noted in Excerpts 3a and 3b, the children's use of, as well as the metastances taken toward knowing, Finnish is distinctly different from Excerpts 1 and 2. In the new Swedish school context, knowing how to speak Finnish is construed as a rare and valued resource among the children in the multiethnic peer group. On lines 1 and 11, the knowledge of Finnish even enables Kristoffer to use it in subversive ways to speak about those present in the third person, displaying a metasociolinguistic stance toward the language used that draws social boundaries concerning the others, who are not assumed to understand Finnish. For Sara and Kristoffer, knowing Finnish is explicitly relied upon for establishing and strengthening in-group social bonds while laying claim to shared bilingual identities and indexing shared cultural feelings of being competent bilinguals in Finnish (despite Sara having some trouble with the morpho-syntax).

The contradictory attitudes displayed toward Sara's use of Finnish in the two different peer group contexts, as demonstrated through her move from Finland to Sweden, provide different resources for shifting the expert–novice configuration in the peer group (cf. Blum-Kulka and Snow 2004: 299). In Finland, Sara was often cast as a linguistic novice by the other children in the bilingual peer group, but in Sweden her participation status in the multilingual peer group has gradually changed from being cast as a language novice to being more of a bilingual expert.

*Solidifying bilingual expertise and expanding
the scope of knowing Finnish*

Next, we will analyze how Sara in this new context orients to and relies on Finnish as something to be taught, and learned, rather than as something expected to be already known, and how the shifting epistemic stance provides for the strengthening of bilingual peer group identities and affiliations. These two aspects will be discussed in Excerpts 4 and 5 below. Both excerpts follow the discussion in Excerpts 3a and 3b.

In Excerpt 4, Sara asks Kristoffer why he does not attend home-language instruction in Finnish, on line 20. In what follows, she tries to persuade him in a stepwise fashion to attend the home language instruction class, mentioning first the attendance of another child, Tom (line 22), and then the fact that Kristoffer would have a Finnish teacher. For her third and final argument she code-switches to Finnish, arguing that by attending, Kristoffer could learn literally anything (line 26). The epistemic stance taken situates her in a teaching position, indexing her epistemic authority relative to her co-participants, who are thus positioned as language learners.

Ex. 4: Solidifying bilingual expertise and expanding the scope of Finnish

20.	Sara:	me:n vafför går du inte på hemspråk (.) på finska (.) hemspråk
		but why don't you go to home language (.) in Finnish (.) home language
21.		(2.6)
22.	Sara:	Tom går också där (.) ja går också
		Tom goes there too (.) I go too
23.		(2.4)
24.	Sara:	å sen du får en finskalärare
		and then you'll get a Finnish teacher
25.		(2.6)
26.	Sara:	sä voit oppii ihan mitä (.) vaan
		you can learn whatever you w- (.) want
27.		(3.0)
28.	Kristoffer:	aattelin et jos mä alkaan tuolla
		what if I started there
29.	Sara:	missä
		where
30.	Kristoffer:	no tuolla: (0.6) hemspråketissa sä ja Tom menee
		well there (0.6) the home language (where) you and Tom go
31.	Sara:	aha:
		oh
32.		(1.5)

In Excerpt 4, the metasociolinguistic stances taken by Sara and the epistemic authority displayed through this stance construe knowing and using Finnish as something valued, and as something one can be taught. Further, the claims she makes to knowing how to learn Finnish characterize her as a recognized and competent speaker of Finnish as her home language. Kristoffer, whose speaking of Finnish in part has provided Sara with the communicative resources for warranting her authoritative claims, responds to her proposal only after a prolonged silence on line 28. His response is also in Finnish, displaying a collective alignment toward the projected stance taken by Sara and exploiting the possibility of his actually beginning the class in the near future. The hypothetical scenario displayed in his response is produced in a grammatically well-formed utterance, but it seems problematic for Sara to align with. She makes a request for clarification of **tuolla** ("there") through the use of the contrastive **missä** ("where") (line 29). In his expansion, Kristoffer has some problems with the production of the Swedish word "hemspråk" ("home language"). It is preceded by hesitation and a pause, finally using the Swedish word but mixing it with some grammatical and phonological features from Finnish: **hemspråketissa**. In these last five turns, we can see that the two children build up collaborative and positive stances toward both learning Finnish in school and themselves as competent speakers of Finnish.

Next (not included as excerpts) Sara and Kristoffer continue their discussion, with Sara alternating between Finnish and Swedish, and Kristoffer using Finnish. The same girl, Carola, again comments on their use of Finnish, exclaiming "va häftit de e" ("it's so cool"). The way Carola takes notice of the two children's use of Finnish adds to the construal of their linguistic expertise in Finnish as valued, but exotic, among the children in this particular multilingual peer-language community. As demonstrated in Excerpts 3b and 4, the two children distinguish themselves from the other children and lay claim to a particular bilingual identity, as well as evaluating others' claims and statuses through the use of an in-group language (Finnish). This stands in contrast to the status of Finnish in the Swedish school setting in Finland, where Finnish was valued but was expected to be known by the children in the bilingual peer group and was therefore not exclusive. In the Finnish setting, Sara's limited proficiency in Finnish renders her at risk of being excluded (as shown in Excerpts 1 and 2). In Sweden, her position in the peer group has changed, though she is still clearly a novice speaker of Finnish, but in this new sociolinguistic setting even her limited proficiency in Finnish is sufficient to warrant her claims of linguistic expertise.

Concluding discussion: cumulative stance taking and learning how to use language across linguistic communities

As we have demonstrated, the ways in which the accumulated record of metasociolinguistic stances taken by and attributed to Sara changes her position in the peer groups and eventually indexes a bilingual identity can be approached from a language socialization perspective. In analyzing what Du Bois (2007: 139–141) describes as "the dialogic and intersubjective dimensions of stance," we have highlighted the complex interplay of "how social actors jointly enact stance, and the mediating frameworks of linguistic structure and sociocultural value they invoke in doing so." As demonstrated, the power hierarchies and values associated with the different linguistic forms in the Swedish-medium preschool context in Finland provide sociolinguistic resources for the children to display their rights to assess Sara's linguistic competence and position themselves as bilingual Finnish–Swedish experts. While bilingual expertise emerges as the salient, oriented-to category among the children in both linguistic communities, it is evident that the evaluations of Sara's language choice, knowledge and competence are resources for identity-making, including realignments and hierarchies, within the different peer group contexts (cf. Evaldsson and Cekaite 2010; Kyratzis 2010). The shifting positions and sometimes contradictory moves made by Sara from bilingual novice to expert are locally accomplished and mobilized interactionally via epistemic authority and subordination, and through the affective and moral stances toward the claims made in respect to her peers.

As we can see, when Sara is in Finland she displays a subordinate and emotionally vulnerable position in the bilingual peer group when language choice and linguistic competence in Finnish are enacted. But when she moves to Sweden, she relies on knowing Finnish for strengthening in-group social bonds with and establishing boundaries concerning the other children in the multilingual peer group, thus positioning herself as a competent bilingual speaker. Sara's shifting participation, reactions and responses to language choice, peer group practices and language policies across linguistic communities underscore the need to account for the agency of individual children and their trajectories of language learning (cf. Garrett and Baquedano-López 2002).

Interestingly, bilingual expertise in Finnish is valued in both peer group contexts (in Finland and in Sweden), while it has marginal status among the adults in both Swedish-medium school settings. However, the fact that Swedish–Finnish bilingualism is more or less taken for granted in the bilingual Swedish–Finnish peer group at the Swedish-medium school in Finland makes it paradoxically hard for a bilingual novice like Sara to learn how to use Finnish in this very setting. The children in the bilingual Swedish–Finnish peer group do not orient to Finnish as a salient language to be learned. Instead, they treat it as something that should already be known and not spoken in school. In the Swedish monolingual school context, the home-language instruction and the children's lack of situated expectations of linguistic expertise in Finnish instead provide a fertile ground for Sara to orient to Finnish as something to be taught and learned, as grounds for claiming linguistic expertise. The evidence presented here demonstrates the varying degrees of access and support that a language learner may experience from others across linguistic communities of practice, and that processes of language socialization are not necessarily linear, entailing consistent progress (Garrett 2007; Schieffelin and Kulick 2004).

As has been demonstrated, metasociolinguistic stance taking – epistemic, affective, moral – in relation to 'knowing Finnish' is an important communicative resource that is used for various practical purposes in processes of peer-language socialization. Metalinguistic stance taking is displayed and relied upon for staging linguistic expertise, claiming authority and displaying subordination, constituting social organization and hierarchies, displaying emotional orientations, establishing social bonds and boundaries, and indexing in- and out-group identities. Through affective and epistemic stances taken toward normatively defined codes, the children constitute themselves as more and less proficient bilingual Swedish–Finnish language users. In so doing, they reorganize social configurations of novice–expert within the peer group (Blum-Kulka and Snow 2004). As demonstrated, the focal child, Sara, recurrently initiated and engaged in language alternation practices in which she code-switched to Finnish as a valued language in interactions with peers with Finnish language backgrounds. Sara's agency as a language learner, displayed in her persistent attempts at learning to use Finnish and her desire to be a competent bilingual Swedish–Finnish speaker, in itself is a crucial resource for the "more durable stance orientations in the individual" child (cf. Jaffe 2009: 20).

What has been described in this chapter, then, is how a learner's emerging communicative and linguistic competence in Finnish is collectively assembled through the peer group's engagement with sociolinguistic forms potentially available in this bilingual community. As noted, Sara's capacity for linguistic creativity and improvisation as well as her persistent attempts to learn to use Finnish, along with the other children's resistance and even glorification of this linguistic code, demonstrate the agency of language learners. Analyzing trajectories of language alternation practices across peer groupings and linguistic communities, we argue, illuminates how this form of agentive language-learning work is ideologically mediated and consequential for the ways children orient to and appropriate sociolinguistic identities in the bilingual social world they inhabit, and how they use linguistic and social actions within it.

TRANSCRIPTION CONVENTIONS

The transcription format used is a simplified version of the one used in CA.

:	prolonged syllable
[ ]	overlapping utterances
?	rising terminal intonation
.	falling terminal intonation
↑	rising pitch
°°	speech in low volume
YES	speech in capitals louder than surrounding speech
hh	laughter
=	latching between utterances
-	abrupt cut-off
(.)	micropause (i.e., shorter than 0.5s)
(2)	numbers in single parentheses represent pauses in seconds
(())	description of non-speech activity
(xx)	inaudible word
mitä	code-switch into Finnish
what	translation into English

The English translations in italics are as close as possible to the Swedish and Finnish verbatim records. All names are fictional.

Acknowledgments

Financial support from the Knut and Alice Wallenberg Foundation, the Bank of Sweden Tercentenary Foundation, the Swedish Research Council, and the Swedish Cultural Foundation in Finland is gratefully acknowledged. We thank the editors for their invaluable comments on an earlier draft.

NOTES

1 In Finland, 5.5% of the inhabitants have Swedish as their first language, and there is a parallel school system, from childcare to university, for the two language groups.

9 "Say princess": the challenges and affordances of young Hebrew L2 novices' interaction with their peers

Shoshana Blum-Kulka and Naomi Gorbatt

Introduction

The goal of this chapter is to map the major steps in the linguistic and social experience of young immigrant children in Israeli preschools and kindergartens, with a specific focus on the contribution of peer interaction to the process. In Israel, as elsewhere, immigrant children may acquire the target language mainly from interaction with their peers at school. Yet there are only a handful of observational studies on second language learning by young children that provide evidence on the ways in which peer interaction promotes language learning (e.g., Tabors 1997; Grøver Aukrust 2004; Cekaite and Aronsson 2004, this volume). Adopting a socio-cultural perspective, the study follows the interactional failures and accomplishments of immigrant children during the first two years of their sojourn in preschool and/or kindergarten.

Language socialization

The language socialization theoretical perspective followed here views children as active agents in their socialization. Children learn language, pragmatic skills and culture through active participation in meaningful interactions with adults and other children (Corsaro 1985; Blum-Kulka and Snow 2002). The major focus of former studies of socialization has been on interaction with adults, from dyads to multi-party and intergenerational talk (Schieffelin and Ochs 1986; Blum-Kulka and Snow 2002). As of the late 1990s, a renewed interest emerged in the crucial role of peer interaction in the process of discursive socialization (Blum-Kulka and Snow 2004). From a learning theory perspective, second language socialization presents a prime case of situated learning. In Lave and Wenger's (1991) terms, the process involves moving from legitimate peripheral participation in the communities' activities to increasingly active participation. Our study was designed to provide support for the role of peer interaction in second language acquisition (SLA), as well as to follow longitudinally the development of the immigrant children's interactive (communicative) competencies and their uses for gaining cultural membership in the new peer culture.

Peer talk and pragmatic development in SLA

To become full members in their new communities of practice, immigrant children need to find ways to interact with their native peers, peer talk becoming a major resource for learning. In moving from peripheral participation in the communities' activities to increasingly active participation, they are aided by different forms of scaffolding performed by the more experienced members, including native and competent bilingual speakers. Gaining full communicative (or pragmatic) competence in a second language entails a range of social, linguistic and pragmatic skills, including social aspects of language use, knowledge of the conversational skills of turn-taking and dialogicity as well mastery of the discursive skills involved in the construction of well-formed texts of extended discourse, like stories and explanations (Grøver Aukrust 2004; Blum-Kulka, Huck-Taglicht and Avni 2004; Cekaite 2007; Zadunaisky Ehrlich and Blum-Kulka, this volume; Rydland, Grøver and Lawrence, this volume).

Our former work on peer interaction in the preschool with native Israeli children demonstrates that children's discursive skills (including conversational, argumentative, storytelling and explanatory skills) are strongly enhanced through daily play and talk with their peers (Blum-Kulka 2005a, 2004; Blum-Kulka, Huck-Taglicht and Avni 2004; Zadunaisky Ehrlich and Blum-Kulka, this volume). Evidence from the field of SLA in natural settings supports the claim that peer talk generates language learning (Tabors 1997; Tabors et al. 2000; Grøver Aukrust 2004; Cekaite 2007; Cekaite and Aronsson, this volume). Tabors (1997) documented the main phases in the acquisition of English by immigrant children and the way English learners use native peers as a source of lexical input; Cekaite and Aronsson (2004) demonstrate that reliance on joking and repetition among non-native peers with poor language skills is a rich source of sociability. Case study reports on young SLA learners document the help peers give in promoting L2 children's second language proficiency by providing adapted, simplified and corrective feedback and by offering young second language learners useful language forms (Huang and Hatch 1978) and language-structured activities (Wong Fillmore 1979) on which they can build further interactions and further learning.

Our findings strongly support the *crucial role of peer interaction in language socialization*. We argue that, to become full members in their new communities of practice, immigrant children need to become engaged in interaction with their native peers, with peer talk becoming a major resource for learning. Yet to be conversant with their native peers, immigrant children *need to have at least rudimentary communicative skills in L2*. To unveil the role of peer interaction in the process of bilingual language socialization, we conducted a longitudinal study that has followed closely a group of immigrant children, starting with their first entrance to a Hebrew-speaking educational institution and continuing for five consecutive years.

Method

The original sample comprised 32 children drawn from immigrant populations of children aged 3 to 7 at the onset of the study, entering preschool or kindergarten in Israel for the first time.[1] Criteria for inclusion in the sample included: (a) first entrance to a Hebrew-speaking school, regardless whether they were born in Israel or not,[2] and (b) being within the normal range of development.[3] Countries of origin included Russia (11), Ethiopia (9), France (9), Korea (1), the US (1) and Germany (1). Parental level of education ranged from a few years of schooling to higher education. Parents' professions included housewives, teachers, computer engineers, farmers and Ulpan (classes for learning Hebrew as a second language in Israel) students.

Observations

As is the custom in Israel, the sample children were immersed in Hebrew L1 preschool and kindergarten classrooms with no or a few (10% to 15%) other immigrant children, not necessarily from the same language background. The observational data[4] were collected during the first two years of the study, with two to four yearly observations for each child during different activity types in the school (free play, assembly time, meals): (a) child-focused audio and video recordings of target children wearing lapel microphones connected to a transmitter (with wireless microphones) and (b) setting-focused audio and video recordings of groups of target and other children identified as being engaged in joint play in various areas of the preschool. All recordings were complemented by field notes taken by the observer present.

Transcription

All data are transcribed in detail, following a modified version of CA conventions (see transcription conventions at the end of the chapter). The data analyzed in this chapter are drawn from ethnographic observations made during the first two years.

Major phases in young children's acquisition of Hebrew as L2

The children's progress in acquiring Hebrew as L2 and moving from peripheral to full participation in the school's social and academic activities can be captured as roughly falling into four main phases:

- the phase of innocence: monolingual chat;
- shock and silence: no communication;
- emergent L2: mainly non-verbal communication with some L2, preference for communication with adults;
- interactional accomplishments in Hebrew interlanguage (mostly communicative yet incomplete mastery of L2): peers as playmates and teachers.

These phases are roughly in line with previous studies of young immigrant children (Saville-Troike 1976; Tabors 1997). The four major phases in young immigrant children's experience in Hebrew-speaking preschool and kindergarten from our data include: (1) the phase of innocence during which the immigrant child continues speaking his or her mother tongue in school, failing to understand it does not 'work' in the new environment; (2) a period of shock and silence for weeks, months and sometimes over a year; (3) emergent mutual attempts at communication with very limited L2 linguistic resources and high reliance on non-verbal means; and (4) the use of basic Hebrew L2 interlanguage, including interactional accomplishments despite limited linguistic resources. Each of these phases offers the novice children a different set of challenges and scaffolds.

In demonstrating the dynamics of interaction at each phase, the emphasis in this chapter is on issues of communication: (1) With whom and to which communicative ends do the novices interact at different phases? (2) What is the nature of the interaction with teachers? Do teachers play a facilitative role? (3) When and how do peers come into play? Can we detect collaborative strategies unique to peer interaction that ease linguistic and socio-cultural socialization for young non-native children?

Age of innocence (a few weeks)

Monolingual young children seem to take it for granted that one language (their own) is the only language used for communication. Hence when confronted for the first time with a new, non-comprehensible language environment, their first reaction is to ignore the new reality and continue speaking their first language (Tabors 1997). Because our first round of observations started a few months into the school year (the time it took to obtain official and parental consent), we only rarely met children during their very first days in the preschool. We were lucky to capture this particular moment in one immigrant child's school life:

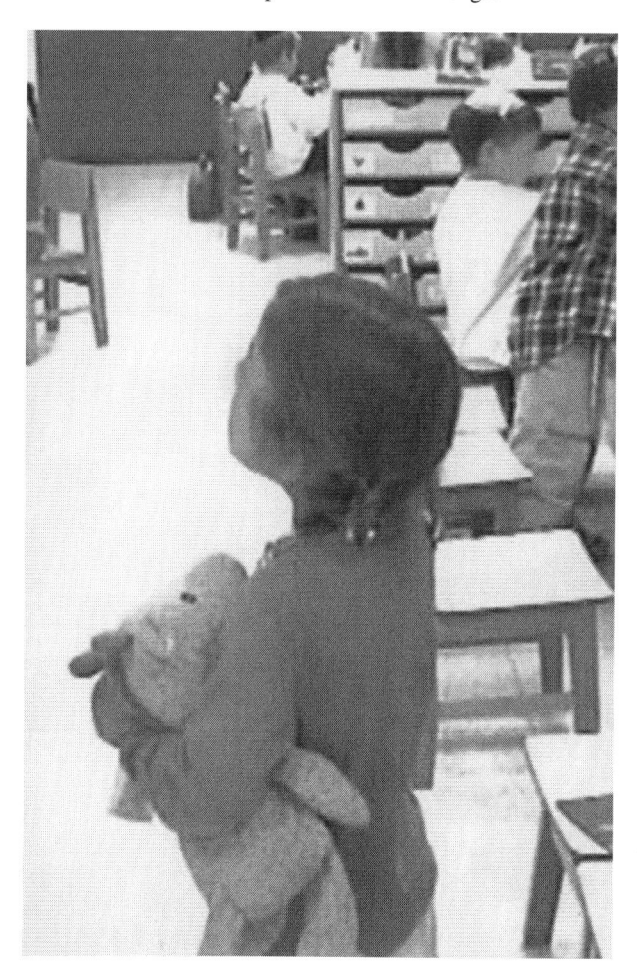

L2 novices' interactions: potentials and challenges 173

Figure 9.1 Sindy: what's going on here?

Sindy, a five-year-old German-speaking girl, who for weeks walked around her preschool chatting happily in German to her peers, teacher and toys alike (Figures 9.1 and 9.2). As the weeks passed, the repeated failure of all her communicative efforts, combined with the non-comprehensibility of the language around her, brought on the painful realization that 'her' German simply does not 'work' in the new environment. Her reaction was one of shock and silence. Her first attempts to communicate in the mother tongue, as for many other children, were followed by a very long phase of almost complete silence. Our field notes from a month after Sindy's arrival at school note: "If Sindy speaks it's only in single words in German she whispered to herself. Otherwise she

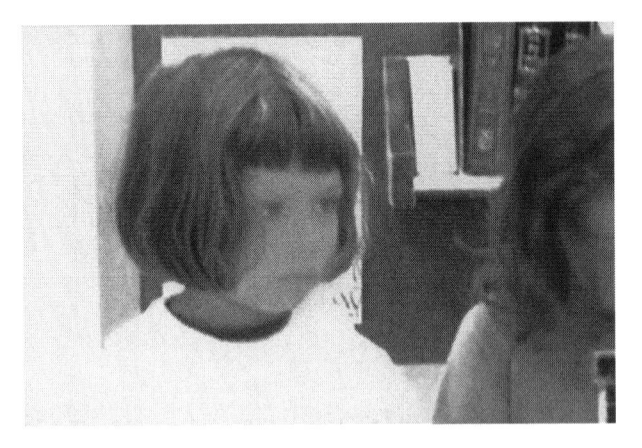

Figure 9.2 Sindy: what's going on here?

fell completely silent. She plays alone" (Naomi, 24 April 2006). Sindy's silent phase lasted seven-and-a-half months.

The 'silent' period: non-verbal interactional success and failure

Several observational studies have noted that once young immigrant children realize that their first language simply does not work in the new surroundings, they enter a period of shock and silence, ranging from eight weeks to two years. This pattern, alternatively called the "nonverbal period" (Tabors 1997), emerged in Greek (Tabors 1997), Korean (Meyer 1989) and Vietnamese (Clarke 1996) two- to six-year-old children acquiring English as L2 and American children acquiring French as L2 (Ervin-Tripp 1974). For the children in our sample, the period of silence lasted from six to twenty months.[5] In one extreme case, a French-speaking boy spent his first year in the kindergarten in almost complete silence, rejecting even attempts of communication from L1 peers in French and, according to his parents, at some point stopping speaking French for a few months at home as well. His first attempts to speak Hebrew with peers emerged only by the end of the second year, around June.

Less attention has been paid to children's attempts during this period to communicate with teachers and peers non-verbally or with extremely minimal linguistic means. Thus, while our observations generally confirm the viability of a relatively long L2 silent period, they also show (a) a rich repertoire of mainly non-verbal communicative strategies employed by the immigrant children in an attempt to establish contact and (b) a very high degree of individual variation in the use of such strategies. Thus the 'silent' period is far from being completely silent.

Figure 9.3 Interactional failures

Non-verbal communicative strategies

On entering a new language environment, young immigrant children are faced with the task of making sense of the world around them – entering a new school culture, meeting new teachers and new kids and, above all, learning a completely new language. Like children in traditional societies, much of the task is achieved more by doing than by saying. Rogoff argues that it is through *keen observation* of the adult world and *intensive participation* in its activities that children in traditional societies are socialized to become full members of their culture (Rogoff 2003). In a similar vein, the immigrant children we observed strive to move from peripheral to full participation in both peer and class activities. They strive to achieve these goals through a rich repertoire of early communicative strategies, using several semiotic resources for communication: direct gaze, or 'spectating' (Tabors 1997), body movement, prosody and single Hebrew words.

Spectating and touch

On one occasion, our camera caught two boys, one of them from our sample and the other a Hebrew L1 speaker, facing each other at the entrance to the preschool room. They looked directly into each other's eyes for several seconds, began to make funny faces at each other, laughed merrily and disengaged, without a word uttered. We observed scenes like the above in different participation structures: both L1 speakers and L2 learners as well as advanced L2 speakers ('veteran' immigrants) and new L2 learners. Notably, the children we studied varied to a great extent in their reaction to such initiations.

Some, like Genetu (Figure 9.3) resisted for many months all attempts at communication with teachers and peers alike. In Figure 9.3, six months after

Figure 9.4 Rough and tender

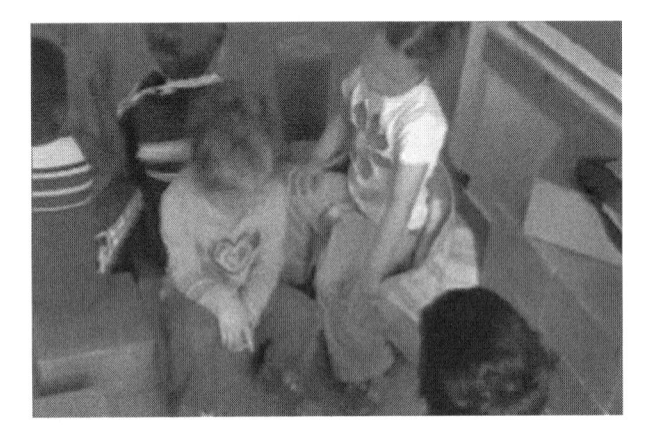

Figure 9.5 Rough and tender

entering the preschool, we see him still keeping his eyes cast down for long periods, resisting any attempt by the Ethiopian girl in front of him to even make eye contact. Thus despite her great eagerness, signaled by her body posture and gaze, and the fact that she speaks to him in Amharic, their shared first language, Genetu's resistance prevails.

Other immigrant children behave very differently during this period, investing great efforts to initiate non-verbal interaction with L1 peers. For example, our video captured a four-year-old immigrant girl (during her ninth month in school) moving, during one long wordless minute, from a rough game of pillow throwing (initiated by her) to a tender moment of reaching out her hand to a (native) boy (Figures 9.4 and 9.5).

L2 novices' interactions: potentials and challenges 177

Emergent L2: participating by doing and first verbal attempts at communication

The first indicators of 'comprehensible input' from the children's point of view are in doing, rather than saying. During Sindy's second month in school, she already followed the teacher's simple instructions for body movement ("hands up, on the shoulders on the head"), and six months later, her teacher reported that she seemed to understand all school routine instructions and was eager to carry them out. Yet she expressed her wishes only by pointing and nodding her head in agreement or disagreement. We noted a similar eagerness for compliance, accompanied by an effort that it should be noticed, across the board for the children in our sample during this period. For example, during our second observation of Akalo, an Amharic-speaking boy (7 months in kindergarten), the children were given maps of Israel to color. Akalo, on seeing that other children received their maps and he did not, followed the teacher around the room for several minutes in silence until she noticed him and gave him his map. Once he had finished coloring, he went up to her, holding it up proudly and saying "Here" (*hine*).

Thus our first field observations often yielded long hours of literally no verbal interaction between the target children and their Hebrew-speaking peers.

Emergent L2: novices with teachers and peers

Interacting with teachers

The novices' first interactional engagements we observed tended to be initiated by the teacher or teacher's aide. The preschool and kindergarten teachers we met share with the general public the belief that young age is an advantage in terms of language learning: immigrant children immersed in the Hebrew-speaking classrooms are expected to master the language easily in a few months.[6] No special provisions exist for facilitating the process, and teachers vary greatly in the types of scaffolding they provide to the novice children.

First attempts by the teacher to engage the novice child in communication are geared toward eliciting agreement or refusal, or are meta-linguistic in nature. For example, towards Saul's (m, L1=French, 4;6) fourth month in school, the teacher is helping a group of children construct a puzzle on the floor; she turns to Saul and asks "are you happy?" Saul nods in agreement, the teacher follows by a confirmation check "yes?" and Saul repeats "yes" (*ken*). Similarly, repeated questions by the teacher to Yeshi (f, L1=Amharic, 7;4, ninth month in school) concerning colors are responded to with a "yes" only when phrased as a 'yes–no' question ("Which color is this?" – no answer. "Is this pink?" – "Yes"). Meta-linguistic prompts also elicit single words: Sandra (f, L1=French, 4;4, three months in school), looking at a picture, is asked "what's this?" and responds "cake" (*uga*); later she engages in a hide-and-seek game with the teacher and is told "say come" and repeats "come." Both teachers and children engage the immigrant children quite frequently in such meta-linguistic "say" rituals, echoing a practice observed in both mothers with young children in New Guinea (Schieffelin 1990) and bilingual families (Blum-Kulka 1997).

A further variation on the repetition ritual is through situated teaching/learning (Pallotti 2001) – cases in which the teacher and the child are engaged in a joint activity in a clearly identifiable context, and the teacher uses the opportunity to introduce new L2 words. Thus in talking about a drawing with Akalo (in his eighth month in school), the teacher asks him to draw a child, points to different body parts on his body ("head," "stomach," "back"), and, after repeating the labels by pointing to herself, Akalo touches the teacher's hair saying "hair" and goes on to draw a child.

The novice children's first attempts at verbal communication with the teachers typically involve attention getters and requests concerning immediate needs. Two frequently used phrases are the vocative *hine* (literally "here is") and the deictic phrase *et ze* ("this one"). Both phrases are heavily contextualized and rely on gestures and objects for interpretation. The first is usually used to show the teacher a drawing or a puzzle, and the second to ask for a specific object. Single words (usually nouns) can also serve a requestive purpose, as when Sandra (f, L1=French, 4;6), in an attempt to free herself from the recording device, goes up to the teacher, touches her, and when the teacher asks "what?" responds with one word: *musiqa!* (emphatically).

The following extract demonstrates a case of early child initiation coupled with a teacher's aid's (first failed) attempts to involve the child in a meta-linguistic "say" ritual. Eva, a French-speaking 5;3-year-old, already ten months in the kindergarten, is trying to draw the teacher's aid's attention to her progress with the Bambi puzzle they have been working on together. She holds up the finished piece announcing proudly "here is!" (turn 25). Rachel, the teacher's aide, launches an implicit "say" ritual: once she gets a positive answer to her query, "you succeeded?" (turn 26), she goes on to pronounce "I succeeded" in past-tense first-person singular, presumably expecting Eva to repeat after her. Eva fails to grasp that the shift in pronouns from "you" to "I" is meant as a meta-linguistic cue for prompting repetition, she points instead to the puzzle and pronounces "here." Only when Rachel inserts the explicit "say" prompt does the child comply. She repeats "I succeeded," receiving indirect praise from the other adult present (turns 31–32).

Ex. 1: The "say" ("tagid") ritual with teachers

Participants: Eva (f, L1=French, 5;3), Rachel (kindergarten teacher's assistant), 20 June 2006.

This episode begins with Eva, two other children, the teacher and her assistant sitting around a table. Eva is putting together a puzzle, encouraged by the teacher and Rachel.

25.	Eva: in::e!	Eva: He::re is! ((happily))
26.	Rachel: ma? tar'i li? Mecuyan! (10.0) iclaxt?	Rachel: What? Show me? Wonderful! (10.0) You succeeded?
27.	Eva: ken.	Eva: Yes.
28.	Rachel: iclaxti.	Rachel: "I succeeded."
29.	Eva: °po°.	Eva: Here. ((pointing at the puzzle))
30.	Rachel: tagidi iclaxti.	Rachel: Say "I succeeded."
31.	Eva: °iclaxti°.	Eva: I succeeded. ((quietly))
32.	Teacher: mecuyan! kol a-kavod la.	Teacher: Wonderful! Well done to her. ((turning to Rachel))

Interacting with peers

"I'm small too to speak this" (*ani miday ktana ledaber ma ze*, meaning: I'm too young to say what this is, implying, I don't know enough Hebrew) is what Masha (f, L1=French, 3;10) told us on our visit during her sixth month in preschool. She was expressing her frustration over communicating in Hebrew, with us, two adults who came to speak to her at a time when she was highly reluctant to initiate interaction with her peers, as were other novice children, presumably for fear of being ridiculed.

First attempts to communicate with peers in Hebrew concern requests for goods (*efshar kcat bacek?* – "Can I have some dough?"), emphatic short refusals ("no"), disputes over objects ("that's mine, that's mine the bucket" – in the sandbox) and vocalizations in enacting roles in pretend play (see turn 32, in Extract 3). Peers pose a serious challenge; what's at stake is not just communicating, but rather finding ways to avoid being ridiculed, to change one's social status within the group, and to move from periphery to center. And indeed, novices' initiatives can result in unpleasant teasing.

On one occasion, sitting around the drawing table, one of the girls asks Sacha (m, L1=Russian, 5;3, seventh month in school) where the cows are. The word 'cow' in Hebrew – *parot* – has an /r/ sound that apparently Sacha is not catching. He responds by asking "what is *palot*?", mispronouncing the word and turning it into a nonce word. His playmate responds by denouncing him: "You don't understand Hebrew." When he protests ("I do"), she insists "Then why don't you understand what 'cows' mean?" Next she responds to his attempt at dismissal ("It's nothing") by offering a definition, "It's an animal," and is followed by another child volunteering an elaboration: "Cows have milk. They give us milk."

The focus on single words is typical of this phase. Teachers and children alike seem to believe that language learning is all about words. In actual practice, the

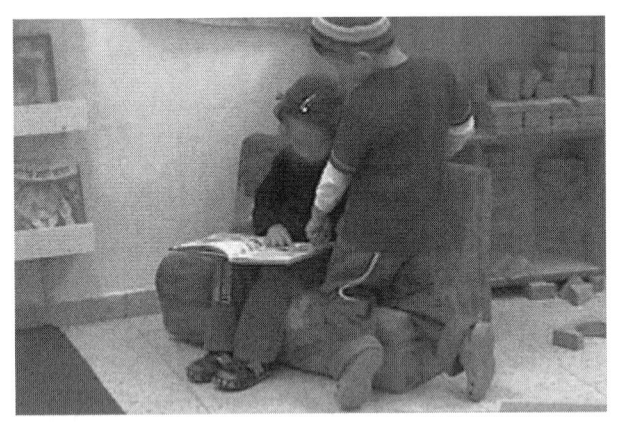

Figure 9.6 Bilingual socialization

Figure 9.7 Bilingual socialization

explicit teaching of words by children to children is a rare phenomenon; the rare occasions on which it occurs are between non-native children, who can use their emergent bilingualism as a resource to facilitate the clarification of word meanings ('how do you say X in Y').

Ex. 2: Bilingual socialization: Saul and the book

Participants: Saul (m, L1=French, 4;7) and Ido (m, L1=French). 12 January 2007. Saul joined the project in its second year. It's his first year in the kindergarten.
Saul and Ido are looking at a picture book of animals.

1.	Saul: Des serpents, des serpents, des souris ((in French))	Saul: ((goes over to Ido, who is looking at a book, and points at two pictures and speaks in French)) the serpents, the serpents, the mice.
2.	Ido: (2.0) xatuli::m, (2.8) pengui::n, cipori::m.	Ido: ((points and says in Hebrew)) (2.0) Ca::ts, (2.8) pengui::n, bi::rds.
3.	Saul: Comment c'est la porte en Hebreu?	Saul: How do you say "door" in Hebrew? ((in French))
4.	Ido: e::, (3.0) je sais pas.	Ido: hm, (3.0) I don't know. (in French)
5.	Saul: Ah tu sais pas, non.	Saul: Ah you don't know. ((in French))
6.	Ido: (2.0) DELET!	Ido: (2.0) DOOR! ((in a triumphant voice, in Hebrew))
7.	Saul: (3.0) C'est ça!	Saul: (3.0) That's it! ((In French, clapping his hands))
8.	Ido:	Ido: ((walks over to Dvir, apparently to ask for more animal names in Hebrew.))

Both children are French L1 speakers; Saul, the child from our sample, whose Hebrew (at his fifth month in school) is extremely weak at this point, approaches Ido, a more veteran child, pointing out animals in his friend's book and labeling them in French (turn 1). The utterance is ambiguous as to its function – is it meant as a request for translation equivalents in Hebrew or as an opening bid for a listing game? By code-switching to Hebrew in the next turn, Ido seems to take upon himself the assigned 'teacher' role; but by naming a completely different set of animals from the ones previously mentioned, he seems to attend to the 'listing' bid (turn 2). Saul's next move leaves no doubt as to his positioning of Ido as the teacher: he switches the language on the floor back to French (turn 3), uttering an explicit meta-linguistic question ("how do you say door in Hebrew") (Blum-Kulka 1997). Ido accommodates by responding in French, admitting his ignorance, and providing Saul with a moment of satisfaction (note how he flags – in French – his friend's ignorance, turn 5) Ido's triumphant moment comes in 6 – when he recalls the word for 'door' in Hebrew and announces it clear and loud. This example shows bilingual children's high language awareness (e.g., Bialystok 2001), and the potential of peer learning and the negotiation for social status even in situations where the parties involved are both still relatively incompetent in the second language.

The next example demonstrates language socialization involving 'book reading' among peers sharing a mother tongue. One child, Rachel, a veteran in the preschool who is at the Hebrew interlanguage stage, engages three other children at the emergent L2 phase in 'reading.' Rachel self-positions herself as the 'expert' and positions the others as 'learners,' thus responding to the Vygotskyan requirement for promoting learning within the zone of proximal development in play (Vygotsky 1978). The participation structure in this case is unique: we are not witnessing L1 peers interacting with novices, but a girl

Figure 9.8 Rachel "reading" to novices

who is a newcomer herself, who, with one year advantage over the others, has by now moved very much to the center of her kindergarten class, often summoned by the teacher to help communication with more novice Amharic-speaking children.

Acting as 'teacher' to her Ethiopian peers, Rachel makes up a story about dogs as she looks at the pictures in the book (Figure 9.8). Two major phenomena stand out here: (a) *Choice of language*: she opts for Hebrew, though Amharic would have been better understood by this specific group. The fact that this is a conscious choice becomes apparent at the end of this episode when she turns away – in fluent Amharic – to reject a fourth child's bid to join the reading. (b) *Accommodating*: the mode of reading accommodates the non-Hebrew-speaking children in several ways: it's very rich in gestures and repetitions, repeating variations on "dog" and "doggie" (*kelev, kalba, klaba, mishpaxat kelev*, in several formations, including ungrammatical ones) no less than thirteen times in two minutes, and it is highly interactive, interpolating the audience several times through direct address and through the use of a transparent non-verbal cue (barking), which the others can join in even without understanding a word (see turn 32). Her strategies echo child-directed speech (CDS) practices typical of care givers addressing young children in Western cultures (Gallaway and Richards 1994).

Ex. 3: 'Reading' to novices

Participants: Rachel (f, L1=Amharic, speaks Hebrew interlanguage); Akalo, (m, L1=Amharic, 6;4, two other L1 Amharic-speaking girls). 21 May 2006.
((continued))

28.	Rachel: sheqet! >pa'am<, >pa'am< ayu. sh::.	Rachel: silence! >Once<, >once< upon a time. sh::. ((silencing the children and starting story))
29.	Akalo: ani kelev.	Akalo: I am a dog. ((to the observer))
30.	SSS: (10.0)	((the kids bark))
31.	Rachel: a-se'ar shela yafe:, xalaqchik, ve-a:-zanav shela kolkax xalaq.	Rachel: () her hair is beautifu:l, smoothy, and he:r tail is so smooth. ((continues to tell the story))
32.	Akalo: [wauwau].	Akalo: [((barks like a dog))]
33.	Rachel: [ve-shel zo:t], camot eze xalaq yoter me-a-klaba: ((mispronouncing dog)). klaba ma shlomex? yesh lanu mar`a kazot. klaba ma shlomex, >hi amra la<. hau hau hau >hi amra< ata kelev, ve-at, (…) niye <u>mishpaxat KELEV</u>! at ka<u>lba</u>, lo roca, ani ka<u>lba</u> >ima aval ani<, at xolat-niqayon, >hau hau hau<, gam ani qoret lax >hau hau hau<.	Rachel: [and he:rs], braids, smoother than the do:g's. dog how are you? We've got that kind of mirror. Dog how are you, >she told her<. ((barking)) >she said< you're a dog, and you, (…) we'll be <u>DOGS family</u>, you're a d<u>og</u>, don't want to, I'm a mother d<u>og</u> but I, you're a cleaning fanatic, ((barking)), I'm also calling you ((barking)).
34.	Rachel: ata kelev, ata gam kelev, hi kalba gam ani kalba, tov?	Rachel: ((turning directly to Akalo)) you're a dog, you're also a dog, she is a dog, I'm also a dog, ok? ((pointing to different kids as she speaks))

Quite typically, the novice child's participation in the event is limited to one utterance (turn 29) and to barking sounds. Nine months into the school year for children in the sample, there is a remarkable degree of variation among the children in level of participation in talk with peers in Hebrew: in recorded sessions of thirty minutes during ten observations in May (lasting 80 to 361 turns), two children contributed between 8 and 16 turns (the first in Amharic and the second in single Hebrew words) to the talk, six children between 40 and 60 turns, and two children between 80 and 112. There is also a parallel variation in length and type of utterances used; thus the division between the 'emergent L2 phase' and the 'interlanguage phase' discussed in the next section is a highly fluid one, varying from child to child.

Table 9.1 summarizes the access strategies of novice children at the 'silent' and emergent L2 periods.

Interactional accomplishments in Hebrew interlanguage: peers as playmates and teachers

One striking difference between adult–child versus peer interaction for young children is in the *keying*, namely, the secondary framing of the interaction in terms of its tone, as serious, playful, ceremonial, etc. (Goffman 1974; Blum-Kulka 2005b). While adult–child interactions are characterized mostly by

Table 9.1 *Nonverbal and verbal strategies of communication*

The 'silent' period	Emergent L2 period
Keen observation and intent participation	Repetition of single words and short utterances
Gaze and touch	Bilingualism: L1 as language learning resource
Compliant behavior	Taking part in "say" ritual with teachers
Song and prayer	Participating in verbal rituals with peers
Joining various play activities	Initiating conversation and responding to
Relying on L1 as a resource for communication	conversational initiatives
	Teasing and humor as a resource

their serious, goal-oriented, matter-of-fact keying, peer interactions with and between the immigrant children tend towards an overall playfulness, ranging from light teasing to ceremonial verbal rituals (Cekaite and Aronsson, this volume). A second difference stems from the unique dynamics of peer interactions as a double opportunity space (Blum-Kulka 2005a; Zadunaisky Ehrlich and Blum-Kulka, this volume): serving simultaneously as an arena for the co-construction of a shared child culture and society, as well as for the development of cognitive, social and linguistic skills. In the case of immigrant children, each interactional episode with peers also necessarily involves the negotiation of the immigrant child's social positioning within the new group, while simultaneously offering opportunities for language learning.

As in native–native peer talk (Blum-Kulka 2005b), explicit language teaching/learning episodes involving novices are rare. Occasionally, native speakers do engage in meta-linguistic repair, as when a friend corrects Eva: "you don't say *madim* (amazing). You say *madhim* with an 'h'"). But such meta-linguistic comments are the exception; most of the time novices gain experience in the new language at this stage through participation in the peer group's regular activities and the genres they entail: such as instrumental talk around the coloring table, meta-talk and 'in frame' talk in pretend play (see also Vardi-Rath et al., this volume), and disputes over property in different games.

In the following, we focus on one central phenomenon typifying the interlanguage phase: novice children's participation in *verbal rituals*. Arguably, verbal rituals, with varying degrees of closure, serve as a language socialization support system for novice children. Such rituals provide rich opportunities for language learning, as well as for subtle negotiations over reciprocal positioning in the peer group.

Verbal rituals

We have defined *verbal rituals* as a recurrent and formulaic activity type, a delimited and scripted speech event that imposes specific rights and duties on its participants. Jewish-American families at dinner, for example, engage regularly in a "how was your day?" ritual, inviting "my day" accounts from all family members, especially children (Blum-Kulka 1997). The verbal rituals observed in the study vary in terms of the allocation of participant roles, their scripts and structure, but share a playful, non-serious keying. Some rituals are specific to the interaction between novices and their more competent peers. Thus in the "say x" ritual –in which Hebrew L1 speakers ask their novice peers to repeat Hebrew words after them – the roles are demarcated and not reversible: the novice child is always positioned as the respondent 'pupil,' expected to recycle the item provided for "x" (see Extract 4). Other rituals are more flexible. For example, when a prompt (like "who likes to eat x?" Extract 5,) is recycled, it opens a slot for confirmation or denial, but also allows for new initiatives. The following examples demonstrate how verbal rituals may act as language socialization support systems, similar to formats of interaction in child–adult discourse (Bruner 1983).

The "say x" ritual among peers, involving a novice child, is quite common. In contrast to adults, for the children the "say x" ritual is a rich source for play and empowerment. For example, on one occasion, a Russian L1 boy (Dion) is seated around the table with four Hebrew L1 girls for lunch; the four girls at the table repeatedly try to elicit repetitions. Dion resists the role he is expected to play of a well-behaved student echoing the words of others; instead, he chooses to be in full control of the situation by responding innovatively to each prompt. Playing on sound and meaning, he manages to transform the keying (tone) of the ritual from teasing at his expense to one that is humorous for all, thereby gaining social status within the group.

Ex. 4: "Say x" rituals

34.	CF2: Dion, tagid "xo:ma↑".	CF2: Dion, say "wa:ll↑". ((in a playful voice))
35–37.	((Three turns omitted.))	((Dion mumbles behind a napkin, another girl leans over and takes it away from his mouth))
38.	CF2: tagid "xoma".	CF2: Say "wall".
39.	Dion: (1.5) <laxmaniya>.	Dion: (0.5) <Bread roll>. ((refers to bread roll Dion is eating. Smiling, and in an amused voice. The girls around the table laugh at his joke))
40.	CF2: (1.5) tagid "xo::ma↑".	CF2: (1.5) Say "wa::ll↑".
41.	Dion: (2.8) laxmaniya.	Dion: (2.8) Bread roll.
42.	CF1: lo, tagid "XO-MA:".	CF1: ((leans towards Dion. Dion looks at her but does not respond)) No, say "WA-LL".
43.	Dion: °laxmaniya°.	Dion: °bread roll°.
44.	CF3: (1.5) tagid "xoma", "xoma".	CF3: (1.5) Say "wall", "wall".
45.	CF4: ta↑gid "Noy".	CF4: Sa↑y "Noy". ((name in Hebrew))

46.	Dion: (1.5) °Poy°.	Dion: (1.5) °Poy°. ((laughs))
47.	CF2: tagid "Li:e:l".	CF2: Say "Lie:l". ((name in Hebrew))
48.	Dion: ma?	Dion: What?
49.	CF2: tagid "Li:e:l". (6.4) tagid "Li:e:l".	CF2: Say "Li:e:l". (6.4) Say "Li:e:l".
50.	Dion: Sapa ktana.(2.0) shuv xoma!	Dion: Small couch. ((the girls laugh again)) (2.0) wall again!
51.	CF1: tagid "Li:".	CF1: Say "Li:".
52.	Dion: (1.6) Pi:.	Dion: (1.6) Pi:.
53.	CF3: (4.3) tagid "pik". (2.0) "pik"! "pik"!	CF3: (4.3) Say "pik".(2.0) "pik"! "pik"!
54.	Dion: >Tiktik<.	Dion: >Tiktik<. ((fast))
55.	CF5: lo, "tik".	CF5: No, "tik" ((bag)).
56.	Dion: (3.2) tiktikpik.	Dion: (3.2) tiktikpik.
57.	CF4: (12.2) tagid "D'iyon".	CF4: (12.2) Say "D'iyon". ((sounds Russian))
58.	Dion: (5.0) kmo Di:-on.	Dion: (5.0) like Di:-òn. ((Hebrew name))
59.	CF4: tagid "D'iyon", tagid "Di::Di::"!	CF4: Say "D'iyon", say "Di:: Di::"!
60.	Dion: lo omrim "D'iy::on" kaxa, omrim Di-òn.	Dion: You don't say "D'iy::on" like this, you say "Di-òn".
61.	CF4: Ayin, ay-i::n, ayin (4.0) ayi::n.	CF4: Ayin, ay-i::n, ayin (4.0) ayi::n. ((sound play, letter name))
62.	Dion: (5.0) Ayin.	Dion: (5.0) Ayin.
63.	CF4: Ayin, ayin. ta- tagid-	CF4: Ayin, ayin. Sa-say-
64.	CF1: (5.5) tagid "sha-yish".	CF1: (5.5) Say "mar-ble".
65.	Dion: sha::yish.	Dion: mar::ble.
66.	CF1: (3.4) tagid nesixa, nesixa.	CF1: (3.4) say princess, princess.
67.	Dion: <xamuda>.	Dion: <cute>
68.	CF1: tagid xamuda.	CF4: say cute.
69.	Dion: (1.3) xe:mada.	Dion: (1.3) cute.
70.	CF2: tagid laxmaniya.	CF2: say bread roll.
71.	Dion: (2.5) (…) xamuda.	Dion: (2.5) (…) cute.
72.	CF2: tagid xamuda.	CF2: say cute.
73.	Dion: (3.4) xamuda laxmaniya.	Dion: (3.4) cute bread roll.
74.	CF2: tagid laxmaniya.	CF2: say bread roll.

A close examination shows that Dion's responses are far from arbitrary – in each case, he chooses whether to attend to sound or meaning, and provides an answer that is cohesive with the prompt regarding sound, rhythm or meaning, but systematically avoids direct echoing.

In response to the first prompt, "say wall," Dion chooses a sound play, replacing *xoma* (wall) by *laxmaniya* (roll, turns 34–44). The girls respond with repeated efforts to gain his compliance in the repetition game: recycling the prompt four times, one of them offering explicit other correction combined with a raised voice (turn 42), but to no avail. The result is a dense triple recycling of the same prompt/response pair, positioning Dion on a more equal footing with the girls than suggested by the initial 'teaching' format of the game. His innovativeness is met by laughter, transforming the keying from

L2 novices' interactions: potentials and challenges 187

Figure 9.9 "Say wall"

Figure 9.10 Who likes to eat x?

(potentially at least) teasing, to something light and playful. The shift to a new prompt (in turn 45) signals concession on the girls' part, an indirect admission of Dion having 'won' the first round of the verbal duel (see also turns 47, 53, 57 and 61). Dion pauses before reacting to the next prompt "say Noy," and then (laughingly) provides a sound play (*poy*), both the pause and laughter reaffirming his keying of the event as playful and enjoyable. The next prompt – "say Liel" – fails: Dion seems to have difficulty processing the sound even when repeated, and chooses to provide a completely unrelated phrase ("small couch") before recycling a former prompt he previously rejected, "wall again" (turn 50). In a further attempt to gain compliance, the next turn repeats the first syllable, "Li," elongating the vowel sound. In response, Dion yet again changes the phoneme from /l/ to /p/, but preserves the rhythm by attending to the syllabic form and the elongated vowel. The repetition of the prompt in the next turn – *pik! pik!* – is echoed in rhythm (but not in sound) in Dion's response – *tiktik* (turn 54). The following other repair prompt – no, *tik* – is different from all previous repairs in that, for the first time, a prompt is derived from Dion's former contribution, but attends not only to the form (one syllable only) but also to the meaning, presumably introducing *tik* (bag) as a lexical item. Dion resists by recycling a combined sequence of nonce syllables, ignoring meaning and attending to form only (turn 56).

The next segment (turns 57–60) represents a shift in keying and an implicit negotiation over cultural identities. The girls ask Dion to repeat his name, voicing (their version of) a Russian pronunciation – stressing the first syllable and inserting a /y/. This blunt attempt at 'othering' is met with strong resistance. Dion resists the attempt to assign him a 'foreign' *membership category* (Sacks 1992) by different means. First, he offers an indirect other repair by providing the Hebrew pronunciation of his name: two syllables with no /y/ sound, and with stress on the second syllable (turn 58). He is met with opposition, with his interlocutor repeating the former prompt, and pronouncing the first syllable by elongating the /i/ vowel (turn 59). Dion responds with an explicit metapragmatic comment, underscoring a shift in keying from playful to serious: "you don't say x" you say y. The shift is ignored (as is the reprimand) and in the next turn the exchange moves back to the verbal game.

The last segment of this event (turns 61–74) testifies to Dion's growing confidence within the group: though in two cases he does repeat the words verbatim (*ayin/shayis*), he continues to play with language, attending to meaning as well as sound ("say princess" – "cute," turns 66–67) and creating novel collocations ("cute bread roll," turn 73). The girls, on the other hand, align with Dion by appropriating his responses and transforming them into prompts: "cute" (turn 68) and "bread roll" (turn 70).

The "say x" ritual examined illustrates the important part played by verbal rituals as a rich resource for sociability in the peer talk of young children, specifically when involving non-native children (Blum-Kulka, Huck-Taglicht and Avni 2004; Cekaite and Aronsson 2004). In the specific event analyzed, sociability is achieved despite the overall oppositional character of the full sequence (see also Zadunaisky Ehrlich and Blum-Kulka, this volume). Though most responsive turns are oppositional, the light keying is co-constructed and preserved through dense across-turn cohesiveness. Cohesiveness is achieved through sound and rhythm, in line with young children's preference for sound play, repetition and prosody as major resources for mutual engagement, and the unexpected word-play twists of most responses. Notably, the segment shows the high resourcefulness of the immigrant child in drawing on language awareness (for both sound and meaning) for playfulness and empowerment.

Like news interviews, the "say" ritual preserves an asymmetrical question (trigger)/response format, with a clear division of discursive roles among participants: the native children as initiators, the novice child as respondent. The format is upheld throughout the exchange, leaving the initiators in the strong position of issuing face-threatening, on-the-record directives ("say x"), expecting passive recyclings, and having the right to accept or reject the given responses. At the onset of the ritual, the native children position the novice child as a 'learner' in need of assistance. In the case examined, this position is challenged by the novice child's playful and oppositional responses, allowing him to reposition himself in face of the others as an equal active player in the verbal ritual.

Verbal rituals are not limited to single words and set phrases; they may also allow for practice in word order and syntactic structure. In one instance, a group of Hebrew L1 and L2 girls, with our sample child (Margarita, 4;4, nine months in school) amongst them, are recycling the phrase "who knows the fairy of x?" (of teeth/of the surprises) using the more advanced, synthetic construct state (*smixut xavura*) noun combination form in Hebrew (*feyat hahafta'ot*) instead of the analytical one (*feya shel ha-hafta'ot*) (Berman 2009). Margarita participates in the first three rounds with brief responses "I don't." Next she attempts to join as an initiator, appropriating the construct state noun-pairing form and recycling "surprises" in a new prompt: "who knows the box of surprises?" (*kufsat hahafta'ot*). Her deviance from the format is corrected ("no, the fairy of surprises"), and she goes on to formulate an elaborated prompt with the expected content and structure: "Who knows the fairy of surprises with presents and sweets? Who knows the fairy of magic?" Thus the clear structure of the verbal game allowed for practice in a relatively complex syntactic structure in Hebrew.

Fixed verbal rituals may also be rich in opportunities for social empowerment. In the next example, the ritual of 'who likes to eat x?' is led by Ester, a monolingual Hebrew L1 speaker and one of the prominent girls in the class. She is the only Hebrew L1 speaker at the table; the other three girls are all Hebrew L2 speakers. As the ritual unfolds, her leadership is challenged by Eva, a French L1 speaker.

Ex. 5: Who likes to eat x?
Participants: Eva (f, L1=French, 5;9), Tami (f, L1=English), Ester (f, L1=Hebrew), Channel (f, L1=French), Ema (f, L1=English, 5;7). 17 January 2007. Around the drawing table.

30.	Ester: MI OHEV LE`EXOL MIKRO:BO:N?	Ester: WHO LIKES TO EAT MICRO:BE:?
31.	Eva: <lo, lo ani>.	Eva: <No, not me>. ((nodding and smiling))

32.	Ester: mi ohev le`exol (karnava:r)?	Ester: Who likes to eat (karliba: r)?
33.	Ema: lo ani.	Ema: Not me. ((laughing))
34.	Ester: mi ohev le`exol e:: >ceva<?	Ester: Who likes to eat >paint<?
35.	Channel: [lo ani.]	Channel: [Not me.]
36.	Ema: [lo ani.]	Ema: [Not me.]
37.	Ester: mi ohev le`exol shoqolad? ANI!	Ester: Who likes to eat chocolate? ME!
38.	Channel: [ANI!]	Channel: [ME!]
39.	Ema: [ANI!]	Ema: [ME!]
40.	Eva: [ANI!]	Eva: [ME!]
41.	Ester: (1.8) mi ohev le`exol e::=	Ester: (1.8) Who likes to eat e::=
42.	Eva: =a! ani- lo- ani- ani yoda'at! MI OHEV LE`EX:O::L (1.0) >pita<?	Eva: =a! I- no- I- I know! WHO LIKES TO E:A::T (1.0) >pita<? ((standing up, talking loudly, sitting again.))
43.	Ema: [ANI!]	Ema: [ME!]
44.	Ester: [ANI!]	Ester: [ME!]
45.	Channel: [ANI!]	Channel: [ME!]
46.	Eva: pica?	Eva: Pizza?
47.	Ema: ANI!=	Ema: ME!=
48.	Ester: =pica ani lo ohevet.	Esther: =I don't like pizza.
49.	Eva: (1.7) yogurt?	Eva: (1.7) Yoghurt? ((smiling voice))
50.	Ester: baa::.	Ester: baa:::. ((disgust onomatopoeia))
51.	Eva: °aval ani gam oxelet yogurt°. (2.3) shokolad?	Eva: °But I too eat yoghurt°. ((wrong word order)) (2.3) Chocolate?
52.	Ester: [A!]	Ester: [A!] ((yells and raises her hands))
53.	Ema: [A!]	Ema: [A!] ((yells and raises her hands))
54.	Eva: nutela?	Eva: Nutella?
55.	Ester: (1.8) yak=	Ester: (1.8) yak= ((disgust))
56.	Ema: =yak.	Ema: =yak.
57.	Eva: (2.3) beycim?	Eva: (2.3) Eggs?
58.	Ester: (3.1) yam.	Ester: (3.1) yam.
59.	Ema: yam=	Ema: yam=
60.	Eva: =pasta?	Eva: =Pasta? ((looking at Ester))
61.	Ester: =yamiyami=	Ester: =Yamiyami=
62.	Ema: =yam m=	Ema: =yam m=
63.	Eva: =chips?	Eva: =Chips? ((looking at Ester))
64.	Ester: chips YAMIYAMI YAM, ani meta alav.	Ester: Chips Yami, yami, I love it.

The episode begins in a playful keying, with nonsense words or absurd suggestions meant to make everybody laugh (microbe/karlibar/paint, turns 30–37). In turn 37, Ester shifts to real food, eliciting happy positive replies in a choir from all four girls present. Eva's move in 42 intercepts the leading girl's next turn – she cuts in with a sound signaling sudden recognition ("A!"), making a meta-comment ("no, I know") before standing up and loudly appropriating verbatim the trigger utterance "who likes to eat?" (Pallotti 2001). The next turns indicate success – the others respond to her in unison.

In turn 46, Eva changes the rules of the game – condensing the prompt to one lexical item referring to real food, she is careful to choose 'easy' words (mostly foreign words used in Hebrew: yoghurt, pasta, chips, pizza, chocolate). The ritual continues with Eva leading the choir, with one brief disruption when Ester's negative reaction to the "yoghurt" prompt (turn 50) triggers an offer of justification on Eva's part (turn 51: probably meaning 'I eat yoghurt too – with other food' – the syntax of her sentence is unclear) and then regains control by opting for the safest option by prompting "chocolate."

The above examples illustrate several important points with regard to peer interaction between novices and their peers: first, peer interaction is colored by a rich range of keyings (like teasing, didactic or sheer playful) absent from most child–adult conversations in the school, second, such interactions necessarily involve negotiations over mutual social positioning, and third, novices have to pass a certain communicative threshold before entering verbal interactions with linguistically competent peers. Once this threshold is passed, interaction with their native and non-native (old-time) peers may become a major resource for language and socio-cultural socialization.

Verbal rituals play an important role in this process. They allow for a high degree of mutual alignment and coordination, manifesting the salience of focus on form rather than content in young children's conversations (Hamo and Blum-Kulka 2007). Their fixed structure facilitates verbal participation, and can be flexible enough to allow for subversive use. As we saw, the novice children find sophisticated ways to resist the *membership categorization*, assigned them by their peers, as non-members (by non-address) or as linguistically incompetent (by teasing or 'teaching' sequences). Verbal rituals give novice children an opportunity to participate and practice sounds, words and new structures in L2, while also allowing them to locally renegotiate the ad hoc social order and their socio-cultural identity.

Summary

We have explored the interactional failures and accomplishments of Hebrew L2 novices with their Hebrew-speaking peers, with a view to language learning, social integration and the negotiation of cultural identities. We have followed young immigrant children's language experience in Hebrew-speaking preschool and school through four key periods: an initial period of innocence, followed by period of shock and silence, the third period of emergent non-verbal and verbal mutual attempts at communication, and the fourth, later period of interactional accomplishments achieved despite limited linguistic resources.

The major focus of our study was on the interactional accomplishments and failures of immigrant children at different phases in their language and culture socialization process. We found that early attempts at communication emerged mainly in interaction with teachers in highly structured contexts, and tended towards didactic keying. In contrast, novice children's interaction with native peers manifests a rich range of keyings and draws on verbal rituals as a major resource for humorous sociability. Expertise in both L1 and L2 serve as warrants for empowerment. Playfulness and humor are richly used even with limited proficiency in the target language, and children exhibit high skillfulness in peer teaching. But importantly, the facilitating role of peer interaction has an important time constraint: it is not available to the L2 children as long as they have not mastered at least rudimentary modes of communication in the new language and do not have enough confidence to use them (see also Rydland, Grøver and Lawrence, this volume, on constraints of peer interaction for L2 learning).

Concurrently, active participation in meaningful interaction with L1 and bilingual peers serves as an arena for the negotiation of social positions and cultural identities. Immigrant children become members in their new communities of practice by constantly repositioning themselves socially and culturally, moving from periphery to center. As expected, peer interaction plays a vital role as a facilitator of social repositioning as well as in the acquisition of L2 communicative competence.

Acknowledgment

The study was supported by Grants no. 338/05 and 1365/08 (2005–2008 and 2007–2011) from the Israeli Science Foundation, Academy of Science. Field observations were carried out by the authors and Maya Shevet. A detailed mapping of the children's progress over the years is to be included in Naomi Gorbatt's doctoral thesis. This chapter draws on data and analyses from the thesis.

TRANSCRIPTION CONVENTIONS

[words]	overlapping talk
=	overlatch
(0.5)	timed intervals
(.)	interval of less than 0.2 seconds
(…)	incomprehensible words
(words)	transcription doubt
.	a falling intonation at the end of an utterance
,	a continuing rising intonation
?	a rising intonation at the end of an utterance
↑	a sharp rise in pitch
↓	a sharp fall in pitch
WORD	high volume
°word°	low volume
<u>word</u>	emphasis
wo::rd	sound stretch

wor-	cut off
>words<	fast rhythm
<words>	slow rhythm
{word}	unusual pronunciation
#words#	unusual tone, indicated in a comment
word/word/word	rhythmic pronunciation
((comment))	transcriber's comments

NOTES

1 The attrition rate was quite high: at the end of the fourth year, the sample included 18 children.
2 In the Russian-speaking community in Israel, parents often send children to Russian-speaking preschools and these children enter kindergarten with no background in Hebrew.
3 Based on teacher reports and a test of non-verbal intelligence.
4 Three further methods of data collection were employed: (a) language proficiency tests comprising two types of vocabulary tests: 1. Peabody Picture Vocabulary Test (PPVT); 2. Expressive One Word Picture Vocabulary Test (EOWPVT) and storytelling using a picture book, administered yearly three times; (b) semi-structured individual child interviews; and (c) case studies of five children during the fifth year.
5 Length of stay (including period of silence) in the school is calculated as of month of entry, which for some children was much later than September.
6 The teachers' role here needs to be understood against major ideological assumptions and beliefs in Israel with regard to child newcomers. For many years, the melting-pot ideology prevailed: newcomers were given new Hebrew names on arrival, and were expected to acquire Hebrew quickly and were discouraged (including the parents) from speaking in their mother tongue (Spolsky and Shohamy Goldberg 1999). In recent years, attitudes have changed to some extent, and educators now employ the discourse of 'multiculturalism,' even if they do not necessarily abide by it in practice. One significant practice that did change is the attitude toward foreign names – children are no longer required to change their name to a Hebrew name. Yet some of the teachers we observed still insisted on Hebrew as the only means of communication between the novice immigrant children (our observations).

10 Language play, peer group improvisations, and L2 learning

Asta Cekaite and Karin Aronsson

Introduction

In work on second language classrooms, researchers with a "ludic" perspective on learning have argued that language play or nonserious language actually constitutes an integral part of second language (L2) use and learning. They have identified a number of ways in which language play may serve as a mediating factor for developing L2 skills. Language play is affectively charged and therefore makes discourse features more noticeable and thus memorable (Peck 1980; Broner and Tarone 2001; Cekaite and Aronsson 2005; Poveda 2005). Creative and innovative language production promotes learners' hypothesis testing and provides triggering episodes that destabilize and restructure the learner's linguistic system (Larsen-Freeman 2010; Tin 2010). It is argued that language play not only encourages students to expand their vocabularies but also generates activities that can be seen as preparations for L2 conversations outside the classroom. One of the implications of such work is that, in order to better understand L2 learning, we must more seriously take into consideration the role of nonserious language, that is, language play.

One of our basic premises is that language play – playful explorations of language variation and language incongruities – constitutes a central feature of peer discourse and children's cultural worlds. Ethnographic studies of children's first-language (L1) use in a broad range of sociocultural contexts have shown that language play activities create multiple and varied opportunities to become aware of and display knowledge of language use (Goodwin 1990; Fasulo et al. 2002; Evaldsson 2005; de León 2007; Howard 2009). When participating in language play, children orient to breaches of linguistic and pragmatic norms. This can be seen as important for their development of lexicon, grammar, and phonology, as well as for their appropriation of sociocultural norms (Nelson 1989). Children's language play thus builds on formal linguistic (phonological, semantic, and syntactic) and pragmatic aspects of language.

In the present study, we demonstrate the relevance of second language play in yet another way. Swain (2000: 112) discussed the formative importance of so-called *collaborative pushed output* in second language learning. One of the

Language play and L2 learning   195

basic arguments in our chapter is that opportunities for social interaction with peers in L2 serves as a core resource for learning. Therefore peer play and other ways of securing and sustaining peer attention become important aspects of second language learning. Language play may trigger extended peer group interactions, and it thus becomes instrumental in creating continued collaborative attention towards both language form and language use (Cekaite and Aronsson 2005).

However, until recently, most work on language play in L2 settings has concerned teacher contributions (van Dam 2002) or language play in adult classroom contexts (e.g., Sullivan 2000; Kim and Kellog 2007; Tin 2010). As yet, only a few studies have been conducted on the role of language play in L2 learning among younger children (but see Peck 1980; Broner and Tarone 2001; Cekaite and Aronsson 2005; Bushnell 2008).

Reflexivity, metalanguage, and collaborative aesthetics

Language play exploits and focuses on the incongruity and ambiguity of language forms, and it is thus closely related to metalanguage, which provides one of the theoretical links between play and language learning. Metalinguistic and metapragmatic functions involve "speaking of language" (Jakobson 1960: 356), that is, speakers' reflexive attitudes towards the formal and pragmatic aspects of language. In other words, reflexivity associated with language involves language users' awareness of, as well as their overt references to, linguistic and pragmatic codes.

In research on children's L2 learning, metalinguistics and metapragmatics have been highlighted as formative factors, contributing to the acquisition of both grammar and pragmatics. Research findings from several sociocultural contexts suggest that bilingual children develop metalinguistic reflexivity about phonological, semantic, and syntactic variation, that is, advanced linguistic awareness (e.g., Bialystok 2009; Poveda 2005).

Metapragmatic play, that is, playful explorations of *the ways in which language is used*, provides important means for expanding the child's pragmatic skills (Blum-Kulka et al. 2004). It involves the child's awareness of pragmatic variations in styles, registers, roles, and communicative genres: *who* is entitled to speak to whom and *how*, that is, in what ways? In L2 language-learning contexts, metapragmatic play mobilizes the learner's creativity in exploring social registers and styles (Cekaite and Aronsson 2004). Metapragmatic play can thus be seen to engage L2 learners' awareness of cultural and social norms for language use, allowing them to try out and explore a broad range of *voices* (Bakhtin 1981).

Playful displays of bilingual knowledge can be seen as one type of manifestation of metapragmatic awareness. In school-yard and other off-task contexts,

Rampton (1995, 2002) has shown that the very presence of several languages may generate language play among adolescents, including so-called *crossing*, that is, code-switching to a language that is not yet part of the speaker's registers. For instance, English-speaking adolescents' peer group play may involve Punjabi–English hybrid constructions or insertions of instructed German for entertainment purposes.

Affective stances, improvisation, and playful repetitions in language play and second language learning

In his work on communication and speech genres, Bakhtin (1978 1981) has shown that there is no "neutral" way of speaking. Our conversations are always impregnated with affects, values, and other perspectives, that is, the speaker's affective stances. Affective stance refers to "a mood, attitude, feeling, and disposition, as well as degrees of emotional intensity vis-à-vis some focus of concern" (Ochs 1996: 410, see also Goodwin and Goodwin 2000; Goodwin, Cekaite, Goodwin 2012). Stanislavskij (1986) has similarly shown that *accentuations* (or affective stances) are constitutive of an actor's performance. Through his/her posture, gestures, and ways of talking (prosody, pauses, loudness, voice qualities), the actor conveys to the audience the role character's feelings and experiences. In multilingual peer-play contexts, it has been documented that, along with lexical resources, repetitions, changes in intonation, speech volume, tempo or voice, code-switching might serve as an expressive and aesthetic resource for marking a variety of affective stances, such as appreciation/affiliation, anger and surprise (Aronsson 1998; Cromdal and Aronsson 2000; Cekaite and Evaldsson 2008).

Speakers thus always orient to and design their contributions to fit a specific audience (Bakhtin 1978, 1981). Performance is an integral element of social life in that speakers embellish and stylize their contributions with different listeners in mind (Bauman and Briggs 1990; Cekaite 2009). This is true even for quite young children (de León 2007). An important part of aesthetic performance and creative improvisation is to switch between novel themes, on the one hand, and repetitions, variations, recyclings, and familiar themes, on the other (Duranti and Black 2012). For instance, in jazz music, there is often a rhythmic variation between solo and group performances, and between old and novel accords and musical themes. Children's play exhibits similar features, displaying constant movements between imitation and repetition, on the one hand, and novelty, on the other, as well as between solo and group performances (Sawyer 1995, 1997). There is always something of a continuum between what is ritualized and what is improvised (Duranti and Black 2012; Sawyer 1995).

Prior work on the social aspects of language play in multilingual contexts has similarly highlighted partial repetitions as a significant resource in the

Ritualized elements   Improvised elements

<----------------->

Figure 10.1 Continuum between old and new elements

dialogical architecture of collaborative aesthetics and performance (Wong Fillmore 1979; Rampton 2002; Cekaite and Aronsson 2004; Piirainen-Marsh and Tainio 2009). Yet variation must entail something more than what Bourdieu has called *intentionless invention* (Duranti and Black 2012). In her work on children's L2 interactions, Cathcart-Strong (1986) has pointed out that, in addition to Grice's conversational maxims, communicative requirements for peer group interactions should include another maxim: "be entertaining!" Similarly, Bushnell (2008) has shown that L2 recyclings and variations are important resources in creating peer group entertainment in language classrooms.

Broner and Tarone (2001) do not explicitly discuss improvisation and performance, but they document resources in language-play performances, such as laughter and shifts in voice quality, in their work on children's language play in a Spanish immersion classroom. Rampton (2002), in his study of UK adolescents' *impromptu peer group Deutsch*, shows that pupils recycle politeness formulae from instructed German, such as *Danke* and *Entschuldigung*, for subversive classroom entertainment.

Repetitions, variation, and experimentation with language elements have been observed to provide means through which second language learners engage with language, analysing it and putting it to use in ways that enable them to develop their linguistic and interactional competences (Pallotti 2001; Rydland and Grøver Aukrust 2005). In early phases of children's second language development, formulaic chunks of talk or phrasal recyclings are important means for generating more talk and for sustaining peer group participation (Wray 2002; Philp and Duchesne 2008).

Prior work by Cekaite and Aronsson (2005) specifically deals with repetitions in second language development, problematizing the acclaimed role of the so-called *communicative language teaching* and authentic dialogues that have been contrasted to "passive" language drills or language use, oriented to formal structures in language. In line with Cook's work on language play (2000), our peer group data, somewhat paradoxically, show that pupils recurrently engaged in spontaneous "language lessons", as it were, repeating and "rehearsing" various teaching routines. Far from being passive, repetitions were used creatively in joint improvisations and classroom performances. Through recyclings and other transformations, the children collaboratively exploited and highlighted the ambiguity, incongruity, and contrastive nature of the linguistic and pragmatic resources employed.

Some of the work cited suggests that repetition and variation are clearly related to creativity, aesthetic performance and joint improvisations. Our present focus is on the ways in which repetition, often with slight variations, and other types of language play provide the means through which children organize their participation in what will here be called *language-play improvisations*. Some of our findings on peer group interactions have been documented in prior studies (Cekaite and Aronsson 2004, 2005). The present chapter extends this work by foregrounding the role of peer group improvisations in language play and L2 learning. We will particularly focus on collaborative aspects of language play and on peer group improvisations, exploring the architecture of language play in a broad sense, including children's attention to both language as such and pragmatics.

The current study

Methodologically, this work has been inspired by ethnographic studies within language socialization paradigms that focus on language learning as a social and situated phenomenon (Duranti, Ochs and Schieffelin 2012).

Setting, participants, and data

For a period of one year, the first author video-recorded classroom life in an L2 immersion classroom (a so-called *mottagningsklass*, literally 'reception classroom') in a Swedish school. The recordings were undertaken during three periods: early and late in the school year, as well as during a mid-period, and they generated about 90 hours of data. The present analyses draw on data from the mid-phase, when the children had spent between four and seven months at school in Sweden.

Swedish was the lingua franca of the classroom, the main language of instruction, as well as the language taught. All children in this class were refugee or immigrant children who had recently arrived from Iraq, Thailand, or Turkey, and they were all beginner learners of Swedish (in all nine children, between 7 and 10 years of age). The names of teachers and students have been anonymized. The classroom teacher, Vera, was a native Swedish speaker. A teacher assistant, Fare, assisted the Arabic-speaking children, and all the children except for Nok, a girl from Thailand, spoke some Arabic, which was an extra unofficial lingua franca in the classroom.

In the classroom, the children's spontaneous contributions were encouraged during individual work as well as during teacher-led activities. Peer group talk was allowed, provided it did not disturb classroom activities. Educational games (e.g., memory cards) were recurrently initiated by the teachers and used for language-teaching practices.

Analytic framework

Participants' perspectives

This chapter draws on so-called *members' perspectives* or *participants' perspectives*. Within conversation analysis, participants' perspectives refer to what the participants themselves say and do within conversations (Sacks 1992) rather than what analysts infer in terms of underlying meaning or intentions. Participants' perspectives are associated with what anthropologists refer to as *emic* approaches, in that they involve analyses based on the participants' own understandings rather than on researchers' pre-defined observational schemes and categories.

In this study, the participants' perspectives also mean the *children's perspectives*, as conveyed through the ways in which the children in the classroom speak and act. Traditionally, children's own standpoints or perspectives have been documented through interview data, mapping children's "voices", as it were (e.g., Prout 2005). During recent decades, however, several researchers have demonstrated that video-recordings offer rich avenues for analysing *children's perspectives*, even if that particular term is not invoked (Goodwin 1990; Whalen 1995; Cromdal and Aronsson, 2000; Evaldsson 2005; Cekaite 2007; Hamo, Blum-Kulka and Hacohen 2004). When working with so-called natural data, that is, data not generated by the researcher, video-recordings are important means for capturing participants' perspectives in that the analyst may follow closely and in sequential detail the ways in which speakers orient to prior interaction.

Analytic unit

The analytic units of our study are *language-play improvisations* (LPs). Within the larger data set, we identified all joking events in which two or more children laughed or commented on something as funny, thereby revealing what was *laughable* (Glenn 1989). Such displays could be: giggles, laughter, repetition, joking uptake, or comments on laughables. Improvisations here involve a minimum of two turns (laughable + uptake) and dialogical features, such as:

LP + giggle
LP + laughter
LP + recycling (repetition or adaptation of laughable)
LP + playful comment
LP + second improvisation/second joke.

Events have thus been classified as funny because of peer responses, that is, other children's uptake. This means that we have deployed a type of "inverted" logic, moving back from the peers' playful uptake to the original improvisation in order to identify laughables. It is not for the analyst to define what is "humorous". Instead, our analyses are based on the dialogues as such, and the participants' (here: the children's) own perspectives, as seen through their uptake.

The LPs were then transcribed in greater detail. Ethnographic field notes have also informed our analysis.

Transcriptions and translations

We viewed the recordings repeatedly and then tried to capture as much as possible of the speakers' affective and expressive stances, in order to re-construe the participants' accentuations, affiliations, and alignments. A basic premise of our study is that affective stances are indexed through verbal, nonverbal, and physical action. Following Ochs and Shieffelin's (1989) seminal paper on affect, we have transcribed indexical aspects of verbal and nonverbal features of conversations, such as prosody, volume, and exaggerated intonation, as features that are deployed in communicating participants' affective stances. Moreover, the present transcriptions and analyses attend to the multimodal complexity of language use (Goodwin et al. 2012), including physical modalities such as gesture and physical action.

The translations have been made by a native speaker, and our ambition has been to preserve the children's original style of speaking to the greatest extent possible, including errors (e.g., number congruency errors as in 'a mittens'). We have, however, not transformed or "translated" mispronunciations and gender errors, such as incorrect choices of Swedish final morphemes (e.g., *-en* or *-et*).

Metalinguistic play

Our findings showed that, besides nonverbal forms of situational humour (e.g., buffoonery, clowning), a large subset of children's spontaneous joking was based on language play, that is, playful mislabellings and puns, drawing on linguistic ambiguity and variation. Language play also involved attention to language in a broader sense, such as ambiguous or incongruous forms of address or unexpected ways of speaking.

In a broad sense, language play covers both play with linguistic structure and play with language use or pragmatics, that is, both metalinguistics and metapragmatics. Six examples will be discussed below: three that deal with children's play with linguistic structure (phonology, semantics, and syntax), that is, language per se, and three that deal with pragmatics, that is, language use. Both cases can be seen to involve language awareness or *reflexivity* (Agha 2007) in that the children can be seen to comment on their own language environment through their ways of playing with language and through their ways of adapting and tailoring their performance to a specific peer group audience.

Metaphonological language play

In their work on language play in second language learning, several scholars have shown ways in which adult second language users orient to phonological language similarities and expressive features of language (Kim and Kellog 2007; Bell 2012).

In her work on young children's interactions with siblings, Keenan (1983) shows that repetition, sound play, and alliteration are important aspects of children's communicative genres. Creative variations and transformations of language provide entertaining resources in peer group improvisations, facilitating and sustaining the young child's conversation with other children ("making it last", Keenan 1983). Similarly, joint improvisations, based on playful recyclings or "format tyings" (Goodwin 1990), seem to be a core part of children's peer group encounters in creating sustained joint attention in peer and sibling teasing, disputes, and play (cf. de León 2007; Howard 2009). In children's early learning of a first language, language-play improvisations in the shape of pattern variations and experimentation actually form an essential part of language development (Nelson 1989; Cook 2000).

At the formal level, there is play with sounds (or with letter shapes, though this is less common) to create patterns of rhyme, rhythm, assonance, consonance, alliteration, etc. and play with grammatical structures to create parallelisms and patterns (Jakobson 1960). At the semantic level there is play with units of meaning, combining them in ways which create worlds which do not exist: fictions. (Cook 2000: 228)

Cekaite and Aronsson (2004) have shown that young L2 learners also orient to phonological features. In the present study on peer group improvisations, the children extensively exploited sound-play-based mislabellings as ways of entertaining their peers, that is, as laughable matters.

In our first example, such a phonological improvisation can, for instance, be found in nonsense constructions or neologisms (Example 1, lines 2 and 4). At the time of the recording, the nominal phrase *ett par x* ('a pair of x') and various plural constructions, such as 'pairs of shoes' or 'pairs of mittens' were frequently practised in the classroom, especially during memory game activities.

Ex. 1

Participants: girls Fusi (7), Layla (10), Rana (8) and a boy, Hiwa (8).
Activity: memory card game.

1.	Hiwa: ->	*E:n- två sko:l*
		A:- two shoe:l ((picks a card of shoes; smiley voice))
2.	Layla:	*En- he he par skor*
		A- he he pair of shoes

3.	Hiwa: ->	*En par skol*
		A pair of shoel ((smiley voice; picks a matching card))
4.	Fusi: ->	*Det [är två skol he he he he he he*
		It is two shoel he he he he he he
5.	Hiwa:	[he he
6.	Layla:	((smiles))

In line 1, Hiwa picks up a memory game card (probably with a picture of a pair of shoes). However, he labels the shoes *e:n två sko:l* ('a: two shoe:l') instead of the target phrase *ett par skor* ('a pair of shoes'; our underlinings). In addition to sound play, he violates the morphological rules for Swedish plurals. The playful affective stance of his nonsensical mislabelling is indicated through the prolonged vowel *sko:l* ('shoe:l') and through his smiley voice. Laughingly, his classmate Layla confirms that these improvisations are indeed funny or laughable. But, she simultaneously repairs his choice of phrase ('a:- two shoes') by providing an alternative phrase (line 2, 'a he he pair of shoes'; our underlining), thus calling attention to the (correct) linguistic form and positioning herself as somebody "in the know".

Hiwa makes use of part of her repair work in his subsequent labelling (line 3), but he still laughingly continues in a playful mode and repeats his phonological improvisation (the neologism *skol*). Fusi aligns with Hiwa's playful affective stance, in that she repeats his original construction (*två skol*, line 4). Fusi's improvisation (a recycling of his original joke) can be seen to convey an affective stance of mutual involvement, understanding, and agreement. By and large, Fusi and Hiwa appear as co-authors of the present improvisation. It is to be noted that the children collaboratively display considerable awareness of fine-grained nuances in Swedish phonology, orienting to phonological distinctions between, for instance, /l/ and /r/. Simultaneously, such sound play involves neologisms and the creation of alternative, imaginary realities.

Metasemantic play

In our first excerpt, the children did not only play with phonological distinctions, they also exploited semantic variation, when they oriented to the difference between 'two shoes' and 'a pair' of shoes. The next example offers another illustration of joking mislabellings during a memory game. While the children of our first example continued to engage in playful spontaneous improvisations, Hiwa picked up a bird card and then made up a nonsense word compound *fågelskol* ('a birdshoel', line 7), exploiting the contrast between real words and the meaning potentials of his nonsense neologism.

Language play and L2 learning

Ex. 2 (continuation of Ex. 1 event)

Participants: girls Fusi (7), Layla (10), Rana (8) and a boy, Hiwa (8).
Activity: memory card game.

7.	Hiwa: ->	*En fågelskol [en fågelskol.*
		A birdshoel a birdshoel. ((picks cards, smiley voice))
8.	Fusi:	*[Ne:j.* ((looks at Hiwa))
		No:.
9.	Layla:	xxx?
10.	Hiwa: ->	**Khani mani** (.) **shanja kani.** he[he
		Hocus pocus(.) **shanja kani.** he he ((playfully labelling the cards; hocus pocus in Arabic + nonsense formula))
11.	Layla:	[he he
12.	Fusi:	*Jag!* ((claims her turn))
		Me!

Hiwa's continued sound play (line 7) is apparently based on assonance, drawing on the phonological parallelism between the two 'l's (*fågelskol*; our underlinings). His neologistic word compound conforms to the rules of Swedish phonology, but it represents a nonsensical derivation. His improvisation thus involves a type of metasemantic commentary, playing with "real" and nonsense meanings. This episode draws on the entertaining potential of varying a simple nominal phrase 'a pair of shoes' in exploiting a series of word parallelisms ('a pair' – 'it is two shoes'; Ex. 1, lines 1–4), as well as metaphonological play, based on sound parallelisms (Jakobson, 1960; here: the phonemic contrasts between /l/ and /r/). Poetic performance is also involved in the nonsense word derivations (fågelskol). This example thus involves both semantic and phonological word play.

Hiwa embellishes his performance (lines 7, 10) through a series of multimodal resources: verbal resources such as repetition and the creation of a novel word compound, and metaphonological word play, as well as nonverbal cues such as a smiley voice and laughter. He also code-switches to Arabic, which is not his native language (line 10). His code-switching or crossing involves the magic Arabic formula *khani mani* ('hocus pocus') and a matching improvised nonsense phrase *shanja kani*, a spontaneous poetic nonsense transformation of the Arabic 'hocus pocus' formula. His code-switching involves sound parallelism in the form of a rhyme, embedded in a grammatical and phonological parallel construction, based on words that have the same length and same alternation of consonants. Hiwa deploys code-switching as an ingredient in a peer-play improvisation as part of the entertainment, and his language play is acknowledged as funny and entertaining in that Layla joins in with his laughing (line 11). Through his code-switching, he can also be seen to exploit an emergent multilingual competence (Rampton 1995, 2002).

On a somewhat speculative note, Hiwa's nonsense formula, as well as his magic Arabic formula, can perhaps also be seen as a parody of the classroom genre as such, that is, as playful commentaries on teachers' classroom picture-labelling practices. The children were playing a memory card game, but within the classroom context this game activity was primarily deployed for picture labelling routines and vocabulary training. These joint improvisations involve both collaborative joking and a poetic use of language, as well as joint exploitations of incongruities and reversals of institutional role expectations.

Metasyntactic play

Children achieve humorous effects when they experiment with language through linguistic improvisations and collaboratively create imaginary and, at times, subversive worlds. Puns and jokes that draw on phrase-level semantic contradictions have been documented in work on children's lore in a variety of sociocultural contexts (Opie and Opie 1959; Howard 2009). In line with work on children's metalinguistic awareness, puns involve developmentally quite complex types of metacognition, in that children have to attend to syntactic ambiguities in language use (Bialystok 2009). This means that the incongruities and what is "fun" are deeply embedded in the sentence structure rather than merely in the semantic or phonological structure of utterances.

In the present recordings, the children did not produce regular puns in Swedish, but they engaged in collaborative production of rudimentary puns. In the following, we will present two such instances involving the child's exploitation of semantic and syntactic ambiguity. Below, Sawan tries to initiate subversive joking, related to the pun *kissar* (our underlining), which may either refer to a plural form of the noun 'kitten' or to the verb 'peeing'.

Ex. 3

Participants: teacher aide, FARE; girls Layla (10), Nok (7), Rana (8), and boys Hiwa (8), Sawan (9), Miran (9).
Activity: Fare and the children are singing a song "We are little ..."

1.	FARE:	*Vi gråter och piper när kissar [oss griper för vi är små råttor vi.*
		We're crying and squeaking when pussies are catching us for we we are little mice. ((singing))
2.	Sawan: ->	[he he he he he he he
3.		((Hiwa and Miran look at Sawan during his laughter))
4.	Miran:	*Varför eh Fare (hon) skrattar?*
		Why eh Fare (she) is laughing? ((looks at Sawan, then FARE, in a harsh voice))
5.	Sawan: ->	*Piper och kissar!* he he he he

		Squeaking and peeing! he he he he
6.	Miran:	*Varför hon xxx Fare skrattar?*
		Why is she xxx laughing Fare? ((irritated voice))
		... ((omission of brief discussion of word meanings))
15.	FARE:	*Kisse! Det är inget att skratta åt.*
		Pussy! It's nothing to laugh about.
16.	Hiwa:	°*Ki:ssssss(e)*°
		°Pee:ssssss°
17.	Nok:	°*Inte kissa kisse*°!
		°Not peeing pussy°! ((smiling at the teacher))
18.	Sawan: ->	*he he he kisse kissa!*
		he he he pussy peeing!
19.	FARE:	*För vi är små grodor vi.*
		Coz we, we are little frogs. ((sings a new couplet))

Sawan immediately starts to laugh when the word *kissar* appears as part of the song (line 2). Evidently, he is orienting to the homophonic qualities of the Swedish plural noun form *kissar* ('kittens') and the verb *kissar* ('peeing'). Miran, another boy in the group, is apparently not aware of the ambiguity of *kissa–kisse* or he is, in fact, aware of the ambiguity, but not amused, which can be seen in his complaint to the teacher, that is, his displayed irritation about Sawan's laughter (lines 4 and 6, Miran incorrectly uses the pronoun 'she'). What is entertaining or not is a highly dialogical affair. But Sawan persists in his attempted joking, and he repeats the subversive song line *piper och kissar he he he he* ('squeaking and peeing', line 5).

Ultimately, the teacher indirectly reproaches Sawan, pointing out that there is 'nothing to laugh about' (line 15). But at this point, Hiwa, in a low voice, subversively makes an equivocal sound imitation of peeing (line 16), aligning with, or even escalating Sawan's nonserious stance. His improvisation is artfully designed in that it contains both collusive semantic elements and a playful exaggeration (of the phonological features of the word *ki:sssse:*). It exploits the onomatopoetic surface resemblance with the target word invoked by the teacher, while it simultaneously conforms to the expected format of a classroom vocabulary exercise. No one laughs at this point, though, and in a sotto voce voice, Nok protests that the word is 'not peeing pussy' (*inte kissa kisse*, line 17). But through a skilful improvisation (line 18), Sawan now reverses the word order of Nok's correction to 'pussy peeing' (*kisse kissa*), thereby managing to design yet another equivocal and subversive joke. But at this point, he is the only person who laughs. As in several other related episodes, the children seem to have a certain sense of timing: subversive giggling, laughing or language-play improvisations go on for a little while and then classroom order is restored. In this way, the children recurrently take "time-out" from on-task activities, as it were, but they then quickly return to their classroom tasks.

Apparently, the present language-play event (rudimentary pun) served the purpose of drawing the other pupils' attention to the ambiguity of language forms, invoking a taboo word in the classroom. Also, Sawan embellished his subversive classroom performance through various nonverbal resources: onomatopoeia, sotto voce subversion, and laughter. However, except for Hiwa, the other participants were somewhat reluctant to align with Sawan's nonserious stance. As in Examples 1 and 2, it can also be seen how peer invitations to laughter are not always accepted. But on the whole, this example shows ways in which the participants designed jokes that drew on poetic parallelisms and onomatopoetic qualities of words, that is, aspects of language that might also enhance the co-participants' metalinguistic skills. Again, it can be noted how collaborative improvisations and language play may facilitate co-participants' attention getting and sustained interactions at the same time as they create "time out" from official classroom business.

Metapragmatic play

Metapragmatic development involves children's acquisition of a variety of speech styles and registers (Agha 2007), that is, their learning of *how* to use language, how to communicate and understand others in a broad range of social contexts and activities, as well as how to take on increasingly complex social roles (Hymes 1972). As will be demonstrated, metapragmatic play provides a locus for experimenting with language styles and registers and, more specifically, for practising authoritative "voices" that are otherwise unavailable to children in asymmetric adult–child interactions (Blum-Kulka et al. 2004).

In their metapragmatic play, the present children exploited breaches of situational expectations about *who* says *what* to *whom*, *when*, and *how* (cf. Cekaite and Aronsson 2004). It was possible to identify two types of metapragmatic play: (i) play with role reversals, social positions and style and (ii) play with hybridities in presentation formats (including hybrid registers). The children played with hybrid presentation modes when they transformed and experimented with classroom genres, deploying such genres in novel ways. This happened when they, for instance, spontaneously initiated and improvised language-play events by importing routines from teacher-led vocabulary training, time-telling, and counting routines. In such recyclings of classroom work, they deployed language drills and other classroom registers for fun and for entertaining peers.

Hybridities (play with registers)

In a well-known play, *The Lesson*, Eugene Ionesco parodies the language-lesson format in foreign language teaching, highlighting absurd elements in routine interchanges in foreign-language classrooms. In the present children's metapragmatic play with hybrid registers, they similarly drew on interactional classroom routines, using them in playful and, at times, parodic ways. For instance, they engaged in spontaneous improvisations where they creatively recycled classroom interactional routines and rituals (e.g., counting sequences, language drills, songs, and greetings). At times, these improvisations took the form of playful transgressions that formed collaborative instances of "mocking subversion" (cf. Aronsson and Thorell 1999, 2002; Blum-Kulka et al. 2004), transforming routine educational activities into peer group entertainment.

In Example 4, the children were engaged in individual (silent) work on maths exercises when Nok deployed a routinely practised nominal phrase ('a pair of trousers/shoes'), embellishing it with an improvised intertextual transformation of this classroom format.

Ex. 4

Participants: girls Nok (7) and Layla (9), and a boy, Hiwa (8), together with other classmates.
Activity: work on individual maths exercises.

1.	Nok:	*Ett par byxor. (.) Ett par strumpor heh heh heh. Ett par byxor ett par strumpor* ((glancing at Hiwa and Layla))
2.		A pair of trousers (.) A pair of socks heh heh heh. A pair of trousers a pair of socks ((glances at H and L))
3.	Hiwa:	((glances at Nok, smiling))
4.	Nok: ->	*Ett par byxor. (0.5) Ett par (.) Fusi.*
		A pair of trousers. (0.5) A pair (.) Fusi.
5.	Hiwa:	[°heh heh°.
6.	Layla:	[°heh heh°.

While working on her maths exercise, Nok engages in language play, glancing at her classmates, Layla and Hiwa. She recycles a vocabulary training routine ('a pair of trouser a pair of socks heh heh heh'), deploying it as a chanting accompaniment to her somewhat repetitive engagement in maths (a counting operation, line 1). Nok's laughter can be seen to invite peer play, and Hiwa responds by smiling back at her.

In the context of the maths task, Nok's improvisation constitutes a (skilful) transgression from the pragmatic norms of situationally appropriate language use. Simultaneously, her repetitive chanting makes use of intertextual ties between the practice of training counting skills and a grammar drill, and it brings forth an implicit parallel between the repetitive (and probably "tedious") character of these educational activities.

Furthermore, Nok transforms the frame of this routine phrase by deploying semantic incongruence when she unexpectedly imports a classmate's name into the language drill: '... a pair of (.) Fusi' (line 4). The substitution, a first name, flouts the expected linguistic structure of the nominal phrase 'pair of x' and involves a semantic contradiction. This means that her language-play improvisation simultaneously capitalizes upon both metasemantic and metapragmatic awareness. But the integration of hybrid genres, here a grammar drill and personal references (the proper name of a peer), is, of course, primarily deployed to invite peer amusement. Nok is successful in that her language-play improvisation is appreciated by her two classmates, Hiwa and Layla, who both laugh, aligning with her playful stance (lines 5–6).

Role reversals and other role appropriations

Role reversals and other types of role appropriation constitute another type of metapragmatic play. In children's first-language development, role reversals are regular features of play: toddlers, for instance, spontaneously play at being their own "mummies" (Gordon 2002), rejoicing in being able to order "their child" around or in being able to undertake other incongruously adult activities. In their joking exchanges, the children in our study inventively experimented with or recycled prior classroom conversations and produced parodic imitations of what in Bakhtinian terms could be called "authoritative discourse" (1981: 345). According to Bakhtin, parody constitutes a "battlefield of opposing intentions": it involves an exploitation of the speech of the other in such a way that it strategically implants "an intention that is directly opposed to the original one" (Bakhtin 1978: 185). In studies of children's role-playing by Andersen (1990) and Aronsson and Thorell (1999), it has, not surprisingly, been found that preschoolers and other young children recurrently chose authoritative positions (doctor, teacher, parent) rather than subordinate roles, such as those of children or pupils.

In the present classroom, the children recurrently exploited their knowledge of teacher talk and teaching routines in joking events that involved *role appropriations* and *role reversals*, children acting as teachers, as it were. In other words, some of these jokes involve impersonations of teachers, where students speak like teachers, engaging in the process of *animation* (Goffman 1981a) of a specific character. For instance, they exploited prosodic repetitions, that is, stylized imitation of the ways the words are spoken, to provide entertaining comments on the current activity (Piirainen-Marsh and Tainio 2009). What is funny about role appropriations is thus not what is said, but *who* says it, and *how* specific language forms or style is used.

Such situational forms of humour in children's peer discourse are built on the inversion of situational expectations and are often accomplished through repetitions: format tyings (Goodwin 1990), and recyclings of recurrent discourse genres. The children exploited *synchronic repetitions* (Tannen 2007) referring to recyclings of the sequentially immediate forms and utterances, as well as *diachronic*, that is, temporally distant repetitions.

The following example demonstrates the children's playful appropriation of teacher registers within peer group interaction. In this case, it involves a diachronic repetition and, more precisely, an improvised stylization of a teacher-type assessment of a pupil's work.

Ex. 5

Participants: a boy, Hiwa (8), and girls Rana (8), Layla (10), and Fusi (7). Activity: the children are playing Memory (picture labelling) on their own.

1.	Rana:	((picks cards))
2.	Layla:	E:h hh xx en kjol (.) en kjol.
		E:h hh xx a skirt (.) a skirt. ((picks matching cards))
3.	Rana: ->	Bra!
		↑Good! ((in a teacher voice and gesture; serious tone))
4.	Hiwa: ->	↑Bra!
		↑Good! ((same pitch register as Rana, falsetto)) he he
5.	Rana:	[°he he°
6.	Layla:	[°he°
7.	Fusi:	[°he he°
8.	Layla:	((picks another card))

In line 3, Rana makes a positive assessment of Layla's successful game move: Layla has just managed to pick a matching pair of cards (something that normally requires both a bit of luck and a good memory for visual configurations). When praising her classmate, Rana deploys a "teacher voice", delivering her talk in a serious mode. Her very act of doing pupil assessments constitutes a recycling of the sequential format of Initiative-Response-Evaluation (I-R-E) routines, prototypical of teacher talk, and it is shaped as a skilful appropriation of a teacher's rights and responsibilities. Teachers are expected to offer praise to their pupils, rather than the reverse. Rana's improvisation can thus be seen as an imitative stylization of teacher talk, including prosodic and lexical elements, typical of teacher talk. Her contribution is shaped as an appropriation of another person's style such that her voice carries the author's original viewpoints and evaluation (Bakhtin 1978: 181).

Hiwa then immediately improvises an escalated teacher performance: he recycles the prior utterance in a falsetto voice, jokingly repeating Rana's teacher-like evaluation (line 4). The recycling capitalizes on several linguistic features: Hiwa designs his utterance as an exact prosodic repetition by imitating not only Rana's lexical choice, but also her high pitch and intonation (see also Goodwin et al. 2012).

210   A. Cekaite and K. Aronsson

The I-R-E routine is thus recycled in a way that involves a playful role reversal of classroom roles, and actually in a parodic or somewhat subversive direction. In any case, Hiwa's escalated re-enactment of Rana's teacher talk proves to be successful as classroom entertainment. Through joint laughter, the three girls can be seen to appreciate and celebrate the laughable qualities of his teacher talk performance (lines 3–7), warming to his playful parody. Their laughing is thus another type of assessment, as it were.

Hiwa's teacher-talk stylization renders a parodic commentary on teacher talk, and perhaps also on the other student's (Rana's) entitlement to a teacher voice, demonstrating his attentiveness to violations of role expectations in educational settings. Such teasing recyclings capitalize on the students' pragmatic awareness, in that different registers signal various degrees of formality/informality, and one aspect of classroom social competence is to master implicit rules of classroom pragmatics. When engaging in metapragmatic play with the I-R-E structure, the children simultaneously display aspects of their classroom competence.

The next example shows another way in which the children took on specific classroom routines associated with teacher talk: in this case, classroom presentation routines. During a recess episode, two girls engaged in playful interaction, creatively deploying their limited L2 resources, as they were getting dressed in the corridor in order to go outside and play. After some joint laughter about Nok's difficulties with her shoes, Nok improvises a (parodic) self-presentation.

Ex. 6

Participants: two girls, Nok and Fusi (both 7).
Activity: recess.

1.	Nok:	A:j
		Ou:ch ((smiling, struggles to put on her shoes))
2.	Fusi:	heh heh heh heh heh eh ((pointing at Nok's shoe))
3.	Nok: ->	*Jag heter du.*
		My name is you. ((smiley voice))
4.	Fusi:	*Van-?* ((producing the first syllable of *van-tar*))
		Mitt-? ((produces first syllable of 'mitt-ens' raising Nok's mittens in front of her))
5.	Nok: ->	*Jag heter Sawan heh heh.*
		My name is Sawan heh heh.
6.	Fusi:	Heh heh heh heh
7.	Nok:	((is about to take back her mittens from Fusi))
8.	Fusi:	*Van-?*
		Mitt-? ((looking at Nok, assuming "teacher" posture))
9.	Nok:	((grabs her gloves from Fusi))
10.	Fusi:	°heh heh° ((Fusi follows Nok))

Nok recycles an educational routine associated with language teaching, 'my name is x' (line 3). It is a conventionalized self-presentation routine, indexical of the social identity of a classroom novice. Nok creatively transforms the formulaic frame by announcing that she is appropriating or taking on the other girl's identity. The role inversion exploits the pragmatic expectation of self-presentation as a resource for establishing a factually correct identity of the speaker. Here, her teasing improvisation (the playful appropriation of her identity) also establishes a play frame, inviting audience laughter or other types of playful uptake.

At this point, Fusi improvises, making yet another impersonation of teacher-talk, deploying a play frame with prosodic, semantic, and interactional means associated with teacher-talk. She actually initiates an I-R-E language-teaching routine, with an incomplete question, requesting that Nok produce a lexical label *van-tar* ('mitt-en'). The intonational contour of her utterance is a fairly accurate performance of a "teacher-talk question" and it is keyed as a playful joking invitation. Combined, her words and actions (the visual display of mittens) are used in a subversive impersonation, in that the teacher question is now primarily exploited for entertainment, as a play-move (in-role talk). In this case, the question also happens to be an examination-type question: the teacher is well aware of the correct response, 'mitten'. The pupil is just expected to fill in the missing morpheme.

The girls then continue their play of role reversals, soliciting peer responses to their playful recyclings of classroom routines. For instance, Nok pursues her earlier role-reversal play frame, this time claiming another classmate's, Sawan's, identity (line 5).

In a classroom context, it is the teacher's prerogative to initiate teaching routines, and to ask "display" questions that examine and evaluate students' knowledge. The present language-play improvisation exploits both intertextual links to classroom routines and inversions of social roles, in that the recyclings can be seen as implicit comments on how, by whom, and when language is used.

Concluding discussion

Through recurrent classroom improvisations, the children worked hard to solicit each other's attention and to secure sustained joint attention and involvement. Participation in such improvisations created entertaining play zones or "time out" (cf. Goffman 1959; Jefferson 1996) within routine classroom activities. During such activities, the children actively exploited their metapragmatic knowledge, that is, their awareness of pragmatic rules about *how* and by *whom* something is said. For instance, the participants engaged in implicit subversive commentaries on their everyday experiences and on the social order in their everyday worlds. Metapragmatic peer play provided the children with opportunities for using social registers that are typically associated with authoritative positions.

But what is perhaps most striking are our findings on children's language play in a narrow sense, that is, children's spontaneous play with phonemes, word meaning and syntax (Examples 1–4) as a type of classroom entertainment.

In terms of language learning, all these language-play improvisations could be seen to provide a type of *double opportunity space* (Blum-Kulka, this volume), in that the participants experimented with and highlighted language matters (sensitizing each other to key factors in language and pragmatics), on the one hand, and engaged in extended entertainment sequences that could be seen to facilitate and sustain the children's L2 conversations, on the other.

Such sustained attention is not something that can be taken as given. There is a great deal of evidence to show that second language learning is quite an extended affair, taking place over many years (Philp, Mackey and Oliver 2008). While the peer group may serve as an important facilitating factor for L2 learning, access to peer group interaction is not something that can be taken for granted (Cekaite 2012; Rydland et al., this volume). Our findings indicate that language-play improvisations in multilingual peer groups can perhaps be seen as key resources for creating sustained peer interaction.

In several ways, the present findings show that spontaneous language play is an important resource in classroom work. In their recyclings of language-lesson routines, the children improvised activities that blurred differences between serious and "nonserious" activities or between school and play activities. In fact, the children often acted as spontaneous "grammarians". This is in close accordance with Vygotsky's (1978) view of play as something serious in children's lives. What is "active" or "passive" in second language teaching has to be recontextualized through analyses of the ways in which the participants themselves (the children) make use of classroom teaching. Moreover, it can be argued that we may need to rethink the dichotomy between play and work in children's lives, that is, the divide between serious and nonserious activities should be reconstrued (cf. Vygotsky 1978; Aronsson 2012).

One of the implications of the present findings is that peer groups or play partners are important social resources. On a societal note, it would seem to be important that children have opportunities to interact with other children in challenging and interesting ways during language learning, and that the school system provide affordances for language-play and peer group improvisations. This might entail teachers and administrators having to rethink or reorganize classroom group compositions or it might mean that children should have a say in terms of finding peers to interact with. Classroom entertainment seems to make learning a seamless and more interesting affair for children. But it might also be important in terms of sustaining children's sense of self and competence, and establishing their trust in schools and classrooms as places worth being in.

TRANSCRIPTION CONVENTIONS

:	prolonged syllable
[ ]	demarcates overlapping utterances
(.)	micropause (i.e., shorter than 0.5s)
(2)	numbers in single parentheses represent pauses in seconds
YES	relatively high amplitude
x	inaudible word
° °	denotes speech in low volume
(( ))	comments from the transcriber
> <	quicker pace than surrounding talk
< >	slower pace than surrounding talk
?	denotes rising terminal intonation
.	indicates falling terminal intonation
=	denotes latching between utterances
Fare	emphatic stress
heh	indicates laughter (number of tokens represent duration)

11 The potentials and challenges of learning words from peers in preschool: a longitudinal study of second language learners in Norway

Veslemøy Rydland, Vibeke Grøver and Joshua Lawrence

Introduction

Vocabulary knowledge has been identified as an important proxy for young children's language development. Even in the preschool period, there is substantial variation in children's vocabulary knowledge that is apparent both between and within groups. In comparing vocabulary levels at group level, it has been found that immigrant children, who are second language (L2) learners, tend to fall behind their monolingual peers (Pagani et al. 2006), and children from low socioeconomic (SES) backgrounds are at a disadvantage compared to children from higher-SES families (Huttenlocher et al. 2007).

Individual and group differences in vocabulary development can to some extent be attributed to variability in the talk offered to young children. A large body of research with monolingual samples has demonstrated that the overall amount (tokens) and/or richness (word types) of talk adults use when interacting with children, both at home (Hart and Risley 1995; Pan et al. 2005) and in educational settings (Dickinson 2001), predict children's growth in vocabulary learning during the preschool period. In particular, the strategies that adults employ during book reading and play with preschoolers (e.g., analytic talk and interaction-promoting talk moves) appear to be of vital importance.

Young immigrant children, who speak a language at home that differs from the language of instruction in school, depend on preschool talk quality to develop a rich second language (L2) vocabulary before entering school. Studies examining the general impact of preschools, which do not discriminate between the importance of teacher and peer talk, suggest that attending preschool is accompanied by accelerated growth in L2 learners' vocabulary knowledge (Leseman 2000; Pagani et al. 2006). Moreover, recent studies have documented the effects of the amount and richness of teacher talk (Grøver Aukrust 2009), as well as teacher-led group talk (Grøver Aukrust and Rydland 2011), on young children's L2 vocabulary acquisition in preschool, both concurrently and longitudinally.

Much less is known about the impact of peer talk per se in preschool. To our knowledge, no studies have examined the potential long-term impacts on L2 vocabulary learning of peer talk during playtime in preschool. To bridge this gap, we aimed to determine whether or not the quality of peer talk (amount and richness in vocabulary use) that target children were exposed to in preschool play was related to their L2 vocabulary, both concurrently and longitudinally. More specifically, we wanted to reveal whether or not the quality of peer talk predicted the short- and long-term L2 vocabulary acquisition of children who were mainly exposed to Turkish (their first language, L1) at home and Norwegian (their L2) in preschool.

The theoretical starting point for examining the short- and long-term implications of peer play talk on children's vocabulary learning is Blum-Kulka and colleagues' conceptual framing of peer talk as a "double opportunity space" (Blum-Kulka et al. 2004). According to them, peer talk functions on two different planes simultaneously. On the first plane, peers construct their way of life through the negotiation of meaning and relationships unique to their childhood culture. The second plane has to do with peer talk constituting a central arena for development. Attention is paid to the opportunities for learning and development that peer talk affords. Blum-Kulka and colleagues have written extensively on how peer talk in "the second space" may be an opportunity for the development of pragmatic skills. In the present study, we consider the second plane by viewing peer talk as an opportunity for word learning. We do this by examining whether or not the quality of talk target children are exposed to when playing with their peers influences their word learning in the short and long term. Then, turning to the first plane and exploring in more detail the ways in which word learning is embedded in peer discussions, we seek to identify the "working ingredients" in peer play talk that potentially support word learning. The first plane reveals the social complexity and fluidity of the peer play context, which is important for delving into the role of peers in young children's language learning. The learning opportunities in preschool play interactions should not be overemphasized, however, as power relations and speaker identities are constantly negotiated in young peer groups. In educational settings where the L2 is used in whole-class communication, the ability to speak the L2 appears to have important social functions, including social acceptance among peers (Willett 1995; Philp and Duchesne 2008; Blum-Kulka and Gorbatt, this volume). As a result, less proficient L2 learners may have problems becoming ratified participants in the challenging and engaging peer conversations from which they learn.

Turning to preschools, the Harvard Home-School Study of monolingual preschoolers from low-SES families demonstrated that the quality of preschool talk, for example, density of extended discourse and rare words, measured as a composite variable of teacher talk and peer talk, was related to the children's vocabulary development in kindergarten (Dickinson 2001). Snow et al. (2007) conducted a follow-up study into the sixth grade based on a sample of the children participating in the Harvard Home-School project. Growth curve analyses revealed that, after kindergarten, all children made gains in vocabulary at essentially the same rate during the elementary years. As a result, the initial differences in children's vocabulary levels associated with preschool talk exposure (density of extended discourse and rare words) remained in subsequent years. Or, put another way, children who had experienced high preschool talk quality did not learn vocabulary at a faster rate during the elementary years compared to children who had experienced low preschool talk quality.

Previous studies of monolingual preschoolers have revealed that it may be beneficial for children to play with peers who use a rich language (Connor et al. 2006; Schechter and Bye 2007). Such findings must be seen in relation to the pragmatic skills enabling children to participate in challenging peer interactions and the characteristics of the peer groups, as well as the quality of the preschool teachers' interactions with the children. However, a study conducted by Henry and Rickman (2007) also demonstrated that the ability level of the peers in a child's preschool classroom (measured as a composite variable of cognitive, pre-literacy, and vocabulary skills) had direct and positive effects on a child's receptive vocabulary skills, after controlling for preschool resources, family characteristics and the child's initial skills when entering preschool. This finding was also supported in a study carried out by Mashburn et al. (2009). In a large sample of four-year-olds, these researchers found a small but significant effect of the classmates' expressive language skills on children's development of expressive and receptive language skills over one year. These large-scale studies do not, however, look at peer talk or single out the peers that children interact with the most in preschool. As the play talk between friends (compared to non-friends) appears to be more complex and cooperative (Howes et al. 1994), it seems imperative to determine whether the unique language contexts children co-construct with their friends have an impact on their L2 vocabulary development.

Many studies accentuate the potential of peer talk in affecting L2 learners' acquisition of vocabulary, for instance, through humorous language play (Blum-Kulka and Gorbatt, this volume; Cekaite and Aronsson, this volume) or pretend-play negotiations (Rydland 2009). However, these studies do not directly address the question of whether or not the talk of L2 learners' preschool play partners constitutes a unique role in shaping their vocabulary learning by, for example, keeping the target child talk and peer talk separate in statistical analyses. Children are, on the one hand, highly motivated to express their viewpoints and understand the messages of their peers when they play together. On the other hand, studies have confirmed the limitations of peers as L2 teachers (Hirschler 1991; Tabors and Snow 1994; Blum-Kulka and Gorbatt, this volume). Tabors and Snow found that non-English-speaking children in US preschools were largely ignored by their peers until they could produce some words in English, and that peers were less willing to repair misunderstandings resulting from non-English-speaking children's lack of word knowledge. Thus, while peers may be powerful sources of word learning, much remains to be learned about the affordances and constraints young L2 learners face when communicating in the target language with peers.

In short, the quality of teacher-led talk (amount and richness) has been found to predict growth in vocabulary acquisition among both monolingual and bilingual samples of children during the preschool period. Moreover, due to a relatively large degree of stability in vocabulary growth during the elementary years, initial differences in children's vocabulary levels associated with preschool talk exposure may persist during elementary school (as demonstrated in the Harvard Home-School Study based on monolinguals). Studies of peer talk effects on L2 learning typically have not identified the unique effect of the L2 learners' play partners. We designed this study to bridge the gap in the research by examining, in particular, the short- and long-term impact of peer talk on L2 vocabulary learning.

The preschool children participating in the study were in their last year of preschool attendance before entering the first grade (the Norwegian school system does not include a kindergarten year). Five-year-olds in Norwegian preschools have typically attended the same preschool classroom for several years. With the transition to school, children join classrooms with new teachers and mostly new peers, necessitating the negotiation of new peer relationships. Children are also continuously influenced by contributors to vocabulary development outside of the preschool context, such as SES factors (for the impact of maternal education on child vocabulary, see Pan et al. 2005; Huttenlocher et al. 2007). Therefore, we did not expect peer talk in preschool to affect the continued growth of the target children's L2 vocabulary during elementary school such that the children who had experienced higher preschool talk quality had a steeper growth curve after leaving preschool. However, we wanted to explore whether or not potential initial differences in children's L2 vocabulary levels associated with peer talk in preschool were sustained during the elementary years. These issues are explored further in the present study, extending previous research regarding the impact of the amount (word tokens) and richness (word types) on vocabulary learning. More specifically, following from the conceptual frame offered by the double opportunity space in peer talk, we sought to answer the following research questions:

1. Addressing the developmental plane in the double opportunity space, we asked, *does the quality of the peer talk in preschool play predict L2 learners' vocabulary knowledge concurrently (at age five) and longitudinally (up to age ten)?*

2. Next, addressing the peer-cultural plane in the double opportunity space, we sought to identify the affordances and constraints that peer-talk discourse in preschool offers L2 learners. More specifically, we asked *how children's various ways of participation in pretend play allowed or inhibited word use and learning.*

We answer the first question by examining the target children's vocabulary trajectories across the study period. As we wanted to examine in the statistical analysis the unique impact of the target children's play partners (the amount and richness of their talk), we decided to control for the target child's talk (drawn from the same play episodes), teacher-led talk in circle time, and maternal education. We answer the second question by analyzing the peer-play participation of two target children drawn from the larger sample who, in spite of many similarities, demonstrated very different ways of play interaction with peers.

Method

Sample

The sample of the present study comprised 26 Turkish–Norwegian-speaking children (15 boys), who were followed from the last year of preschool (age 5) up to the fifth grade (age 10). The children's mean age at the first observation was 5.11 (range 5.3–6.4). At the outset of this study, all target children had attended preschool for a minimum of two years. The children were drawn from twenty different preschool classrooms, and they entered twenty-two different first-grade classrooms located in multiethnic neighborhoods in two of the larger cities in Norway. The children in these classrooms spoke many different L1s at home, for example, Urdu, Turkish, Arabic, various African languages, and so forth, but the common language was Norwegian.

The children were all born in Norway, while their parents were born in Turkey. Interviews and questionnaires conducted with parents and children in the first and fifth grade confirmed that the families spoke mainly Turkish at home. The parental education level was relatively low (ranging from five years of schooling up to the completion of high school), and most of the parents held jobs with relatively low educational demands.

Procedure

When the target children were visited as five-year-olds in their preschool classrooms, they were preparing to enter the first grade. The target children were observed in their classrooms three or four times over a period of five years, which spanned the last year of preschool (age five, N = 26), the first grade

Table 11.1 *Target children's PPVT-III raw scores*

PPVT	N	Mean	SD
Age 5	26	43.62	7.64
Age 6	26	50.77	7.10
Age 7	10	56.20	7.21
Age 10	24	93.88	16.98

(age six, N = 26) and the fifth grade (age ten, N = 24). We lost two children in the fifth grade for reasons unrelated to this research project. Because of limited resources, only ten of the students were visited in the second grade (age seven).

Assessing oral language skills in Norwegian

Target children's receptive vocabulary knowledge was assessed individually during each year of observation using a translated version of the Peabody Picture Vocabulary Test-III (PPVT-III, Dunn and Dunn 1997). In this test, children have to recognize an orally presented word and point to the picture (out of four pictures) corresponding to the word. The reported reliability for the PPVT-III (English version) is 0.94. The validity of the translated version applied on five-year-olds has been checked against the receptive language scales of the Reynell Developmental Language Scales and found satisfactory (Grøver Aukrust 2009). As seen in Table 11.1, there was a much wider range in target children's receptive vocabulary scores at age ten (fifth grade) than at age five (preschool).

Observing peer play in preschool

Peer play was videotaped during free playtime in preschool (when the target children were five years old). Teachers asked target children to bring their peers to the playroom to make sure that they interacted with close friends of their choice. The peer groups usually comprised three to four children, but the number of play participants at a given time point varied from two to six, as some children would leave and other children would enter the playroom. All the peer groups played in rooms equipped with different toys aimed at encouraging pretend play. Each group was typically videotaped for 30 to 60 minutes, out of which the consecutive 20 minutes characterized by the most joint pretend-play talk was selected for transcription. Twenty-five play episodes were sampled as two target children played together.

The talk occurring in the peer-play episodes was transcribed following the transcription conventions of the Child Language Data Exchange System (CHILDES, MacWhinney 1995).

Table 11.2 *Tokens and types per minute for target children and peers (in play) and in teacher-led talk (in circle time)*

Measure	Mean	SD
TokensChild	27.67	16.97
TokensPeers	45.03	21.78
TokensTeacher	89.51	33.37
TypesChild	3.12	1.80
TypesPeers	4.84	2.26
TypesTeacher	9.18	3.30

Note: N = 26

Identifying amount and richness of peer play talk

Based on the transcripts, the amount (tokens) and richness (types) of talk in peer play was analyzed using Computerized Child Language Analysis (CLAN, see MacWhinney 1995). For amount of talk, we identified the number of word tokens per minute produced by the target child and the peers in each play episode respectively. To identify vocabulary richness, we similarly identified the number of word types per minute produced by the target child and his or her play partners (for procedure, see Grøver Aukrust and Rydland 2011). As can be seen in the standard deviations in Table 11.2, there was a wide variation in target children and their play partners' talkativeness in play with respect to the production of both tokens and types.

Control variables: teacher-led group talk and maternal education

Teacher-led group talk was videotaped during the daily circle time when the preschool teacher discussed various topics with the whole class (15–18 children). The measure of teacher-led group talk comprised the talk produced by the teacher as well as the children (teachers offered two-thirds of the tokens on average). The procedure for identifying the amount and richness of teacher-led group talk was similar to the procedure used to identify talk in peer play (Grøver Aukrust and Rydland 2011). Table 11.2 provides the means and standard deviations for density of tokens and types in teacher-led group talk.

Maternal education was divided into three main categories:

1. Five years of schooling (N = 13);
2. Middle school (N = 7); and
3. High school (N = 6).[1]

Learning words from peers: potentials and challenges 221

Table 11.3 *Intercorrelations between PPVT, tokens and types per minute for target children and peers (in play), teacher-led talk (in circle time) and maternal education*

	Variables	1	2	3	4	5	6	7	8	9
1.	PPVT age 5	–								
2.	PPVT age 6	0.54**	–							
3.	PPVT age 10	0.36~	0.38~	–						
4.	TokensChild	0.23	0.15	0.23	–					
5.	TypesChild	0.34	0.27	0.27	0.94***	–				
6.	TokensPeers	0.43*	0.27	0.23	0.05		–			
7.	TypesPeers	0.51**	0.44*	0.23	0.18	0.31	0.94***	–		
8.	TokensTeacher	0.30	0.65***	0.25	-0.23	-0.18	0.28	0.29	–	
9.	TypesTeacher	0.27	0.63**	0.08	-0.10	-0.04	0.25	0.29	0.88***	–
10.	MaternalEd	0.29	0.49*	0.46*	0.22	0.28	0.18	0.16	0.37~	0.36~

Note: N = 26 (except at age 10, N = 24). ~ $p < 0.10$, *$p < 0.05$, **$p < 0.01$, ***$p < 0.001$

Results

Table 11.3 presents the intercorrelations between the main variables of the present study. As seen in the table, the target children's receptive vocabulary scores (PPVT-III) were moderately correlated across time. Moreover, the density of tokens and types were very highly correlated, both at the target child level and at the peer level. In spite of this substantial relationship between the amount (tokens) and richness (types) of words used in play, vocabulary richness appeared to be more strongly related to the target children's oral language skills. The concurrent relationship between the types produced by the target children in play and their receptive vocabulary knowledge was only marginally significant. However, the peers' contribution of types in play demonstrated a moderately strong relation to the target children's receptive vocabulary at age five and six, but not at age ten. It is interesting to note that the target children's tokens and types were not significantly related to the peers' tokens and types. This suggests that some of the more talkative target children were observed in play with peers who were less talkative compared to the peers in the other play episodes, and vice versa (this will be expanded further in the Discussion section).

The richness of talk (types) produced by the target children or by their peers was not significantly related to teacher-led group talk or to maternal education. However, there appeared to be a relation between teacher-led talk and maternal education, on the one hand, and the target children's L2 vocabulary scores across time, on the other. As longitudinal growth modeling is more appropriate for exploring these relationships over time, we now turn to the growth analyses to explore research question one.

Table 11.4 *Results of fitting a taxonomy of multi-level models for change predicting raw vocabulary scores*

Variable	Model A	Model B	Model C	Model D
Fixed effects				
Intercept	48.61*** (1.19)	41.38*** (1.26)	41.37*** (1.25)	27.52*** (3.53)
Age		10.24*** (0.63)	8.97*** (0.75)	9.10*** (0.79)
MaternalEd X age			1.86** (0.69)	1.63* (0.71)
TypesTeacher				0.57 (0.31)
TypesPeers				1.24** (0.48)
TypesChild				0.82 (0.57)
Variance components				
Age	107.6*** (29.89)	7.15*** (2.97)	5.71*** (2.62)	5.83*** (2.71)
Intercept	74.10*** (52.27)	19.57*** (13.41)	18.57*** (13.18)	1.61 (9.54)
Residual	41.22*** (9.78)	42.02*** (9.80)	42.11*** (9.84)	43.43*** (10.33)

Note: Standard errors in parentheses. $^*p < 0.05$, $^{**}p < 0.01$, $^{***}p < 0.001$

The effect of peer talk on vocabulary knowledge

In order to answer the first research question, we fit a series of longitudinal models, including the covariates and variables of interest (Table 11.4). Model A is the unconditional means model, and demonstrates that the true mean for students across the study (when accounting for the nesting of observations within students) is $M = 48.6$. Model B is the unconditional growth model. This model demonstrates that at the start of the study, children had PPVT-III scores of roughly 41 and then increased roughly 10 raw score points each year across the study (not accounting for other covariates).

Model C includes an interaction between maternal education and child age. The parameter estimates associated with that interaction term suggest that students coming from homes in which the mother has received more schooling tend to learn Norwegian vocabulary more quickly up to age ten.

Model D presents the final fitted model in the series. This model includes parameter estimates for baseline vocabulary knowledge, yearly vocabulary growth, and the maternal education by age interaction term. The model also includes estimates of age-five vocabulary knowledge related to the vocabulary richness of the peers. The model demonstrates that the vocabulary richness of the peers in play was associated with higher vocabulary scores for the target children at age five, even accounting for the target child's vocabulary richness in play, teacher-led group talk, and maternal education. Furthermore, we

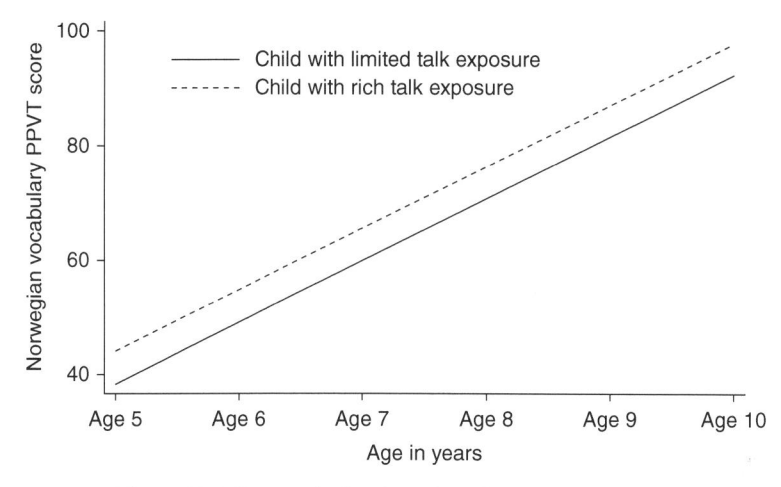

Learning words from peers: potentials and challenges 223

Figure 11.1 Prototypical trajectories of two children
Note: The "limited talk exposure" illustrates a child who is one SD below the mean and the "rich talk exposure" illustrates a child who is one SD above the mean in terms of peers' richness of vocabulary use in play.

explored interactions between the vocabulary richness of the peers and age to see if early participation in specific peer play groups resulted in changes in the target children's long-term vocabulary growth trajectories. As expected, we did not find that the vocabulary richness of the peers in preschool play affected long-term changes in the target children's vocabulary growth during the elementary school years. In sum, these models suggest that playing with peers who use a rich vocabulary is associated with a stronger target child vocabulary knowledge at the end of preschool and that this early effect does not attenuate in subsequent years (controlling for other covariates in the model).

These results are demonstrated in Figure 11.1, which plots the predicted trajectories of two prototypical children from high maternal-education homes with access to average levels of vocabulary richness in teacher-led group talk, and who themselves produce an average range of different words in play. As seen in the figure of L2 vocabulary development, the initial benefits of playing with peers who use a rich vocabulary in preschool do not attenuate over the following five years.

We now turn to the second research question. In the following, we present the cases of two target children and their play with peers in preschool. These target children were selected because they were relatively similar across some important dimensions:

1. Their vocabulary skills in Turkish were relatively similar both at age five and ten;[2]
2. The educational levels of their parents were relatively similar; and

3. They both played with peers that used a rich vocabulary in play compared to the peers in the other sampled play episodes.

However, while the first case demonstrates a target child, Yusuf, who himself produced many different words during preschool peer play at age five, the second target child, Aylin, produced relatively little talk when playing with her peers.

Peer play as a context for word use and word learning

When Yusuf was five years old, his mother and father had lived in Norway for twelve and twenty years, respectively. Both parents had finished elementary school. Yusuf's mother was working part time as a preschool assistant, while his father was unemployed. According to Yusuf and his parents, both his mother and father used predominantly Turkish when communicating to Yusuf, while Yusuf used both Turkish and Norwegian when addressing his parents. Moreover, Yusuf used mostly Norwegian when interacting with his two older siblings and his peers (independent of whether his peers were Turkish-speaking or not). Yusuf entered preschool when he turned four years old; he had therefore been in preschool for approximately two years when the present observation was conducted. At the ages of five and ten, Yusuf's raw scores on the PPVT-III were 50 and 107, respectively, which were both above the mean raw scores in the sample of target children (within the 75th percentile).

Introducing new words through pretend transformations

In the play episode analyzed in this section, Yusuf is in the playroom with Frank and Mary, who are both monolingual speakers of Norwegian. Yusuf and Frank are pretending they are riding horses and being warriors in what appears to be a Pokémon war. They talk about missiles, explosions, lava, and magma. Mary is occupied with her dolls and a baby trolley that she has brought to the playroom. Maybe in an attempt to negotiate a space for Mary in the male-dominated play scenario, Mary and the boys are constantly teasing each other; for example, the boys pretend to eat the baby trolley. The first extract from this play episode begins with Mary throwing her doll at Frank while the boys are pretending to be riding their horses.

Ex. 1[3]

1.	Frank:	*Du kaster en brennmanet ass.*
		[You are throwing a jellyfish.] (Angry, he opens the door and throws the doll out of the playroom.)
2.	Yusuf:	*Hade ## det er no mer enn baby +/.*
		[Bye-bye ## it is something other than a baby +/.]

Learning words from peers: potentials and challenges 225

As seen in line 1, Frank verbally transforms Mary's teasing act of throwing the doll at him to represent something else within the imaginary world. According to him, Mary was throwing a jellyfish. Yusuf follows up on this idea by explicating that the doll Frank is throwing out the door is something other than a baby (line 2). The idea of the doll representing something other than a baby is revisited by the children many times in this play episode.

Expanding word meaning by co-constructing pretend-play ideas

In the next excerpt, Mary leaves the room – telling the boys that she will be back soon – while the boys continue their pretend scenario of riding horses.

Ex. 2

1.	Mary:	*Jeg kommer tilbake.*
		[I'll be back.]
2.	Frank:	*Ikke hent de babyene asså.*
		[Do not bring back the babies.] (Strict tone of voice)
3.	Mary:	*/Nei ditt # frø.*
		[/No you # seed.]
4.	Yusuf:	*Det går # fortere ## enn noensinne.*
		[It goes # faster ## than ever.] (Pretends to be riding)
5.	Frank:	*Det går fort # raskere og fortere enn deg ## når jeg kan sunke fart.*
		[It goes fast # speedier and faster than you ## then I can slow down.]
6.	Yusuf:	*Da kommer # bak # bran # da kommer brakfra ## m hesten min # bak.*
		[Then comes # back # bran # then comes from the brack ## with my horse # back.]

As seen in line 2, Frank warns Mary that she should not bring the babies to the room again, and his strict tone of voice underscores that the dolls may still represent something dangerous. Mary answers Frank with a teasing remark, calling him a "seed" (in Norwegian, this word can be used to undermine someone), before she leaves the room (line 3). In line 4, Yusuf verbally elaborates on the boys' current play enactment of riding horses by stating that they are going "faster than ever." Frank follows up on this idea in line 5 – he is going "speedier and faster" than Yusuf, but then he slows down his speed. Yusuf (although stuttering a bit) expands on the idea that Frank is slowing down by saying that his horse is coming up "from the back" (line 6). Eager to pretend, Frank extends the meaning of the word "faster" introduced by Yusuf by repeating the word as well as by providing a synonym ("speedier") and an antonym for the word ("slow down"). Yusuf demonstrates comprehension of this message by elaborating on Frank's idea. When Frank's horse is slowing down, his horse is coming up from the back. Frank does not appear to pay attention to Yusuf's problems, pronouncing the phrase "from the back." One reason for this may be that Yusuf manages to self-repair and communicate his message in a way that appears comprehensible in the context of pretending.

Introducing a rich vocabulary through teasing and humor

In the final extract from this play episode, Mary is back in the room with the doll under her arm. Once again, the idea that the doll represents something other than a baby becomes the topic of conversation.

Ex. 3

1.	Yusuf:	*Men vet du hva # hun /har en fisk.*
		[But do you know what # she /has a fish.] (Teasing voice)
2.	Mary:	*Nei.*
		[No.]
3.	Yusuf:	*Jo.*
		[Yes.]
4.	Mary:	*/Du har en fisk # og du har en fisk.*
		[/You have a fish # and you have a fish.] (She points to Yusuf first, and then to Frank)
5.	Yusuf:	*Jeg har en /løve jeg mens du vet.*
		[I have a /lion you know.]
6.	Mary:	<*Du har en xxx*> [>].
		[<You have a xxx> [>].] (Teasing voice)
7.	Frank:	<*xxx tiger*> [<].
		[<xxx tiger> [>].]
8.	Yusuf:	*Dere har en # jeg har en slange hvis du vet kobra.*
		[You have a # I have a snake if you know cobra.]
9.	Mary:	*Vet du hva du er en elefant.*
		[Do you know what you are an elephant.] (To Yusuf)

In line 1, Yusuf starts teasing Mary, who is holding the doll, by saying that she has a fish. This turns into a game in which the children call each other by different animal names, and claim to have different animals. In lines 5 and 8, Yusuf claims to have both a "lion" and a "cobra snake," while Mary calls Yusuf an "elephant" (line 9). Thus, the intriguing play theme introduced by Frank at the beginning of this play episode – that Mary's doll was something other than a baby – was revisited by the children many times for different purposes (humor and teasing), enabling the introduction of a wide variety of words.

In this way, the play episode with Yusuf and his peers exemplifies a phenomenon that was evident across the play episodes in this study: the symbolic pretend-play frame established between peers seemed to allow the introduction of words that would otherwise not be relevant in the immediate situation. Moreover, certain words may be powerful in shaping the co-construction of meaning within the pretend-play frame. While some words (like 'jellyfish') may be introduced only once without much explanatory context in play with peers, other words (like 'faster') may be picked up and repeated among participants in a way that expands on the word's meaning. By building on each other's ideas (even for the purposes of teasing or competition), the children elaborated on word meanings both in a broad sense (introduction of the word 'jellyfish' in Example 1, line 1, initiated conversations about scary animals throughout the play episode), and within adjacent utterances (in Example 2, line 5, Frank elaborated on Yusuf's idea of going faster).

The limitations of peer play as a context for word use and word learning

Similar to the case of Yusuf, the next target child, Aylin, also played with peers who used a relatively rich vocabulary. However, while Yusuf contributed new ideas and words to the play talk with his peers, Aylin was less talkative.

When Aylin was five years old, her parents had lived in Norway for about thirty years. Both her mother and father had graduated middle school and worked fulltime. While Aylin's mother worked as an assistant in a nursing home, her father worked as a cleaner. In the interview conducted with Aylin in the first grade, she was very clear that she spoke Turkish with her parents and that she preferred to speak Turkish when playing with her friends. Aylin entered preschool when she was two years old. There were many Turkish-speaking children in Aylin's preschool classroom, allowing her to use both Turkish and Norwegian in informal peer interactions. In the fifth grade, however, Aylin reported using mostly Norwegian when spending time with her peers. At age five, Aylin's raw score on the PPVT-III was 43, which was slightly below Yusuf's score but above the mean among the target children. At age ten, however, her raw score on the PPVT-III was 89, slightly below the mean scores of the target children in the present study.

In the play episode with Aylin at age five, she is in the playroom with Leyla, Sara and Emily. While Leyla also speaks Turkish as her L1, Sara's L1 is Swahili, and Emily is a monolingual speaker of Norwegian. As was also the case with some of the other target children in this study, Aylin seemed to have problems with occupying the floor and elaborating on her ideas in peer play when the common language was Norwegian – even after many years in the same preschool classroom.

The constraints of using the L1 in L2-speaking peer groups

In this episode, the girls are playing in a large playhouse with movable walls. The playhouse contains a well-equipped play kitchen. Emily seems to move between different roles, for example, announcing that she is the mom working outside the home, or a guest who comes to visit. She also moves in and out of the playhouse to offer her ideas and explanations of the play theme to the other girls. For example, she enunciates how the other girls should behave when she comes in as a guest, how she constructs a trap outside the family home to deter burglars, and how her children need to clean their rooms in order to get different benefits. Aylin is mostly in the play kitchen, setting the table with Sara and Leyla. They label the food they put on the table, such as sugar, pancakes and omelets. In the first extract, Aylin addresses Leyla in Turkish, asking her if they are going to make food.

Ex. 4

1.	Aylin:	*Yemek mi yapacak?*
		[Are we going to make food?] (In Turkish to Leyla)
2.	Leyla:	*Ya yemek yapacagiz.*
		[Yes, we are going to make food.] (In Turkish to Aylin)
3.	Leyla:	*Ja vi skal lage mat!*
		[Yes, we are going to make food!] (Repeats her message loudly in Norwegian)

As seen in line 1, Aylin addresses Leyla in Turkish to establish the pretend-play frame of making food. Leyla first answers Aylin in Turkish, and then announces their agreement in Norwegian (line 3). This act of translation suggests that Leyla is highly aware that the common language needs to be Norwegian in order for all four girls to play together. Although this example demonstrates how, in order to ensure collaborative play, peers may afford word learning through translation from the L1 to the L2, the way the present play episode evolved underscores the challenges involved in becoming a ratified participant in L2 pretend-play interactions.

L2 skills are put on display

In the next extract, Aylin puts a cup on the table while using the word "teddy bear."

Ex. 5

1.	Aylin:	*Bamse.*
		[Teddy bear] (Not clear what she is referring to here)
2.	Sara:	*Neei!*
		[Noo!]
3.	Aylin:	*Joo!*
		[Yes!] (Angry tone of voice)
4.	Sara:	*Men det ser ut som det er vann.*

		[But it looks like it is water.] (She peeks into the small mug on the table, her voice soft, and looks at Aylin)
5.	Leyla:	*Jeg skal gå med mamma # en tur.*
		[I am going with mommy # a trip.] (She leaves the kitchen)
6.	Aylin:	*Det er melk.*
		[It is milk.] (Softer voice)
7.	Sara:	*Men melk er ikke så svær.*
		[But milk is not that big.] (Aylin does not respond)
		(… the talk of Leyla and Emily is focused on establishing the broader play scenario of the mom working outside the home)
8.	Aylin:	*Ahh!*
		[Ohh!] (Very dissatisfied tone of voice)
9.	Sara:	*Hva er det?*
		[What is it?]
10.	Aylin:	*Jeg må ha.*
		[I need.]
11.	Leyla:	*Hva må du ha?*
		[What do you need?]
		(She comes back into the kitchen)
12.	Aylin:	*Kac tane catal?*
		[How many forks?] (In Turkish to Leyla)
13.	Leyla:	*Kan du si # norsk?*
		[Can you say # Norwegian?]
14.	Sara:	*Kan du snakke på norsk # jeg forstår ikke hva du mener.*
		[Can you speak in Norwegian # I don't understand what you mean.]
15.	Aylin:	*Ja.*
		[Yes.]

As seen in line 1, Aylin says the word "teddy bear" while putting a cup on the table. The context of this word is difficult to understand, and Sara does not follow up. Instead, Sara corrects the way Aylin has set the cup on the table (line 2), but Aylin refuses to comply with this with an angry rebuke "no," and puts the cup back (line 3). Maybe in an attempt to explain why she wanted to move the cup and to restore cooperation, Sara changes her tone of voice and says to Aylin that it looks like the mug contains water (line 4). As a response to this, Aylin explains in a softer voice that the mug contains milk (line 6). As seen in line 7, Sara attempts to argue for her idea (that the mug contains water) by stating that the mug is too big to contain milk. Aylin, however, does not respond to this contention.

As seen in line 8, Aylin suddenly expresses great dissatisfaction with a complaining "ohh." Sara asks her what it is, but, as seen from Aylin's response, she does not seem to find the word for what it is that she needs (line 10). Leyla seems to be sensitive to the fact that Aylin may have problems expressing herself, because she comes back into the play kitchen and asks Aylin what she is looking for (line 11). Aylin switches to Turkish when telling Leyla that she needs the forks (line 12). Leyla responds to this switch to Turkish by answering her in Norwegian and encouraging Aylin to speak Norwegian. Sara follows up on this suggestion, explaining that she does not understand Aylin if she does not speak Norwegian.

As this extract demonstrates, Aylin appears to have more problems than her peers with explicating her ideas, for example, she cannot remember the Norwegian word for fork, lines 8–10), and building an argument during opposition in Norwegian, for example, when discussing whether the mug contains milk or water (lines 5–7). When Aylin tries to clarify her goal in Turkish to Turkish-speaking Leyla (line 12), she is not getting much help (line 14). At this point, Leyla seems to be highly conscious that everyone must speak Norwegian or else the common play will break down.

L2 skills are intertwined with the negotiation of power relations

In the next extract, the girls have begun to look for clothes with which to play dress-up. Aylin finds a string of hearts and asks her peers what it is. Once again, Aylin's Norwegian language competency becomes the topic of conversation.

Ex. 6

1.	Aylin:	*Hvem er det?* [Who is that?] (She shows Leyla the string of hearts)
2.	Leyla:	*Jo det det er # det er /belte # kan du ikke /norsk?* [Yes it it is # it is /belt # don't you know Norwegian?]
3.	Aylin:	*Det er ikke /belte.* [It is not /belt.]
4.	Leyla:	*/Jo det er /belte!* [/Yes it is /belt!]
5.	Sara:	*Jo # det er /belte # man pleier å gjøre +...* [Yes # it is /belt # one usually does +...] (She takes the string of hearts and tries to knit it around her own waist)
6.	Leyla:	*Sånn # ja man /pleier å gjøre sånn # det er /belte.* [Like that # yes one /usually does like that # it is /belt.] (Mature tone of voice directed at Aylin)
7.	Sara:	*Sånn.* [Like this.] (Tries to put on the belt)
8.	Leyla:	*Og den # og vi /knute den.* [And it # and we /knit it.] (Mature tone of voice directed at Aylin)
9.	Sara:	*Ser du?* [Do you see?] (She shows how the string of hearts is placed around her waist)
10.	Leyla:	*Se.* [Look.] (To Aylin)
11.	Sara:	*Nå ble det /belte.* [Now it is/belt.]
12.	Aylin:	xxx. (Inaudible)

13.	Leyla:	*Hvorfor du sa at det er ikke /belte da # på /tyrkisk?*
		[Why did you say that it isn't /belt then # in Turkish?]
14.	Sara:	*Kanskje hun # kanskje hun /visste ikke det.*
		[Maybe she # maybe she didn't /know.]

When Aylin finds the belt and asks what it is (line 1), she formulates the question slightly incorrectly by asking "who" it is instead of "what" it is. Although Aylin's question may be more related to the function of the string of hearts (and not the Norwegian word for belt), Leyla's response puts Aylin's lack of Norwegian vocabulary on display by confronting her with the question "don't you know Norwegian?" (line 2). Aylin, however, clarifies that she does not believe that the string of hearts is a belt (line 3). When Leyla states that it is a belt, without explaining any further, Sara demonstrates how the string of hearts can be placed around the waist (lines 5, 7, 9, and 11). Leyla follows up by explaining Sara's demonstration to Aylin in a way that signals an alliance with Sara ("we knit it"). After this careful demonstration, Leyla confronts Aylin once more (line 13). This time, Sara appears to defend Aylin, suggesting that maybe she just did not know (line 14).

As stated by Aylin herself in the interview, she preferred to speak Turkish with her peers. Attending a classroom with many Turkish–Norwegian speakers probably also allowed her to use Turkish in preschool pretend-play to some degree. Throughout the play episode analyzed here, Aylin made many attempts to address Leyla (the other Turkish–Norwegian speaker) in Turkish, although the other two girls did not know Turkish. The first time (Example 4, line 1), Leyla solved this potential threat to collaborative play by translating Aylin's Turkish utterance into Norwegian (Example 4, line 2). After that, Leyla attempted to persuade Aylin to speak Norwegian as the common language in play, sometimes in an encouraging manner (Example 5, line 16) and sometimes in a more demeaning tone of voice (Example 6, lines 2 and 13). Thus, Leyla seemed to be torn between the desire to include Aylin in the common play (Example 4, lines 2–3) and the desire to dissociate herself from Aylin (Example 6, lines 2 and 13), in case Aylin should end up being excluded. Aylin made many attempts to speak Norwegian (Example 5, lines 1 and 13, and Example 6, lines 1 and 3). When these initiatives were not successful, however, Aylin was often met with some type of feedback from the other girls indicating that they did not fully understand her (Example 5, lines 14 and 17, and Example 6, lines 13–14).

Discussion

In this study, we looked at the vocabulary trajectories of Turkish-speaking children who were learning Norwegian as their L2 in preschool, following them over a period of five years from preschool to fifth grade. When first observed at age five, all these children had attended a minimum of nearly two years in Norwegian preschool. As a result, none of the children was a newcomer to their classroom or to a Norwegian-language context when we observed them in peer play.

The first main finding, based on our growth analyses, was that the richness of the peer talk in pretend-play predicted where the target children started out in terms of L2 vocabulary knowledge at the end of preschool (controlling for the target child's talk in play, teacher-led talk in circle-time, and maternal education level in the statistical analysis). By looking at the L2 talk the target children had access to in their play interactions with peers, the present study adds to recent large-scale studies by demonstrating the effect of classmates' vocabulary scores on preschoolers' vocabulary development (Henry and Rickman 2007; Mashburn et al. 2009).

Secondly, by following the target children into elementary school, we were able to detect a long-term effect of peer talk in preschool. An inspection of the individual growth curves in the present study uncovered a relatively large degree of stability in the target children's L2 vocabulary development during elementary school, indicating that the trajectories of vocabulary learning set by the end of preschool may be difficult to alter later on.

As expected, we did not find that playing with peers who used a rich vocabulary in preschool resulted in steeper vocabulary growth curves across subsequent years. However, we did find that the initial differences in vocabulary levels related to peer talk at age five were maintained up to age ten (they did not attenuate as children got older). These longitudinal findings are similar to what Snow et al. (2007) detected when they investigated the long-term effects of preschool talk quality on vocabulary development in a sample of monolingual children from low-SES homes (although they did not look specifically at the role of peers).

A third finding of this study was the lack of a strong relationship between the target children's and their play partners' verbal production in play (see Table 11.3), reflecting that a child's L2 verbal production is only one of many factors affecting his or her access to peer language models. Some of the target children in the present study were among the main contributors of a rich vocabulary in peer play (as was the case for Yusuf), suggesting that they had managed to attain a central position in their peer group that could potentially afford them access to a rich vocabulary in pretend-play discussions or position them as language models for their peers. Other target children in our sample contributed little talk to the pretend-play dialogue with peers, even after many years of attending the same classroom. While some of these less talkative children also played in peer groups that contributed relatively low levels of vocabulary richness, some children had access to play with peers who used a wide range of words in play (as was the case for Aylin).

Through the cases of Yusuf and Aylin, this study demonstrates how the pretend-play frame allows the use of a wide variety of words with peers. Peer play may contribute to L2 learners' vocabulary learning because of the opportunities for children to make sense of novel words and receive feedback on their production – most often indirectly to attain a shared meaning, or through humorous play with language (as reported by Blum-Kulka and Gorbatt, this volume; Cekaite and Aronsson, this volume). L1 use among peers may additionally aid comprehension of the L2, for instance, through translations, but it may also restrict access to the L2 peer community. The case of Aylin points to the complexities of looking at the peer-play context as an arena for L2 vocabulary acquisition. While adult-led conversations are often aimed at scaffolding L2 learners' verbal productions and building their self-esteem as language users, peer-driven conversations may be less accommodating and inclusive (see also Tabors and Snow 1994). As the case of Aylin reveals, children work to position themselves vis-à-vis others in peer group play. Compared to adult-led conversations, the language use among peers in play is more clearly intertwined with the emotional layers of belonging and relationships (see discussion in Philp and Duchesne 2008). Aylin's peers were sometimes helpful; for instance, when Leyla translated Aylin's Turkish utterance into Norwegian so that the other girls would understand (Example 4), and when Sara demonstrated to Aylin how the string of hearts could be used as a belt (Example 6). At the same time, Leyla and Sara also placed Aylin's lack of Norwegian proficiency on display (Examples 5 and 6), challenging her to speak Norwegian in a more demanding tone of voice. Leyla appeared to be highly sensitive to the fact that Aylin's use of Turkish in this peer context might threaten the collaborative play. Moreover, the way in which Leyla collaborated with Sara while simultaneously challenging Aylin's Norwegian language competence (Example 6) suggested that she was trying to build an alliance with Sara and dissociate herself from Aylin. The case of Aylin, then, demonstrates a trend we saw among many of the children in our study: that becoming a ratified participant and gaining self-confidence as an L2 speaker in vocabulary-rich peer conversations in preschool may not be an easy task – even for children who have attended the same preschool classroom with the same peers for a long time. Time per se is probably not sufficient to attain a central position in peer play; Aylin had attended two more years of preschool than Yusuf.

In summary, we believe that the results of the present study underscore the importance of the preschool period in general, and the peer-play context in particular, for L2 learners' vocabulary acquisition. Moreover, by shedding light on the challenges of becoming a ratified participant in L2 peer play, this study points to the need for more knowledge about how teachers can supervise and scaffold children's participation in peer play without disrupting the unique qualities (or active ingredients) of these interactions for L2 learning.

TRANSCRIPTION CONVENTIONS

Transcription conventions are based on a simplified version of the Child Language Data Exchange System (MacWhinney 1995).

<text>	demarcates overlapping utterances
#	small pause within an utterance
##	longer pause within an utterance
/text	stressed word
xxx	inaudible word
?	rising intonation
!	demanding utterance
+...	demarcates unfinished utterance
+/.	demarcates abrupt cut-off from others

NOTES

1 Based on these categories, two dummy variables were created and used in the growth analysis.
2 At ages five, six and seven, Turkish vocabulary skills were assessed with a translated version of the Peabody Picture Vocabulary Test-III (PPVT-III, Dunn and Dunn 1997). At age ten, Turkish vocabulary skills were assessed with a translated version of the British Picture Vocabulary Scale-II (BPVS-II, Dunn et al. 1997).
3 See Transcription conventions above.

Part IV

Conclusion

12 What, when, and how do children learn from talking with peers?

Katherine Nelson

In addressing the central questions of this chapter's title, the authors and editors of this volume have gone beyond the main lines of research on children's language learning as these were established over past decades. Centrally, they have situated their inquiry in social-cultural experiences that constitute the everyday learning contexts for children of all ages and all communities. In the introductory chapter, Cekaite and her colleagues lay out the social-cultural theory that informs their research (see also Blum-Kulka's chapter in this volume.) It is worth restating some of the themes I resonated to in the Introduction before embarking on a brief review of the beginnings of our field.

First, the focus on "*peers* as a discourse community" and on "peer talk as a locus for the acquisition of discursive language skills" is not only new in child language studies but provides a model for developmental studies of many other topics, taking the focus beyond that of individual achievements. In specific, research on children's social cognitive development during the pre-school years calls out for this kind of work (see later discussion of Bogdan 2013). A second point of departure is the notion put forth by Blum-Kulka of peer talk as a "double opportunity space for the co-construction of children's social worlds." This idea emphasizes that children's experience and development are multi-dimensional, with many different aspects taking place in the same space at the same time – language, pretense, problem solving, and social relationships all mixed together in time. Development in these contexts takes place through interaction. A third point to emphasize is the child's perspective on the environment of interaction, and how peer culture may influence that perspective. These themes (and others) recur throughout the volume.

From the perspective of a historical understanding of the field of child language development, this approach is essential to account for findings that have been before our eyes for more than half a century, but which have not generally been properly understood, as I document in the first section of this chapter. I begin here with an informal overview of the origins of the field of child language that speaks to the processes of both child learning and scholarly understanding of the process, as backdrop to the main problems addressed in these works. Later sections discuss peer culture, and the role of peer speech in language learning and social and cognitive development, both extending and elaborating on some of the main themes, with the aim of rethinking where we are and where we might be going.

Looking back

Fifty years ago there was little scholarly interest in children's language or how it was acquired. A few pioneers had kept diaries of their children's acquisition of words, and even recorded early sentence constructions by individual children (e.g., Lewis 1951). Except for Roger Brown's (1958) pioneering venture into the "word learning game" there were no theories about how language was acquired by children; that it appeared regularly in all children of "normal" development was apparent and seemingly not in need of explanation. This lack of interest vanished when Chomsky's theory of the "language acquisition device" (LAD) appeared on the linguistics scene (Chomsky 1965). Chomsky claimed that language was "built in" to the human brain, as a language module that managed the learning of grammar from examples in the surrounding environment, examples that were held to be too deficient in themselves to serve as reliable guides to the underlying "deep" syntactic structures that generated all possible grammars.

The ensuing excitement within the linguistic, philosophical, and psychological communities in response to Chomsky's elegant theory supported ongoing radical changes in psychology as well as linguistics, specifically in the establishment of computation-based Cognitive Psychology (later Cognitive Science) as the dominant theoretical position and area of study, with cognitive orientations extending into developmental, social, personality, clinical, and indeed all sub-fields of the discipline. For our purposes here, the main result was an understanding that language acquisition was a (child's) "head-driven" enterprise, unfolding according to innately specified principles. The job of scholars was assumed to be to document the emergence of the principles in children's speech productions.

Early in this period, social psychologists at Harvard – Susan Ervin-Tripp, Roger Brown – and their students extended the new inquiry into language acquisition, making recordings and transcripts of children at home producing first two-word combinations (around two years of age). The data analysis focused almost exclusively on the child's productions in terms of a minimal beginning grammar (Brown 1973). Thus was born a new interdisciplinary field – child language – drawing on researchers in linguistics, developmental, social and cognitive psychology, speech and hearing, and anthropology. The new field soon had its own journal, and before long many books, monographs, and articles. As is usually the case, the beginnings influenced how the field developed, and the beginnings here were situated primarily in experimental psychology.

In both psychology and linguistics research practice centered on context-free child speech samples, based on an unacknowledged assumption that language learning is a *within-child achievement of a context-free standard adult grammar*. It is not surprising that the child's acquisition of a more or less complete mastery of English grammar by the age of four years was considered to be automatic, rapid, and impossible to achieve without the guidance of a built-in language acquisition device, the LAD that Chomsky proposed.[1]

From the beginning, experimental and statistical practices in psychology have had a far-reaching influence on what is acceptable (literally in terms of journal publications) within this and other related fields of study. Where possible, work is carried out in the laboratory where variables can be manipulated and controlled, rather than in natural settings where uncontrolled context may interfere with clear-cut results. Such control may be essential to construction of causal theories. However, I will argue that in the previously unexplored domain of language development – and presumably in other newly opening domains – the rush to the experimental laboratory may prematurely close a field to exploration and to new discoveries bearing on alternative ways of understanding and explanation.

The model of language acquisition in many experimental laboratories was and is that of the infant and child as an automatic acquirer of the pieces of the language: first, sound discriminator and producer, pattern processor, then word learner, receptive and productive, learning first nouns, next verbs, adjectives and other parts of speech, with grammatical constructions built up piece by piece. This is a seductive model. It suggests a regularity that must have an underlying structural base in the natural cognitive structure of the child's brain. The problem is that this model does not work because the data are not consistent with its regularity. It has been contradicted by the evidence from real-world data almost since the beginning of child language study in the 1960s and 1970s. The very first attempts to model child grammars of two-word productions resulted in different grammars from different investigators (McNeill 1970; Ervin-Tripp 1971; Brown 1973; Braine 1976). The problem was not that the different grammars competed to explain the same constructions; it was that different children produced two-word constructions that required different grammars to describe them.

Two widely accepted practices in particular obscured the social and contextual influences on child language learning from the outset. Here I cite examples from first-word learning for two reasons. It has been a focus of research and theory from the beginning of child language studies and it exemplifies the tendencies at work in the field rather clearly. One practice widely shared in psychology is the focus on means of a distribution as the sole meaningful value, rather than viewing variations for further insight. This focus was evident with respect to both the *rate* of number of words acquired by infants during the second year (with the number "50 words" peaking between 17 and 19 months), and the *kinds* of words learned in that period, the greatest number being nouns, specifically object names. Both of these widely accepted means obscured the broad variation in paths to a first vocabulary among normally developing language learners, some of whom do not reach the 50-word standard until after their second birthday, and others who learn very few object names among their first 50 words. I argued that these variable pathways (documented in Nelson 1973) require explanation within a general theory of word learning. Instead, the 50-word count has achieved "milestone" status, and the noun emphasis has been enshrined in theory and its causes tested extensively in child development laboratories, where, it is agreed, object names are learned on the basis of perceptual features (but see recent work by Kemler Nelson 1999). First word learning is still most frequently described as consisting primarily of object names (Gentner 1982; Bloom 2000), and the most widely used assessment instrument (Fenson et al. 1993) appears to support this (but see Nelson, Hampson and Shaw 1993 for a different analysis). Yet theories that attempt to explain why children learn mainly nouns do not account for all the children in the world who do not, including those learning Japanese (Gopnik and Choi 1990), Mandarin (Tardif 1996), and other verb-centered languages.

Another drawback in psychological research is ignoring the *process* of first language learning while focusing on its *products*. Products such as names of objects, verbs, and verb endings can be reproduced and studied in experimental settings, but how these products are learned and used is inaccessible to most experimental methods. There are exceptions where researchers have taken care to replicate as closely as possible the natural conditions of interaction (e.g., Baldwin 1991; Tomasello and Kruger 1992). Tomasello's (1992) study of his daughter's first verbs as documented in a diary is an excellent example of alternative methods. Others were similarly oriented to process. For example, Bates and her colleagues (Bates et al. 1988, Bates 1993) regularly used diaries and other observational methods. Lois Bloom (1973, 1993) constructed an environment and a peer group for the study of the process of word learning in situ that revealed the child's emotional and attentional states in producing early words, among much else. Budwig's (1995) analysis was based on close observation over time and was construed in terms of a functional-developmental model. These classical investigations (and others) are rich in both data and theory. They are mostly confined to the earliest phases of L1 learning (with some other investigators venturing to track simultaneous learners of L1 and L2). It is important that both L. Bloom and Budwig followed children over quite long spans of time and viewed their results in a developmental framework. However, a social-cultural model of development was not fully embraced by the field during this time period.

The first move of documenting the special role of adults in the language-learning process (Snow and Ferguson 1977) was recognition of the unique characteristics of adult speech with young children, termed "motherese" (e.g., use of high pitch, emphatic and rhythmic prosody, short sentences), which has been shown to be virtually universal across cultures (Fernald 1992), and thus was seen as a "natural" aid to the child's learning. Importantly, however, the contribution of motherese was initially viewed within the continuum of assumptions that failed to distinguish the child's perspective from that of the adult. The adult was seen as adapting a special "code" that made aspects of what is to be learned easily accessible to the learning child, but in what way the child's specific language uses are affected by motherese has not been sufficiently established. How children's learning is or is not advanced through motherese requires a focus on the interactive unit, on both the child's ability and interest at a particular moment in time in conjunction with what the mother is offering. Without attending to the child's position in the duet performance, we cannot extrapolate or evaluate the other's influence. Learning to use a language is a temporally occurring process in social and spatial context.

Paul Bloom's (2000) account of word learning is regarded as a definitive summary of the state of the art. In that work he concludes that children's ability to "read adult minds" and "to map words to concepts" explains their acquisition of words from first to last. That is, the process is "head-driven," as cognitive science and Chomsky assumed. Bloom did consider the effects of maternal language and scaffolding on the child's learning of words and concluded that efforts to teach words had no significant effects on children's progress. This conclusion overrides a great deal of research focused on social-class differences and children's language experience (e.g., Hart and Risley 1995). Of course, there is much more to learn of language than what words to use, but the point here is that even this first step is viewed in this theoretical framework as basically under the control of the child's head, independent of the social-cultural or linguistic environment. In my view, this is not just a simplification for theoretical reasons but a distortion of the reality that needs to be explained. Strangely, although this view sees the child as determiner of learning, it is not the child as actor but the child's hidden brain that does the work.

This long introduction on the earliest phase of L1 learning may seem out of context with the main themes of this volume. However, the point is that the entire learning process must be understood in terms of a social-cultural and developmental model, and that much research from the beginning of the field (and of the learning process) has not been carried out or examined from this perspective. A final note on missing pieces in the story of children's language learning is that primary attention has been focused on word learning and grammar. How children use language with others, how they learn to converse and to acquire knowledge through language during the years from two to four are largely unexplored. Yet we find in the chapters here children of 3 and 4 years speaking naturally with both peers and adults, hearing and acting out stories, aiding children who do not yet speak their language in learning it, teasing, arguing, and generally displaying an impressive range of social and cognitive knowledge in speech. How these skills are acquired is as little known or attended to as word learning was 50 years ago. I turn, then, to the main topics of this volume.

Learning language in social-cultural context

The social-cultural theory adopted in this volume recognizes the necessary participation of the child in the learning process as well as the necessary support and contributions from social, cultural, and linguistic sources that make possible continuous advance through the complexities of learning to use language effectively. Language acquisition and use is a social and cultural enterprise in which the child is not alone, but is part of a community of speakers whose practices include extended discourse, including explanation, narrative, arguments, and expressions of emotional feelings, as well as humor and disciplinary remarks. (These discourse functions are well represented in this volume: see Nicolopoulou et al. on narrative, Zadunaisky Ehrlich and Blum-Kulka on argument, Monaco on Pontecorvo on explanations, Cekaite and Aronsson on emotion and humor.) For the learner, language is not a structure to be acquired in parts, but a form of discourse that is available to grasp when context and familiarity support readiness to learn. This approach to language learning is consistent with emerging socio-constructivist models of distributed cognition (as noted by Monaco and Pontecorvo, this volume). Entry into language takes off from more primitive communicative components involving facial expression, touching, movement, gesture (e.g., raising arms for a hug), singing. Although we do not know what aspects of parental speech or actions may be helpful to the child, we can observe the appeal of certain sounds and patterns, especially of rhythm and tonality. The productions of the two-year-old Emily, an advanced language learner whose talk to herself in her crib at night suggested to me the important role of prosody in her gaining control of extended discourse structures – in sentence and paragraph – that make up literate speech (Nelson 2004). I suspect that this dimension is equally important to the acquisition of first words and phrases. Early observers often noted the occurrence of "sentence-like" productions of sound streams by toddlers who were not yet word users. Some of these may be meaningful productions for the child but are not understood by the listener. For example, Peters (1983) documented such cases, including the productions of a second-born girl whose babble was viewed as uninterpretable, until close listening of singsong phrases revealed meaningful patterns (e.g., "op-en duh door") repeated over and over. These individual "solutions" to language acquisition problems can only be explained within a social-cultural paradigm.

The larger conception of the language-learning process conveyed in the social-cultural approach has a central place for the child as a *participant* in a cultural community of interactors, *using* language in its social practices and in the course of this acquiring the whole, social piece by piece. Conversations display discursive practices that broaden, enrich, and enlighten the learning of the linguistic system. Constructive mental processes in conjunction with language in use do the work of learning for the individual child, whose eventual achievement of a working system of language may retain a number of idiosyncratic "mistakes" or inventions (see Tomasello 2003). As Tomasello observed, the adult language that the child hears in speech serves as a resource for the work of the child's constructive processes. It is neither an imitative model nor a language of instruction but a model of language in context.

Peer speech as a learning environment for L1 and L2

Within these communities, peer cultures can emerge that contribute another context for learning, both for the L1 learners who are advancing in the use of extended discourse practices, and for L2 learners in their midst who have a double task of acquiring the new medium and of mastering new ways of expressing intentions that become increasingly complex. Peer speech differs from "motherese" and ongoing adult language, although it may have many of the same sound contours of standard adult speech. It may also have its own characteristic rhythms, patterns, and use of volume (e.g., whispering, yelling). Young children may also use aspects of "motherese" in speaking to dolls, pets, or babies, but not to peers. We may expect quite different interactions in speech and behavior between peers and adults with young language learners. For L1 children, peer talk may be seen as favorable insofar as these children have acquired the rudiments of their language and are ready for new challenges. For L2 learners, the situation might be less favorable, being challenged on all fronts at the same time. So far as I know, these differences between L1 and L2 learning in childhood have not been systematically addressed. These dimensions of language in use – both maternal and peer – may or may not influence the child's formal learning of an initial or later language. Nonetheless they contextualize the learning experience and may motivate the learner to take part in what is a varied and valuable social practice.

The early phases of L1 learning are relevant to many aspects of the research reported here in considering what is similar and what is different. For example, the social-cultural context of learning in the first phase differs from later points in virtue of the developmental status of the learner and of the social environment that supports learning. In regard to the difference between learning L1 and L2, the L2 learner also needs to learn words, but having acquired a first language and entered into the language-using community she knows *what words do*. This difference is one among several that relate to the "how" question of this chapter. To what extent do the learners of any language at any age benefit from direct help with structure or meaning from others who are expert in the language use? Are parents ideal teachers or helpers? In what way? Can peers play the same or a specific related role? As discussed in the first section of this chapter, it appears that a rethinking of the early stages of acquisition of words and phrases may be needed to shed light on these differences. How might peer speech relate better or less well than adult speech for the child learner? What aspects of child culture might be relevant to these questions? Some of the chapters in this volume begin to answer these questions. For example, Blum-Kulka and Gorbatt found that native children engaged the immigrant children in "say" rituals echoing the practice of mothers of young children (see also Cekaite and Aronsson on this topic). Rydland et al. (Chapter 11) found that peer talk predicted vocabulary of immigrant children at the beginning of learning and that variations in vocabulary were maintained up to age ten.

In this volume, *peer culture* is proposed as an important constituent of the larger cultural community and has a unique contribution to make to the child's acquisition of the varied layers of language use within his or her community. What is peer culture? Childhood in modern societies follows ancient patterns of socialization and enculturation to some degree, but there are distinctive differences that make the idea of a distinctive child culture appropriate. Children live within an oral world situated within a literate community, many of whose materials and practices are obscure at best. At the same time, they share in aspects of the literate space, for example in listening to the reading of stories and other materials. Many of the materials that adults provide include written symbols and instructions. The infant progresses from being a limited interactor and observer of some of these practices and materials as well as of the sound of oral language, and gradually enters into what may be thought of as the oral component of the literate culture. The practices of oral cultures have been contrasted with those of literate ones, with an emphasis on group decision making and argumentation and the passing on of knowledge and arts through oral tradition (Nelson 1996). These contrasts are helpful in conceptualizing the organization of peer culture among contemporary children, such as those observed in these chapters.

The natural use of language within a cultural community displays a variety of modes of discourse that incorporate references to cultural roles and practices unique to different situations and environment. For example, the discourse of shopping is distinct from that of exchanges in the home, involving monetary values, people in defined roles such as cashier, and choices among a variety of goods that may be absent from the child's home experience. In a supermarket, talk with the cashier is likely to be limited to a few standardized exchanges about prices and packaging, whereas in another type of store it may focus on merchandise choices. Young children readily learn the "shopping script," including its verbal components, as well as many other everyday routines and scripts with their own settings, participants, and verbal practices (Nelson 1986). As the child's out-of-home experiences expand to include daycare or pre-school, new scripts and roles, and accompanying vocabulary and discourse conventions, come into play. Importantly, these include increasing opportunities for engaging with other children in peer groups.

Children new to a language may be introduced to the practices of a child culture through its use by peers in play and other activities. Such a process may apply both to a first language (as young children newly enter into a group or school setting) as well as to the second language learners studied in this volume (Blum-Kulka and Gorbatt; Cekaite and Aronsson; Evaldsson and Sahlström). An assumption here is that peer culture is an important contributor to children's acquisition of language practice and how language works to effect social goals. The documentation of this process is of great interest and value. Yet, for the most part, both peer culture and peer speech or language remain somewhat unspecified in relation to adult culture and language.

Perhaps the first point to be addressed is the idea that peer culture exists separate from, or as a sub-component of, the larger cultural community. The general assumption both among researchers and the larger community is that young children are enculturated through their interactions with adults, primarily parents and teachers. To the extent that peers are influential on behaviour, it is in support of cultural practices and processes, although there may be practices among peers at odds with those approved by the adults. Even within the cultural participation framework (Rogoff 2003), the typical situation of early childhood is visualized as that of the child as observer of adult practices and as participator in these in a child-adapted fashion. This model of the single child persists despite the widespread modern practice of early childhood education centers and of the traditional sibling and neighborhood peer groups.

Many observers will resonate with and value the work reported in this volume, no doubt agreeing that the role of peers in contributing to social, cognitive, and linguistic developments has been under-recognized and neglected as a research topic. Nonetheless, the question of whether there is something we can legitimately call "peer culture" among pre-schoolers (as there might be, say, among adolescents) remains open. Traditionally, as described in the literature from an earlier period, groups of children of different ages came together within small neighborhood gatherings for games and general social occasions. Within such groups, distinctive ways of social life, including games, contests, and projects were carried on, constituting what could legitimately be referred to as peer culture. The requisite knowledge and ways of engaging were passed on from older to newer and younger members through their participation. Common practices among such groups endured through generations and were often similar across geographically separated groups. An extensive repertoire of games, songs, poems, and practical skills, as well as social expertise and knowledge was acquired through such groups. As younger children became older they maintained and passed on the order and practices of the peer culture to the next younger ones, before themselves entering into the adult world.

A major change has taken place over the past decades in many communities around the globe, such that there is less overlap of ages within any given peer group. For example, there are distinctive peer practices within pre-kindergarten and kindergarten groups, and again in the pre-teen age group (Maybin, this volume), which in turn is divided by gender into a girls' and boys' culture. The mixture of ages and genders in the activities of neighborhood groups – if they exist – is much less common now than earlier. Rather, the peer group, from pre-school on, is typically organized by age and school grade. The wisdom of the eldest group members cannot therefore be expected to be passed on in the same way as previously. In this respect, peer groups among children are in fact more like adult groups, where general cultural knowledge is assumed across a wide span of ages, and older members do not have superior knowledge and social standing than younger. Indeed, in some respects, the younger appear to have the advantage. However, to the extent that each age group has its own peer practices and serves to "enculturate" those who join its membership, or evolves new ways of being over time as different members contribute to it, the peer culture that emerges is definitely a sub-culture within that of the general school culture overseen by the adults, teachers. As most readers know from their own childhood experience, this mode of being simultaneously situated in two cultural scenes, the peer subordinate to the school for most of the day and the peer then taking on superiority outside the school context, can be a source of considerable strain for individuals who are not skilled in the demands of both. Fortunately, the examples presented in this volume represent cases where the peer culture fills in gaps that are left open by the school program and its demands. This may be a typical organization for children of pre-school age, but with older children and different social groups one may find more challenging of the school culture by peers, and more conflict among the expectations of each.

All of this is quite speculative and in no way serves to mitigate the real contribution that is made in bringing the construct of peer culture into the analysis of how young children learn to engage with extended discourse, in teasing, argumentative, or narrative forms. Indeed, that children need to gain the knowledge and skills involved in such contexts, and that such achievements include the advancement of their cognitive, linguistic, and social development is apparent.

How do children learn from talking with peers?

I believe that the assumption that there is distinct peer group culture and language practice in most children's experience and at most ages of three years and beyond is probably correct and that its contribution to language acquisition, cognitive development, enculturation, and cultural innovation must become part of social constructivist theorizing. A major problem for this position is the changing nature of child culture with the changing age and developmental status of the children. Here, most of the attention has been focused on the pre-school period, but, as Maybin's chapter reveals, cultural practices and social organization among peers in the later school years provide unique challenges beyond those of the adult world. These observations are hardly new, but their study has not been sufficiently deep within the linguistic and psychological spheres of development.

For example, a major new consideration of the role of peers and peer culture in the social-cognitive development of pre-schoolers has been advanced by Radu Bogdan (2013), who emphasizes the socio-political challenges and strategizing evoked in the peer environment of the pre-school. These challenges demand of children greater language facility and cognitive abilities to reason about others' actions and motivations than were needed in the more protected home context of the very young. As a consequence, children advance in social-cognitive thinking and in speech practices involving extended discourse, such as argumentation. Such challenges for L1 and L2 speakers alike are in fact evident in some of the situations documented by several of the chapters in this volume. Bogdan argues, as do these authors (e.g., Kyratzis; Vardi-Rath et al., Nicolopoulou et al.) that pretense play is an invaluable source of practice for the cognitive requirements of thinking and learning in school and later life. Indeed, he asserts that pretense play may be a unique human adaptation that undergirds the higher levels of human thinking (a position similar to Vygotsky 1978). In this regard, the language of extended discourse is essential to its achievement. A related general argument has been put forth by Daniel Hutto (2008), with an emphasis not on peer culture but on narrative, citing the work of Nelson (2003) and supported as well by Nicolopoulou and Weintraub (1998).

In addition to the idea of peer culture as a positive environment for development of competence, it is possible to see the emergence of different "language games," in Wittgenstein's sense, arising in different "forms of life" during the pre-school and school years. In each move to a new peer group, newcomers must learn the specific practices, including specific uses of language, as they begin to take part. This is clearest with the L2 learners (Rydland, Grøver and Lawrence, this volume), but is also evident in the description of story telling and enacting practice described by Nicolopoulou et al. (this volume). The story telling and enacting is instigated and organized by teachers, but the children themselves organically construct the practice as the year proceeds. As Wittgenstein (1953) noted, words may take on new roles in different socially organized settings, where the specifics of the organization determine what is meant within that setting. His reference was to such examples as legal arguments or philosophical discourse, but the same may be said for differentiating children's school and play talk.

In this volume, the culture most in focus is that of very young children in pre-schools. We might think of it as pre-school culture, and indeed, although the societies studied here are somewhat diverse, the pre-school children are likely to seem quite familiar to most readers. Sub-cultures arise when participants in organizations come to common understandings of how to negotiate status-and-exchange relationships, among others. Children entering pre-school are new to these kinds of informal practices among groups of peers, which are common also throughout later childhood. The youngest age groups, if separated from those older, may find it necessary to establish their own patterns, and may find it expedient to rely on adults (teachers, aides) for guidance. Thus the youngest groups may revolve around the adult by default. When moving on or up they may find that their interests are served by mutual agreement among the group and may find practices already in place that bear that out. Leaders may then arise and stabilize practices.

Thus peer culture endures, but the guidance and continuity supplied by older more experienced children is probably less effective than it was in previous generations. This inference reflects the fact that in much of the US there are no longer neighborhood play groups in the old sense, and many fewer families with a range of sibling ages – perhaps only an older–younger sibling pair separated by two or three years. Thus the continuity of child culture is being replaced by distinctive age cultures. To the extent that this is the case, it is likely to place more of a challenge to many young children in adjusting to different groups, and to give opportunities for the most socially adept peers to establish leadership styles and group norms for better or worse.

A different perspective is provided by the idea of the pre-school as constituting a distinctive sub-population of non-literate oral culture (Nelson 2007). As noted previously, oral cultures are distinctive in the use of speech in social groups to achieve both individual and social ends, such as exchange relationships and obligations (Ong 1982). Most notably, knowledge is conveyed personally, not through written works. However, reading aloud to children from written works modifies this restriction and provides a platform for entering the more literate world. This perspective is relevant to the claims that pre-school talk in pretense play incorporates literate forms that aid in moving into the literate environment of primary school (Kyratzis, this volume). Literate discourse – borrowed in part from written stories – may supplement "plain speech" patterns in pretense before becoming common in other social activities. As pretense builds on narrative forms (see Vardi-Rath et al., this volume), both contexts may provide a platform for "vaulting" (to use Bogdan's term) to the higher level of literate culture. Older school children may then be viewed as a sub-group of, or apprentices within, adult literate culture. These observations have obvious relevance for the importance of reading aloud to young children at home and in the pre-school as platforms for the movement into the literate school world. As Hutto (2008) argued, such reading and discussing is important as well for the development of social-cognitive knowledge.

It is tempting to point out, however, that the literate adult world became more orally oriented during the last century with the aid of the telephone and radio first, then television, all indirect but oral in nature. The recent effect of the electronic world of emails, social media and so on appears to be a remix of oral messages in written form. It appears that we now live in a world that merges the two, where literate discourse no longer exhibits the widespread formality of expression that it did in the nineteenth and earlier centuries, but has to a very large extent become "oralized." The very nature of "literate" appears to have changed over time. These developments need much more analysis, including their widespread social and artistic influences, but this is not of primary importance for the present project.

Convincing as these chapters focused on peer speech are in conveying the message of its social and cultural contribution to the young (and older) child's means for dealing with the world, there is not much consideration here of the interface between the child and adult communities. In focusing on the ways that young children manage their social and political concerns in peer speech, the roles of adults (teachers, parents) tend to disappear. Given the vast amount of attention that has been given in the literature to parent–child talk in early language learning and in such pursuits as memory sharing and book reading, this research neglect is understandable. However, the longer-run project of the child's enculturation and education involves a successful merge into the adult culture. As Rogoff (2003) has argued strongly, different cultures promote this process in different ways. The question then is how peer groups and peer speech may interface with child–adult social-cultural activities in the larger community.

The issue of the interface of adult and child culture is raised by some of the work in this volume (e.g., in Kyratzis's chapter). Nicolopoulou (this volume) describes peer group activities as products of adult direction, and in some of her other work, Nicolopoulou (1996) has traced the story-creation and acting activities as emergent from children's engagement with story listening and pretend play, taken under the direction of a creative teacher. In the present chapter, she is concerned with a group of children from less literate home backgrounds than those previously studied. The studies of Nicolopoulou et al. and Kyratzis seem to call for a within-group comparison of how the language used in pretend play (as in Kyratzis' work) is or is not carried over into story construction and action (as in Nicolopoulou et al.). Nonetheless, the evidence offered here of active peer contributions to learning and development of language, knowledge, and thinking, as well as social understanding, is overdue and very welcome.

To return to the account in the first section of this chapter, a full accounting of the process of early language development, from first words to simple conversations, requires the acknowledgment of the significance of the social-cultural context within which each child begins to learn to speak his or her own language. Of great value in the work reported here is the close observation of children in these contexts. As awareness of the complexity of developmental processes and their temporal dependence increases, it has become obvious that much of the research tradition that has emerged from experimental psychology (as construed in the first section of this chapter) is not applicable to the research questions arising in pursuit of a social-cultural understanding of human development. The implication is that only different research methods – including those cited earlier – focused on context and interaction can form the basis for informative theories of how learning in natural environments proceeds.

I have touched on many different issues in reflecting on the work presented here and have not attempted to extract a single overall message. I believe that among the values of the studies here is the reflection of diversity – of children, of contexts, of challenges, of cultures and languages. The diversity of uses of language in child culture draws attention to how different aspects of the language–culture interface are revealed in practice. Play and stories are not only useful contexts for observing language in its move toward mature forms and practices, but are revealed to be central to the child culture. I come back to an earlier conclusion: we need to explain the causes of diversity as much as we need explanations for regularities. Close observation of pre-school children making advances in language, cognition, and social understanding proves a good place to start.

NOTES

1 It soon became clear that 4-year-olds had not mastered all the intricacies of the adult grammar and that adults learning a second language were often faster than children in gaining competence, but these amendments failed to move the field substantially in a different direction.

References

Agha, A. 2007. *Language and social relations*. Cambridge University Press.
Andersen, E. 1990. *Speaking with style: the sociolinguistic skills of children*. London: Routledge.
Angelova, M., Gunawardena, D. and Volk, D. 2006. 'Peer teaching and learning: co-constructing language in a dual language first grade', *Language and Education* 20: 173–190.
Arendt, H. 1977. *The life of the mind*, vol. 1: Thinking. New York: Harcourt Brace Jovanovich.
Aronsson, K. 1998. 'Identity-in-interaction and social choreography', *Research on Language and Social Interaction* 31: 75–89.
　2012. 'Language socialization and verbal play', in A. Duranti, B. Schieffelin and E. Ochs (eds.), *The handbook of language socialization*, pp. 464–483. Malden, NJ: Wiley-Blackwell.
Aronsson, K. and Thorell, M. 1999. 'Family politics in children's play directives', *Journal of Pragmatics* 31: 25–47.
　2002. 'Voice and collusion in adult–child talk: toward an architecture of intersubjectivity', in S. Blum-Kulka and C. Snow (eds.), *Talking with adults: the contribution of multi-party talk to language development*, pp. 277–295. Mahwah, NJ: Lawrence Erlbaum.
Astington, J. W. 1993. *The child's discovery of the mind*. Cambridge, MA: Harvard University Press.
Bakhtin, M. 1978. 'Discourse types in prose', in L. Mateika and K. Pomorska (eds.), *Reading in Russian poetics*, pp. 176–96. Ann Arbor, MI: University of Michigan Press.
　1981. *The dialogic imagination: four essays*. C. Emerson and M. Holquist, (transl.). Austin, TX: University of Texas Press.
　[1935]1981. 'Discourse in the novel', in M. Holquist (ed.), C. Emerson and M. Holquist (trans.), *The dialogic imagination: four essays by M. M. Bakhtin*, pp. 259–422. Austin, TX: University of Texas Press.
　[1929]1984. *Problems of Dostoevsky's poetics*. C. Emerson (ed. and trans.). Minneapolis, MN: University of Minnesota Press.
Baldwin, D. 1991. 'Infants' contributions to the achievement of joint reference', *Child Development* 62: 875–890.
Barnes, D. 1976. *From communication to curriculum*. Harmondsworth: Penguin Books.
Barthes, R. 1980. *La chambre claire. Note sur la photographie*. Paris: Gallimard Seuil.

Barton, D. 2007. *Literacy: an introduction to the ecology of written language* (2nd edn). Oxford: Blackwell.
Bates, E. 1993. 'Comprehension and production in early language development', *Monographs of the Society for Research in Child Development* 58(3–4): 222–242.
Bates, E., Bretherton, I. and Snyder, L. 1988. *From first words to grammar*. Cambridge University Press.
Bauman, R. and Briggs, C. 1990. 'Poetics and performance as critical perspectives on language and social life', *Annual Review of Anthropology* 19: 59–88.
Bell, N. 2012. 'Formulaic language, creativity, and language play in a second language', *Annual Review of Applied Linguistics* 32: 189–205.
Berentzen, S. 1984. 'Children constructing their social world: an analysis of gender contrast in children's interaction in a nursery school', *Bergen Occasional Papers in Social Anthropology*, No. 36. University of Bergen, Department of Social Anthropology.
Berman, R. A. (ed.) 2004. *Language development across childhood and adolescence: psycholinguistic and crosslinguistic perspectives*. Amsterdam: John Benjamins.
   2009. 'Children's acquisition of compound constructions', in R. Lieber and P. Stekauer (eds.), *The Oxford handbook of compounds*, pp. 298–322. Oxford University Press.
Bettleheim, B. 1987. 'The importance of play', *The Atlantic Monthly*, March, pp. 35–46.
Bialystok, E. 2001. *Bilingualism in development*. Cambridge University Press.
   2009. 'Bilingualism: the good, the bad, and the indifferent', *Bilingualism: Language and Cognition* 12: 3–11.
Björk-Willén, P. 2007. 'Participation in multilingual preschool play: shadowing and crossing as interactional resources', *Journal of Pragmatics* 39: 2133–2158.
Bloom, L. 1973. *One word at a time*. The Hague: Mouton.
   1993. *The transitions from infancy to language: acquiring the power of expression*. New York: Cambridge University Press.
Bloom, P. 2000. *How children learn the meaning of words*. Cambridge, MA: MIT Press.
Blum-Kulka, S. 1997. *Dinner talk*. Mahwah, NJ: Lawrence Erlbaum.
   2002. 'Do you believe that Lot's wife is blocking the road (to Jericho)? Co-constructing theories about the world with adults', in S. Blum-Kulka and C. E. Snow (eds.), *Talking to adults*, pp.85–115. Mahwah, NJ: Lawrence Erlbaum.
   2004. 'The role of peer interaction in later pragmatic development: the case of speech representation', in R. Berman (ed.), *Language development across childhood and adolescence: psycholinguistic and crosslinguistic perspectives*, pp. 191–211. Amsterdam: John Benjamins.
   2005a. 'Modes of meaning-making in children's conversational storytelling', in J. Thornborrow and J. Coates (eds.), *The sociolinguistics of narrative*, pp. 149–171. Amsterdam: John Benjamins.
   2005b. 'Rethinking genre: discourse genres as a social interactional phenomenon', in K. Fitch and R. Sanders (eds.), *Handbook of language and social interaction*, pp. 231–275. Mahwah, NJ: Lawrence Erlbaum.
   2010a. 'Introduction: communicative competence, discursive literacy and peer talk', in S. Blum-Kulka and M. Hamo (eds.), *Child peer talk*, pp. 5–42. Tel Aviv: The Center for Educational Technology [in Hebrew].

References

2010b. 'Genres and keyings in child peer talk at preschool and at school', in S. Blum-Kulka and M. Hamo (eds.), *Child peer talk*, pp. 42–86. Tel Aviv: The Center for Educational Technology [in Hebrew].

Blum-Kulka, S. and Dvir, S. 2010. 'Peer interaction and peer learning', in E. Baker, B. McGaw and P. Peterson (eds.), *International encyclopedia of education* (3rd edn). Oxford: Elsevier.

Blum-Kulka, S. and Hamo, M. (eds. and co-authors) 2010. *Child peer talk: patterns of communication*. Tel-Aviv: The Center for Educational Technology [in Hebrew]. (forthcoming) *Kids' peer talk*. Oxford University Press.

Blum-Kulka, S., Huck-Taglicht, D. and Avni, H. 2004. 'The social and discursive spectrum of peer talk', *Discourse Studies* 6(3): 307–328.

Blum-Kulka, S. and Snow, C. E. (eds.) 2002. *Talking to adults*. Mahwah, NJ and London: Lawrence Erlbaum.

2004. 'Introduction: the potential of peer talk', *Discourse Studies* 6(3): 291–306.

Bodrova, E. and Leong, D. J. 2007. *Tools of the mind: the Vygotskian approach to early childhood education* (2nd edn). Columbus, OH: Merrill/Prentice Hall.

Bogdan, R. J. 2013. *Mindvaults: sociocultural grounds for pretending and imagining*. Cambridge, MA: MIT Press.

Braine, M. D. S. 1976. 'Children's first word combinations', *Monographs of the Society for Research in Child Development* 41(1).

Briggs, C. L. 1988. *Competence in performance: the creativity of tradition in Mexican verbal art*. Philadelphia, PA: University of Pennsylvania Press.

Brofenbrenner, U. and Ceci, S. J. 1994. 'Nature-nurture reconceptualized in developmental perspective: a bioecological model', *Psychological Review* 101: 568–586.

Broner, M. and Tarone, E. 2001. 'Is it fun? Language play in a fifth-grade Spanish immersion classroom', *The Modern Language Journal* 85: 363–379.

Brown, R. 1958. *Words and things: an introduction to language*. Free Press.

Brown, R. 1973. *A first language: the early stages*. Cambridge, MA: Harvard University Press.

Bruner, J. 1983. *Child's talk: learning to use language*. Oxford University Press.

Budwig, N. 1995. *A developmental-functionalist approach to child language*. Mahwah, NJ: Erlbaum.

Bushnell, K. 2008. '"Lego my keego!": an analysis of language play in a beginning Japanese as a foreign language classroom'. *Applied Linguistics* 30: 49–69.

Butler, C. and Weatherall, A. 2006. '"No we're not playing families": membership categorization in children's play', *Research on Language and Social Interaction* 39(4): 441–470.

Butler, J. 1990. *Gender trouble: feminism and the subversion of identity*. New York and London: Routledge.

Cathcart-Strong, R. 1986. 'Input generation by young second language learners', *TESOL Quarterly* 20: 515–530.

Cazden, C. B., John, V. and Hymes, D. 1972. *Function of language in the classroom*. New York: Teachers College Press.

Cekaite, A. 2007. 'A child's development of interactional competence in a Swedish L2 classroom', *The Modern Language Journal* 91: 45–62.

2009. 'Soliciting teacher attention in an L2 classroom: embodied actions and affective displays', *Applied Linguistics* 30: 26–48.

2012. 'Affective stances in teacher-novice student interactions: language, embodiment, and willingness to learn in a Swedish primary classroom', *Language in Society* 41: 641–670.

Cekaite, A. and Aronsson, K. 2004. 'Repetition and joking in children's second language conversations: playful recyclings in an immersion classroom', *Discourse Studies* 6: 373–392.

2005. 'Language play, a collaborative resource in children's L2 learning', *Applied Linguistics* 26: 169–191.

Cekaite, A. and Björk-Willén, P. 2013. 'Peer group interactions in multilingual educational settings: co-constructing social order and norms for language use', *International Journal of Bilingualism* 17: 174–188.

Cekaite, A. and Evaldsson, A.-C. 2008. 'Staging linguistic identities and negotiating monolingual norms in multiethnic school settings', *International Journal of Multilingualism* 5: 177–196.

Chen, D. W., Fein, G. G., Killen, M. and Tam, H. P. 2001. 'Peer conflicts of preschool children: issues, resolution, incidence and age-related patterns', *Early Education and Development* 12(4): 523–544.

Chomsky, N. 1965. *Aspects of a theory of syntax*. Cambridge MA: MIT Press.

Clarke, P. 1996. *Investigating second language acquisition in preschools: a longitudinal study of four Vietnames-speaking Children's acquisition of English in a bilingual preschool*. Ph.D. dissertation, La Trobe University, Melbourne.

Cobb-Moore, C., Danby, S. and Farrell, A. 2009. 'Young children as rule makers', *Journal of Pragmatics* 4(8): 1477–1492.

Connor, C. M., Morrison, F. J. and Slominski, L. 2006. 'Preschool instruction and children's emergent literacy growth', *Journal of Educational Psychology* 98: 665–689.

Cook, G. 2000. *Language play, language learning*. Oxford University Press.

Cook-Gumperz, J. and Gumperz, J. 1978. 'Context in children's speech', in N. Waterson and C. E. Snow (eds), *The development of communication*, pp. 3–23. New York: John Wiley and Sons.

Cooper, P. 2009. *The classrooms all young children need: lessons in teaching from Vivian Paley*. University of Chicago Press.

Corsaro, W. A. 1985. *Friendship and peer culture in the early years*. Norwood, NJ: Ablex.

1992. 'Interpretive reproduction in children's peer cultures', *Social Psychology Quarterly* 58: 160–177.

1993. 'Interpretive reproduction in children's role play', *Childhood* 1: 64–74.

1997. *The Sociology of Childhood*. Thousand Oaks, CA: Pine Forge Press.

2003. *We're friends, right?* Washington, DC: Joseph Henry Press.

2005. *The sociology of childhood* (2nd edn). Thousand Oaks, CA: Pine Forge Press.

2012. Peer cultures. In *Childhood Studies, Oxford Bibliographies*. www.oxfordbibliographies.com/page/childhood-studies.

Corsaro, W. A. and Rizzo, T. 1990. 'Disputes in the peer culture of American and Italian nursery school children', in A. Grimshaw (ed.), *Conflict talk: sociolinguistic investigations of arguments in conversation*, pp. 21–66. Cambridge University Press.

Coupland, N., Garrett, P. and Williams, A. 2005. 'Narrative demands, cultural performance and evaluation: teenage boys' stories for their age-peers' in J. Thornborrow

and J. Coates (eds.), *The sociolinguistics of narrative*, pp. 67–88. Amsterdam: John Benjamins.
Cromdal, J. 2001. 'Can I be with? Negotiating play entry in a bilingual school', *Journal of Pragmatics* 33: 515–543.
  2004. 'Building bilingual oppositions: codeswitching in children's disputes', *Language in Society* 33: 33–58.
  2009. 'Childhood and social interaction in everyday life: introduction to the special issue', *Journal of Pragmatics* 41: 1473–1476.
Cromdal, J. and Aronsson, K. 2000. 'Footing in bilingual play', *Journal of Sociolinguistics* 4(3): 435–457.
Crookal, D. 2007. 'Second language acquisition and simulation', *Simulation and Gaming* 38: 6–8.
Danby, S. and Theobald, M. (eds.) 2012. *Disputes in everyday life: social and moral orders of children and young people*. Studies of Children and Youth, Special Volume 15. New York: Emerald.
Dascal, M. 2000. 'Types of polemics and types of polemical moves', in H. S. Hill and G. Manetti (eds.), *Signs and significations*, vol. 2, pp. 127–150. New Delhi: Bahri.
De León, L. 1998. 'The emergent participant: interactive patterns in the socialization of Tzotzil (Mayan) infants', *Journal of Linguistic Anthropology* 8: 131–161.
  2007. 'Parallelism, metalinguistic play, and the interactive emergence of Zinacantec Mayan siblings' culture', *Research on Language and Social Interaction* 40: 405–535.
Department for Education 2011. *Bailey Review of the Commercialisation and Sexualisation of Childhood*. London: Department for Education.
Dickinson, D. 2001. 'Large-group and free-play times: conversational settings supporting language and literacy development', in D. Dickinson and P. Tabors (eds.), *Beginning literacy with language*, pp. 223–256. Baltimore, MD: Paul Brookes.
Di Cori, P. 1999. *Insegnare di storia*. Turin: Trauben Edizioni.
Dressler, W. U. and de Beaugrande, R. 1981. *Introduction to text linguistics*. London: Longman [original: *Einführung in die Textlinguistik*. Tübingen: Niemeyer].
Du Bois, J. 2007. 'The stance triangle', in R. Englebretson (ed.), *Stance in discourse: subjectivity and interaction*, pp. 13–182. Amsterdam: John Benjamins.
Dunn, J. 1999. 'Introduction: new directions in research on children's relationships and understanding', *Social Development* 8(2): 137–142.
Dunn, L. and Dunn, L. 1997. *Peabody Picture Vocabulary Test (PPVTIII)* (3rd edn). Circle Pines, MN: American Guidance Service.
Dunn, L., Dunn, L., Whetton, C. and Burley, J. 1997. *The British Picture Vocabulary Scale: Second Edition*. Windsor: NFER, Nelson.
Duranti, A. and Black, S. 2012. 'Language socialization and verbal improvisation', in A. Duranti, E. Ochs and B. Schieffelin (eds.), *The handbook of language socialization*, pp. 443–463. Malden, NJ: Wiley-Blackwell.
Duranti, A., Ochs, E. and Schieffelin, B. (eds.) 2012. *The handbook of language socialization*. Malden, NJ: Wiley-Blackwell.
Dyson, A. H. 2003. *The brothers and sisters learn to write: popular literacies in childhood and school cultures*. New York: Teachers College Press.
Edwards, D. 1993. 'Toward a discursive psychology of classroom education', prepared for a special issue of *Infancia y Aprendizaje*.

1997. *Discourse and cognition*. London: Sage.
Edwards, D. and Potter, J. 1992. *Discursive psychology*. London: Sage.
Enfield, N. J. and Levinson, S. C. 2002. 'Introduction: human sociality as a new interdisciplinary field', in N. J. Enfield and S. Levinson (eds.), *Roots of human sociality: culture, cognition and interaction*, pp. 1–35. Oxford and New York: Berg.
Ervin-Tripp, S. 1971. 'An overview of grammatical development', in D. Slobin (ed.), *The ontogenesis of grammar*. New York: Academic Press.
  1974. 'Is second language learning like the first?', *TESOL Quarterly* 8: 111–127.
  1986. 'Activity structure as scaffolding for children's second language learning', in W. Corsaro, J. Cook-Gumperz and J. Streeck (eds.), *Children's worlds and children's language*, pp. 327–58. Berlin: Mouton de Gruyter.
  1991. 'Play in language development', in B. Scales, M. C. Almy, A. Nicolopoulou and S. Ervin-Tripp (eds.), *Play and the social context of development in early care and education*, pp. 84–97. New York: Teachers College Press.
Ervin-Tripp, S. and Mitchell-Kernan, C. (eds.) 1977. *Child discourse*. New York: Academic Press.
Ervin-Tripp, S. M. and Reyes, I. 2005. 'Child-code-switching and adult content contrasts', *International Journal of Bilingualism* 9(1): 85–102.
Evaldsson, A.-C. 2002. 'Boys' gossip telling: staging identities and indexing (non-acceptable) masculine behavior', *Text* 22: 1–27.
  2005. 'Staging insults and mobilizing categorizations in a multiethnic peer group', *Discourse in Society* 16: 763–786.
  2007. 'Accounting for friendship: moral ordering and category membership in preadolescent girls' relational talk', *Research on Language and Social Interaction* 40(4): 377–404.
Evaldsson, A.-C. and Cekaite, A. 2010. '"SCHWEDIS he can't even say Swedish": subverting and reproducing institutionalized norms for language use in multilingual peer groups', *Pragmatics* 20: 587–604.
Fassler, R. 1998. 'Room for talk: peer support for getting into English in an ESL kindergarten', *Early Childhood Research Quarterly* 13: 379–409.
Fasulo, A., Girardet, H. and Pontecorvo, C. 1998. 'Historical practices in school through photographical reconstruction', *Mind, Culture and Activity* 5: 253–271.
Fasulo, A., Liberati, V. and Pontecorvo, C. 2002. 'Language games in the strict sense of the term: children's poetics and conversation', in S. Blum-Kulka and C. E. Snow (eds.), *Talking to adults: the contribution of multiparty discourse to language acquisition*, pp. 209–240. Mahwah, NJ: Lawrence Erlbaum.
Fasulo, A. and Pontecorvo, C. 1999. 'Discorso e istruzione', in C. Pontecorvo (ed.), *Manuale di psicologia dell'educazione*, pp. 67–90. Bologna: Il Mulino.
Fenson, L., P. Dale, et al. 1993. *MacArthur Communicative Development Inventories: User's guide and technical manual*. San Diego, CA: Singular Publishing.
Fernald, A. 1992. 'Human maternal vocalizations to infants as biologically relevant signals: an evolutionary perspective', in J. H. C. Barkow, L. Cosmides and J. Tooby (eds.), *The adapted mind: evolutionary psychology and the generation of culture*, pp. 391–428. New York: Oxford University Press.
Fielder, F. 1978. 'Leadership effectiveness', *American Behavioural Scientist* 24: 619–632.
Frith, S. 1996. 'Music and identity', in S. Hall and P. du Gay (eds.), *Questions of cultural identity*. London: Sage.

References

Galda, L. and Pellegrini, A. (eds.) 1985. *Play, language, and stories*. Norwood, NJ: Ablex.

Gallaway, C. and Richards, B. J. (eds.) 1994. *Input and interaction in language acquisition*. Cambridge University Press.

Garrett, P. 2007. 'Language socialization and the (re)production of bilingual subjectivities', in M. Heller (ed.), *Bilingualism: a social approach*, pp. 233–255. Hampshire: Palgrave Macmillan.

Garrett, P. and Baquedano-Lopez, P. 2002. 'Language socialization: reproduction and continuity, transformation and change', *Annual Review of Anthropology*: 31 339–361.

Garvey, C. 1977. 'Play with language and speech', in S. Ervin-Tripp and C. Mitchell-Kernan (eds.), *Child discourse*, pp. 27–49. New York: Academic Press.

  1990. *Play*. Cambridge, MA: Harvard University Press.

Geertz, C. 1973. 'Thick description: towards an interpretative theory of culture' in C. Geertz, *The interpretation of cultures: selected essays*, pp. 3–30. New York: Basic Books.

Genishi, C. and Di Paolo, M. 1982. 'Learning through argument in a pre-school' in L. C. Wilkinson (ed.), *Communication in the classroom*, pp. 49–68. New York: Academic Press.

Genishi, C. and Dyson, A. H. 2009. *Children, language, and literacy: diverse learners in diverse times*. New York: Teachers College Press.

Gentner, D. 1982. 'Why nouns are learned before verbs: linguistic relativity versus natural partitioning', in S. A. I. Kuczaj (ed), *Language development*, vol. 2: Language, thought, and culture, pp. 301–334. Hillsdale, NJ: Lawrence Erlbaum.

Georgakopoulou, G. 2007. *Small stories, identity and interaction*. Amsterdam: John Benjamins.

Gergen, K. J. and Gergen, M. M. 1986. *Social psychology*. New York: Springer Verlag.

Gibson, J. J. 1982. 'The theory of proprioception and its relation to volition: an attempt at clarification', in E. S. Reed and R. Jones (eds.), *Reasons for realism: selected essays of James J. Gibson*, pp. 385–388. Hillsdale, NJ: Lawrence Erlbaum.

Girardet, H. 1991. 'Spiegare i fenomeni storici', in C. Pontecorvo, A. Ajello and C. Zucchermaglio, *Discutendo si impara. Interazione sociale e conoscenza a scuola*. Rome: La Nuova Italia Scientifica.

Glenn, P. J. 1989. 'Initiating shared laughter in multi-party conversations', *Western Journal of Speech Communication* 53: 127–149.

Goffman, E. 1959. *The presentation of self in everyday life*. New York: Anchor.

  1967. *Interaction ritual: essays in face to face behavior*. Garden City, NY: Doubleday.

  1974. *Frame analysis: an essay on the organization of experience*. New York: Harper and Row.

  1978. 'Response cries', *Language* 54: 787–815.

  1981a. 'Footing', in E. Goffman (ed.), *Forms of talk*, pp. 124–159. Philadelphia, PA: University of Pennsylvania Press.

  1981b. *Forms of talk*. Cambridge, MA: Harvard University Press.

Goldberg, T., Schwarz, B.B. and Porat, D. 2011. '"Could they do it differently?" narrative and argumentative changes in students' writing following discussion of "hot" historical issues', *Cognition and Instruction* 29(2): 185–217.

Goldman, L. R. 1998. *Child's play: myth, mimesis, and make-believe*. Oxford: Berg.
González, N., Moll, L. C. and Amanti, C. 2005. *Funds of knowledge: theorizing practices in households, communities, and classrooms*. Mahwah, NJ: Lawrence Erlbaum.
Goodwin, C. 1984. 'Notes on story structure and the organization of participation', in J. M. Atkinson and J. Heritage (eds.), *Structures of social action*, pp. 25–46. Cambridge University Press.
　1994. 'Professional vision', *American Anthropologist* 96: 603–633.
　2000. 'Action and embodiment within situated human interaction', *Journal of Pragmatics* 32: 1489–1522.
　2007. 'Participation, stance and affect in the organization of activities', *Discourse in Society* 18: 53–73.
Goodwin, C. and Goodwin, M. H. 2004. 'Participation', in A. Duranti (ed.), *A companion to linguistic anthropology*, pp. 222–244. Oxford: Basil Blackwell.
Goodwin, M. H. 1990. *He-said-she-said: talk as social organization among black children*. Bloomington, IN: Indiana University Press.
　1993. 'Accomplishing social organization in girls' play: patterns of competition and cooperation in an African American working-class girls' group', in S. T. Hollis, L. Pershing and M. J. Young (eds.), *Feminist theory and the study of folklore*, pp. 149–165. Urbana, IL: University of Illinois Press.
　2006. *The hidden life of girls: games of stance, status, and exclusion*. Oxford: Blackwell.
Goodwin, M. H., Cekaite, A. and Goodwin, C. 2012. 'Emotion as stance', in A. Peräkylä and M.-J. Sorjonen (eds.), *Emotion in interaction*, pp.16–42. Oxford University Press.
Goodwin, M. and Goodwin, C. 2000. 'Emotion in situated activity', in N. Budwig, I. C. Uzgiris and J. Wertsch (eds.), *Communication: an arena of development*, pp. 33–53. Stamford: Ablex.
Goodwin, M. H. and Kyratzis, A. 2007. 'Children socializing children: practices for negotiating the social order among peers', *Research on Language and Social Interaction* 40: 279–289.
　2012. 'Peer language socialization', in A. Duranti, E. Ochs and B. Schieffelin (eds.), *The handbook of language socialization*, pp. 365–390. Malden, NJ: Wiley-Blackwell.
Gordon, C. 2002. '"I'm mommy and you're Natalie": role-reversal and embedded frames in mother-child discourse', *Language in Society* 31: 679–720.
Gopnik, A. 2009. *The philosophical baby: what children's minds tell us about truth, love, and the meaning of life*. London: The Bodley Head.
Gopnik, A. and Choi, S. 1990. 'Language and cognition', *First Language* 10: 199–216.
Govier, T. 2001. *A practical study of argument* (5th edn). Belmont, CA: Wadsworth/Thomson Learning.
Grimshaw, A. D. (ed.) 1990. *Conflict talk: sociolinguistic investigations of arguments in conversations*. Cambridge University Press.
Grøver Aukrust, V. 2001. 'Talk-focused talk in preschools – culturally formed socialization for talk?', *First Language* 21: 57–82.

References

2004. 'Explanatory discourse in young second language learners' peer play', *Discourse Studies* 6: 393–412.

2009. 'Young children acquiring second language vocabulary in preschool group-time: does amount, diversity, and discourse complexity of teacher talk matter?', *Journal of Research in Childhood Education* 22: 17–37.

Grøver Aukrust, V. and Rydland, V. 2009. '"Does it matter?" Talking about ethnic diversity in preschool and first-grade classrooms', *Journal of Pragmatics* 41: 1538–1556.

2011. 'Preschool classroom conversations as long-term resources for second language and literacy acquisition', *Journal of Applied Developmental Psychology* 32: 198–207.

Grøver Aukrust, V. and Snow, C. E. 1998. 'Narratives and explanations during mealtime in Norway and U.S.', *Language in Society* 27: 221–246.

Gumperz, J. 1982. 'Conversational code-switching', in J. Gumperz, *Discourse strategies*, pp. 59–99. Cambridge University Press.

1996. 'The linguistic and cultural relativity of inference', in J. Gumperz and S. C. Levinson (eds.), *Rethinking cultural relativity*, pp. 374–406. Cambridge University Press.

Gumperz, J. and Cook-Gumperz, J. 2005. 'Making space for bilingual communicative practice', *Intercultural Pragmatics* 2(1): 1–24.

Hamo, M. and Blum-Kulka, S. 2007. 'Apprenticeship in conversation and culture: emerging sociability in preschool peer talk', in J. Valsiner and A. Rosa (eds.), *The Cambridge handbook of sociocultural psychology*, pp. 423–444. New York: Cambridge University Press.

Hamo, M., Blum-Kulka, S. and Hacohen, G. 2004. 'From observation to transcription: theory, practice and interpretation in the analysis of children's naturally occurring discourse', *Research on Language and Social Interaction* 37: 71–88.

Harris, P. L. 2000. *The work of the imagination*. Oxford: Blackwell.

Harris, P. L., Johnson, C., Hutton, D., Andrews, G. and Cooke, T. 1989. 'Young children's theory of mind and emotion', *Cognition and Emotion* 3: 379–400.

Harris, P. L. and Kavanaugh, R. D. 1993. 'Young children's understanding of pretense', *Society for Research in Child Development Monographs*. (Serial No. 231).

Harré, R. and Van Langenhoeve, L. 1991. 'Varieties of positioning', *Journal for the Theory of Social Behaviour* 21: 393–407.

Hart, B. and Risley, T. R. 1995. *Meaningful differences in the everyday experience of young American children*. Baltimore, MD: Paul Brookes.

He, A. W. 2002. 'Speaking variedly: socialization in speech roles in Chinese heritage language classes', in R. Bailey and S. Schecter (eds.), *Language socialization and bilingualism*. Clevedon, UK: Multilingual Matters.

Heath, S. B. 1983. *Ways with words*. Cambridge University Press.

1986. 'Taking a cross-cultural look at narratives', *Topics in Language Disorders* 7: 84–94.

Hedegaard, M., Aronsson, K., Höjholt, C. and Ulvik, O. (eds.) 2012. *Children, childhood, and everyday life*. Charlotte, NC: Information Age Publishing.

Heller, M. (ed.) 2007. *Bilingualism: a social approach*. New York: Palgrave Macmillan.

Henry, G. and Rickman, D. 2007. 'Do peers influence children's skill development in preschool?', *Economics of Education Review* 26: 100–112.

Hickmann, M. 2003. *Children's discourse*. Cambridge University Press.
Hirschler, J. 1991. *Preschool children's help to second-language learners*. (Unpublished doctoral dissertation, Harvard University).
Hoff, E. 2006. 'How social contexts support and shape language development', *Developmental Review* 26: 55–88.
Hoyle, S. M. 1998. 'Register and footing in role play', in S. M. Hoyle and C. T. Adger (eds.), *Kids talk: strategic language use in later childhood*, pp. 47–67. Oxford University Press.
Howard, K. M. 2009. 'Breaking in and spinning out: repetition and decalibration in Thai children's play genres', *Language in Society* 38: 339–363.
Howes, C., Droege, K. and Matheson, C. C. 1994. 'Play and communicative processes within long- and short-term friendship dyads', *Journal of Social and Personal Relationships* 11: 401–410.
Huang, J. and Hatch, E. 1978. 'A Chinese child's acquisition of English', in E. Hatch (ed.), *Second language acquisition: a book of readings*, pp. 383–400. Rowley, MA: Newbury House.
Hummelstedt, I. 2010. '"Ja har Afrika å du har Asia": etnicitet som resurs i flerspråkiga elevers vardagsinteraktion'*, Pedagogiska fakulteten, Vasa: Åbo Akademi.
Hunston, S. and Thompson, G. 2000. 'Evaluation: an introduction', in S. Hunston and G. Thompson (eds.), *Evaluation in text: authorial stance and the construction of discourse*, pp. 1–27. Oxford University Press.
Huttenlocher, J., Vasilyeva, M., Waterfall, H. R., Vevea, J. L. and Hedges, L. V. 2007. 'The varieties of speech to young children', *Developmental Psychology* 43: 1062–1083.
Hutto, D. D. 2008. *Folk psychological narratives: the sociocultural basis of understanding reasons*. Cambridge, MA: MIT Press.
Hymes, D. H. 1972. 'On communicative competence' in J. B. Pride and J. Holmes (eds.), *Sociolinguistics*, pp. 269–293. Harmondsworth: Penguin.
Hymes, D. 1974. *Foundations in sociolinguistics: an ethnographic approach*. Philadelphia, PA: University of Pennsylvania Press.
Ilgaz, H. and Aksu-Koc, A. 2005. 'Episodic development in preschool children's play prompted and direct-elicited narratives, *Cognitive Development* 20: 526–44.
Jakobson, R. 1960. 'Closing statement: linguistics and poetics', in T. A. Sebeok (ed.): *Style in language*. Cambridge, MA: MIT Press.
Jaffe, A. 2009. 'Introduction: the sociolinguistics of stance', in A. Jaffe (ed.), *Stance: sociolinguistic perspectives*, pp. 3–28. Oxford University Press.
Jefferson, G. 1996. 'On the poetics of ordinary talk', *Text and Performance Quarterly* 16:1–61.
Kampf, Z. and Blum-Kulka, S. 2007. 'Do children apologize to each other? Apology events in young Israeli peer discourse', *Journal of Politeness Research* 3(1): 11–27.
  2011. 'Why Israeli children are better at settling disputes than Israeli politicians', in F. Bargiela-Chiappini and D. Kádár (eds.), *Politeness across cultures*, pp. 85–105. Basingstoke: Palgrave Macmillan.
Karrebæck, M. 2008. *At blive et børnehavebarn: en minoritetsdrengs sprog, interaktion og deltagelse i børnefællesskabet*. [Becoming a preschool child: a minority boy's language, interaction and participation in children's community]. Copenhagen: Faculty of Humanities, Copenhagen University.

References

Kärkkäinen, E. 2006. 'Stance taking in conversation: from subjectivity to intersubjectivity', *Text and Talk* 26: 699–731.
Keenan, E. 1983. 'Making it last: repetition in children's discourse', in E. Ochs and B. Schieffelin (eds.), *Acquisition of conversational competence*, pp. 26–39. Boston, MA: Routledge & Kegan Paul.
Kemler Nelson, D. G. 1999. 'Attention to functional properties in toddlers' naming and problem-solving', *Cognitive Development* 14: 77–100.
Kim, Y. and Kellogg, D. 2007. 'Rules out of order: differences in play language and their developmental significance', *Applied Linguistics* 28: 25–45.
Kirschenblatt-Gimblett, B. 1979. 'Speech play and verbal art', in B. Sutton-Smith (ed.), *Play and learning*, pp. 219–238. Philadelphia, PA: University of Pennsylvania Press.
Koven, M. 2002. 'An analysis of speaker role inhabitance in narratives of personal experience', *Journal of Pragmatics* 34: 167–217.
Kyratzis, A. 1993. 'Pragmatic and discourse influences on the acquisition of subordination-coordination', *Proceedings of the 25th Annual Meeting of the Stanford Child Language Research Forum*, pp. 324–332. Stanford, CA: CSLI Publications.
  1999. 'Narrative identity: preschoolers' self-construction through narrative in same-sex friendship group dramatic play', *Narrative Inquiry* 9: 427–455.
  2004. 'Talk and interaction among children and the co-construction of peer groups and peer culture', *Annual Review of Anthropology* 33: 625–649.
  2007. 'Using the social organization affordances of pretend play in American preschool girls' interactions', *Research on Language and Social Interaction* 40(4): 321–352.
  2010. 'Latina girls' peer play interactions in a bilingual Spanish-English US preschool: heteroglossia, frame-shifting, and language ideology', *Pragmatics* 20: 557–586.
Kyratzis, A. and Guo, J. 2001. 'Preschool girls' and boys' verbal conflict strategies in the US and China: cross-cultural and contextual considerations', *Research on Language and Social Interaction* 3: 445–475.
Kyratzis, A., Reynolds, J. and Evaldsson, A.-C. 2010. 'Heteroglossia and language ideologies in children's peer play interactions', *Pragmatics* 20(4): 457–466.
Kyratzis, A., Tang, Y. and Köymen, S. B. 2009. 'Codes, code-switching, and context: style and footing in peer group bilingual play', *Multilingua-Journal of Crosscultural and Interlanguage Communication* 28(2–3): 265–290.
Küntay, A. and Ervin-Tripp, S. 1997. 'Conversational narratives of children: occasions and structures', *Journal of Narrative and Life History* 7: 113–128.
Labov, W. 1972. *Language in the inner city*. University of Philadelphia Press.
Ladd, G. 2009. 'Trends, travails, and turning points in early research on children's peer relationships: legacies and lessons for our time?', in K. H. Rubin, W. M. Bukowski and B. Laursen (eds.), *Handbook of peer interactions, relationships, and groups*. New York: Guildford.
Larsen-Freeman, D. 2010. 'Having and doing: learning from a complexity theory perspective', in P. Seedhouse, S. Walsh and C. Jenks (eds.), *Conceptualising learning in Applied Linguistics*, pp. 52–68. Hampshire, UK: Palgrave Macmillan.
Lave, J. and Wenger, E. 1991. *Situated learning: legitimate peripheral participation*. Cambridge University Press.

References

Leseman, P. P. M. 2000. 'Bilingual vocabulary development of Turkish preschoolers in the Netherlands', *Journal of Multilingual and Multicultural Development* 21: 93–112.

Levinson, S. 2002. 'On the human interactive engine', in N. J. Enfield and S. Levinson (eds.), *Roots of human sociality: culture, cognition and interaction*, pp. 39–70. Oxford and New York: Berg.

Lewis, M. M. 1951. *Infant speech: a study of the beginnings of language*. New York: The Humanities Press.

Lillard, A. 2011. 'Mother–child fantasy play', in A. D. Pellegrini (ed.) *The Oxford handbook of play*, pp. 284–295. New York: Oxford University Press.

Livingstone, S. 2002. *Young people and new media*. London: Sage.

Livingstone, S. and Bober, M. 2004. *UK Children Go Online: Final Report of Key Project Findings*. London: London School of Economics and Political Science.

Logan Kelin, N. 2011. 'Doing gender categorization: non recognitional person reference and the omnirelevance of gender', in S. A. Speer and E. Stokoe (eds.), *Conversation and gender*, pp. 64–82. Cambridge University Press.

Maas, F. K. and Abbeduto, L. 2001. 'Children's judgements about intentionally and unintentionally broken promises', *Journal of Child Language* 28(2): 517–529.

Maccoby, E. 2002. 'Gender and group process: a developmental perspective', *Current Directions in Psychological Science* 11: 54–58.

MacWhinney, B. 1995. *The CHILDES project: Tools for analyzing talk*. Hillsdale, NJ: Erlbaum.

Mail Online 2009. www.dailymail.co.uk/tvshowbiz/article-1167995/EastEnders-fans-uproar-41-000-tell-producers-bring-Danielle-dead.html, April 7.

Mandler, J. M. and Johnson, N. S. 1977. 'Remembrance of things parsed: story structure and recall', *Cognitive Psychology* 9: 111–191.

Martin, J. R. 2000. 'Beyond exchange: appraisal systems in English' in S. Hunston and G. Thompson (eds.), *Evaluation in text: authorial stance and the construction of discourse*, pp. 142–175. Oxford University Press.

Martin, J. R. and White, P. R. R. 2005. *The language of evaluation: appraisal in English*. Basingstoke: Palgrave Macmillan.

Mashburn, A. J., Justice, L. M., Downer, J. T. and Pianta, R. C. 2009. 'Peer effects on children's language achievement during pre-kindergarten', *Child Development* 80: 686–702.

Maybin, J. 2006. *Children's voices: talk, knowledge and identity*. Houndmills: Palgrave Macmillan.

McNamee, G. 1987. 'The social origins of narrative skills', in M. Hickmann (ed.), *Social and functional approaches to language and thought*, pp. 287–304. Orlando, FL: Academic Press.

McNeill, D. 1970. *The acquisition of language: the study of developmental psycholinguistics*. New York: Harper & Row.

McTear, M. 1985. *Children's conversation*. Oxford: Blackwell.

Mercer, N. 1992. 'Culture, context, and the construction of knowledge', in P. Light and G. Butterworth (eds.), *Context and cognition: ways of learning and knowing*, pp. 28–46. London: Harvester Wheatsheaf.

    2004. 'Sociocultural discourse analysis: analysing classroom talk as a social mode of thinking', *Journal of Applied Linguistics* 1(2): 137–168.

Meyer, C. A. 1989. *The role of peer relationships in the socialization of children to preschool: a Korean example*. Ph.D. dissertation, Ohio State University, Columbus.

Minks, A. 2010. 'Socializing heteroglossia among Miskitu children on the Caribbean Coast of Nicaragua', *Pragmatics* 20: 495–522.

Monaco, C. 2007. '"Poi devi trovare anche la risposta logica". Pensare storicamente in quarta elementare: un'esperienza di lavoro in piccolo gruppo', *Rivista di Psicolinguistica Applicata* VII(1–2): 39–68.

Monnot, C. 2010. 'The female pop singer and the "Apprentice" girl: learning femininity through pop music role models in France', *Journal of Children and Media* 4(3): 283–297.

Mor, E. 2010. 'Between fiction and reality in preschoolers' pretend play', in S. Blum-Kulka and M. Hamo (eds.), *Child talk: patterns of communication in peer talk*, pp. 209–261. Tel-Aviv: The Center for Educational Technology [in Hebrew].

Muller Mirza, N. and Perret-Clermont, A. N. (eds.) 2009. *Argumentation and education: theoretical foundations and practices*. Dordrecht: Springer.

Muntigl, P. and Turnbull, B. 1998. 'Conversational structure and facework in arguing', *Journal of Pragmatics* 29(3): 225–256.

Nelson, K. 1973. 'Structure and strategy in learning to talk', *Monographs of The Society for Research in Child Development*, Serial 143, vol. 38.

  1986. *Event knowledge: structure and function in development*. Hillsdale, NJ, Lawrence Erlbaum Assoc.

  1989. *Narratives from the crib*. Cambridge, MA: Harvard University Press.

  1996. *Language in cognitive development: the emergence of the mediated mind*. New York: Cambridge University Press.

  2003. 'Narrative and self, myth and memory', in R. Fivush and C. Haden (eds.), *Autobiographical memory and the construction of a narrative self: developmental and cultural perspectives*, pp. 3–28. Mahwah, NJ: Erlbaum.

  2004. 'Construction of the cultural self in early narratives', in C. Daiute and C. Lightfoot (eds.), *Narrative analysis: studying the development of individuals in society*, pp. 87–110. London: Sage.

  2007. *Young minds in social worlds: experience, meaning, and memory*. Cambridge, MA: Harvard University Press.

Nelson, K., Hampson, J. and Shaw, L. 1993. 'Nouns in early lexicons: evidence, explanations, and implications', *Journal of Child Language* 20: 61–84.

Nicolopoulou, A. 1996. 'Narrative development in social context', in D. Slobin, J. Gerhardt, J. Guo and A. Kyratzis (eds.), *Social interaction, social context, and language: essays in honor of Susan Ervin-Tripp*, pp. 369–390. Mahwah, NJ: Erlbaum.

  1997. 'Worldmaking and identity formation in children's narrative play-acting', in B. Cox and C. Lightfoot (eds.), *Sociogenetic perspectives on internalization*, pp. 157–187. Mahwah, NJ: Erlbaum.

  2002. 'Peer-group culture and narrative development', in S. Blum-Kulka and C. E. Snow (eds.), *Talking to adults: the contribution of multiparty discourse to language acquisition*, pp. 117–152. Mahwah, NJ: Erlbaum.

Nicolopoulou, A., McDowell, J. and Brockmeyer, C. 2006. 'Narrative play and emergent literacy: storytelling and story-acting meet journal writing', in D. Singer, R. Golinkoff and K. Hirsh-Pasek (eds.), *Play=learning: how play motivates and enhances children's cognitive and social-emotional growth*, pp.124–144. New York: Oxford University Press.

Nicolopoulou, A. and Richner, E. 2004. '"When your powers combine, I am Captain Planet": the developmental significance of individual- and group-authored stories by preschoolers', *Discourse Studies* 6: 347–371.

Nicolopoulou, A., Scales, B. and Weintraub, J. 1994. 'Gender differences and symbolic imagination in the stories of four-year-olds', in A. H. Dyson and C. Genishi (eds.), *The need for story: cultural diversity in classroom and community*, pp. 102–23. Urbana, IL: NCTE.

Nicolopoulou, A. and Weintraub, J. 1998. 'Individual and collective representations in social context: a modest contribution to resuming the interrupted project of a sociocultural developmental psychology', *Human Development* 41: 215–235.

Ninio, A. and Snow, C. 1996. *Pragmatic development*. Boulder, CO: Westview Press.

Ochs, E. 1988. *Culture and language development*. Cambridge University Press.

　　1993. 'Constructing social identity: a language socialization perspective', *Research on Language and Social Interaction* 26: 287–306.

　　1996. 'Linguistic resources for socializing humanity', in J. Gumperz and S. Levinson (eds.), *Rethinking linguistic relativity*, pp. 407–437. New York: Cambridge University Press.

　　2002. 'Becoming a speaker of culture: language socialization and language acquisition: ecological perspectives', in C. Kramsch (ed.), *Language acquisition and language learning*, pp. 99–120. New York: Continuum Press.

Ochs, E. and Schieffelin, B. (eds.) 1979. *Developmental pragmatics*. New York: Academic Press.

　　1989. 'Language has a heart', *Text* 9(1): 7–25.

Ochs, E., Smith, R. and Taylor, C. 1989. 'Detective stories at dinnertime: problem-solving through co-narration', *Cultural Dynamics* 2: 238–257.

OECD 2006. *Starting strong II: early childhood education and care*. Paris: OECD.

Oliver, R. and Grote, E. 2010. 'The provision and uptake of different types of recasts in child and adult ESL learners: what is the role of age and context?', *Australian Review of Applied Linguistics* 33: 26.1–26.22.

Olson, D. R. 1994. *The world on paper: the conceptual and cognitive implications of writing and reading*. Cambridge University Press.

　　1996. 'Language and literacy: what writing does to language and mind', *Annual Review of Applied Linguistics* 16: 3–13.

　　2009. 'Language, literacy and mind: the Literacy Hypothesis', *Psykhe [online]* 18, N1: 3–9.

Ong, W. J. 1982. *Orality and literacy: the technologizing of the word*. New York: Routledge.

Opie, I. and Opie, P. 1959. *Children's games in the street and playground*. Oxford: Clarendon Press.

Orsolini, M. and Pontecorvo, C. 1992. 'Children's talk in classroom discussions', *Cognition and Instruction* 9: 113–136.

Pagani, L. S., Jalbert, J., Lapointe, P. and Hérbert, M. 2006. 'Effects of junior kindergarten on emerging literacy in children from low-income and linguistic-minority families', *Early Childhood Education Journal*, 33: 209–215.

Painter, C. 2003. 'Developing attitude: an ontogenetic perspective on appraisal', *Text* 23(2): 183–209.
Paley, V. 1986. *Mollie is three: growing up in school*. University of Chicago Press.
  1990. *The boy who would be a helicopter: the uses of storytelling in the classroom*. Cambridge, MA: Harvard University Press.
Pallotti, G. 2001. 'External appropriations as a strategy for participating in intercultural multi-party conversation', in A. Di Luzio, S. Gunthner and F. Orletti (eds.), *Culture in communication: analyses of intercultural situations*, pp. 295–334. Amsterdam: John Benjamins.
Pan, B. A., Rowe, M. L., Singer, J. D. and Snow, C. E. 2005. 'Maternal correlates of growth in toddler vocabulary production in low-income families', *Child Development* 76: 763–782.
Paugh, A. 2005. 'Multilingual play: children's code-switching, role-play, and agency in Dominica, West Indies', *Language in Society* 34: 63–86.
  2012. *Playing with languages: children and change in a Caribbean village*. New York: Berghah Books.
Peck, S. 1980. 'Language play in child second language acquisition', in D. Larsen-Freeman (ed.), *Discourse analysis in second language research*. Rowley, MA: Newbury House.
Pellegrini, A. D. 1985. 'The relations between symbolic play and literate behavior', *Review of Educational Research* 55: 107–121.
  2009. *The role of play in human development*. New York: Oxford University Press.
  2010. 'Play and games mean different things in an educational context', *Nature* 467: 27.
Pellegrini, A. D. and Galda, L. 1998. *The development of school-based literacy: a social ecological perspective*. London: Taylor and Francis.
Peters, A. 1983. *The units of language acquisition*. Cambridge University Press.
Peterson, C. 1994. 'Narrative skills and social class', *Canadian Journal of Education* 19: 251–269.
Philp, J. and Duchesne, S. 2008. 'When the gate opens: the interaction between social and linguistic goals in child second language development', in J. Philp and R. Oliver (eds.), *Child's play? Child second language acquisition*, pp. 83–104. Amsterdam: John Benjamins.
Philp, J., Mackey, A. and Oliver, R. 2008. 'Child's play? Second language acquisition and the young learner in context', in J. Philp and R. Oliver (eds.), *Child's play? Child second language acquisition*, pp. 3–26. Amsterdam: John Benjamins.
Piaget, J. 1962. *Play, dreams, and imitation in childhood*. New York: Norton.
  1995. *Sociological studies*. London: Routledge.
Piirainen-Marsh, A. and Tainio, L. 2009. 'Other-repetition as a resource for participation in the activity of playing a video-game', *Modern Language Journal* 93: 153–169.
Plantin, C. 2002. 'Argumentation studies and discourse analysis: the French situation and global perspectives', *Discourse Studies* 4(3): 343–368.
Pontecorvo, C. 1985. 'Discutere per ragionare: la costruzione della conoscenza come argomentazione', *Rassegna di psicologia* 2(1–2): 23–45.
  1991. 'Il contributo della prospettiva vygotskiana alla psicologia dell'istruzione', in C. Pontecorvo, A. M. Ajello and C. Zuccermaglio (eds.), *Discutendo si impara:*

interazione sociale e conoscenza a scuola, pp. 21–38. Rome: La Nuova Italia Scientifica.
  (ed.) 1999. *Manuale di psicologia dell'educazione*. Bologna: Il Mulino.
Pontecorvo, C. and Arcidiacono, F. 2010. 'Development of reasoning through arguing in young children', *Cultural-Historical Psychology* 4: 19–29.
Pontecorvo, C. and Girardet, H. 1993. 'Arguing and reasoning in understanding historical topics', *Cognition and Instruction* 11: 365–395.
Pontecorvo, C. and Pontecorvo, M. 1986. *Psicologia dell'educazione: conoscere a scuola*. Bologna: Il Mulino.
Pontecorvo, C. and Sterponi, L. 2002. 'Learning in educational setting', in G. Wells and G. Claxton (eds.), *Learning for life in the 21st century*, pp. 127–140. Oxford: Blackwell.
  2006. 'Explication et justification dans les séquences de rendre compte (accountability): moralité et raisonnement dans les discours familiaux', in C. Hudelot, A. Salazar Orvig and E. Veneziano (eds.), *L'explication: enjeux cognitifs et interactionnels*, pp. 245–254. Paris: Peeters Edition.
Potter, J. and Wetherell, M. 1987. *Discourse and social psychology*. London: Sage.
Poveda, D. 2005. 'Metalinguistic activity, humour and social competence in classroom discourse', *Pragmatics* 15: 89–107.
Premack, D. G. and Woodruff, G. 1978. 'Does the chimpanzee have a theory of mind?', *Behavioral and Brain Sciences* 1(4): 515–526.
Prout, A. 2005. *The future of childhood: towards the interdisciplinary study of children*. London: Falmer Press.
Rampton, B. 1995. *Crossing: language and ethnicity among adolescents*. London: Longman.
  2002. 'Ritual and foreign language practices at school', *Language in Society* 31: 491–525.
  2006. *Language in late modernity*. Cambridge University Press.
Ravid, D. and Tolchinsky, L. 2002. 'Developing linguistic literacy: a comprehensive model', *Journal of Child Language* 29(2): 417–447.
Raymond, G. and Heritage, J. 2006. 'The epistemics of social relations: owning grandchildren', *Language in Society* 35: 677–705.
Reynolds, J. F. 2007. 'Buenos dias'(military salute): the natural history of a coined insult', *Research on Language and Social Interaction* 40: 437–466.
  2010. 'Enregistering the voices of discursive figures of authority in Antonero children's socio-dramatic play', *Pragmatics* 20: 467–493.
Richner, E. and Nicolopoulou, A. 2001. 'The narrative construction of differing conceptions of the person in the development of young children's social understanding', *Early Education and Development* 12: 393–432.
Rindstedt, C. and Aronsson, K. 2002. 'Growing up monolingual in a bilingual community', *Language in Society* 31: 721–42.
Robinson, E. J. and Beck, S. R. 2000. 'What is difficult about counterfactual reasoning?', in P. Mitchell and K. J. Riggs (eds.), *Children's reasoning and the mind*, pp. 101–119. Hove, UK: Psychology Press.
Rogoff, B. 1998. 'Cognition as a collaborative process', in D. Kuhn and R. S. Siegler (eds.) *Handbook of child psychology*, vol. 2: Cognition, Perception, and Language (5th edn), pp. 679–744. New York: Wiley.
  2003. *The cultural nature of human development*. Oxford University Press.

Rogoff, B., Mistry, J., Göncü, A. and Mosier, C. 1993. 'Guided participation in cultural activity by toddlers and caregivers', *Monographs of the Society for Research in Child Development* 236(58, no. 8): 1–179.
Roskos, K. A., Christie, J. F., Widman, S. and Holding, A. 2010. 'Three decades in: priming for meta-analysis in play-literacy research', *Journal of Early Childhood Literacy* 10(1): 55–96.
Rubin, K. H., Fein, G. and Vandenberg, B. 1983. 'Play', in E. M. Hetherington (ed.), *The handbook of child psychology: social development*, pp.693–774. New York: Wiley.
Ruble, D. N., Martin, C. L. and Berenbaum, S. A. 2006. 'Gender development', in W. Damon and N. Eisenberg (eds.), *Handbook of child psychology*, vol. 3: Social, emotional, and personality development, pp. 858–932. Hoboken, NJ: Wiley.
Rydland, V. 2009. '"Wow – when I was going to pretend drinking it tasted Coke for real!": second-language learners' out-of-frame talk in peer pretend play. A developmental study from preschool to first grade', *European Journal of Developmental Psychology* 6: 190–222.
Rydland, V. and Grøver Aukrust, V. 2005. 'Lexical repetition in second language learners' peer play interaction', *Language Learning* 55: 229–253.
Sacks, H. 1992. *Lectures on conversation* (vols. I and II). Oxford: Basil Blackwell.
Sacks, H., Schegloff, E. A. and Jefferson, G. 1974. 'A simplest systematics for turn taking', *Language* 50: 696–735.
Sahlström, F., Forsman, L., Hummelstedt, I., Pörn, M., Rusk, F. and Slotte-Lüttge, A. 2013. *Inga konstigheter* [Nothing special]. Stockholm: Liber.
Sale, M. 1992. 'Call and response as critical method: African-American oral traditions and beloved', *African American Review: Women Writers Issue* 26(1): 41–50.
Saville-Troike, M. 1976. *Foundations for teaching English as a second language: theory and method for multicultural education*. New Jersey: Prentice Hall.
Sawyer, R. K. 1995. 'A developmental model of heteroglossic improvisation in children's fantasy play', *Sociological Studies of Children* 7: 127–153.
  1997. *Pretend play as improvisation: conversation in the preschool classroom*. Mahwah, NJ: Lawrence Erlbaum.
  2001. 'Play as improvisational rehearsal – multiple levels of analysis in children's play', in A. Goncu and E. Klein (eds.), *Children in play, story and school*, pp.19–38. New York: Guilford Press.
  2002. 'Improvisation and narrative', *Narrative Inquiry* 12(2): 321–351.
  2005. 'Music and conversation', in D. Miell, R. Macdonald and D. Hargreaves (eds.), *Musical communication*, pp. 45–60. Oxford University Press.
Schechter, C. and Bye, B. 2007. 'Preliminary evidence for the impact of mixed-income preschools on low-income children's language growth', *Early Childhood Research Quarterly* 22: 137–146.
Schegloff, E. A. 2007. *Sequence organization in interaction:. a primer in Conversation Analysis I*. New York: Cambridge University Press.
Schegloff, E. A., Jefferson, G. and Sacks, H. 1977. 'The preference for self-correction in the organization of repair in conversation', *Language* 53(2): 362–382.
Schiefelbusch, R. and Pickar, R. 1984. *The acquisition of communicative competence*. Baltimore, MD: University Park Press.
Schieffelin, B. 1990. *The give and take of everyday Kaluli children*. Cambridge University Press.

1994. 'Code-switching and language socialization: some probable relationships', in J. Felson Duchan et al. (eds.), *Pragmatics: from theory to practice*, pp. 20–43. New York: Prentice Hall.
Schieffelin, B. and Kulick, D. 2004. 'Language socialization', in A. Duranti (ed.), *Companion to linguistic anthropology*, pp. 349–368. London: Blackwell.
Schieffelin, B. and Ochs, E. (eds.) 1986. *Language socialization across cultures*. Cambridge University Press.
Schiffrin, D. 1985. 'Everyday argument: the organization of diversity in talk', in T. A. van Dijk (ed.), *Handbook of discourse analysis*, vol. 3: Discourse and dialogue, pp. 35–46. London: Academic Press.
Scollon, R. and Scollon, S. 1981. *Narrative, literacy and face in interethnic communication*. Norwood, NJ: Ablex.
Segal, M. 2008. *What's the story? On the development of narrative competence*. Tel Aviv: The Mofet Institute Press, [in Hebrew].
2011. *The tower falled (the tower fell down): word innovations created by children and their analysis*. Tel Aviv: The Mofet Institute Press [in Hebrew].
Seidman, S., Nelson, K. and Gruendel, J. 1986. 'Make believe scripts: the transformation of ERs in fantasy', in K. Nelson (ed.), *Event knowledge: structure and function in development*, pp. 161–187. Hillsdale, NJ: Lawrence Erlbaum Associates.
Sheldon, A. 1996. 'You can be the baby brother but you aren't born yet: preschool girls' negotiation for power and access in pretend play', in Constituting gender through talk in childhood: conversations in parent-child, peer, and sibling relationships (special issue) *Research on Language and Social Interaction* 29:57–80.
Silverstein, M. 1993. 'Metapragmatic discourse and metapragmatic function', in J. Lucy (ed.), *Reflexive language*, pp. 33–58. New York: Cambridge University Press.
Siraj-Blatchford, I. and Mani, L. 2008. '"Would you like to tidy up now?" An analysis of adult questioning in the English Foundation Stage', *Early Years* 28: 5–22.
Slotte-Lüttge, A. 2005. *'Ja vet int va de heter på svenska.' Interaktion mellan tvåspråkiga elever och deras lärare i en enspråkig klassrumsdiskurs*. ['I don't know how to say it in Swedish.' Interaction Between Bilingual Students and their Teachers in a Monolingual Classroom Discourse]. Dissertation, Åbo Akademi University Press.
Slotte-Lüttge, A., Pörn, M. and Sahlström, F. 2013. 'Learning how to be a *tähti*: a case study of language development in everyday situations of a seven-year-old multilingual Finnish child', *Internation Journal of Bilingualism* 17: 153–173.
Smith, P. K. 2005. 'Play types and functions in human development', in B. J. Ellis and D. F. Bjorklund (eds.), *Origins of the social mind: evolutionary psychology and child development*, pp. 271–291. New York: Guilford.
Smith, P. K. and Vollstedt, R. 1985. 'On defining play: an empirical study on the relationship between play and various play criteria', *Child Development* 5: 1042–1050.
Snow, C. E. 1984. 'Parent-child interaction and the development of communicative ability', in R. Schiefelbush and J. Pickar (eds.), *Communicative competence: acquisition and intervention*, pp. 69–107. Baltimore, MD: University Park Press.
1999. 'Facilitating language development promotes literacy learning', in L. Eldering and P. P. M. Leseman (eds.), *Effective early education: cross-cultural perspectives*, pp. 141–162. New York: Falmer Press.

2004. 'What counts as literacy in early childhood?' in K. McCartney and D. Philips (eds.), *Handbook of early child development*. Oxford: Blackwell.
Snow, C. and Ferguson, C. A. (eds.) 1977. *Talking to children: language input and acquisition*. Cambridge University Press.
Snow, C. E., Porche, M. V., Tabors, P. O. and Harris, S. R. 2007. *Is literacy enough? Pathways to academic success for adolescents*. Baltimore, MD: Paul Brookes.
Sperber, D. and Wilson, D. 1995. *Postface to the second edition of Relevance*. Oxford: Blackwell.
Spolsky, B. and Goldberg Shohamy, E. 1999. *The languages of Israel: Policy, ideology, and practice*. Clevedon, UK: Multilingual Matters.
Stanislavskij, C. 1986. *Building a character*. London: Methuen.
Statistics Finland, 2009. *The largest groups by native language 1998 and 2008*, retrieved June 3, 2009, www.stat.fi/til/vaerak/2008/vaerak_2008_2009-03-27_kuv_005_en.html.
Stein, N. L. and Albro, E. 2001. 'The origins and nature of arguments: studies in conflict understanding, emotion, and negotiation', *Discourse Processes* 32: 113–133.
Sterponi, L. 2009. 'Accountability in family discourse: socialization into norms and standards and negotiation of responsibility in Italian dinner conversations', *Childhood* 16: 441–459.
Sullivan, P. N. 2000. 'Spoken artistry: performance in second language classroom', in J. K. Hall and L. S. Verplaetse (eds.), *Second and foreign language learning through classroom interaction*. Mahwah, NJ: Lawrence Erlbaum.
Sutton-Smith, B. 1986. 'The development of fictional narrative performances', *Topics in Language Disorders* 7:1–10.
  [1998] 2001. *The ambiguity of play*. Cambridge, MA: Harvard University Press.
Swain, M. 2000. 'The output hypothesis and beyond: mediating acquisition through collaborative dialogue', in J. Lantolf (ed.), *Sociocultural theory and second language learning*. Oxford University Press.
Sylva, K., Bruner, J. and P. Genova 1976. 'The role of play in the problem solving of children 3+5 years old', in J. Bruner, A. Jolly and K. Sylva (eds.), *Play: its role in development and evolution*, pp. 244–257. New York: Basic Books.
Szymanski, M. 1999. 'Re-engaging and dis-engaging talk in activity', *Language in Society* 28(1): 1–23.
Tabors, P. 1997. *One child, two languages*. Baltimore, MD: Paul H. Brookes.
Tabors, P., Aceves, C., Bartolomé, L., Pcez, M. and Wolf, A. 2000. 'Language development of linguistically diverse children in Head Start classrooms: three ethnographic portraits', *NHSA Dialog* 3: 409–440.
Tabors, P. and Snow, C. E. 1994. 'English as a second language in preschools', in F. Genesee (ed.), *Educating second language children: the whole child, the whole curriculum, the whole community*, pp. 103–125. New York: Cambridge University Press.
Tannen, D. 2002. 'Agonism in academic discourse', *Journal of Pragmatics* 34(10–11): 1651–1669.
  2007. *Talking voices: repetition, dialogue, and imagery in conversational discourse* (2nd edn). New York: Cambridge University Press.
Tardif, T. 1996. 'Nouns are not always learned before verbs: evidence from Mandarin speakers' early vocabularies', *Developmental Psychology* 32: 492–504.

Tartas, V., Baucal, A. and Perret-Clermont, A.-N. 2010. 'Can you think with me? The social and cognitive conditions and the fruits of learning', in K. Littleton and C. Howe (eds.), *Educational dialogues: understanding and promoting productive interaction*, pp. 64–82. Oxford: Routledge.

Tetreault, C. 2009. '*Cité* teens entextualizing French TV host register: crossing, voicing, and participation frameworks', *Language in Society* 38(2): 201–31.

Tin, T. B. 2010. 'Language creativity and co-emergence of form and meaning in creative writing tasks', *Applied Linguistics* 32: 215–235.

Tomasello, M. 1992. *First verbs: a case study of early grammatical development*. New York: Cambridge University Press.

2002. 'Some facts about primate (including human) social learning and communication', in A. Cangelosi and D. Parisi (eds.), *Simulating the evolution of language*, pp. 327–340. London: Springer Verlag.

2003. *Constructing a language: a usage-based theory of language acquisition*. Cambridge, MA: Harvard University Press.

Tomasello, M. and Kruger, A. C. 1992. 'Joint attention on actions: acquiring words in ostensive and non-ostensive contexts', *Journal of Child Language* 19: 313–333.

Turino, T. 2008. *Music as social life: the politics of participation*. University of Chicago Press.

van Dam, J. 2002. 'Ritual, face, and play in a first English lesson', in C. Kramsch (ed.), *Language acquisition and language socialization*. London: Continuum.

Verschueren, J. 2004. 'Notes on the role of metapragmatic awareness in language use', in A. Jaworski. N. Coupland and D. Glasinski (eds.), *Metalanguage: social and ideological perspectives*, pp. 53–73. Berlin: De Gruyter.

Verschueren, J., Östman, O. and Blommaert, J. (eds.) 1995. *Handbook of pragmatics*, pp. 367–371. Amsterdam: John Benjamins.

Voloshinov, V. N. [1929]1973. *Marxism and the philosophy of language*. Trans. L. Matejka and I. R. Titunik. Cambridge, MA: Harvard University Press.

Vygotsky, L. S. 1978. 'The role of play in development', in M. Cole, V. John-Steiner, S. Scribner and E. Souberman (eds.), *Mind in society: the development of higher psychological processes*, pp. 92–104. Cambridge, MA: Harvard University Press.

[1920s – 30s] 1978. *Mind in society: the development of higher psychological processes*, ed. M. Cole et al. Cambridge, MA: Harvard University Press.

1986. *Thought and language*. Cambridge, MA: MIT Press.

Wagner, D. A., Venezky, R. L. and Street, B. V. (eds.) 1999. *Literacy: an international handbook*. Boulder, CO: Westview Press.

Watson-Gegeo, K. A. and Gegeo, D. W. 1989. 'The role of sibling interaction in child socialization', in P. G. Zukow (ed.), *Sibling interaction across cultures: theoretical and methodological issues*, pp. 54–76. New York: Springer-Verlag.

Weigand, E. 2006. 'Argumentation: the mixed game', *Argumentation* 20: 59–87.

Wellman, H. M., Cross, D. and Watson, J. 2001. 'Meta-analysis of theory of-mind development: the truth about false belief', *Child Development* 72: 655–684.

Wells, G. 1985. 'Preschool literacy-related activities and success in school', in D. R. Olson, N. Torrance and A. Hildyard (eds.), *Literacy, language, and learning: the nature and consequences of reading and writing*, pp. 229–255. New York: Cambridge University Press.

Wenger, E. 1998. *Communities of practice: learning, meaning, and identity*. Cambridge University Press.

Whalen, M. R. 1995. 'Working toward play: complexity in children's fantasy activities', *Language in Society* 24: 315–348.
Willett, J. 1995. 'Becoming first graders in an L2: an ethnographic study of L2 socialization', *TESOL Quarterly* 29: 473–503.
Wittgenstein, L. 1953. *Philosophical investigations*. New York: Macmillan.
Wolf, D. and Hicks, D. 1989. 'The voices within narratives: the development of intertextualitiy in young children's stories', *Discourse Process* 12: 329–53.
Wong Fillmore, L. 1979. 'Individual differences in second language acquisition', in C. Fillmore, D. Kempler and W. Wang (eds.), *Individual differences in language ability and behavior*. New York: Academic Press.
  1991. 'Second-language learning in children: a model of language-learning in social context', in E. Bialystok (ed.), *Language processing in bilingual children*, pp. 49–69. Cambridge University Press.
Wray, A. 2002. *Formulaic language and the lexicon*. Cambridge University Press.
Zadunaisky Ehrlich, S. and Blum-Kulka, S. 2010. 'Peer talk as a "double opportunity space": the case of argumentative discourse', *Discourse and Society* 21(2): 1–23.
Zentella, A. 1997. *Growing up bilingual: Puerto Rican children in New York*. Oxford: Blackwell.
  2005. 'Premises, promises, and pitfalls of language socialization research in Latino families and communities'. in A. C. Zentella (ed.), *Building on strength: language and literacy in Latino families and communities*, pp.13–30. New York: Teachers College Press.
Zosuls, K. M., Lurye, L. E. and Ruble, D. N. 2008. 'Gender: awareness, identity, and stereotyping', in M. M. Haith and J. B. Benson (eds.), *Encyclopedia of infant and early childhood development*, vol. 2, pp. 1–12. London: Elsevier.

Index

accentuations, 196
adult–child interactions
  characteristics of, 9–10, 42
  discourse effects, 3
  and motherese, 241
  and peer-group culture, 248–249
  and traditional learning, 88
affect, judgement and appreciation, 107–108, 109, 111–118, 123–125
affective displays, 108, 124
affective stance
  and identity, 157, 162–163
  indexical aspects of, 200
  in peer play contexts, 196
  playful, 202
  positive affect, 7, 65, 85, 89–90
Andersen, E., 208
argumentative discourse
  over abstract issues, 36–38
  conflict avoidance, 28
  and cooperation, 27–28
  and cultural co-construction, 31–32, 39–40
  de-escalation strategies, 30–31
  defined, 25
  and discursive literacy, 83–84, 85
  as double-opportunity space, 24–25, 39
  within double-opportunity space, 23
  metaphor serving opposing goals, 23
  and reality–fiction resolution, 29–30
  and small group activity, 89
  and sociality, 27
  study background, 25–26
Aronsson, K. and Thorell, M., 208

Bakhtin, M., 111, 196, 208
Barnes, D., 87, 89, 90, 93, 102
Barthes, R., 91
Bayeux Tapestry, 91
bilingual resources, *see also* code-switching
  explicit verbal statements, 130–131, 140, 145–146
  hybrid statements, 142–143
  and literacy skills, 147–148
bilingualism, *see also* code-switching; language play (second language learning); metasociolinguistic stances; pretend play, bilingual settings; second language learning; vocabulary knowledge, second language learners
bilingual expertise, 163–165, 166, 228–230
bilingual identities, 149–152, 157–159, 161, 163, 166–167
bilingual knowledge, 163–165, 230–231
  and discursive literacy, 147–148
  and epistemic stances, 157–159, 160–163, 166–167
  heteroglossic utterances, 142–143
  knowledge displays, 157–159, 160–163, 203
  and language play, 194–195, 198
  peer play and vocabulary learning, 214–215, 216–221
  play frames, 133–134, 228
Blum-Kulka, S., 4–5, 33, 64, 237
Bogdan, R., 247
Bourdieu, Pierre, 197
Brown, R., 238
Bushnell, K., 197

call–response format, 38
Cathcart-Strong, R., 197
Cekaite, A. and Aronsson, K., 170, 197, 201
Chomsky, N., 238
code-switching
  bilingual knowledge displays, 145, 157–159, 203
  and changes of play frame, 140, 145, 147
  contesting linguistic expertise, 155–157
  epistemic stances, 160–163
  and language play, 196
  within multilingual peer groups, 14, 151
  as paralinguistic clue, 132, 133
collaborative emergence, pretend play, 7–8, 42–43

Index

conflict resolution, 27–31
constructivism, 39
Cook, G., 201
Cook-Gumperz, J., 131
Corsaro, W. A., 6, 27
cultural identities and peer interaction,
 155–157, 188

decontextualized language, 129–130
developmental tradition, 24
Di Cori, P., 91–92
discursive literacy, *see also* literacy
 and argumentative events, 83–84, 85
 and bilingual children, 147–148
 and decontextualized language, 129–130
 defined, 32, 64, 130
 distancing, 33, 35–38
 links with pretend play, 11–12, 63–64,
  84–85, 147
 and narrative competence, 130
 textuality, 33–34
discursive practices
 links with peer-group culture, 5, 6–7, 8,
  237, 245–247
 and peer talk, 23, 237
 in preadolescents, 6–7, 12
 in preschool children, 6–7
 and small group activity, 89–90
 in the school setting, 88
distancing
 abstract issues, 36–38
 and discursive literacy, 33, 35–38
 and speech acts, 35–36
double-opportunity spaces
 and argumentative discourses, 23,
  24–25, 39
 peer talk as, 4–5, 23, 215, 237
 in second language learning, 184, 212
 and vocabulary acquisition, 215
Du Bois, J., 150, 165

Ehrlich, Z. and Blum-Kulka, S., 130
emotional engagement
 friendship bonds, 119–123
 popular culture and evaluative language,
  112–113, 115–116, 117–118
Enfield, N. J. and Levinson, S. C., 26
environmental design studies, 66
epistemic stances
 affiliative epistemic stances, 160–163
 bilingual knowledge displays, 157–159,
  160–163
 claiming authority, 155–157
 contesting linguistic expertise, 154–155
 epistemic authority displays, 157–159

 solidifying bilingual expertise, 163–165
Evaldsson, A.-C., 151
evaluative language, 107–108, 109, 111–118,
 123–124
expert–novice interactions, 9, 42, 61, 184,
 see also verbal rituals
exploratory talk, 93–94, 102, 104,
 see also small group activity

fantasy play, *see* pretend play (PP)
Fasulo, A. and Pontecorvo, C., 88, 89
Fasulo, A. *et al.* (1998), 91
footing (alignment), 131–132, 137–140,
 146–147, *see also* stance, theory of
framing, *see* play frames
friendship bonds
 and alignment, 118, 119–121
 and argumentative events, 27, 39
 expression through musical alignment,
  121–123, 124
 and mutual reassurance, 121
 and narrative storytelling, 54–55, 61
 and second language learning, 216–217
Frith, S., 121

games, defined, 65
Garrett, P., 151
Geertz, C., 107
gender
 and argumentative events, 31–32
 gender roles and popular culture, 122–123
 and narrative storytelling, 46–47,
  52–53, 58–60
 and small group activity, 95–96, 104
Girardet, H., 87
Goffman, E., 131, 132, 150, 153
Goldman, L. R., 130, 140, 145
Goodwin, C., 91, 131, 144, 151
Goodwin, C. and Goodwin, M. H., 132,
 144, 153
Goodwin, M. H., 140
Gopnik, A., 28
Gumperz, J. H., 131

Harris, P. L., 65
Harris, P. L. *et al.* (1989), 34
Harvard Home-School Study, 215
Heath, S. B., 130, 145
Henry, G. and Rickman, D., 216
here-and-now discourse, 69–70, 74–75
historical reasoning
 development of, 87, 91–92
 and small group activity, 99–104, 105
Hutto, D., 247
Hymes, D. H., 25

instructional design studies, 66

Jaffe, A., 149, 151, 153

Kärkkäinen, E., 154–155
Keenan, E., 201
keying, 117, 184, 185–187, 191
Koven, M., 111–112
Kyratzis, A., 151

Labov, W., 111
language learning, *see also* second language learning
　developmental research, 3
　diversity of, 250
　experimental research, drawbacks in, 239–240, 250
　first stages and peer talk, 243–244
　and gender construction, 32
　historical overview, 238–239
　and identity, 149
　as independent and child-driven, 238, 239, 241
　ludic perspective, 194
　and peer-group culture, 212–213, 244–245
　through pretend play in the wake of a story, 85
　and reflexivity, 195
　verbal rituals, 38, 184–191
　and vocabulary, 214
language play (second language learning)
　hybridities (play with registers), 206–208
　improvisations, 199–200, 212
　as learning resource, 212–213
　and metalinguistics, 195
　metaphonological play, 201–202
　metapragmatic play, 206–212
　and metapragmatics, 195–196
　metasemantic play, 202–204
　metasyntactic play, 204–206
　and reflexivity, 195
　use of repetition and improvisation, 196–198
　role reversals, 208–211
　second language and peer interaction, 194–195, 226–227
　study background, 198–200
　verbal rituals, 185–188
Lave, J. and Wenger, E., 152, 169
leadership roles, 94–95
Levinson, S., 26
literacy, *see also* discursive literacy
　exposure to books, 61
　and kindergarten schooling, 63
　knowledge acquisition and visual documents, 91, 248–249

written and oral, 248–249
literate capacity, 65

Martin, J. R., 107
Mashburn, A. J. *et al.* (2009), 216
metacognitive discourse
　and character enactment, 83–84
　defined, 83
　and the original story text, 83
metaplay discourse, 69–70, 85
metasociolinguistic stances
　and bilingual knowledge, 149, 163–165, 166–167
　defined, 149
　and peer-group culture, 149–150, 153
　and sociolinguistic identities, 150–151, 157–159, 161, 163, 166–167
mocking-subversive keying, 117
motherese, 241
multilingual settings, 151, 165–166
music
　and emotional entrainment and friendship bonds, 119–123, 124
　and films, 118–119

narrative development
　analysis (table), 50
　and audience response, 55
　narrative competence (bilingual settings), 130, 137–138, 143, 146
　narrative trajectories, 50–51, 54
　and peer-group culture, 60, 109
　playful experimentation in, 53–56
　and pretend play, 129–131
narrative skills
　and gendered sub-cultures, 46–47
　social class factors, 46
narrative storytelling
　boys and conflict narratives, 59
　and gender, 46–47, 52–53, 58–60
　peer-oriented narratives, 43–45, 60, 249–250
　performance aspect, 44, 45, 60
　preschool children, studies, 45–48
　sociocultural contexts, 54–55, 58–59, 60
　study background, 48–51
narrative styles
　first-person, 51–52
　selection of narrative elements, 46
　third-person fictional stories, 55–56
narrative themes
　cross-fertilization of, 53, 57–60, 61
　family-genre stories, 52–53, 59–60
　shared narrative genre, 57–59

Index

Ochs, E., 196
Ochs, E. *et al.* (1989), 43
Olson, D. R., 78
opportunity spaces, *see also* double-opportunity spaces
   narrative storytelling, 60
   peer talk, 4–5, 43
oral performance, 11, 44, 45, 60, 196
original story text (OST), *see also* pretend play in the wake of story reading (PPWS)
   adherence to the text, 78–79
   awareness of, 75–78
   as constraining factor, 68
   impact on pretend play, 67–68
   interactions with, 64, 75
   and metacognitive discourse, 83
   as source of authority, 80–81

Painter, C., 107–108
participants' perspectives, 199
Paugh, A., 151
peer-group culture
   children's deep involvement within, 7–8, 31, 237
   collaboration within, 42–43
   concept of promises, 35
   emotions and evaluative language, 118
   and friendship bonds, 27, 39, 61, 216–217
   importance for language learning, 4, 212–213, 244–245
   links with wider language communities, 5, 6, 8, 237, 245–247
   meaning negotiation within, 4–5
   metasociolinguistic stances, 149–150, 153
   in multilingual settings, 151, 166–167
   and narrative storytelling, 249–250
   and popular culture, 107, 108
   pre-teenage children, 108, 123–125
   social status within, 83–84
   and storytelling, 109
peer language socialization
   bilingual knowledge displays, 157–159
   contesting linguistic expertise, 155–157
   epistemic authority displays, 157–159
   epistemic stances, 160–163
   keying (tone), 184, 185–187, 191
   in a monolingual Swedish school, 159–160, 166
   and peer interaction, 170–171
   solidifying bilingual expertise, 163–165
   studies of, 169–170
   study background, 152–154
peer talk
   affordances, 23–24
   and vocabulary knowledge, 214–217
   characteristics of, 9–10, 243
   as double-opportunity space, 4–5, 23, 215, 237
   egalitarian nature of, 5, 8–9
   and first stages of language learning, 243–244
   linguistic anthropologic studies, 4
   literate features, 11–12
   oral features, 11
   and second language learning, 170, 243
   sociocultural benefits, 9, 40
Pellegrini, A. D., 11–12, 65, 129, 130, 138
Pellegrini, A. D. and Galda, L., 69
Peters, A., 242–243
Piaget, Jean, 5, 8–9, 63
play frames
   in bilingual settings, 133–134
   cohesion devices, 140–142
   here-and-now discourses (out-of-frame), 69, 74–75
   in-frame and out-of-frame mobility, 73–74
   in-frame discourse, 69
   joint orientation within, 136, 137–140
   metaplay discourses, 69–70, 85
   out-of-frame role negotiations, 71–73
   within pretend play, 65–66, 131, 132–133
   underscoring, 135–136, 142–143, 145–146
   and vocabulary knowledge, 226–227, 232–233
play, defined, 65, *see also* pretend play (PP)
popular culture
   and evaluative language, 112–113, 115–116, 117–118
   films, 118–119
   and gender roles, 122–123
   music, 119–123, 124
   and peer-group culture, 109–110
   popular drama, 111–118
   study background, 110–111
positive affect
   and peer interaction, 7, 89–90
   and the role of play, 65, 85
pretend play (PP), *see also* code-switching; play frames
   collaboration within, 7–8, 42–43
   conflict resolution, 28–30
   and discursive literacy, 11–12, 147
   and extended discourses, 11–12, 247
   and narratives, 129–131
   norms of and argumentative discourse, 28
   play frames, 131, 132–133
   shared make-believe, 28–30
   speech representation in, 12

pretend play in the wake of story reading (PPWS)
  and argumentative discourse, 83–84, 85
  defined, 64, 65–66
  and discursive literacy, 63–64, 84–85
  in-frame and out-of-frame mobility, 73–74
  interactions with the original story text (OST), 64, 67–68, 75
  interpretive reproduction in, 81–82
  and language learning, 85
  and literacy skills, 63–64
  and metacognitive argumentative discourse, 83–84
  out-of-frame discourses, 71–73, 74–75
  play frames, 65–66
  research formats, historical, 66
  study background, 67
  use of distanced discourse, 68
pretend play, bilingual settings
  character motives, 143–144
  and decontextualized language, 129–130
  embodied practices, 132, 139, 144–145
  and literacy skills, 129–131
  narrative competence in, 130, 137–138, 143, 146
  need for verbal explicitness, 130–131, 140, 145–146
  and participation (footing), 131–132, 137–140, 146–147
psycholinguistic development, 4–5

Ravid, D. and Tolchinsky, L., 64
reflexivity
  in discursive literacy, 33, 139, 147
  and language learning, 195, 200
  and metacognition, 83–84
repetition rituals, 177–178, 196, 208–210
research
  future research directions, 15–16
  scope of studies, this volume, 15
Rogoff, B., 175
Roskos, K. *et al.* (2010), 66

Sawyer, R. K., 7
second language learning, *see also* language play (second language learning)
  bilingual socialization, 180–181
  interaction with teachers, 177
  ludic perspective, 194
  non-verbal communication, 174
  novice phases, 172
  novices, access strategies, 184
  participation by doing, 177
  and peer-group positions, 13, 14, 215, 230–231, 233

peer interaction, benefits, 12–13, 194–195, 218, 223–227, 233
peer interaction, drawbacks, 13–14, 216–217, 227–230, 233
peer interaction, novices, 179–180
peer reading to novice children, 181–184
and peer talk, 170
peers as teachers, 184
phase of innocence, 172–174
repetition rituals, 177–178
silent phase, 173–174, 184
study background, 171
use of repetition and improvisation, 197–198
verbal rituals, 184–191
and vocabulary knowledge, 214–215
Seidman, S. *et al.* (1986), 144
small group activity
  collaborative/oppositional aspects in, 89, 90, 96–99, 104
  egalitarian nature of, 89–90, 95, 104
  and exploratory talk, 102
  and historical reasoning, 99–104, 105
  leadership types, 94–95, 104
  as learning tool, 88–89
  study background, 87, 90–91, 92–93
  value of, 105
Smith, P. K., 63
Snow, C. E., 129–130, 144
Snow, C. E. *et al.* (2007), 215–216
social interaction
  and gender construction, 31–32
  Piagetian theory, 8–9
  Vygotskyan theory, 9
sociality
  and argumentative events, 27–31, 39
  and evaluative language, 108
  and human interaction, 26–27
sociocultural aspects
  argumentative discourse research, 24, 39
  and language learning, 242–243
  narrative construction of reality, 48
  of peer talk, 4–5, 6–7, 9, 40, 43
  in research, 240, 241–242, 250
sociolinguistic identities
  in bilingual settings, 150–151, 157–159, 161, 163, 166–167
  in multilingual settings, 151–152, 230–231
  in peer talk, 14
speech events, 23–24, 25, 35–36
stance, theory of, 150–151, *see also* affective stance; epistemic stances
Stanislavskij, C., 196
storytelling, *see* narrative storytelling

Swain, M., 194
symbolization, 63, 91

Tabors, P., 170
textuality
  in argumentative discourse, 33–35
  in discursive literacy, 33
Theory of Mind, 34
Turino, T., 121

verbal rituals
  and empowerment, 189–191
  and grammatical learning, 189
  and language learning, 184–185
  and sociability, 185–189
visual documents, 91, 248–249
vocabulary knowledge, second language learners
  acquisition within a double-opportunity space, 215
  expanding word meanings, 225–226
  expansion through humour, 226–227
  growth rate and preschool talk exposure, 215–216, 217, 223, 232
  intercorrelations between PPVT, tokens and types (table), 221
  introducing new words, 224–225
  and language learning, 214
  longitudinal models, 222–223
  and peer interaction, 218, 223–230
  and peer talk, 217, 218, 222–223, 232
  and preschool children, 215–216
  results of fitting a taxonomy of multi-level models for change predicting raw vocabulary scores (table), 222
  study background, 217–221
  target children's PPVT-III raw scores (table), 219
  through teacher-led talk, 214, 217
  token and types per minute for target children (table), 220
Vygotsky, L., 9, 63, 107, 181

Wittgenstein, L., 247–248

Printed in Great Britain
by Amazon